Conducting Research in Developmental Psychology

This comprehensive guide offers a rich introduction to research methods, experimental design and data analysis techniques in developmental science, emphasizing the importance of an understanding of this area of psychology for any student or researcher interested in examining development across the lifespan.

The expert contributors enhance the reader's knowledge base, understanding of methods, and critical thinking skills in their area of study. They cover development from the prenatal period to adolescence and old age, and explore key topics including the history of developmental research, ethics, animal models, physiological measures, eye-tracking, and computational and robotics models. They accessibly explore research measures and design in topics including gender identity development, the influence of neighborhoods, mother–infant attachment relationships, peer relationships in childhood, prosocial and moral development patterns, developmental psychopathology and social policy, and the examination of memory across the lifespan. Each chapter ends with a summary of innovations in the field over the last ten years, giving students and interested researchers a thorough overview of the field and an idea of what more is to come.

Conducting Research in Developmental Psychology is essential reading for upper-level undergraduate or graduate students seeking to understand a new area of developmental science, developmental psychology, and human development. It will also be of interest to junior researchers who would like to enhance their knowledge base in a particular area of developmental science, human development, education, biomedical science, or nursing.

Nancy Aaron Jones, Ph.D., is an associate professor in the Department of Psychology and Behavioral Neuroscience, the FAU Brain Institute and the Center for Complex Systems, Florida Atlantic University, US. Her research focuses on the integration of infant brain and emotional development in the family system, particularly in the context of maternal mood disorders.

Melannie Platt, Ph.D., is a researcher and instructor at Florida Atlantic University, US. Her main research interests include emotional development, social and emotional learning, and relationships in early childhood.

Krystal D. Mize, Ph.D., is an affiliate faculty member in the Department of Psychology and Behavioral Neuroscience at Florida Atlantic University, US. Her primary interest is in the correlates and determinants of non-optimal and optimal emotional and social development across the lifespan.

Jillian Hardin, Ph.D., is a psychology researcher and adjunct instructor at Florida Atlantic University, US. Her main research interest is how early experiential factors influence biobehavioral development and later functioning.

Conducting Research in Developmental Psychology

A Topical Guide for Research Methods Utilized Across the Lifespan

Edited by Nancy Aaron Jones, Melannie Platt, Krystal D. Mize, and Jillian Hardin

NEW YORK AND LONDON

First published 2020
by Routledge
52 Vanderbilt Avenue, New York, NY 10017

and by Routledge
2 Park Square, Milton Park, Abingdon, Oxon, OX14 4RN

Routledge is an imprint of the Taylor & Francis Group, an informa business

© 2020 Taylor & Francis

The right of Nancy Aaron Jones, Melannie Platt, Krystal D. Mize, and Jillian Hardin to be identified as the authors of the editorial material, and as the authors for their individual chapters, has been asserted in accordance with sections 77 and 78 of the Copyright, Designs and Patents Act 1988.

All rights reserved. No part of this book may be reprinted or reproduced or utilized in any form or by any electronic, mechanical, or other means, now known or hereafter invented, including photocopying and recording, or in any information storage or retrieval system, without permission in writing from the publishers.

Trademark notice: Product or corporate names may be trademarks or registered trademarks, and are used only for identification and explanation without intent to infringe.

Library of Congress Cataloging-in-Publication Data
A catalog record for this title has been requested

ISBN: 978-0-367-34020-9 (hbk)
ISBN: 978-0-367-34022-3 (pbk)
ISBN: 978-0-429-35206-5 (ebk)

Typeset in Sabon
by Swales & Willis, Exeter, Devon, UK

www.routledge.com/9780367340223

To my family and friends, especially my wonderful husband and beautiful and talented children (Keara and Samuel Casey). Thank you for supporting me, including helping me with this book and encouraging me to be a developmental scientist ... as it is hard not to wonder how you became the wonderful people you are! And to all my colleagues and students, some of whom also helped me with this book. Every day I'm humbled by your dedication, creativity, and knowledge. Thank you for all you do!

N.A.J.

To Randy and Martha, for always inspiring me to grow.

M.P.

To my mom, Chris: I now realize how many sacrifices you made for us and I appreciate the life you created out of almost nothing. Your intuitive wisdom taught me to love learning. To Nick: You taught me to question everything. To Shannon: thank you for all of your support as I completed my education and learned to conduct research. Without the three of you, I would not be writing this book. To Mark, Branden, and Devin: All I do is for you! My apologies for the sacrifices we had to endure but my hope is that because of those, your families have to make fewer sacrifices. And finally, to future researchers: Go out and design some amazing developmental research! I look forward to seeing what you create.

K.D.M.

To my flowers, Averie Annelise and Arlyn Shea: Helping you grow is my life's greatest work. To my love, Rodney, and my family, Marianne and Lila: Thank you for your unconditional support and love. To my brother, Darius: Learning to live in a world without you taught me a strength I never believed I possessed. Thank you for that one last gift.

J.H.

Contents

Preface		ix
List of Contributors		xii
1	A Century of Research in Child Development: The Emergence of a New Science JOHN W. HAGEN, CARLY A. LASAGNA, AND SHERRI E. PACKETT	1
2	Overimitation across Development: The Influence of Individual and Contextual Factors BRUCE RAWLINGS, NATÁLIA DUTRA, CAMERON TURNER, AND EMMA FLYNN	26
3	Ethics in Developmental Research DIANA J. METER AND MARION K. UNDERWOOD	40
4	Prenatal Animal Models of Behavioral Development GALE A. KLEVEN AND SEANCERAY A. BELLINGER	50
5	Physiological and Behavioral Research Methods across Prenatal and Infant Periods NANCY AARON JONES AND KRYSTAL D. MIZE	70
6	Studying Perceptual Development in Infancy FABRICE DAMON, NICHOLAS J. MINAR, AND ANNE HILLAIRET DE BOISFERON	84
7	Studying Children's Verb Learning across Development JANE B. CHILDERS, SNEH LALANI, BLAIRE PORTER, SOPHIA ARRIAZOLA, PRISCILLA TOVAR-PEREZ, AND BIBIANA CUTILLETTA	104
8	Developmental Robotics for Language Learning ANGELO CANGELOSI AND MATTHEW SCHLESINGER	113

Contents

9 Attachment Theory and Research in a Developmental Framework 122
PATRICIA CRITTENDEN AND SUSAN SPIEKER

10 Social Ecological Influences: The Role of Residential
Neighborhoods in the Development of Children and Youth 134
MARGARET O'BRIEN CAUGHY*

11 Measuring Peer Relationships During Childhood:
Exploring the Benefits of Using Peer Nominations 148
CHRISTOPHER D. AULTS

12 Gender Identity Development 157
MADHAVI MENON AND SARA M. GORMAN

13 Methodological Issues in Cross-Cultural Research on Prosocial
and Moral Development 171
GUSTAVO CARLO AND SAHITYA MAIYA

14 Translational Science: Developmental Psychopathology
and Social Policy 189
ROSS A. THOMPSON

15 Methodological Considerations in Collaborative
Memory and Aging Research 200
MICHELLE L. MEADE, SUMMER R. WHILLOCK, AND KATHERINE M. HART

Index 210

---

*Dr. Tammy Leonard contributed the activities/supplemental materials that are a part of this chapter and included on the Taylor and Francis website.

Preface

Students in psychology traditionally strive to acquire information and ultimately their degrees in the clinical field and tend to shy away from research. While clinical practice is a noble endeavor, all students require training and information in research methods to be informed and knowledgeable. In addition, developmental science is a necessary skill for parents, clinicians, colleagues, and even employers as understanding how we develop is understanding others in the world around us. This book originally was developed to inform students in the process of obtaining a college-level degree as to the methods of developmental science; however, it is for anyone who wants to understand others and their process of development. The focuses are on research methods (how to/ what to do to collect data), experimental designs (how to evaluate the data collected), and data analysis techniques (how to interpret the data and the processes studied) related to various topics in developmental psychology spanning from prenatal development to research on aging. Each chapter is written by experts, some that have worked in the field for years and some who are just starting out in the field and have already obtained a reputation for quality work. All authors conduct developmental research in their particular field of science! They have boiled down their expertise and crafted each chapter with the goal of enhancing the reader's knowledge base, understanding of methods, and critical thinking skills in their area of study.

In Chapter 1, John Hagen reviews the history of developmental research. Dr. Hagen and his colleagues have skillfully analyzed the historical roots and have worked with the SRCD history project over the years. Their analysis of this project is a must-read to understand where developmental science has originated from and where to go in the future.

Bruce Rawlings, Natália Dutra, Cameron Turner, and Emma Flynn wrote Chapter 2 and their focus is on overimitation in infancy. Their chapter is specifically designed to discuss the broader concept of stability and change across development.

In Chapter 3, Diana J. Meter and Marion K. Underwood take on and discuss conducting ethical research during development. This work is timely, in that notable changes to the Common Rule (which guides ethical conduct of research in the US) were just enacted. Meter and Underwood skillfully discuss the overall ethical issues that should be considered in developmental science with a specific focus on vulnerable populations and research in developmental ethics.

Chapter 4 by Gale A. Kleven and Seanceray A. Bellinger discusses the vital contributions that animal models offer developmental researchers due to some of the limitations of human developmental research. Animal models allow for studies involving not only observations (e.g. ultrasounds) but also alterations in the trajectory of development during the prenatal period.

In Chapter 5, Nancy Aaron Jones and Krystal D. Mize discuss how physiological measures (i.e., infant EEG) that reveal notable brain and neuro-hormonal influences (i.e., cortisol and oxytocin—both maternal–fetal and maternal–infant) serve as potential biomarkers of future patterns of regulation and dysregulation. The overarching theme of this chapter is to highlight the significant meaning that fetal-to-infant behavioral and neurodevelopment has for understanding change. This chapter also aims to inform the next generation of researchers as to the innovative designs that can serve to advance the field of developmental science.

In Chapter 6, Fabrice Damon, Nicholas J. Minar, and Anne Hillairet de Boisferon, set out to acquaint the reader with both traditional and modern research methods that are utilized in the field of perceptual development. The authors discuss the need for critical thinking skills when conducting research with preverbal infants.

Chapter 7, co-authored by Jane B. Childers, Sneh Lalani, Blaire Porter, Sophia Arriazola, Priscilla Tovar-Perez, and Bibiana Cutilletta reviews language development in early childhood and presents novel research using eye-tracking in the area of verb acquisition.

Chapter 8, by Angelo Cangelosi and Matthew Schlesinger offer an interdisciplinary approach to studying cognitive development by integrating computational and robotics models into developmental research. This chapter briefly analyzes a set of examples of developmental robotics models of the acquisition and learning. The authors outline how using "baby" robot platforms, artificial neural networks, and machine learning techniques can inform the developmental field about scientific modeling as well as educational and assistive applications.

Renowned experts in the conceptualization of mother–infant attachment relationships, Patricia Crittenden and Susan Spieker co-authored Chapter 9. They provide an overview of previous research in attachment as well as discussing the Dynamic-Maturational Model of Attachment and Adaptation. They also present novel ideas designed to lead attachment research into the future by producing unique and innovative measures that merge science and clinical ideas and processes.

Chapter 10, by Margaret O'Brien Caughy, focuses on child development from an ecological context and highlights the importance of assessing the influence of neighborhoods. This chapter is pivotal as the assessment of whole areas of the community and their effect on outcomes is a direction for future scientists to understand. (Dr. Caughy and Dr. Tammy Leonard co-authored the activities for this chapter, providing complex and cutting-edge designs for studying neighborhoods.)

Christopher D. Aults authored Chapter 11 and he covers methods for measuring peer relationships during childhood and adolescence including peer nominations, teacher nominations, and self-reporting. His expertise on these topics provides significant meaning to the understanding of child peer relationships for future scientists.

Chapter 12 speaks to that all important question asked about newborns, "Is it a boy or a girl?" Developmental psychologists have a long history of interest in gender because it plays a role in our behavior, attitudes, traits, abilities, and self-presentation. Madhavi Menon and Sara M. Gorman review the factors that influence gender identity development and present us with some of the measures and designs used to study this important topic.

Preface xi

Chapter 13, co-authored by Gustavo Carlo and Sahitya Maiya, discusses the debate over whether prosocial and moral development patterns are universal or vary as a function of culture. This chapter introduces the reader to a report of efforts to develop and validate two measures: the Prosocial Reasoning Objective Measure (PROM) to test prosocial moral reasoning and the Prosocial Tendencies Measure (PTM), which measures prosocial measures. Through the use of these and other culturally sensitive measures, future research will be able to provide us with an accurate description of prosocial and moral development in children.

Ross A. Thompson in Chapter 14 uses his notable expertise to discuss developmental psychopathology and social policy. This chapter is the very definition of the focus on translational research that the field has yearned for in understanding the impact of development on the world of clinical outcomes.

In Chapter 15 Michelle L. Meade, Summer R. Whillock, and Katherine M. Hart discuss the research issues important to research on aging and memory. They provide a review of the methods and measures used to examine memory across the lifespan. The authors suggest collaborative scaffolding as a potential tool for addressing the memory decline humans face as they age. The authors also discuss methodological factors that should be considered surrounding levels of analysis and accurate and false memories.

There are also a series of activities and supplemental materials that will be added to the Taylor and Francis website where those reading this book can see and in some cases can practice the research described in that particular chapter.

Contributors

Arriazola, Sophia – Trinity University
Aults, Christopher D. – King's College
Bellinger, Seanceray A. – Florida Atlantic University
Cangelosi, Angelo – University of Manchester
Carlo, Gustavo – University of Missouri
Childers, Jane B. – Trinity University
Crittenden, Patricia – Family Relations Institute
Cutilletta, Bibiana – Trinity University
Damon, Fabrice – Université Bourgogne Franche-Comté
Dutra, Natália – Durham University, and The Capes Foundation, Ministry of Education of Brazil
Flynn, Emma – Queen's University, Belfast
Gorman, Sara M. – Nova Southeastern University
Hagen, John W. – University of Michigan, Ann Arbor
Hart, Katherine M. – Montana State University
Hillairet de Boisferon, Anne – Université Paris Descartes
Jones, Nancy Aaron – Florida Atlantic University
Kleven, Gale A. – Wright State University
Lalani, Sneh – Trinity University
Lasagna, Carly A. – University of Michigan, Ann Arbor
Leonard, Tammy – University of North Texas*
Maiya, Sahitya – University of Missouri
Meade, Michelle L. – Montana State University
Menon, Madhavi – Nova Southeastern University

Meter, Diana J. – Utah State University

Minar, Nicholas J. – NAF Educational Network[**]

Mize, Krystal D. – Florida Atlantic University

O'Brien Caughy, Margaret – University of Georgia

Packett, Sherri E. – University of Michigan, Ann Arbor

Porter, Blaire – Trinity University

Rawlings, Bruce – Durham University and The University of Texas at Austin

Schlesinger, Matthew – Southern Illinois University

Spieker, Susan – University of Washington

Thompson, Ross A. – University of California, Davis

Tovar-Perez, Priscilla – Trinity University

Turner, Cameron – Australian National University

Underwood, Marion K. – Purdue University

Whillock, Summer R. – Montana State University

[*]Dr. Tammy Leonard contributed the activities/supplemental materials that are a part of this chapter and included on the Taylor and Francis website.

[**]The majority of this work was done when the author was affiliated with the Institute for the Study of Child Development—Rutgers Robert Wood Johnson Medical School

1 A Century of Research in Child Development
The Emergence of a New Science

John W. Hagen, Carly A. Lasagna, and Sherri E. Packett

A Century of Research in Child Development: The Emergence of a New Science

The developmental sciences' concern with investigating changes across the lifespan has been driven by the aim to describe and explain in order to optimize development since their founding in the early 20th century (Baltes, Reese, & Lipsitt, 1980). The methodologies used to achieve this goal, however, have undergone great change over the years. To properly understand these changes, it is crucial to consider the history of the field, including the movements involved in the rapid onset of child study in the 1920s and the circumstances that preceded the origins of developmental research in the late 1800s. The evolution of developmental science, despite being a sub-discipline of psychology is a whole, is distinct from that of adult psychology. Developmental psychology has different roots and foci than experimental or other branches. There has not been a "pure" theory-driven period, but rather real-life concerns, interest in application, and policy that goes back to its early years in the late 19th and early 20th century. While some developmentalists were more focused on theory-driven, value-neutral approaches, this path has never been the dominant one.

The field's unique history is the result of contextual factors and socio-political circumstances that converged on the study of child development. These factors set the stage for the field of developmental psychology to emerge, shaping turn-of-the-century perspectives on children in a way that drove scientific interest in their development. The betterment of children and families, whether it be through understanding of education, health, or child welfare, has been and continues to be a motivator for pursuing research. In this chapter, we provide a brief overview of the many periods and phases in the history of developmental study, emphasizing the types of design, methods, and data obtained to bring the particular foci of child development.

Precursors to Child Study: Perspectives on Childhood throughout History

Before the rapid emergence of child study in the early 20th century, there was little interest in childhood and misperceptions about the nature of development were widespread. In fact, throughout much of history, it was not understood that children were meaningfully different from adults. Without the notion of qualitatively different stages of development, there was no perceived need to study children in their own right (Smuts, 2008).

The writings of John Locke and Jean Jacque Rousseau were among the first to spark interest in the study of childhood. Locke's idea of the *tabula rasa* (or blank slate) stressed the importance of the environment in shaping development, which gained popularity in education and parenting practices (Crain, 1992). Rousseau was the first to describe development in terms of discrete stages and his work would later inspire psychologists such as Jean Piaget and Maria Montessori (Rousseau, 1979; Thompson, Hogan, & Clark, 2012).

During the late 1700s, there was growing interest in developmental changes during infancy. This prompted the first attempts at non-scientific child study. German Philosopher Dietrich Tiedemann (1748–1803) published a diary of daily observations made throughout the first two years of his son's life (Thompson et al., 2012): "For the first time in human history, someone thought it worthwhile to record and publish a description of the behavioral development of a normal child" (Borstelmann, 1983, p. 34). These written analyses by parents became known as **baby biographies**, which consisted of detailed, daily observations of infants recorded by parents or family members. They are considered among the methodological precursors to scientific child study.

Paving the Way for Child Study: A Changing Socio-Political Backdrop

In the mid-1800s, all levels of government began to take on societal concerns such as work environment and education. The role of children, the family, and education were understood to be key to the future of the nation. Thus, greater consideration was given to the nature of development in order to raise and educate the nation's children more effectively for the country's welfare (Smuts, 2008). The role of the mother—considered to play the central role in a child's upbringing—began to evolve. Mothers were expected to do a good job raising their children such that it might, ultimately, benefit the future of America (Smuts, 2008).

Women utilized these newfound expectations as justification for their desire to participate more actively in policy movements in the private and public sectors (Thompson et al., 2012). It became acceptable for women to exert their influence on policy with obvious relevance to family and home life. At the end of the Civil War, women's organizations, with more influence and structure than they ever had, began to grow (Smuts, 2008). The largest and most powerful of these was the Woman's Christian Temperance Union (WCTU), which operated under the motto "Save the child today and you have saved the nation tomorrow" (Smuts, 2008).

Social Reform

The well-being of the child that gained attention in the mid-19th century was fully embraced by the social reformers of American progressivism, who placed it at the forefront of their agenda. The socio-political changes that occurred before and during the progressive era of reformation set the stage for the child study movement of the 1920s to emerge. The efforts of social reformers, scientists, and philanthropists drew attention to the importance of the study of children in ways that called for an interdisciplinary, lifespan approach. The social reform goal would come to shape the nature of the research itself, influencing the topics of interest, methodologies employed, and demographics of children that were studied (e.g. chronological age and social class).

American Social Science Association

Professional associations, such as the American Social Science Association (ASSA), were established to create a link between the female reformers and those conducting scientific investigations, leading the associations to thrive throughout the 1870s and 1880s (Smuts, 2008). In 1881, the Boston chapter of the ASSA issued the first child study initiative. A call was issued asking parents to record observation of their young children, with the plan that the data collected would be of later use (Smuts, 2008). Other similar, large-scale studies began. A subset of philanthropic efforts focused on the funding of research was deemed worthwhile. This practice came to be known as "scientific philanthropy," before it was replaced with the term "social work" (Bremner, 1956; Smuts, 2008).

Child-Centered Movements

Settlement House Movement

In 1884, the Settlement House Movement began with the goal of helping children cope with issues related to abuse, neglect, and abandonment. Their efforts led to a new investigative approach to support their cause (Addams, 1910; Smuts, 2008). The approach was coined the "social survey" and it proved crucial for demonstrating connections between urban environments and poverty, child labor, and other urban issues at the forefront of reformists' agendas. The social survey built upon approaches used by ASSA and other groups in the past, but with significant improvements. Survey researchers carried out work in the homes and communities of the people they studied, collecting detailed accounts and comprehensive information based on geographic location. Thus, they were able to collect measures of health, family, and social structure (Bulmer, Bales, & Sklar, 1991).

Child Welfare Movement

The child welfare movement emerged from concerns surrounding the child's general health and physical well-being. Child welfare reform started to gain popularity and needed financial support from philanthropists during the early 1900s, focusing on topics such as feeding practices and hygiene (Hilgard, 1987; Thompson et al., 2012). A crucial pillar of the movement was the establishment of the Iowa State Child Welfare Research Station in 1917. A group of women in Iowa had campaigned for the state's commitment to the institution under the slogan "Forty thousand for hogs and nothing for children" (Smuts, 2008). It became the first institution in the world dedicated to the study of the "normally" developing child (Bradbury & Stoddard, 1933; Cravens, 1993; Smuts, 2008). Its work focused on physical, mental, and emotional development, and assumed an interdisciplinary approach.

Origins of Widespread Scientific Child Study

The field of experimental psychology became a self-contained area of scientific research in 1879 when German scholar William Wundt opened the first laboratory in the world dedicated to conducting psychological experiments (Smuts, 2008). Considered the first "psychologist," Wundt is credited with establishing psychology as an academic discipline, conducting experimental studies in laboratory settings. Subjects were excluded if researchers believed they lacked (1) abilities to make accurate inferences about their experiences, and (2) adequate communication skills.

It was assumed that only reports made by adults could be trusted, so children, animals, and those considered "atypical" or "deviant" were excluded throughout much of this period (Smuts, 2008). G. Stanley Hall, a student of William Wundt, was the first to question this assumption.

G. Stanley Hall's Child Study Movement

G. Stanley Hall believed that there was much *to learn* and much that *could be learned* from research involving children; he believed scientific research on children was both possible and worthwhile (Smuts, 2008). Hall brought the discipline to the United State and established the first American psychology laboratory at Johns Hopkins University in 1883. That same year, Hall published *The Contents of Children's Minds*, which is considered the first publication in the history of scientific child study (Hall, 1883). He argued that the scientific study of children was possible and thus became a landmark in the child study movement—a movement that paved the way for the emergence of modern developmental psychology (Thompson et al., 2012).

Throughout the 1890s, Hall oriented the focus of research on children against a backdrop of progressivism and social reform. His aim was two-fold: expanding our understanding of the child *and* improving the practices and methodologies used in the study of children. Hall sought to make improvements to child study in order to benefit the future of the country. These goals aligned with many of the female reformers, philanthropists, welfare advocates, and recently established organizations of mothers at the time (e.g. ASSA). Hall also established key pillars of modern psychology including the American Psychological Association, which he founded in 1887 with just 31 members. By 1893, Hall's child study movement had officially begun, driving research focused on school-aged children and adolescents for the purpose of furthering the understanding of children and creating more effective methods of study (Smuts, 2008).

With the launching of the child study movement, the stage was set for the beginning of child sciences as World War I ended. Hall argued for the study of both cognitive and social development and founded the Children's Institute at Clark University in 1909. The institute served as a center for research and also included a children's clinic (Lerner, Wertlieb, & Jacobs, 2003; Ross, 1972; Thompson et al., 2012). It was the first university-based institution dedicated to research on children.

There were issues with the methodologies used in early child research. The availability of research on children that could be considered "scientific" was limited, and some work was problematic given the limitations of some methods as well as the assumption that methods in adult psychology could be translated to research on children (Smuts, 2008). In 1901, the American psychologist Edward Thorndike offered the following critique: "That child-study has few exact statements as yet is due to the incompetence or thoughtlessness of its students, and not to the nature of the subject" (Thorndike, 1901, p. 20). The converging efforts in the two decades that followed gave the field what was necessary to bridge the gap between rudimentary child study and an established field of scientific research on development.

The Beginning of the Child Study Movement

At the start of the 20th century, there was agreement within society and the scientific community: children could be studied scientifically, but this alone was not sufficient for developmental psychology to emerge as it did. Unlike other fields of psychology, which gained gradual popularity as research disciplines over the decades, child development rose to prominence at an impressive rate. In 1918, only three psychologists and two psychiatrists in the United States were dedicated to full-time research on children (Smuts, 2008). A decade later, these numbers had grown to exceed 600 scholars, and by 1935, the study of children's development was an established, thriving domain. The establishment of land grant universities by the federal government in the 1860s was especially crucial in the child study movement. Parents were eager to obtain advice on child rearing, and *Parents' Magazine* was established in 1926 and continues to thrive today. However, a more troubling set of circumstances played a role as well.

After World War I, it became apparent that over half of the nation's young men were found to be unfit to serve in the military. These results came from standardized measures for mental testing, which began in the United States with the Stanford-Binet IQ test (Smuts, 2008). In 1917, the US army began to administer the Army Alpha, designed to evaluate the intellectual and emotional functioning of 2 million soldiers during World War I (Colman, 2008). Concern had been expressed at both government and private levels about low performance, and ways to remedy young people's mental and physical health issues were sought (Smuts, 2008).

Shortly after WWI, many philanthropic foundations shifted their resources to child programs and from charity to scientific endeavors. There was a strong belief that a better society could be created by applying social science and emphasizing the importance of childhood experiences on development (Smuts, 2008). The goal was "to reform the child for the benefit of society" (Smuts, 2008, p. 4). The efforts of social reformers, scientists, and philanthropists drew attention to a multidisciplinary, lifespan approach to studying development.

The Three Parts of the Child Study Movement

The child study movement, as it later came to be known, was actually made up of three separate movements whose efforts worked in parallel, but from within distinct domains using different strategies (Smuts, 2008): (1) the child guidance movement, (2) the US Children's Bureau and other efforts of the US federal government to study children and their development, and (3) the child development movement. These three movements were unified by the goal of furthering knowledge of children and development to better serve the future of the nation.

> The 1920s, usually seen as the decade of the flapper and the bootlegger, was actually the decade of the child. More than in any other period of American history, before or since, trends in science and society converged to place the child at center stage.
> (Smuts, 2008, p. 2).

Child Guidance Movement

The child guidance movement sought to understand children's emotional and behavioral problems, using multidisciplinary teams—including psychiatrists, psychologists, and social workers—that carried out their work in "guidance clinics," established by the private sector (Smuts, 2008). The first child guidance clinic was the Chicago Juvenile

Psychopathic Institute, founded in 1909 (Snodgrass, 1984). Psychiatrist William Healy was appointed as its first director. The clinic, renamed the Institute for Juvenile Research, provided diagnostic assessment and some forms of treatment to juvenile offenders referred from the courts.

> That just goes to show you how much at that time I was under the influence of everybody else—there was something the matter with the kid mentally or he wouldn't be such an offender. So we called it the Juvenile Psychopathic Institute which is really a silly name for it because we didn't find out that most of them were psychopathic.
> (Snodgrass, 1984, p. 5). *William Healy (1869–1963)*

Repeat offenders, whose behaviors were thought to result from underlying psychopathology, were also referred to the institute so they could be studied by researchers. Healy later directed a clinic in Boston in 1917—the now famous Judge Baker Clinic—where the large-scale study of juvenile delinquents was carried out (Smuts, 2008). This clinic served as the model for all child guidance clinics that came after it.

The Federal Government and the Children's Bureau

The federal government in the United States dedicated important effort to studying children and development in the 1900s and their efforts increased following WWI. The US Children's Bureau was founded in 1912 with an annual budget of $25,600, and Julia Lathrop was appointed Chief (Smuts, 2008). It pioneered in using the survey techniques developed by urban social reformers during the progressive era. The Bureau studied infant and maternal health during its first ten years and also studied child labor, dependency, and delinquency. Child welfare research was its primary activity (Smuts, 2008). The Bureau used social survey techniques to draw parallels between issues experienced by the child with conditions of poverty. By using a sociological rather than a medical approach, it was demonstrated that much of infant mortality was positively correlated with living in poverty.

President Woodrow Wilson proclaimed 1918 to be the Year of the Child (Smuts, 2008). The Federal Government also provided financial support for White House Conferences on Children held every ten years. The first White House Conference was in 1930 and by 1934, over 200 lifespan studies on American children were completed and the findings were integrated into the Social Security Act passed in 1935 (Bradbury, 1962; Smuts, 2008).

Child Development Movement

After World War I, new goals came to the forefront of the social agenda. Early childhood was assigned greater importance along with the many influences on development (Smuts, 2008). The support of philanthropy expanded to include *all* children, not just the disadvantaged.

A pioneering effort was the previously mentioned Iowa Child Welfare Research Station (see Figure 1.1), which institutionalized research on the physical, mental, and emotional development of normal children from conception to maturity (Smuts, 2008). The goal was to understand the child through the coordination and integration of research from various disciplines. At that time, most developmentalists worked in

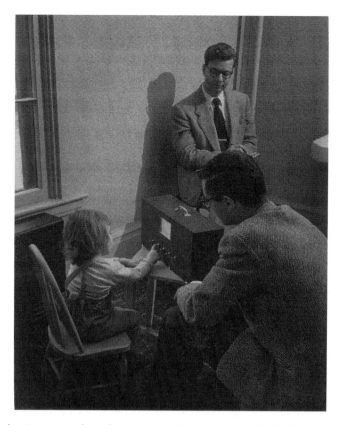

Figure 1.1 Conducting research with a young girl at the Iowa Child Welfare Research Station, 1950s.
Reprinted from Frederick W. Kent, *Conducting research with a young girl*, The University of Iowa, 1950s. Frederick W. Kent Collection, the University of Iowa Libraries (Iowa City, Iowa), and published with the approval of the University Archives at the University of Iowa Libraries, Iowa City, Iowa. Retrieved from http://digital.lib.uiowa.edu/cdm/compoundobject/collection/ictcs/id/7781/rec/203.

autonomous institutes, sometimes associated with universities, rather than academic departments or scientific laboratories.

"The Child's Conception of the World" by Jean Piaget (1925) prompted increased interest in the study of cognition in the decades that followed. Another landmark study from 1920 was John Watson's "Little Albert," which provided evidence of classical conditioning and was one of the first well-known studies that used children as subjects (Smuts, 2008). Prior to that, the majority of research on children was confined to observational methods.

Many studies were conducted on the physical development of children during this time (Thompson et al., 2012). Researchers began studying topics such as reaction speed, left or right handedness, and perceptual motor development (Goodenough, 1935; Gutteridge, 1939; Halverson, 1931; Hildreth, 1949; Thompson et al., 2012). Social development also became a topic of interest. Charlotte Buhler, one of the founders of modern lifespan psychology, conducted famous studies on social development and behavior in infancy

(Thompson et al., 2012). Freud's psychoanalytic theory was also influential on child study during the late 1930s.

The Establishment of the Five Child Research Institutes

The original child development research institutes were founded by the Laura Spelman Rockefeller Memorial (LSRM) between 1923 and 1929 (Smuts, 2008). During this time, Lawrence K. Frank established five research institutes based in major universities across the United States and Canada: Iowa State University, Columbia University at Teachers College, University of California-Berkeley, University of Minnesota, and the University of Toronto.

By 1927, Frank began to question the direction that some of the institutes were taking (Thompson et al., 2012). He felt that with emphasis placed on developing group norms, the research was missing an understanding of the individual child. As a result, new foci for some of the work were established. For example, the focus at Berkeley was to be on longitudinal research. Membership of the Committee on Child Development (CCD) was enlarged to encourage the evolution of child development research into an interdisciplinary endeavor that same year (Smuts, 2008).

The Founding of the Society for Research in Child Development (SRCD)

The consequences of the three parts of the child study movement are evident in the emergence and founding ideals of the field. The perspectives of the relevant disciplines strongly influenced both the type of research and the findings. The SRCD, perhaps the leading professional organization on research in child development, emerged from the CCD established by the National Research Council (NRC) in 1924. The NRC was the research arm of the National Academy of Sciences. The reasons that the CCD was formed had to do with the newly established goals of the time, aimed at preventing, rather than ameliorating, social ills. The newly emerging social and behavioral sciences were to be employed in accomplishing these goals. Research and education were highly regarded, and thus funds from philanthropy, as described above, became available to expand new endeavors (Smuts & Hagen, 1986).

Robert Woodworth, a leader in psychology and faculty member at Columbia University, was recruited to chair the CCD and several other prominent scholars were appointed. Monies from the LSRM were made available to fund initial activities. The activities were restricted to research and it was to be "as rigidly a scientific enterprise as possible and minimize references to child welfare implications and obligations" (Smuts & Hagen, 1986, p. 112). Twelve hundred questionnaires were sent to members of the American Psychological Association (APA) and to other organizations such as Anthropology to determine who was engaging in research relevant to children and young animals. A conference of thirty people was convened, and future goals were established.

Perhaps the major outcome was the establishment of the journal *Child Development* (*CD*) in 1930, which became the flagship journal in the field, with a multidisciplinary approach. The wide range of topics included: biochemistry, dentistry, education, pediatrics, psychiatry, psychology, parent education, public health, sociology, anatomy, and anthropometry. The committee also identified ways to standardize techniques for conducting research and a scholarship program was established.

The CCD then recommended to its parent group that a new professional society, independent of the NRC, should be established, and in 1933 the SRCD was founded. Since its inception the SRCD had dual principles: to foster research on child development from the perspectives of all relevant disciplines and to encourage the implementation of findings for the betterment of society's children and families. This was an exciting time, and even though the United States was at the beginning of the national depression of the 1930s, considerable progress was made, which continued until the country entered World War II, at which point much of the world of science greatly slowed down or came to a grinding halt (Smuts & Hagen, 1986).

Trends in Modern Developmental Research (1930–present)

The journal *Child Development* has become a major source for the study of the trends on research in children over the past eight decades.

Historical Trends: (1930–1979)

By the 1970s, the field had experienced nearly four decades of growth and maturation, settling into its own as a discipline. There was growing interest in the way the field had changed and whether the types of research conducted in the early decades still seemed pertinent. Later, the approach used involved secondary analyses of published research to examine trends that could highlight where the field had been, how it may have changed, and the direction it appeared to be going.

It is important to note that content analyses of published research assume that a scientific field is defined by the research it publishes (Kail & Herman, 1977). Historical publications, then, serve as an "archive of the paradigms of research in that field" (McLoyd & Randolph, 1985, p. 79). Though publications in no way provide a complete depiction of the research being conducted, we maintain a perspective that was well-articulated by Graham (1992): "There can be little doubt that these journals depict the current zeitgeist, mirror the scholarly interests of our academic leadership, and disseminate the products of what funding agencies deem worthy of support" (p. 629). While various social and political factors no doubt contributed to the rise of child development research, similar circumstances also greatly influenced the content of the research being produced. As the research focused on children grew, there was increasing interest in research trends in the field, in terms of the topics that researchers focused on, attributes of the methodologies they employed, and the ways in which these areas experienced change across decades. Using various forms of **content analyses**, developmental researchers have been able to take an introspective look at the field by examining the key features of the articles in leading journals.

Secular Research Trends

Charles Super, an American developmentalist, conducted one of the first large-scale content analyses of published research (Super, 1982). Super took a secular approach to the trends in research, analyzing articles published in *CD* from 1930 to 1979. He randomly selected ten articles from among those published each year and each article was coded for: characteristics of the study, sample, and authors.

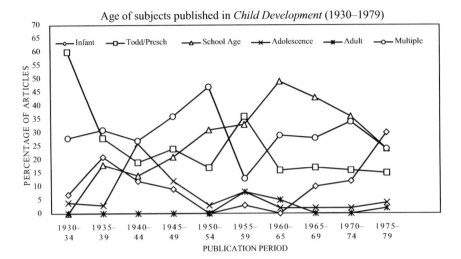

Figure 1.2 Age of subjects published in *Child Development* (1930–1979).
Adapted from Super, C. M. (1982). Secular Trends in Child Development and the Institutionalization of Professional Disciplines. *Newsletter of the Society for Research in Child Development*, Spring 1982.

Samples

Super (1982) found that the age groups of interest varied over time, such as the increase in the number of infant studies in the 1960s, followed by a rise in adolescent research the following decade (see Figure 1.2).

Studies with few subjects (< 10) virtually disappeared over time (see Figure 1.3). Further, many studies did not specify data on ethnicity/SES (socioeconomic status) of their subjects, a topic discussed below.

Authors

Changes in the characteristics of authors revealed a trend in the sociology of research on children. Studies from the first three decades had primarily one author, while more recent publications had multiple authors, as shown in Figure 1.4 (Super, 1982). Most early publications (1930–1960) were produced by authors affiliated with research institutes. Post-1960 publications were most often authored by scholars in university settings.

Methods

It was also revealed that approaches to data collection changed over time. Research from the 1930s to the 50s frequently utilized tests, interviews, archives/records, and naturalistic observations (see Figure 1.5). Beginning in the 1960s, the use of experimental paradigms increased dramatically.

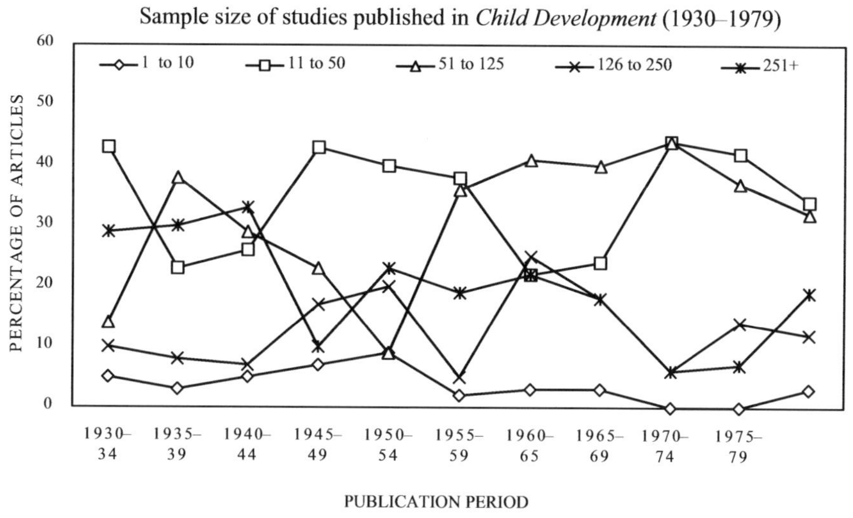

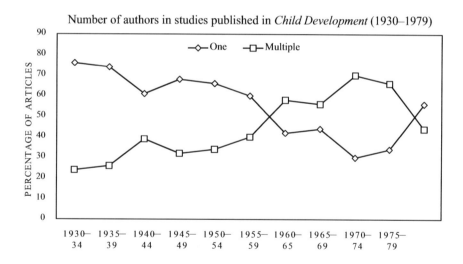

Figure 1.3 Sample size of studies published in *Child Development* (1930–1979).
Adapted from Super, C.M. (1982). Secular Trends in Child Development and the Institutionalization of Professional Disciplines. *Newsletter of the Society for Research in Child Development*, Spring 1982.

Figure 1.4 Number of authors in studies published in *Child Development* (1930–1979).
Adapted from Super, C.M. (1982). Secular Trends in Child Development and the Institutionalization of Professional Disciplines. *Newsletter of the Society for Research in Child Development*, Spring 1982.

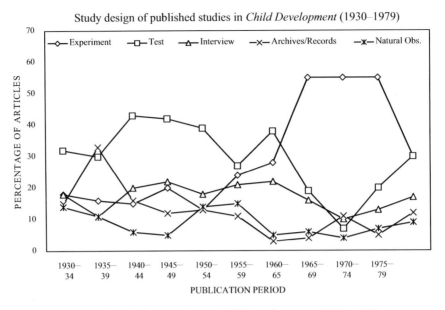

Figure 1.5 Study design of published studies in *Child Development* (1930–1979).
Adapted from Adapted from Super, C.M. (1982). Secular Trends in Child Development and the Institutionalization of Professional Disciplines. *Newsletter of the Society for Research in Child Development*, Spring 1982.

Changes in the topics studied have seen increasing numbers of studies focused on issues related to social/emotional and/or cognitive development, while earlier studies contained a range of different topics (see Figure 1.6).

Historical Relevance

In the context of the Cold War (1947–1991), the Korean War (1950–1953), and the Vietnam War (1955–1975), interest in studying the resilience of the child arose. The launch of Sputnik in 1957 by the Soviet Union instilled fear in America that prompted the need for greater research on effective teaching and learning. Shortly thereafter, there was a revival of interest in child rearing. According to Baldwin (1956), half of the research during that time addressed the connections between personality of the child and parenting practices. There was also considerable work on attachment and temperament (Thomas, Chess, & Birch, 1968). Famous examples include the seminal work of John Bowlby on attachment theory, Harry Harlow's research on mother–child relationships, and Mary Ainsworth's development of the Strange Situation paradigm which was used to highlight different attachment styles. Piaget's work on cognitive development was published in English during the late 1950s, sparking interest in the study of cognition (e.g. Inhelder & Piaget, 1958). The social activism that came with the civil rights movement in the United States from the late 1950s forward also impacted science and academia.

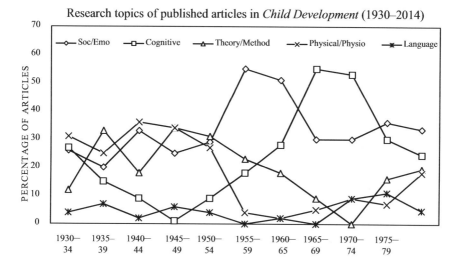

Figure 1.6 Research topics of articles published in *Child Development* (1930–1979).
Adapted from Super, C.M. (1982). Secular Trends in Child Development and the Institutionalization of Professional Disciplines. *Newsletter of the Society for Research in Child Development*, Spring 1982.

Conclusions

The findings from Super's work on trends are important in the context of what was to come in the field of child development. One can speculate that such changes occurred, at least in part, as a response to the converging factors discussed: the rapid expansion of research in the behavioral sciences, the infusion of federal and private funds to support these endeavors, and a large increase in the number of programs, departments, centers, and institutes devoted to the study of children and families.

Characteristics of Children Studied

Following Super's work, there was increased interest in examining the characteristics of children, including race/ethnicity and nationality. Taken together, "[The] social unrest of the 1960s stimulated psychologists to turn their attention toward the study of socially relevant topics, particularly ethnic minority groups" (Caplan & Nelson, 1973).

McLoyd and Randolph (1984, 1985) suggested there may be biases in procedures and instruments in studies on African American children. They examined trends in the study of African American children from research published in *CD* from 1936 to 1980. They found few studies were conducted on African American children before 1960, and race-comparative studies (in which African American children were compared with white children on some factor or factors) gained popularity over this time.

Graham (1992) carried out a content analysis of leading APA journals, appropriately titled "Most of the Subjects were White and Middle Class." She found just 3% of studies focused on African Americans, calling for more attention to a problem in published research at the time:

> ... academic psychologists face serious challenges as the 1990s unfold ... social concerns demand increased understanding of the psychological functioning of Black Americans, and pedagogical needs call for cultural diversity in our academic curricula ... these challenges are ... not likely to be met without a strong empirical literature on African Americans from which psychologists can draw. It therefore seems appropriate to stop and take stock of the status of African American research in the journals of mainstream psychology,
>
> (Graham, 1992, p. 629)

Studies of this kind highlighted the need for increased diversity in developmental research. Demand for change in the methods and subjects employed were called for.

Trends in Research in Child Development: (1980–present)

Background

Before the 1980s, race, ethnicity, and socioeconomic status of children were not available in most published research. Today, most articles provide this information. In the 1990s, the governing board of SRCD responded to the lack of diversity. A special issue of *CD* was published in 1990, focusing on minority children (Spencer & McLoyd, 1990). *Child Development's Special Issue on Minority Children* provided an outlet for researchers of minority issues to publish work.

> It is suggested that the most critical legacy of the special issue is the conceptual and ideological zeitgeist it fostered. The issue set culture and ecological context in the foreground of analyses, advanced a cultural-variant perspective, and further discredited the deficit perspective that long dominated the study of ethnic minority children and families. The special issue is also significant for its role in shaping post-1990 research agenda. In addition, it underscored the need for more nuanced articulations of what cultural or ethnic characteristics are of special relevance for understanding specific domains of development and the need for well-crafted methodological tools with which to test these ideas, ...
>
> (McLoyd, 2006, p. 1)

In 1991, developmental psychologist Susan Somerville became the editor of *CD* and was given a mandate to increase diversity in its published studies. Somerville stressed how diversity would be valued by the journal in future publications in order to promote change (Somerville, 1991). SRCD governance established a policy concerning the descriptive information that all submitters of manuscripts to *CD* must provide about the children in their studies. The work of SRCD committees and programs at biennial meetings at this time also expressed the commitment of SRCD to issues related to diversity and minority issues.

Finally, to assess the impact of the mandate on future publications in *CD*, a project was undertaken by then executive director John W. Hagen to examine trends in research. Since that time, the project has continued to track trends in research and was expanded to include other journals and a more sophisticated coding scheme. Hagen and Conley (1994), as the first endeavor, pursued analyses of changes in the research, while more recent analyses include data through 2017. The results discussed in subsequent sections come from this project that has been active for over 25 years. Basic criteria for coding are presented below and a more detailed explanation of the coding used in the publications is available in the supplementary materials for Activity 1.

Early Work

Hagen and Conley (1994) focused on tracking diversity of subject populations and methodological changes over time. Articles published in *CD* from 1980 to 1993 were analyzed using a coding scheme drawn from Super (1982). Specific race/ethnicity categories were added. Articles were coded for whether race/ethnicity was reported (Yes/No), whether the sample was "predominantly white" (Yes/No), and the race/ethnicity of subjects.

Results

The majority of articles through the 1980s provided little to no information about the race/ethnicity of subjects whatsoever (see Figure 1.7; Hagen & Conley, 1994). Beginning in 1990, more authors in *CD* provided race/ethnicity information.

Due to increases in reporting, a striking rise in the percentage of studies that included white or predominantly white subjects was observed. A steady increase in studies that specified percentages of subject ethnicities also began at the same time. Lastly, Hagen and Conley also noted that the proportion of studies examining only African American, Asian, or Hispanic children remained low and fairly constant.

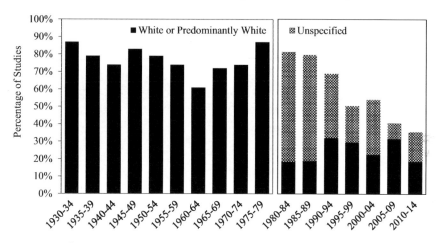

Figure 1.7 Research Topics in CD Published Articles (1930–2014).
Left panel: adapted from Super, C.M. (1982). Secular Trends in Child Development and the Institutionalization of Professional Disciplines. *Newsletter of the Society for Research in Child Development*, Spring 1982. Right panel: Data from 1980 to 1993 adapted from Hagen, J.W., & Conley, A.C. (1994). Ethnicity and Race of Children Studied in Child Development, 1980–1993. *Newsletter of the Society for Research in Child Development*, Spring 1994; data from 1994 to 2004 adapted from Hagen, J.W., Velissaris, N.G., & Nelson, M.J. (2004, August). The Emergence of the Child Research Movement. *Presentation at the 28th International Congress of Psychology Conference*. Beijing, China; data from 2005 onward adapted from Hagen, J.W., & Lasagna, C.A. (2018, June). A Look at Research Published in Child Development Over Time: Historical and Recent Trends in the Scientific Investigation of Children. *Poster presented at the 2nd annual meeting of the National Research Conference on Early Childhood (formerly the National Head Start Conference)*, Arlington, VA.

Later Work. (1995-early/mid-2000s)

Subsequent studies showed increased focus on the differential treatment of participants of certain demographics on the basis of study attributes such as content and risk status. A consequence of the growing number of studies reporting race/ethnicity was the appearance of an increase in studies on predominantly white subjects. It is unlikely that this represents a true rise in the number of studies using such heterogeneous samples. Instead, this is likely an emergence of a trend that was there all along–it was simply unable to be seen without authors providing details. Analyses conducted have provided the first evidence of differential treatment of subjects in recently published research (CD 1995–2003) on the basis of subjects' age and race/ethnicity (e.g. Hagen, Germack, McCartney, & Lignell, 2000; Hagen et al., 2004).

Hagen et al. (2000) looked at articles published in CD from 1980 to 1999 and noted differential treatment of certain age groups. Adolescents were more likely to be the subjects of studies on at-risk youth as compared to other age groups. School-aged children and younger were more frequently included in studies of normally developing children.

Hagen et al. (2004) looked at differences in race/ethnicity distributions of children studied that emerged when studies were divided into two groups: (1) "normal," which includes children considered to have typical development, and "at-risk," which refers to children at-risk for a particular developmental problem, that are studied to obtain data on these children. This work also highlighted that articles in CD focused predominantly on middle-class children (over half of children studied were reported at middle class and above in terms of SES) that resided in the United States (76% of children studied; Hagen et al., 2004). Approximately one out of every four studies published in CD during this time did not report the SES of children studied. Findings also suggested that research on what is considered to be normal child development was based on samples lacking ethnic diversity (see Figure 1.8).

These results provide a basis to question whether differential criteria may be used in the studying of children of different race/ethnicity groups and to pursue more detailed trends analyses in order to find answers to these questions.

Current Work (2007–2016)

The most recent studies continue the pursuit of previous investigations and make additions to the coding scheme where needed to keep the methods germane to the times. Current studies examine trends in *Child Development* (CD) and *Developmental Psychology* (DP), as well as the European journal *Developmental Science* (DS), to examine trends with possible broader representations. From 2007–2016, 890 studies from these journals have been coded and analyzed for aspects of their methodology, subject characteristics, and content.

In the past decade, study methodologies and subject populations have continued to increase in complexity, necessitating refinements to the coding scheme. For example, as more studies are specifying the socioeconomic statuses of participants, it was apt to include a complete percentage breakdown of SES by social class in the revised scheme. While a goal of the study is to analyze past methods and their relation to historical events, the focus here is on what changes have occurred over time leading to present day. More specifically, how far child development research has come in its quest for diversity and inclusion.

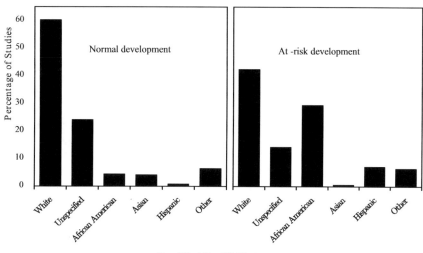

Figure 1.8 Race/Ethnicity distributions in "normal" versus "at-risk" studies. Adapted from Hagen, J.W., Velissaris, N.G., & Nelson, M.J. (2004, August). The Emergence of the Child Research Movement. Presentation at the 28th International Congress of Psychology Conference. Beijing, China.

Preliminary analyses revealed few differences between the two American journals but extreme differences in their comparison to articles in *DS*. To simplify discussion, analyses are presented using combined data from *CD* and *DP* (see Tables 1 and 2), unless otherwise noted, with select comparisons of interest described in relation to *DS*. Notably, greater diversity was observed, but this may be attributed at least in part to rising numbers of studies on at-risk populations.

Age groups ranging from infancy to adolescence were well represented among these publications. Most of the children studied resided in North America, and the majority of articles were from the United States. Issues concerning social-emotional and cognitive development continued to dominate. In this publication period, 20% of studies included at-risk subjects and 80% were considered normal. Sixty-four percent of studies reported SES of their subjects: parental education level, household income, and social class were the most frequently reported indices. Of the 80% of articles reporting race/ethnicity, the average sample from this period had the following ethnic makeup: 59% White, 12% African American, 10% Hispanic, 8% Asian and 6% other/mixed ethnicity.

Results showed interactions between certain characteristics and study attributes; most notably, differential treatment of participants of different ethnicities based on risk status. Consistent with previous findings, children from minorities were more often included in at-risk studies. White and Asian children were more likely to be included in normal studies. Thus, the ethnic distribution of normal studies from 2007 to 2016 lacks ethnic diversity, since the subjects are predominantly white. The

Table 1 Characteristics of studies among published research on children: descriptive information for variables of interest examined by Hagen and Lasagna (2018)

	Comparison by publication period						Totals for entire publication period		
	2007–2009			2014–2016			2007–2016		
Variable	No. of valid cases	N	M (%)	No. of valid cases	N	M (%)	No. of valid cases	N	M (%)
Content area									
Social/emotional	164	115	70.0	210	134	64.0	613	384	63.0
Intellectual/cognitive	164	79	48.0	210	95	45.0	613	284	46.0
Parent–child interaction	164	52	32.0	210	50	24.0	613	162	26.0
Physiological	164	21	13.0	210	32	15.0	613	74	12.0
Academic	164	25	15.0	210	29	14.0	613	97	16.0
Intervention	164	7	4.0	210	19	9.0	613	41	7.0
Cultural	164	20	12.0	210	25	12.0	613	74	12.0
Country									
United States	164	110	67.1	210	150	71.4	613	423	69.0
United Kingdom	164	9	5.5	210	18	8.6	613	41	6.7
Canada	164	13	7.9	210	21	10.0	613	50	8.2
Other countries by region:									
W. Europe	164	0	0.0	210	1	0.5	613	63	10.3
E. Asia	164	0	0.0	210	1	0.5	613	23	3.8
Australasia	164	4	2.4	210	7	3.3	613	22	3.6
N. Europe	164	4	2.4	210	6	2.9	613	14	2.3
Middle East	164	4	2.4	210	7	3.3	613	14	2.3
S. Europe	164	10	6.1	210	25	11.9	613	12	2.0

E. Europe	164	0	0.0	210	1	0.5	613	3	0.5
S.E. Asia	164	5	3.1	210	11	5.2	613	2	0.3
Africa	164	7	4.3	210	7	3.3	613	1	0.2
Demographic Reporting									
Age reported	164	210	100.0	210	210	100.0	613	613	100.0
Ethnicity reported	164	143	87.0*	210	149	71.0*	613	491	80.8
Gender reported	164	155	94.5	210	194	92.4	613	582	94.9
SES reported	164	90	55.0*	210	145	69.0*	613	390	64.0

Notes: adapted from Hagen, J.W., & Lasagna, C.A. (2018, June). A Look at Research Published in *Child Development* Over Time: Historical and Recent Trends in the Scientific Investigation of Children. Poster presented at the 2nd annual meeting of the National Research Conference on Early Childhood (formerly the National Head Start Conference), Arlington, VA. Based on sample of (N = 613) articles published in *CD* (n = 272) and *DP* (n = 341) from 2007 to 2016. * = Significant difference between T1 and T2 (p <.05) according to results of independent samples t-test of mean differences between time periods.

Table 2 Characteristics of samples among published research on children: descriptive information for variables of interest examined by Hagen and Lasagna (2018)

Variable	Comparison by publication period						Totals for entire publication period		
	2007–2009			2014–2016			2007–2016		
	No. of valid cases	N	M (%)	No. of valid cases	N	M (%)	No. of valid cases	N	M (%)
Age									
Infancy	164	36	21.7	210	34	16.1	613	118	19.2
Toddler/preschool	164	31	19.0	210	47	22.5	613	142	23.1
School age	164	37	22.8	210	57	27.1	613	151	24.7
Adolescence	164	46	28.1	210	54	25.6	613	154	25.2
Adulthood	164	14	8.5	210	18	8.8	613	47	7.7
Ethnicity									
White	142	87	61.0	149	83	55.6	491	288	58.6
African American	142	16	11.2	149	21	13.9	491	60	12/3
Hispanic	142	13	9.3	149	16	10.8	491	47	9.6
Asian	142	12	8.4	149	11	7.5	491	39	8.0
Other/mixed	142	8	6.0	149	10	7.0	491	31	6.4
Unspecified	142	7	5.6	149	9	4.7	491	26	5.4
Gender									
Male	155	79	51.0	194	100	51.5	582	285	49.0
Female	155	76	49.0	194	94	48.5	582	297	51.0
Geographic Location									
N. American	164	120	72.9	210	141	67.3	613	435	70.9
Europe	164	25	15.5*	210	50	23.8*	613	119	19.4
Asia	164	7	4.4	210	8	4.0	613	25	4.1

	n	Count	%	n	Count	%	n	Count	%
Africa	164	0	0.0	210	2	0.8	613	2	0.3
Middle East	164	3	1.8	210	1	0.5	613	8	1.2
S. Pacific	164	6	3.7	210	7	3.3	613	21	3.4
Cen. & S. America	164	3	1.6	210	1	0.3	613	3	0.6
Risk Status									
At-risk	164	29	17.7	210	52	24.8	613	121	19.7
Normal	164	135	82.3	210	158	75.2	613	274	80.3

Notes: adapted from Hagen, J.W., & Lasagna, C.A. (2018, June). A Look at Research Published in *Child Development* Over Time: Historical and Recent Trends in the Scientific Investigation of Children. Poster presented at the 2nd annual meeting of the National Research Conference on Early Childhood (formerly the National Head Start Conference), Arlington, VA. Based on sample of $N = 613$ articles published in *CD* ($n = 272$) and *DP* ($n = 341$) from 2007 to 2016. * = Significant difference between T1 and T2 ($p < .05$) according to results of independent samples t-test of mean differences between time periods.

overrepresentation of adolescent subjects in at-risk studies was found to be lower during this period.

Though recent evidence from *CD* and *DP* supports the notion that demographic reporting practices are improving, this tendency is not characteristic of *all* journals in the field. *DS*, for instance, still reports participant demographics such as race/ethnicity and SES infrequently compared with *CD* and *DP*. Key analyses involving *DS* demonstrate that not all trends observed in *CD* and *DP* are represented in *DS*. Another finding was that increases in correlational studies occurred in *CD* and *DP*, while *DS* continues to publish experimental articles.

Note that SES has not been addressed in the present analyses. Though approximately two-thirds of studies reported an indicator of participant SES, the measures provided are inconsistent and often not comparable, making between-study SES comparisons unreliable. A standardized approach to measuring and reporting SES is clearly needed. The relatively few that do report SES often used basic class distinctions such as lower, middle, and upper class. Recent advances have shown SES to be a complex, multifaceted measure. Work in this area typically includes indicators such as parental education level and family income levels. While these measures provide improvement, the result is that many measures claim to be indicators of this but are variable (e.g. Duncan, Daly, McDonough, & Williams, 2002; Winkleby, Jatulis, Frank, & Fortmann, 1992). With many new measures available and yet few standards to guide their use, the recent inclusion of purposeful SES measures is "progress" that comes with unfavorable consequences.

An aspect of design and methodology that our project has yet to include concerns the changes in sample size over time, and how these patterns relate to the methodology used as well as the ethnic composition of some samples. In the 1960s through the 1990s, there was increased use of experimental designs that was seen as increased rigor in developmental research. However, other changes in research began to appear as well. The increased availability of secondary sources of data which considerably increased sample sizes and better descriptions of the subjects, as well as the increased emphasis on longitudinal study designs, have all occurred over the past two decades or so. According to Davis-Kean and Jager (2017), in the past, developmental science relied on small sample sizes of children. The small samples are limited in power to detect differences as well as the lack of demographic diversity, which limits generalization. The sophistication of the new approaches to conducting developmental research that allow for more conclusions and inferences is changing rapidly and it is important to monitor the changes as they appear in current published research. These changes have inspired us to include a project examining the relationships among new correlational variables over two decades. A preliminary analysis examined the aforementioned 2007–2016 data from *CD* in this light and additional data from 2017 as well. A subsample of the total number of articles (n=95) from *CD* over the past decade was selected and coded for the following variables: Sample Size by Group (200 or less and over 200), Race Proportions (White, African American, Hispanic, Asian, and Other/Mixed), Years (Early and Late), and Study Design (Experimental and Correlational).

Consistent with previous findings of increasing racial diversity, subjects were less predominately white and more diverse as sample size increased. Specifically, the proportion of white subjects decreased and the proportion of African American subjects increased with increasing sample size. This finding could be due to racial stratification techniques available in the larger studies or the number of race-specific studies may have increased. Since the previous analyses found that at-risk studies had also increased, this finding could also contribute to the increase in African American subjects noted. In addition, the proportion of Hispanic participants showed a nonsignificant increase. Again, these findings point to increased diversity.

Racial/ethnic distribution was not the only aspect of method/design that showed change over the past decade or so. Of special note, for the 95 studies included in the analyses to 2007–2017, 27 were classified as experimental and 68 were correlational. These numbers reflect the dramatic shift towards studies using predominately newer correlational designs in the past ten years. In total, 72% of all studies were classified as correlational. When examining the variation based on sample size, we found that studies with samples of less than 200 relied more on experimental (47%) than larger studies (10%). There was a significant relationship between a study's sample size and its elected design. This could be due to an increase in longitudinal studies and use of secondary data analysis over the decade, which future analyses could determine by investigating if studies with larger sample sizes are more likely to be non-experimental studies.

Conclusions

Results from this work on trends in published research on children has provided evidence for positive changes in publications found in major journals in the field. The goal to increase diversity of both subjects and topics by editorial boards in the 1990s has been partially achieved. More studies of normal minority children are needed, and efforts should be made to include samples representing a larger continuum of children to promote diversity.

The research conducted in child development and developmental science over the past five decades has shown great changes in the topics of study, the design and methods employed, and in sensitivity to the subject populations studied. It is evident that for *CD* in particular, the mandates of the governing council of SRCD were effective in bringing about more inclusiveness and diversity in the children and youth studied. Other journals have shown promising trends as well. While progress is needed, the concerns expressed by Jeffrey Arnett (2008) are being addressed and the future for improving our understanding of our nation's and the world's children looks bright.

References

Addams, J. (1910). Charity and social justice. *The North American Review*, 192(656), 1–5.
Arnett, J. J. (2008). The Neglected 95%: Why American psychology needs to become less American. *American Psychologist*, 63(7), 609–613.
Baldwin, A. L. (1956). Child psychology. *Annual Review of Psychology*, 7(1), 259–282. doi:10.1146/annurev.ps.07.020156.001355
Baltes, P. B., Reese, H. W., & Lipsitt, L. P. (1980). Life-span developmental psychology. *Annual Review of Psychology*, 31(1), 65–110. doi:10.1146/annurev.ps. 31.020180.000433
Borstelmann, L. J. (1983). Children before psychology: ideas about children from antiquity to the late 1800s. In P. H. Mussen (Ed.) *Handbook of Child Psychology*, 4th ed., vol. 1: History, theory and methods (pp. 1–40). New York: Wiley.

Bradbury, D. (1962). *Five Decades of Action for Children: A History of the Children's Bureau*. Washington, DC: U.S. Department of Health, Education, and Welfare.

Bradbury, D., & Stoddard, G. (1933). *Pioneering in Child Welfare: A History of the Iowa Child Welfare Research Station, 1917–1933*. Iowa City: State University of Iowa Press.

Bremner, R. H. (1956). *From the Depths; The Discovery of Poverty in the United States*. New York: New York University Press.

Bulmer, M., Bales, K., & Sklar, K. K. (Eds.). (1991). *The Social Survey in Historical Perspective, 1880–1940*. Cambridge, UK: Cambridge University Press.

Caplan, N., & Nelson, S. D. (1973). On being useful: the nature and consequences of psychological research on social problems. *American Psychologist, 28*, 199–211.

Colman, A. (2008). *Army Alpha and Beta Tests: A Dictionary of Psychology*. Oxford University Press. Retrieved 16 January 2019, from www.oxfordreference.com.proxy.lib.umich.edu/view/10.1093/acref/9780199534067.001.0001/acref-9780199534067-e-632.

Crain, W. C. (1992). *Theories of Development: Concepts and Applications* (3rd ed.). Englewood Cliffs, NJ: Prentice-Hall, Inc.

Cravens, H. (1993). *Before Head Start: The Iowa Station & America's Children*. Chapel Hill, NC: University of North Carolina Press.

Davis-Kean, P. E., & Jager III, J. (2017). From small to big: methods for incorporating large scale data into developmental science. *Monographs Society Research in Child Development, 82*, 31–45. doi:10.1111/mono.12297.

Duncan, G. J., Daly, M. C., McDonough, P., & Williams, D. R. (2002). Optimal indicators of socioeconomic status for health research. *American Journal of Public Health, 92*(7), 1151–1157.

Goodenough, F. L. (1935). Selected references on preschool and parental education. *The Elementary School Journal, 35*(7), 540–548. doi:10.1086/457218.

Graham, S. (1992). Most of the subjects were white and middle class: trends in published research on African Americans in selected APA journals, 1970–1989. *American Psychologist, 47*(5), 629.

Gutteridge, M. (1939). A study of motor achievements of young children. *Archives of Psychology, 244*, 1–178.

Hagen, J. W., & Conley, A. C. (1994). Ethnicity and race of children studied in *Child Development*, 1980–1993. *Newsletter of the society for research in child development*, Spring 1994.

Hagen, J. W., Germack, M. C., McCartney, J. R., & Lignell, B. W. (2000, June) Research on Children: Trends in Substantive Areas and Subject Characteristics. *Presented at the 5th National Head Start Conference*, Washington, DC.

Hagen, J. W., & Lasagna, C. A. (2018, June). A Look at Research Published in *Child Development* over Time: Historical and Recent Trends in the Scientific Investigation of Children. *Poster presented at the 2nd annual meeting of the National Research Conference on Early Childhood (formerly the National Head Start Conference)*, Arlington, VA.

Hagen, J. W., Velissaris, N. G., & Nelson, M. J. (2004, August). The Emergence of the Child Research Movement. *Presentation at the 28th International Congress of Psychology Conference*. Beijing, China.

Hall, G. S. (1883). The contents of children's minds. *Princeton Review, 11*(May), 249–272.

Halverson, H. (1931). An experimental study of prehension in infants by means of systematic cinema records. *Genetic Psychology Monographs, 10*(2–3), 107–286.

Hildreth, R. (1949). Donald E. Emerson. *The Journal of Philosophy, 46*(14), 452.

Hilgard, E. R. (1987). *Psychology in America: A Historical Survey*. New York: Harcourt Brace.

Inhelder, B., & Piaget, J. (1958). *The Growth of Logical Thinking from Childhood to Adolescence*. New York: Basic Books.

Kail, R. V., & Herman, J. F. (1977). Structure in developmental psychology: an analysis of journal citations. *Human Development, 20*, 309–316.

Lerner, R. M., Wertlieb, D., & Jacobs, F. (2003). Historical and theoretical bases of applied developmental science. *Handbook of Applied Developmental Science: Historical and Theoretical Foundations, 1*, 1–28.

McLoyd, V. C. (2006). The legacy of child development's 1990 special issue on minority children: an editorial retrospective. *Child Development, 77*, 1142–1148. doi:10.1111/j.1467-8624.2006.00952.x.

McLoyd, V. C., & Randolph, S. M. (1984). The conduct and publication of research on Afro-American children. *Human Development, 27*(2), 65–75.

McLoyd, V. C., & Randolph, S. M. (1985). Secular trends in the study of Afro-American children: a review of *Child Development*, 1936–1980. *Monographs of the Society for Research in Child Development, 50*, 65–75.

Piaget, J. (1925). La représentation du monde chez l'enfant (The Child's Conception of the World). *Revue de Theologie et de Philosophie, 13*(56), 191–214.

Ross, D. (1972). *G. Stanley Hall: The Psychologist as Prophet*. Chicago, IL: University of Chicago Press.

Rousseau, J. (1979). *Emile: Or, On Education*. New York: Basic Books.

Smuts, A. B. (2008). *Science in the Service of Children, 1893–1935*. New Haven, CT: Yale University Press.

Smuts, A. B., & Hagen, J. W. (1986). *History and Research in Child Development*. Chicago, IL: University of Chicago Press.

Snodgrass, J. (1984). William Healy (1869–1963): pioneer child psychiatrist and criminologist. *Journal of the History of the Behavioral Sciences, 20*(4), 332–339.

Somerville, S. C. (1991). Editorial. *Child Development, 62*, 873–874.

Spencer, M. B., & McLoyd, V. C. (Eds.) (1990). *Child Development: Special Issue on Minority Children. 61*(2).

Super, C. M. (1982). Secular trends in child development and the institutionalization of professional disciplines. *Newsletter of the Society for Research in Child Development*, Spring 1982.

Thomas, A., Chess, S., & Birch, H. G. 1918–1973. (1968). *Temperament and Behavior Disorders in Children*. New York: New York University Press.

Thompson, D., Hogan, J. D., & Clark, P. M. (2012). *Developmental Psychology in Historical Perspective*. New York: John Wiley & Sons.

Thorndike, E. L. (1901). *Notes on Child Study* (Vol. 8, No. 3–4). New York: Macmillan Company.

Winkleby, M., Jatulis, D., Frank, E., & Fortmann, S. P. (1992). Socioeconomic status and health: how education, income, and occupation contribute to risk factors for cardiovascular disease. *American Journal of Public Health, 82*, 816–820.

2 Overimitation across Development
The Influence of Individual and Contextual Factors

Bruce Rawlings, Natália Dutra, Cameron Turner, and Emma Flynn

Introduction to the Topic

Children are extremely effective at acquiring information from others (termed social learning) and exhibit a remarkable proclivity to reproduce witnessed behaviour. From nine months, children readily imitate others (Meltzoff & Moore, 1989), and throughout childhood they prefer copying others over attempting to solve novel problems themselves (Flynn, Turner, & Giraldeau, 2016; Rawlings, 2018). Copying others allows children to navigate their physical and social environments by rapidly learning the affordances, and the appropriate social behaviour, of our complex world. Social learning has potential advantages when compared to individual learning, which is inherent with risks associated with discovery, such as being the first to eat a particular item or navigating dangerous environments (Legare & Nielsen, 2015). Such is children's proclivity to copy others, they frequently engage in what has become known as 'overimitation'.

Overimitation is the act of imitating actions that are causally unnecessary in a goal-directed sequence of actions, such that task efficiency appears decreased (Lyons, Young, & Keil, 2007). This propensity, thought to be unique to humans, develops early in life and is maintained into adulthood. For example, after witnessing an adult demonstrate actions irrelevant to success on novel puzzles (such as tapping on top of a box which only requires opening a door to retrieve a reward), young children (Nielsen, 2006), adolescents (Whiten et al., 2016) and adults (Flynn & Smith, 2012) have been shown to copy these irrelevant actions with remarkable fidelity. Overimitation in children has been documented when apparatuses are transparent such that the irrelevance actions are highly salient (Horner & Whiten, 2004), when children are told to ignore 'silly' actions by a demonstrator (Lyons et al., 2007), in laboratory (McGuigan, Makinson, & Whiten, 2011) and non-laboratory settings (Whiten et al., 2016) as well as across tasks other than puzzleboxes (Frick, Clément, & Gruber, 2017) including gestures (Clay, Over, & Tennie, 2018).

This chapter will present the overimitation literature – particularly focusing on its development across childhood – and the methods used to examine overimitation. We begin by describing key theories of why children overimitate, before explaining how overimitation is typically measured by developmental psychologists, and what this has told us about the developmental trajectory of overimitation. The conventional perspective is that the propensity to overimitate continually increases across development. However, a central theme of this chapter is to advocate that innovations in methods used to examine overimitation suggest that the trajectory of overimitation is actually more complex than a simple broadly linear developmental pathway. Specifically, we focus on two factors that seem especially pertinent to the expression of overimitation across development: extrinsic factors, relating to the conditions in which experiments are conducted, and intrinsic individual differences distinct to the child.

Summary of the Topic (and Age-Related Changes)

The copying of instrumentally *irrelevant* actions distinguishes overimitation from imitation, defined here as matching the bodily actions of a model (Whiten & Ham, 1992). Imitation, which due to its proximity to overimitation will also feature throughout this chapter, is a useful strategy to quickly acquire complex social and instrumental information. Yet, humans' propensity to overimitate presents a puzzle; on face value, copying irrelevant actions appears to be an over-effortful and irrational strategy. Why, then, do we so readily overimitate?

Broadly, there are two principal accounts attempting to explain overimitation. Causal accounts (also termed instrumental) claim that by faithfully copying others, children acquire causal information about their behaviour and the objects they interact with (Lyons, Damrosch, Lin, Macris, & Keil, 2011). These accounts propose that children copy with high fidelity because they are unable to reliably understand the link between actions and results in goal-directed behaviours. Thus, by encoding witnessed behaviours as causally relevant, children rapidly acquire understanding of the affordances of our complex tool-rich world. Supporting evidence comes from studies showing that children do not display overimitation for actions performed on a detached, separate container to the one holding the reward (Lyons et al., 2007) and that children are less likely to imitate actions not performed directly on an apparatus (i.e. clapping above a puzzlebox) than those performed on the apparatus (Hoehl, Zettersten, Schleihauf, Grätz, & Pauen, 2014). Moreover, children still overimitate even when explicitly instructed to exclude unnecessary actions (Lyons et al., 2011).

In contrast, social based accounts of overimitation (also termed affiliative or conventional) propose that overimitation results from social motivations, and that children perform irrelevant actions to affiliate with or 'be like' others (Over & Carpenter, 2012). Studies show that children overimitate more when the demonstrator is present rather than out of sight (Nielsen & Blank, 2011) and when observing live versus video demonstrations (Marsh, Ropar, & Hamilton, 2014). Further, when tasks are framed such that normativity is salient (emphasising how things ought to be done), children's propensity to overimitate increases (Clegg & Legare, 2016b). Children's imitation is also facilitated by a range of social cues including pedagogical intentions (Bonawitz et al., 2011) and being primed with ostracism (Watson-Jones, Legare, Whitehouse, & Clegg, 2014). Consequently, it has been argued that children attribute causally non-functional behaviour as cultural conventions (i.e. socially driven), resulting in high-fidelity copying (Legare & Nielsen, 2015).

While instrumental and social hypotheses are currently the dominant accounts, overimitation may serve other purposes. Imitation is known to play an important role in communicative development (Eckerman & Peterman, 2004) and language learning (Toth, Munson, Meltzoff, & Dawson, 2006), and thus it may be important to consider the role of overimitation in communication (Clay et al., 2018). Indeed, three-year-old children reproduce redundant novel words in utterances (Bannard, Klinger, & Tomasello, 2013) and, having learned a selection of correct words, three- to five-year-olds repeated a model's 'mispronounced' words with marked fidelity, even after they have correctly named the appropriate words before testing (Subiaul, Winters, Krumpak, & Core, 2016). Given that language is inherently conventional, children's vocal overimitation, violating their own linguistic knowledge, is suggestive of social motivations (Subiaul et al., 2016).

Overimitation thus likely serves several functions across multiple domains, which each may manifest in different circumstances (Keupp, Behne, Zachow, Kasbohm, & Rakoczy, 2015). Our propensity to overimitate may also be a contributing factor to our species' striking cultural success. Humans are the most cultural species on earth and in tandem, high-fidelity imitation (including overimitation) and innovation are proposed to be the dual mechanisms allowing human culture to accumulate across generations (Legare & Nielsen, 2015). Innovation (the generation of novel and useful behaviours) generates variation in skillsets, technology and social practices, and high-fidelity imitation facilitates the dissemination of these behavioural variants. Indeed, there is no concrete evidence of overimitation in nonhuman animals; lack of overimitation has been found with chimpanzees (Horner & Whiten, 2004), bonobos (Clay & Tennie, 2018), orangutans (Nielsen & Susianto, 2009) and two canid species (Johnston, Holden, & Santos, 2017). These results suggest that unlike humans, other species are driven by reproducing the outcome of observed actions. Conversely, children attribute social and/or instrumental importance to witnessed non-functional actions, which in turn facilitates preservation of cultural products.

The Developmental Trajectory of Overimitation

The initial demonstration of overimitation evoked much exploration of its development across childhood. Overimitation emerges early in life; by around two years children replicate irrelevant actions (McGuigan, 2013; Clay et al., 2018). Several studies examining age differences in the propensity to overimitate have found that it appears to follow a linear progression: increasing throughout childhood, with some evidence that even adults display higher rates of overimitation than children. Marsh et al. (2014) found that rates of overimitation increased with age in five- to eight-year-old children across three separate tasks, including making a paper fan, building tower blocks and retrieving toys from boxes. McGuigan et al. (2011) investigated three- and five-year-olds and adults' propensity to copy irrelevant actions on a novel transparent puzzlebox before obtaining a reward. Adults overimitated at the highest rate, followed by five-year-olds, with three-year-olds displaying the lowest overimitation rate. Moreover, recent work by Whiten et al. (2016) in a 'real life' scenario (a public zoo) found that four- to fifteen-year-old children and adults showed equally high rates of reproducing irrelevant actions on a puzzlebox apparatus. Thus, these studies, in which different-aged participants are presented with the same apparatus in the same conditions, appear to indicate that we overimitate across the lifespan, and that the tendency to do so increases with age.

Possible Measurement and Designs

The typical experimental paradigm to study overimitation involves an experimenter presenting children with a novel apparatus – commonly a puzzlebox. The experimenter performs a predetermined set of actions on the apparatus (e.g., tapping the box or manipulating non-functional parts; see Additional Activity 2.1 for examples) before the child, and the number of observed irrelevant actions participants reproduce are measured. Children are usually assessed individually, out of sight of others, such as in a quiet area of their school or in a university laboratory.

Researchers can employ various manipulations to explore the cognitive and social underpinnings of high-fidelity copying. For instance, one possible manipulation is to use peer models instead of adults. Children experience many situations in which they observe peers rather than adults performing solutions to novel problems. Some evidence suggests that children show higher-fidelity imitation of peers than adults (Zmyj, Aschersleben, Prinz, & Daum, 2012), that male and female children may differ in their propensity to overimitate when observing peers (Gruber, Deschenaux, Frick, & Clément, 2017), and that copying peers may be a strategy to determine group cohesion in varying social contexts (Zmyj et al., 2012). Manipulations of different ages of model allows researchers to assess whether, and why, children preferentially or more faithfully copy specific others.

Another possible manipulation is to present tasks to children in social settings, such as in their school class. This affords assessment of children's social learning in a natural, dynamic social environment, to track the diffusion of behaviours throughout groups and to measure whether children preferentially copy specific others in group contexts. Flynn and Whiten (2012) found that popular children were more likely to copy and be copied than less-popular children in a nursery school setting, while demonstrations by older children were more likely to be copied than those by younger children in several large groups of pre-school children (McGuigan et al., 2017). Group testing offers interesting insights into the dynamics of imitation in social groups, although surprisingly, to date, overimitation has been little assessed in non-individual settings.

Investigation of age differences in overimitation involves testing children of different age groups within the same study and measuring age-related differences in performance. Studies of overimitation may investigate small age groups (e.g., 3–4 years, 5–6 years) or larger age groups (e.g., 4–9 years, 10–15 years). Comparisons between smaller age groups allows a more fine-grained assessment of developmental changes in overimitation, while larger age groups allow a broader appraisal of age-differences in copying behaviours.

There are various other manipulations researchers can explore, such as live versus video demonstrations, how the task is framed or the level of experimenter communication. Each manipulation is designed to ask a different question, and should thus be carefully considered. Moreover, how the experiment is conducted has implications for its validity, a topic to which we now turn.

Core Methodologies

Overimitation is typically assessed using an experimental approach, where researchers test hypotheses by manipulating independent variables (e.g. task framing or age of participants) and measuring the effect these manipulations have on a dependent variable (overimitation behaviours). Experiments contrast with observational methods, whereby researchers observe participants without manipulations. Experiments provide high internal validity (the ability to rule out alternative explanations by controlling extraneous variables) but often lack external validity (how well findings can be generalised to real-world settings). Yet even within experiments, researchers face a trade-off between higher or lower internal and external validity.

Testing children individually provides high internal validity by allowing systematic control of extraneous variables, and thus isolation of the mechanisms, conditions and experimental manipulations that shape overimitation. Individual testing removes potential difficult-to-control confounds related to group testing, such as monitoring who observes what and whom, and individual differences in social relationships with present others (Rawlings, Flynn, & Kendal, 2017). Moreover, individual testing allows researchers to select demonstrators based on specific characteristics, which allows assessment of model-based biases. This level of internal validity is not typically possible with group testing.

Yet, individual testing may lack external validity. Social group testing provides a naturalistic and dynamic context in which individuals learn from others; children frequently acquire social information with multiple peers, family or community members present (Flynn & Whiten, 2010). Further, in unfamiliar laboratory settings, children may defer to adult experimenter's behaviours (or behaviours they feel are expected), and thus testing among peers may elicit more natural behaviours. However, group testing is logistically difficult (requiring a lot of video-coding and parental consent, for example) and faces the concerns of internal validity outlined above. Indeed, group testing is sometimes labelled quasi-experimental to highlight the lack of direct experimental control of the diffusion of behaviours.

One method of bridging internal and external validity is to conduct individual testing in natural settings. In one example, a puzzlebox task was presented as an exhibit in a public zoo (Whiten et al., 2016). When 'participants' approached, an experimenter acting as a fellow visitor performed relevant and irrelevant actions on the puzzlebox before allowing unsuspecting participants to interact with the apparatus (see Accompanying Activity 2 for more details of the experimental set-up). Here, adults and children overimitated at similar rates to laboratory studies, suggesting that overimitation is not an artefact of unfamiliar settings or children deferring to unfamiliar researchers.

Regardless of where experiments are conducted, a researcher either live-codes or, preferably, video-records the interaction for later coding. Participants' performances are scored to calculate their fidelity to the observed demonstrations (see Accompanying Activity 2 for a discussion of different approaches to scoring). Ideally, a subset of videos – typically at least 20% – coded by one researcher are also coded by another researcher unaware of the study aims. This inter-rater reliability measures agreement among those coding the videos (of whether an action is an overimitation behaviour or not, for example), and there should be high agreement between researchers. Further, experiments should include an asocial control condition, in which children are presented with the apparatus without any demonstrations. If asocial participants do not perform irrelevant actions, this indicates that effects in experimental groups are due to social learning.

Overimitation researchers face many decisions when deciding on their study methodology. They must consider theoretically derived experimental manipulations and trade-offs between internal and external validity. These are not simple decisions, yet carefully planned experiments have progressed our understanding of the social and cognitive mechanisms underlying overimitation and indeed our understanding of the developmental progression of overimitation.

Experimental Innovations and Their Implications for Our Understanding of Age-Differences of Overimitation

Since the discovery of overimitation in children over a decade ago (Horner & Whiten, 2004), there has been a vast amount of research investigating this phenomenon across infants, children, adults and other animals. We have collated important findings on who, when and why individuals overimitate, providing a large pool of knowledge about this curious, human-specific phenomenon. For much of its relatively short history, it was thought that the propensity to overimitate increases with age, even into adulthood. In the following sections, we focus on studies revealing that extrinsic factors – relating to the specific conditions in which experiments are conducted – and intrinsic individual differences specific to the participant influence both the overall propensity to overimitate and the pattern of age differences in overimitation.

Contextual Factors

Children learn from others in a multitude of contexts. Where testing takes place, the type of behaviour being learned, who children observe and the nature (or lack) of information provided all vary from one learning event to another. Manipulating the conditions in which testing occurs allows researchers to examine the role context plays on children's copying behaviour.

Characteristics of the Demonstrator(s)

Demonstrators (models) differ in a range of characteristics that inform learners about the value of the information they transmit (e.g. teachers, parents, peers, siblings); effective social learning therefore requires copying demonstrators selectively (Laland, 2004). Indeed, children exhibit a range of learning biases dictating that they are more likely to copy models who are similar to themselves, more familiar, more proficient and who have a high status (for a review see Price, Wood, & Whiten, 2017). These copying heuristics allow humans to efficiently extract the most useful information from those they observe (Wood, Kendal, & Flynn, 2013).

Nonetheless, evidence is mounting that different-aged children react divergently to specific model characteristics. While higher-fidelity copying of same-sex peers has been found in three-year-old children (Shutts, Banaji, & Spelke, 2009), female three- to five-year-olds were more likely to overimitate than males when the model was designated as a 'member of their team', suggesting females' overimitation is more sensitive to in-group effects than males (Gruber et al., 2017). Relatedly, whereas seven- to eleven-year-old females were much more likely than males to elect to observe a male demonstrator over directly attempting to solve a task themselves (Rawlings, 2018), no such effect was found in three- and five-year-olds (Flynn et al., 2016).

The number of, or presence or absence of, demonstrators markedly influences children's proclivity to overimitate. Evans, Laland, Carpenter, & Kendal (2017) varied whether all (four of four), the majority (three of four), or the minority (one of four) models performed causally relevant and irrelevant actions when solving a puzzlebox. Four- to six-year-old children were 'selective overimitators' such that they copied all behaviours with more fidelity when all models performed them, yet reproduced relevant, but not irrelevant actions, with more fidelity in the majority condition.

Further, older children were less likely than younger children to overimitate in the minority condition, indicating that with age the social influence becomes stronger. Indeed, adults also only reproduce irrelevant actions when both models perform them compared to when only one model does (McGuigan, 2012). In contrast, children and adults behave differently when the presence or absence of the demonstrator is manipulated during performance: children only reproduce irrelevant actions when the demonstrator remains in the room (Nielsen & Blank, 2011), while adults are not influenced by the presence or absence of models (McGuigan, 2012).

Task Framing

In everyday learning events, the instructions provided to children can vary dramatically. Adjusting how tasks are framed and/or the instructions given allows experimenters to increase the salience of instrumental or social elements of the task and, in turn, measure how this affects copying behaviour.

Clay et al. (2018) manipulated the framing so that four- to six-year-old children experienced either a communicative, an instrumental or a normative framing to puzzle-box tasks. Overall, overimitation was highest in the normative condition. However, although overimitation in the normative context showed an age-related increase, younger children were more likely than older children to overimitate in the instrumental condition. Similarly, Flynn, Turner and Giraldeau (2018) found that three-year-old children imitated an adult majority more when the task framing was arbitrary (i.e. little information provided) than when there was a correct or more rewarding way to do the task. Yet, whereas five-year-olds generally overimitated more than three-year-olds, this did not differ across normative judgment domains. Accordingly, these studies suggest that older children are more driven by social cues than younger children.

Task Type

As outlined, studies using a puzzlebox paradigm have provided a wealth of information about why we overimitate, when it emerges and the conditions in which overimitation is more or less likely to occur. However, experiments varying task type allow scrutiny of how the specific task type influences children's overimitative behaviour across development.

Frick and colleagues presented five- to twelve-year-old children with a task in which children had to use a pipe cleaner to retrieve a bucket containing a reward from within a transparent tube (Frick et al., 2017). Some of the children who did not successfully retrieve the reward were demonstrated the solution, but which included an irrelevant action (circling the tube with a piece of string before retrieving the reward with the pipe cleaner). These children overimitated at a lower rate than same-aged children in the puzzlebox studies outlined above. Moreover, in contrast to puzzlebox studies there was no age effect; the youngest children were as likely as the oldest children to overimitate. Whether or not the task involves tools also affects the rate at which children overimitate. Taniguchi and Sanefuji (2017) found that overimitation is higher in tool-based tasks compared to those without tools, which may be indicative of children copying to gain affordance understanding. These studies thus highlight the need for researchers to continue to expand beyond puzzlebox tasks to assay different motivations and age differences underlying overimitation.

In summary, evidence based on novel study designs is increasingly suggestive that younger and older children react differently to specific contextual factors. Most pertinently, it appears that age positively correlates with increased sensitivity to social cues (indeed, in five- to eight-year old children, older children were more sensitive to demonstrator eye contact [Marsh et al., 2014]). It is likely that younger children rely on copying others to rapidly acquire causal information, while older children, who have greater causal understanding of the relation between actions and outcome, are more motivated by the need to follow conventions and rules (Kenward et al. 2011) as their social environment becomes more complex.

Individual Differences

Scientists interested in individual differences study how differences in stable, personal characteristics influence our behaviours. Although individual differences in overimitation has received comparatively little attention compared to other influences, innovative studies increasingly suggest that a range of factors including sex, personality and cultural background may be important predictors of children's copying behaviour (Mesoudi, Chang, Dall, & Thornton, 2016; Rawlings et al., 2017). We explore these factors next.

Sex Differences

Until recently, there has been little attention on sex differences in human social learning, and studies frequently omit data on the performance of males and females separately. Nonetheless, some recent work provides tentative evidence of sex differences in both overimitation and the use of social information (the propensity to use information acquired from others). Interestingly, results from studies of social information use and overimitation have, so far, revealed opposite patterns of findings.

Just one study has documented sex differences in overimitation. The study previously described by Frick et al. (2017), which incorporated demonstrations of irrelevant actions on an innovation challenge, found that in both urban France and rural Serbia males were more likely than females to overimitate. The authors suggested that because the irrelevant action incorporated an additional item (a piece of string) not required for reward retrieval, the putative male bias for tools may explain why, in contrast to other overimitation studies (where typically a single, necessary, tool is used), males were more likely than females to overimitate.

Conversely, several studies of social information use suggest females are more likely than males to use social information. Brand, Brown, and Cross (2018) and Cross, Brown, Morgan, and Laland (2017) found that female adults copied others more than males on a mental rotation and computer-based task requiring the building of spaceships, respectively. Task-confidence (Cross et al., 2017) and risk-aversion (Brand et al., 2018) were offered as mediating factors in females' greater use of social information. Further, as noted previously, 70% of seven- to eleven-year-old females elected for a (male) demonstration before attempting to solve a puzzlebox, yet males of this age showed no preference for electing for demonstrations or not (Rawlings, 2018), and no such sex differences were found with three- and five-year-olds (Flynn et al., 2016). Interestingly, the findings of a female bias for social information resonate with studies of chimpanzees showing that females are more likely to engage in social learning than males (Lonsdorf, 2017; Watson et al., 2018).

Frick and colleagues' (2017) remains the only study to report sex differences in overimitation. Perhaps given that in Frick et al. (2017) the model demonstrated how to solve the task and the redundant actions, the uncertainty of how to succeed is eliminated (i.e. elements of task-confidence/risk should be nullified). This may explain their contrasting results to studies of social information. Further work is needed to verify and explore these findings and their relation to age differences, and it is important for researchers to explicitly investigate hypotheses concerning potential sex differences in overimitation.

Personality

Personality refers to stable, inter-individual differences in thought, behaviour and emotion across time and situations (Roberts & DelVecchio, 2000). Personality is typically measured in children by asking caregivers (and occasionally schoolteachers) to complete rating-scales of children's personality. Personality predicts children's social interactions (Tani, Greenman, Schneider, & Fregoso, 2003) and scholastic achievement (Poropat, 2014) and thus intuitively plays a role in children's copying fidelity.

Most studies investigating the role of personality on children's copying behaviour have focused on extraversion (which encompasses being bold, dominant, social and active) or closely related traits, generally reporting a positive relation between these traits and copying. Parental ratings of infants' extraversion positively predicted overimitation in a toy-playing game (Hilbrink, Sakkalou, Ellis-Davies, Fowler, & Gattis, 2013), while two- to four-year-olds rated as dominant observed peers more on a puzzlebox task (Flynn & Whiten, 2012). Given the interpersonal nature of extraversion it is possible that high scorers are more likely to copy others because of sheer exposure to others (Flynn & Whiten, 2012). Indeed, individuals scoring high in measures of extraversion are more attracted to social stimuli than low scorers (Feiler & Kleinbaum, 2015).

There is very little work on personality traits beyond these traits and this gap in the overimitation literature means we can only make predictions through indirect evidence. For instance, characteristics such as openness to experience and creativity may negatively correlate with overimitation. This is because openness to experience – being curious, inventive and imaginative – is strongly linked with innovation (see Rawlings et al., 2017), and since innovation requires at least some asocial learning (Carr, Kendal, & Flynn, 2016) children scoring highly on openness may be less likely to overimitate. Moreover, it is unknown whether personality influences overimitation differently across development. Children's personalities develop across childhood, with extraversion typically decreasing with age (Van den Akker, Deković, Asscher, & Prinzie, 2014) and thus feasibly there may be a personality–age interaction in overimitative propensity. These ideas are unsubstantiated with regards to overimitation but provide theoretical motivation for future studies.

Cultural Background

Recent years have seen a growing acceptance that developmental psychology is overreliant on samples from so-called WEIRD (Western, Educated, Industrialised, Rich and Democratic) societies (Nielsen, Haun, Kärtner, & Legare, 2017). This has spurred an increased research effort to examine children from 'non-WEIRD' societies, including from scientists interested in children's social learning. If overimitation is a human universal, it should be present in children across all populations regardless of cultural background. However, if it is a product of something socio-culturally specific to certain societies, we would expect cultural variation.

The evidence so far suggests that overimitation is universal, although the developmental trajectories of overimitation vary across cultures. Three- to six-year-old children from urban Australian, aboriginal Australian and South African Bushman populations exhibited equivalent rates of overimitation on a puzzlebox task (Nielsen, Tomaselli, Mushin, & Whiten, 2014). Similarly, two- to six-year old Kalahari Bushman children and urban Australian children produced similar overimitation rates on three puzzleboxes (Nielsen & Tomaselli, 2010). While these studies suggest overimitation is present cross-culturally, the lack of age differences contrasts findings from Western populations.

Some populations are less likely to overimitate than others. Aka children and adults and Ngandu children, both of the Congo Basin, Africa, did exhibit overimitation on a puzzlebox task, but rates were lower than found in Western populations (Berl & Hewlett, 2015). Interestingly, as with some findings with Western populations, Aka adults were more likely to overimitate than Aka children. Different populations may also be differentially influenced by task framing. Clegg and Legare (2016a) presented six- to eight-year-old children from the United States and Ni-Vanuatu with a necklace-making overimitation task. Both populations displayed overimitation, but when the task was framed instrumentally (compared to normatively), Ni-Vanuatuan children were more likely than US children to overimitate. This study hints that cultural variation in children's socialisation practices may predict cultural variation in sensitivity to social cues.

Therefore, evidence from a growing set of non-WEIRD populations points towards an early, universal human tendency to overimitate. However, populations appear to vary in the extent to which they overimitate, their sensitivity to framing and the age-trajectory of overimitation. Yet, more evidence is needed to determine the degree to which culture is representative of similarities and differences across these groups (Nielsen et al., 2014). Moreover, cultural influences (or the lack of them) may be confounded by demographic variables; early life stresses may be important for determining population differences in social learning (Mesoudi et al., 2016). Thus, despite these exciting findings, more comprehensive efforts are required to assess whether, and how, culture impacts the development of overimitation across societies.

In sum, there is an increasingly large set of individual-specific factors that moderate age differences in copying fidelity. There is tentative evidence that male children may be more likely to overimitate, yet females are more likely to use social information generally. Further, younger children show no sex differences in electing for demonstrations, yet older females are more likely than males to do so. Personality also predicts overimitation, with socially ground traits related to extraversion predicting the propensity to copy others; although personality–age interactions are yet to be investigated. Finally, there is cultural variation in the overall, and developmental pattern of, expressions of overimitation as well as the influence of task framing.

Conclusions

The focus of overimitation research has begun to change. Early studies investigated the developmental progression of this phenomenon by investigating different age groups with the same task in the same conditions. These studies indicated that across childhood the propensity to overimitate continually increases. The shift in focus, however, means scientists are devising ingenious experimental manipulations to investigate the underlying motivations and influences on children's overimitation. These innovations show that while the overall magnitude of propensity to overimitate might increase with age, contextual and individual variables moderate this effect. With age, children become more sensitive to social cues such as the framing of the task or characteristics of the demonstrator. Sex, cultural background and potentially personality are also just some important individual predictors of age-differences in overimitative behaviours.

These progressions are highly encouraging, even if they do imply that we need to refine our initial conclusions. Yet, much still remains to be done. There are countless different contexts in which social learning can take place, and the number of factors that may affect copying behaviours is vast. Scientists need to use carefully planned, theoretically driven experiments to continue building upon these recent progressions to advance our understanding of the developmental trajectory of overimitation.

References

Bannard, C., Klinger, J., & Tomasello, M. (2013). How selective are 3-year-olds in imitating novel linguistic material? *Developmental Psychology*, 49(12), 2344–2356. doi:10.1037/a0032062.

Berl, R. E. W. & Hewlett, B. S. (2015). Cultural variation in the use of overimitation by the Aka and Ngandu of the Congo Basin. *PloS One*, 10(3), e0120180. doi:10.1371/journal.pone.0120180.

Bonawitz, E., Shafto, P., Gweon, H., Goodman, N. D., Spelke, E., & Schulz, L. (2011). The double-edged sword of pedagogy: Instruction limits spontaneous exploration and discovery. *Cognition*, 120(3), 322–330. doi:10.1016/j.cognition.2010.10.001.

Brand, C. O., Brown, G. R., & Cross, C. P. (2018). Sex differences in the use of social information emerge under conditions of risk. *PeerJ*, 6, e4190.

Carr, K., Kendal, R. L., & Flynn, E. (2016). Eureka!: What is innovation, how does it develop, and who does it? *Child Development*, 87(5), 1505–1519. doi:10.1111/cdev.12549.

Clay, Z., Over, H., & Tennie, C. (2018). What drives young children to over-imitate? Investigating the effects of age, context, action type, and transitivity. *Journal of Experimental Child Psychology*, 166(2), 520–534. doi:10.1016/j.jecp.2017.09.008.

Clay, Z. & Tennie, C. (2018). Is overimitation a uniquely human phenomenon? Insights from human children as compared to bonobos. *Child Development*, 89(5), 1535–1544. doi:10.1111/cdev.12857.

Clegg, J. M. & Legare, C. H. (2016a). A cross-cultural comparison of children's imitative flexibility. *Developmental Psychology*, 52(9), 1435–1444. doi:10.1037/dev0000131.

Clegg, J. M. & Legare, C. H. (2016b). Instrumental and conventional interpretations of behavior are associated with distinct outcomes in early childhood. *Child Development*, 87(2), 527–542. doi:10.1111/cdev.12472.

Cross, C. P., Brown, G. R., Morgan, T. J. H., & Laland, K. N. (2017). Sex differences in confidence influence patterns of conformity. *British Journal of Psychology*, 108(4), 655–667. doi:10.1111/bjop.12232.

Eckerman, C. O. & Peterman, K. (2004). Peers and infant social/communicative development. In G. Bremner & A. Fogel (Eds.), *Blackwell Handbook of Infant Development* (pp. 326–350). Oxford, UK: Blackwell Publishing Ltd. doi:10.1002/9780470996348.ch12.

Evans, C. L., Laland, K. N., Carpenter, M., & Kendal, R. L. (2017). Selective copying of the majority suggests children are broadly "optimal-" rather than "over-" imitators. *Developmental Science*, e12637. doi:10.1111/desc.12637.

Feiler, D. C. & Kleinbaum, A. M. (2015). Popularity, similarity, and the network extraversion bias. *Psychological Science*, 26(5), 593–603. doi:10.1177/0956797615569580.

Flynn, E. & Smith, K. (2012). Investigating the mechanisms of cultural acquisition: How pervasive is overimitation in adults? *Social Psychology*, 43(4), 185–195. doi:10.1027/1864-9335/a000119.

Flynn, E., Turner, C., & Giraldeau, L.-A. (2016). Selectivity in social and asocial learning: Investigating the prevalence, effect and development of young children's learning preferences. *Philosophical Transactions of the Royal Society of London. Series B, Biological Sciences*, 371(1690), 688–699. doi:10.1098/rstb.2015.0189.

Flynn, E., Turner, C., & Giraldeau, L.-A. (2018). Follow (or don't follow) the crowd: Young children's conformity is influenced by norm domain and age. *Journal of Experimental Child Psychology*, 167, 222–233. doi:10.1016/j.jecp.2017.10.014.

Flynn, E. & Whiten, A. (2010). Studying children's social learning experimentally "in the wild". *Learning & Behavior*, 38(3), 284–296. doi:10.3758/LB.38.3.284.

Flynn, E. & Whiten, A. (2012). Experimental "microcultures" in young children: Identifying biographic, cognitive, and social predictors of information transmission. *Child Development*, 83(3), 911–925. doi:10.1111/j.1467-8624.2012.01747.x.

Frick, A., Clément, F., & Gruber, T. (2017). Evidence for a sex effect during overimitation: Boys copy irrelevant modelled actions more than girls across cultures. *Royal Society Open Science*, 4(12), 170367. doi:10.1098/rsos.170367.

Gruber, T., Deschenaux, A., Frick, A., & Clément, F. (2017). Group membership influences more social identification than social learning or overimitation in children. *Child Development*, 90(3), 728–745. doi:10.1111/cdev.12931.

Hilbrink, E. E., Sakkalou, E., Ellis-Davies, K., Fowler, N. C., & Gattis, M. (2013). Selective and faithful imitation at 12 and 15 months. *Developmental Science*, 16(6), 828–840. doi:10.1111/desc.12070.

Hoehl, S., Zettersten, M., Schleihauf, H., Grätz, S., & Pauen, S. (2014). The role of social interaction and pedagogical cues for eliciting and reducing overimitation in preschoolers. *Journal of Experimental Child Psychology*, 122(1), 122–133. doi:10.1016/j.jecp.2013.12.012.

Horner, V. & Whiten, A. (2004). Causal knowledge and imitation/emulation switching in chimpanzees (Pan troglodytes) and children (Homo sapiens). *Animal Cognition*, 8(3), 164–181. doi:10.1007/s10071-004-0239-6.

Johnston, A. M., Holden, P. C., & Santos, L. R. (2017). Exploring the evolutionary origins of overimitation: A comparison across domesticated and non-domesticated canids. *Developmental Science*, 20(4). doi:10.1111/desc.12460.

Kenward, B., Karlsson, M., & Persson, J. (2011). Over-imitation is better explained by norm learning than by distorted causal learning. *Proceedings of the Royal Society B: Biological Sciences*, 278(1709), 1239–1246. doi:10.1098/rspb.2010.1399.

Keupp, S., Behne, T., Zachow, J., Kasbohm, A., & Rakoczy, H. (2015). Over-imitation is not automatic: Context sensitivity in children's overimitation and action interpretation of causally irrelevant actions. *Journal of Experimental Child Psychology*, 130, 163–175. doi:10.1016/j.jecp.2014.10.005.

Laland, K. N. (2004). Social learning strategies. *Animal Learning & Behavior*, 32(1), 4–14. doi:10.3758/BF03196002.

Legare, C. H. & Nielsen, M. (2015). Imitation and innovation: The dual engines of cultural learning. *Trends in Cognitive Sciences*, 19(11), 688–699. doi:10.1016/j.tics.2015.08.005.

Lonsdorf, E. V. (2017). Sex differences in nonhuman primate behavioral development. *Journal of Neuroscience Research*, 95(1–2), 213–221. doi:10.1002/jnr.23862.

Lyons, D. E., Damrosch, D. H., Lin, J. K., Macris, D. M., & Keil, F. C. (2011). The scope and limits of overimitation in the transmission of artefact culture. *Philosophical Transactions of the Royal Society of London. Series B, Biological Sciences*, 366(1567), 1158–1167. doi:10.1098/rstb.2010.0335.

Lyons, D. E., Young, A. G., & Keil, F. C. (2007). The hidden structure of overimitation. *Proceedings of the National Academy of Sciences of the United States of America, 104*(50), 19751–19756. doi:10.1073/pnas.0704452104.

Marsh, L. E., Ropar, D., & Hamilton, A. F. de C. (2014). The social modulation of imitation fidelity in school-age children. *PloS One, 9*(1), e86127. doi:10.1371/journal.pone.0086127.

McGuigan, N. (2012). The role of transmission biases in the cultural diffusion of irrelevant actions. *Journal of Comparative Psychology, 126*(2), 150–160. doi:10.1037/a0025525.

McGuigan, N. (2013). The influence of model status on the tendency of young children to over-imitate. *Journal of Experimental Child Psychology, 116*(4), 962–969. doi:10.1016/j.jecp.2013.05.004.

McGuigan, N., Burdett, E., Burgess, V., Dean, L. G., Lucas, A., Vale, G., & Whiten, A. (2017). Innovation and social transmission in experimental micro-societies: Exploring the scope of cumulative culture in young children. *Philosophical Transactions of the Royal Society of London. Series B, Biological Sciences, 372*(1735), 20160425. doi:10.1098/rstb.2016.0425.

McGuigan, N., Makinson, J., & Whiten, A. (2011). From over-imitation to super-copying: Adults imitate causally irrelevant aspects of tool use with higher fidelity than young children. *British Journal of Psychology, 102*(1), 1–18. doi:10.1348/000712610X493115.

Meltzoff, A. N. & Moore, M. K. (1989). Imitation in newborn infants: Exploring the range of gestures imitated and the underlying mechanisms. *Developmental Psychology, 25*(6), 954–962. doi:10.1037/0012-1649.25.6.954.

Mesoudi, A., Chang, L., Dall, S. R., & Thornton, A. (2016). The evolution of individual and cultural variation in social learning. *Trends in Ecology & Evolution, 31*(3), 215–225. doi:10.1016/j.tree.2015.12.012.

Nielsen, M. (2006). Copying actions and copying outcomes: Social learning through the second year. *Developmental Psychology, 42*(3), 555–565. doi:10.1037/0012-1649.42.3.555.

Nielsen, M. & Blank, C. (2011). Imitation in young children: When who gets copied is more important than what gets copied. *Developmental Psychology, 47*(4), 1050–1053. doi:10.1037/a0023866.

Nielsen, M., Haun, D., Kärtner, J., & Legare, C. H. (2017). The persistent sampling bias in developmental psychology: A call to action. *Journal of Experimental Child Psychology, 162.* doi:10.1016/j.jecp.2017.04.017.

Nielsen, M. & Susianto, E. W. E. (2009). Failure to find over-imitation in captive orangutans (Pongo Pygmaeus): Implications for our understanding of cross-generation information transfer. In J. Håkansson (Ed.), *Developmental Psychology* (pp. 153–167). New York, NY: Nova Science Publishers.

Nielsen, M. & Tomaselli, K. (2010). Overimitation in Kalahari Bushman children and the origins of human cultural cognition. *Psychological Science, 21*(5), 729–736. doi:10.1177/0956797610368808.

Nielsen, M., Tomaselli, K., Mushin, I., & Whiten, A. (2014). Exploring tool innovation: A comparison of Western and Bushman children. *Journal of Experimental Child Psychology, 126,* 384–394. doi:10.1016/j.jecp.2014.05.008.

Over, H. & Carpenter, M. (2012). Putting the social into social learning: Explaining both selectivity and fidelity in children's copying behavior. *Journal of Comparative Psychology, 126*(2), 182–192. doi:10.1037/a0024555.

Poropat, A. E. (2014). Other-rated personality and academic performance: Evidence and implications. *Learning and Individual Differences, 34,* 24–32. doi:10.1016/j.lindif.2014.05.013.

Price, E., Wood, L. A., & Whiten, A. (2017). Adaptive cultural transmission biases in children and nonhuman primates. *Infant Behavior and Development, 48,* 45–53. doi:10.1016/j.infbeh.2016.11.003.

Rawlings, B. (2018). *Establishing predictors of learning strategies; an investigation of the development of, and evolutionary foundations of, intrinsic and extrinsic factors influencing when we learn from others and from whom we learn.* Durham University. http://etheses.dur.ac.uk/12800/

Rawlings, B., Flynn, E., & Kendal, R. L. (2017). To copy or to innovate? The role of personality and social networks in children's learning strategies. *Child Development Perspectives*, *11*(1), 39–44. doi:10.1111/cdep.12206.

Roberts, B. W. & DelVecchio, W. F. (2000). The rank-order consistency of personality traits from childhood to old age: A quantitative review of longitudinal studies. *Psychological Bulletin*, *126* (1), 3–25. doi:10.1037/0033-2909.126.1.3.

Shutts, K., Banaji, M. R., & Spelke, E. S. (2009). Social categories guide young children's preferences for novel objects. *Developmental Science*, *13*(4), 599–610. doi:10.1111/j.1467-7687.2009.00913.x.

Subiaul, F., Winters, K., Krumpak, K., & Core, C. (2016). Vocal overimitation in preschool-age children. *Journal of Experimental Child Psychology*, *141*, 145–160. doi:10.1016/j.jecp.2015.08.010.

Tani, F., Greenman, P. S., Schneider, B. H., & Fregoso, M. (2003). Bullying and the big five. *School Psychology International*, *24*(2), 131–146. doi:10.1177/0143034303024002001.

Taniguchi, Y. & Sanefuji, W. (2017). The boundaries of overimitation in preschool children: Effects of target and tool use on imitation of irrelevant actions. *Journal of Experimental Child Psychology*, *159*, 83–95. doi:10.1016/j.jecp.2017.01.014.

Toth, K., Munson, J., Meltzoff, A. N., & Dawson, G. (2006). Early predictors of communication development in young children with autism spectrum disorder: Joint attention, imitation, and toy play. *Journal of Autism and Developmental Disorders*, *36*(8), 993–1005. doi:10.1007/s10803-006-0137-7.

Van den Akker, A. L., Deković, M., Asscher, J., & Prinzie, P. (2014). Mean-level personality development across childhood and adolescence: A temporary defiance of the maturity principle and bidirectional associations with parenting. *Journal of Personality and Social Psychology*, *107*(4), 736–750. doi:10.1037/a0037248.

Watson, S. K., Vale, G. L., Hopper, L. M., Dean, L. G., Kendal, R. L., Price, E. E., ... Whiten, A. (2018). Chimpanzees demonstrate individual differences in social information use. *Animal Cognition*, *21*(5), 639–650. doi:10.1007/s10071-018-1198-7.

Watson-Jones, R. E., Legare, C. H., Whitehouse, H., & Clegg, J. M. (2014). Task-specific effects of ostracism on imitative fidelity in early childhood. *Evolution and Human Behavior*, *35*, 3. doi:10.1016/j.evolhumbehav.2014.01.004.

Whiten, A., Allan, G., Devlin, S., Kseib, N., Raw, N., & McGuigan, N. (2016). Social learning in the real-world: "Over-imitation" occurs in both children and adults unaware of participation in an experiment and independently of social interaction. *PLOS ONE*, *11*(7), e0159920. doi:10.1371/journal.pone.0159920.

Whiten, A. & Ham, R. (1992). On the nature and evolution of imitation in the animal kingdom: Reappraisal of a century of research. In P. J. Slater, J. S. Rosenblatt, C. Beer, & M. Milinski (Eds.), *Advances in the Study of Behavior* (Vol. 21, pp. 239–283). doi:10.1016/S0065-3454(08) 60146-1.

Wood, L. A., Kendal, R. L., & Flynn, E. (2013). Whom do children copy? Model-based biases in social learning. *Developmental Review*, *33*(4), 341–356. doi:10.1016/j.dr.2013.08.002.

Zmyj, N., Aschersleben, G., Prinz, W., & Daum, M. (2012). The peer model advantage in infants' imitation of familiar gestures performed by differently aged models. *Frontiers in Psychology*, *3*, 252. doi:10.3389/fpsyg.2012.00252.

3 Ethics in Developmental Research

Diana J. Meter and Marion K. Underwood

A Lesson from History

Developmental research involves the study of humans from conception to death as they grow physically, emotionally, and behaviorally across the lifespan. As a student of the scientific method knows, research in most other sciences typically entails controlled experiments, which include experimental manipulation of certain factors that allow a researcher to conclude causality. Although some developmental science researchers employ these methods, much developmental research is correlational—researchers observe development as it unfolds naturally over time and can make connections between factors occurring across development without manipulating developmental trajectories. These types of studies are particularly useful when investigating factors that may impact development negatively, because research that influences human development in ways that lead to negative outcomes for participants is deemed unethical. However, there have been times when researchers directly influenced participants in ways that caused incidental and long-term harm. Although the field of developmental research is relatively new compared to other sciences, the history of the study of human development is stained by a past that includes unethical treatment of child and adult human subjects. Researchers should be aware of these mistakes in developmental science and learn from the past so that they are able to produce ethically and morally executed research that supports the wellbeing of participants and populations under study.

In 1939, researcher Wendall Johnson and his team investigated the effect of labeling children as "stutterers" or "normal speakers" on their speech fluency. This study, only published in student Mary Tudor's master's thesis in 1939, has become known as the "Monster Study" because of the researchers' behavior toward the human subjects. The participants were children from preschool to high-school age who resided in an orphanage in Iowa. Tudor (1939) reported that several of the children were unable to read and most of the children's IQs were low. The research team designed an experiment to understand the behavioral influence diagnosis might have on stuttering. Groups of children with speech problems and typically developing children were assigned to different conditions. In addition to a series of speaking, reading, and other tasks, within each condition the children were either encouraged to speak freely and told that they would outgrow speech problems or that they have a great deal of trouble with their speech, which was undesirable. Orphanage staff were also told the child's "diagnosis." Children who were deemed "stutterers" were provided the following message:

The staff has come to the conclusion that you have a great deal of trouble with your speech. The type of interruptions which you have are very undesirable. These interruptions indicate stuttering. You have many of the symptoms of a child who is beginning to stutter. In fact, you are beginning to stutter. You must try to stop yourself immediately. Use your will power. Make up your mind that you are going to speak without a single interruption. It's absolutely necessary that you do this. Do anything to keep from stuttering. Try very hard to speak fluently and evenly. If you have an interruption, stop and begin over. Take a deep breath whenever you feel you are going to stutter. Don't ever speak unless you can do it right. You see how [the name of a child in the institution who stuttered rather severely] stutters, don't you? Well, he undoubtedly started this very same way you are starting. Watch your speech every minute and try to do something to improve it. Whatever you do, speak fluently and avoid any interruptions whatsoever in your speech.

(Tudor, 1939, pp. 10–11)

Tudor (1939) describes in her discussion how easily influenced the orphanage teachers and matrons were, accepting the researchers' diagnosis even though in many cases it was purposefully incorrect. She also describes the effect of being labeled a stutterer on the children's verbalizations, as well as their social behavior in response to speech interruptions.

This study has multiple flaws that deem it unethical by contemporary standards. First, the children in this study were not voluntary participants, nor did they have guardians who could have provided informed consent on their behalf. The children did not know the true reason behind the experiment, and it seems they were not debriefed about the study purpose until after the experiment was over and psychological damage had been committed. These children were also in some cases young and of low intelligence, and likely would have needed help interpreting and understanding informed consent information, even if it was presented to them. The researchers could not know whether their experimental paradigm could negatively affect the psychological and speech development of children in the different conditions, and there was not a procedure in place for safeguarding their development, although contemporary researchers would likely recognize the potential for harm in delivering an untrue diagnosis. The researchers also seemed to have power in the orphanage; Tudor herself reports that the staff accepted her conclusions. The orphanage staff were also manipulated in that they were told of the children's diagnoses and to act in accordance with different treatments for the children, even though the treatments may have been inappropriate and harmful to some children.

Unfortunately, the Monster Study is only one of many studies that have denied participants basic rights. Physicians in Nazi Germany performed such barbaric medical experiments that a code of ethics resulted from their trial, known as the Nuremberg Code (1949). The Nuremberg Code states "voluntary consent to research is essential, that subjects must have the capacity to consent, that they be provided with sufficient information and comprehend that information, and that they are able to exercise their free choice without duress or deceit" (Stanley & Guido, 1996).

The following sections will describe improvements that have been made to protect human subjects, particularly those who are vulnerable to abuse or coercion. First, we will introduce the contemporary Institutional Review Board's role, along with responsibilities of researchers. We will discuss informed consent procedures and appropriate incentives. We end with ethical considerations for new research methodology and recommendations for researchers working with Institutional Review Boards. Ensuring ethical treatment of human participants in developmental science is an essential and ever-changing practice as research methodology develops and changes.

Where We Are Now: Institutional Review Boards, Vulnerable Populations, Responsibilities of Researchers

Currently in the United States, federal law requires that research with human participants can only be conducted if it has been approved by an Institutional Review Board (IRB; Office for Human Research Protections, 2009). IRBs exist to protect the basic rights of human beings who participate in research: informed consent, the right to decline or cease participation without penalty, confidentiality, and decent treatment. An IRB is responsible for reviewing and monitoring research involving human subjects, both in advance before the study begins and periodically throughout the study. IRBs are designed to be knowledgeable and impartial in their reviews of research procedures; they must include at least five members, with appropriate expertise to review the types of research proposals submitted to the IRB. IRB members must not have any involvement or other conflict of interest with proposals reviewed. IRB members must be from diverse backgrounds with relation to race, gender, and culture, and be sensitive to community attitudes. An IRB must include one member whose concerns primarily focus on science and one whose primary concerns do not focus on science, and must include one member not affiliated with the institution sponsoring the IRB. IRB members are responsible for following written guidelines to review all research procedures. In order to approve a research protocol, an IRB must determine that risks to participants are reduced to the extent possible, risks are reasonable in relation to the benefits of the research, participants are selected in an equitable manner, participants give informed consent and that consent is documented, data are monitored for safety as procedures are carried out, and additional safeguards are in place for protected or vulnerable populations (for details of the federal requirements, see Office for Human Research Protections, 2009).

Investigators are responsible for designing research that meets these criteria, for overseeing every phase of the study to make sure that all procedures are followed, for ensuring that no harm to participants occurs, and for reporting immediately to the IRB any deviation from the research procedures and any harm to participants. Researchers are also responsible for understanding the special risks for research participation by vulnerable populations.

Vulnerable populations that require special protections under these federal laws include pregnant women and fetuses, prisoners, and children. If IRBs regularly review investigations of vulnerable populations, they are required to have members with expertise in those groups, including children. Specifically with respect to research in children and other vulnerable groups is whether members of those groups can provide informed consent. To be able to provide informed consent, research participants must be able to express their wish to participate or not, understand what participation requires and other relevant information, use rational reasoning to reach a decision about participation, understand the research and what it will involve enough to be able to make a choice about participation, and make a decision consistent with that of a reasonable person (Stanley & Guido, 1987). Because children under 18 are not believed to be able to meet these criteria, parents must provide consent for the research participation of children under 18. To the extent possible, given the age of the child, cognitive abilities, and emotional maturity, youth should provide informed assent, meaning their agreement to participate in the research.

Other vulnerable groups may not be able to meet these criteria for informed consent because of intellectual or psychological limitations, including those with developmental disabilities, serious mental illness, or Alzheimer's disease. For these individuals, just as for children, consent must be provided by legal guardians, but the person participating still must be provided with information about the study to the extent possible and provide their own assent. For all vulnerable groups, guardian consent is necessary but not sufficient; vulnerable persons must also provide their own assent to participate in research.

In considering whether research procedures involving children meet the criteria for approval, the federal guidelines require that the research does not require greater than minimal risk, defined as "that the probability and magnitude of harm or discomfort anticipated in the research are not greater in and of themselves than those ordinarily encountered in daily life or during the performance of routine physical or psychological examinations or tests" (see Office for Human Research Protection, 2009). However, given that children in some social contexts regularly experience violence and abuse in their daily lives, experts have argued that minimal risk is not an acceptable criterion for whether research can be safely conducted with children and adolescents (Thompson, 1990). A higher, more sensitive standard for an appropriate level of risk for research with minors is whether the research involves decent treatment of children (Thompson, 1990). What counts as decent treatment requires a sophisticated understanding of developmental changes in vulnerability (i.e., which experiences could be most challenging to children at different stages of development). Developmental researchers are responsible for designing research that constitutes decent treatment of children, given the special developmental strengths and vulnerabilities of the participants being studied.

Developmental researchers also have a responsibility to study the impact of their research procedures on children as they carry out their investigation, to assess children's understanding of informed consent and their perceptions of the impact of the research. These studies can be conducted as part of ongoing investigations or even in response to concerns raised by community members to contribute to the complicated developmental calculus of what constitutes decent treatment of children. One example of such a study was of nine-year-old children's perceptions of sociometric testing conducted in their school classrooms, which was halted by the school district when a small number of parents became alarmed (Mayeux, Underwood, & Risser, 2007). Both children and teachers in the schools where sociometrics were conducted before the testing was halted were interviewed about children's responses to the research procedures. Children and teachers reported that children were not distressed by the sociometric testing, did not perceive that their peers treated them differently after sociometric testing, understood the research procedures, and comprehended that their responses would be kept confidential and that they could stop participating if they wanted.

Participants' Understanding of Informed Consent Procedures

Before an individual consents to participate in research, they must be provided with information including risks and benefits, their rights to privacy and autonomy, that researchers will be honest and fair, and that steps will be taken to ensure no harm is committed. When this information is shared without undue coercion from researchers, parents, or inappropriate incentives, participants can make an informed decision about participation (Fisher, 2004; Scherer, Annett, & Brody, 2007).

As online studies become more common, some researchers question: a) whether participants read consent information and more specifically, b) what can be done to ensure participants' understanding of informed consent information. This question is particularly important for research conducted among youth. Many researchers support ensuring informed assent from minors along with their caregivers' informed consent, and that minors should be able to autonomously assert their choice to participate or not without coercion from parents or researchers (Miller, Drotar, & Kodish, 2004; Tait, Voepel-Lewis, & Malviya, 2003). In the case that parental consent may put youth at risk, such as in the case of abuse or neglect, or in studies of runaway or homeless youth, it may be waived, leaving the minor's assent the only consent to participate in research (Fisher, Arbeit, Dumont, Macapagal, & Mustanski, 2016; Meade & Slesnick, 2002). In one study of parents of LGBTQ youth, 74% of parents did not think parental permission should be required for research about HIV behavioral surveillance (Newcomb, Clifford, Greene, & Mustanski, 2016). There are multiple issues that may impact whether youth can autonomously consent for themselves.

First, if children will be put in harm's way if their parent or guardian is contacted in general or because of the topic of a study, it may not be appropriate to involve these adults in the research process. In some cases, children are under the guardianship of the state, not a parent or caregiver, and a caseworker may not be knowledgeable about how risks and benefits of research participation may impact a particular youth (Meade & Slesnick, 2002). One population that may be asked to participate in research unbeknownst to parents is LGBTQ youth.

In a study of gay and bisexual boys ages 14–17, researchers investigated different approaches to gaining online assent to better understand the impact of assent on participation (Friedman et al., 2016). Participants were assigned to an "assent as usual" condition, or were required either to answer two questions about potential risks and the voluntary nature of the study, or to answer seven questions from the assent information. The participants who completed the assent questions had a significantly better understanding of the study information presented in the assent document, but those in these groups also dropped out at significantly higher rates prior to even completing the assent process. The authors concluded that posting assent materials online is not enough. This is an important conclusion, but fewer participants from the sample completing the study also suggests decreased generalizability of the findings. It is important for researchers in the future to learn whether drop-out due to quizzes such as this is because of participant laziness or their discomfort with the study protocol leading to their autonomous decision not to participate.

To answer the question of at what age minors are able to comprehend informed consent information, researchers in the medical, clinical, and developmental science fields have compared youth of different ages in cross-sectional designs. Issues that can make the ability to assent more difficult for minors or individuals from vulnerable populations include the difficulty of the language in the document, whether the language is the native language of the potential participant, the complexity of the study protocol, and the level of confidentiality the researchers can guarantee (Miller et al., 2004).

Many studies of youth's ability to consent or assent comes from medical research studies that have implications for social science researchers working with similar populations. Among a sample of sixty 14–17-year-old sexual minority youth, 96% of participants said it would be easy to ask questions about the intervention study, and 87% said it would be easy to refuse participation (Fisher et al., 2016). The authors concluded that according to focus group discussions, the participants were able to maturely reflect on risks and benefits of participation. Children have reported understanding that they can stop participating in other samples of youth, 2nd, 4th, and 6th graders in one study (Hurley & Underwood, 2002), 12–17-year-olds in another (Vitiello et al., 2007), and 7–12 years-old in a third (Chu, DePrince, & Weinzierl, 2008).

Whether adolescents should be allowed to give their consent and participate in research without guardian assent is an important question because the participants are minors whose care should be the responsibility of their parent or guardian. However, when minors are limited in their ability to autonomously decide to participate in research, this undermines their own ability to make decisions for themselves.

In all, most studies find that the majority of children and adolescents comprehend research protocol, risks and benefits to participation, and that their participation is voluntary, and their understanding seems to increase with age (Bruzzese & Fisher, 2003; Hurley & Underwood, 2002), with older adolescents' comprehension similar to that of adults (Crane & Broome, 2017). Even most younger children have a good understanding of research rights (Crane & Broome, 2017).

Recommendations that have come from research on informed consent and assent with minors includes the following. First, assent quizzes and lessons on research rights have been shown to be effective in enhancing understanding among youth participants (Crane & Broome, 2017). Second, because children and adolescents can comprehend informed consent information, often to the same degree as adults, researchers should provide the opportunity for youth to assent using language that is appropriate for child and adolescent participants (Crane & Broome, 2017). Burke and colleagues conclude from their study of children and adolescents' understanding of medical research that by providing age-appropriate informed consent information, even young children can understand risks and benefits associated with research participation (Burke, Abramovitch, & Zlotkin, 2005).

Overall, very few participants (about 5%) tend to report negative experiences resulting from research participation, and report important benefits including learning something new for the benefit of themselves or others and enjoying sharing information about themselves for the research project (Crane & Broome, 2017). One important question that remains is whether youth are able to autonomously act on their understanding of their research rights in the event that they do not assent to part of the study protocol or change their mind while participating in research. An interesting descriptive example of an adolescent explaining to a peer that she was comfortable having her text messages used for research, but not her Facebook communication is shared below:

(11:28:23am) Participant A says to Participant B:
Did you let the <BlackBerry Project> link up with your Facebook?
(11:28:32am) Participant B says to Participant A:
Yes
(11:41:10am) Participant A says to Participant B:
Ehh I didn't
(11:41:30am) Participant B says to Participant A:
Haha that is like the whole point for the [project]

(11:41:34am) Participant A says to Participant B:
They already have my phone ... I don't want them on my fb too
(11:41:41am) Participant B says to Participant A:
Haha ok

(Meter, Ehrenreich, Carker, Flynn, & Underwood, 2019).

This adolescent participant was able to autonomously choose how much of her personal communication she was willing to share for research purposes.

Incentives

The use of incentives is important for recruiting and retaining participants. Some incentives are payments that reimburse participants for out-of-pocket expenses that may discourage participants from taking part in research. Other incentives are meant to encourage participants to take part in a study (Bagley, Reynolds, & Nelson, 2007) and decrease attrition, which may be especially important when, in order for a study to be successful, participants need to be retained for a number of months or years (Rice & Broome, 2004). However, the use of incentives can be controversial because it may be an important factor in whether individuals choose to participate or continue their participation in a research study; children and adolescents commonly cite incentives as a reason for participating in research (Crane & Broome, 2017).

Although incentives are often approved by IRBs and funding agencies, this is unlikely to be the case if incentives are "overly enticing" to participants and would potentially lead participants to take part in research that they otherwise would not, the result of a "corruption of judgement" (Grant & Sugarman, 2004, p. 733). In other words, individuals who desire the monetary incentive may accept the terms of study despite their own judgement in order to receive the compensation. In some cases, funders may have limitations on appropriate incentives that may depend on the population (e.g.www.nij.gov/funding/Pages/research-participant-costs-and-incentives.aspx). One approach to decrease the chances of enticing participants through incentives is to follow a wage payment model.

The wage payment model involves compensating participants using an hourly wage for the duration of time it takes to complete the research task. The payment is generally commensurate to that of a low-wage, unskilled, essential job (Bagley et al., 2007). Although this model applies to adults who typically have experience weighing the costs and benefits of participating in work for a certain wage, there is little understanding of whether this model is appropriate for compensating children for their participation in research. A qualitative study of children and adolescents who were asked about their hypothetical participation in medical research found that children younger than nine years as measured by the Peabody Picture Vocabulary Test had a poor understanding of the value and role of money (Bagley et al., 2007). The results suggest that this model of compensation or incentivizing research may be inappropriate for children with a developmental age older than nine.

Ethical Considerations for New and Uncommon Research Methodology

One way researchers have harnessed the power of technology as a research method to study human development is through investigation of publicly posted communication via social media (Calvin, Bellmore, Xu, & Zhu, 2015; Moreno, Grant, Kacvinsky, Moreno, &

Fleming, 2012). Because the "data" included in these studies is publicly published on the internet, it is no longer deemed private information but instead freely accessible (Zimmer, 2010), and informed consent is considered unnecessary. However, when individuals post to social media sites, they likely are unaware of the potential and are do not intend for their media content to be used in research (Moreno, Fost, & Christakis, 2008).

Moreno and colleagues (2012) tested young adult college students' comfort with this research method for learning information about individuals. About 27% of participants supported this approach, 36% were "fine" with it, 29% felt neutral about it, 9% were uneasy, and 9% were concerned. Those who were concerned in many cases were unaware that their information was currently being posted publicly. Although in this study most participants seemed comfortable with the approach, this does not mean that the use of these data in research does not put the participants at risk.

In 2008, public Facebook profiles from a cohort of students at a university in the US were used in research. After the researchers deidentified the data and took other steps to protect "participant" privacy, the data were publicly released. The institution where these individuals were students was quickly discovered. Although individual information was not released, which individuals from which cohort from the university was discovered. One argument for this sort of research is that there was no information gathered or discovered that could put the participants at risk—the individuals could not be victimized because of the information that was now public. However, another argument is one for dignity-based privacy, one's "ability to control the flow of their personal information" (Zimmer, 2010, p. 321). Whether publicly available data *should* be used by researchers without the consent of participants is an ethical debate up for discussion (boyd & Crawford, 2012).

Another approach to harnessing the power of technology to study human development is through notifying participants of how their digital communication data will be monitored and recorded and requiring informed consent. The BlackBerry Project was the first ambulatory assessment study of its kind to capture sent and received text messages from adolescents in the US (Underwood, Rosen, More, Ehrenreich, & Gentsch, 2012). In this study, a great deal of personal communication was captured, and researchers were concerned with whether high-school-aged adolescents were able to understand the information shared during the informed consent procedure to allow them to make an informed decision about study participation without undue influence from parents or researchers. In an exit interview which occurred at the final year of data collection, participants' responses confirmed their understanding of the meaning of confidentiality and their right to withdraw without anything bad happening. They were less aware of the special circumstances when confidentiality might need to be broken, and the specific steps taken to protect the data. Although the participants were aware that the research team recorded and could read any of their text message communication, 96% of participants reported that nothing about the project ever upset or worried them. The evidence suggests that older adolescents do understand and can consent to their participation in ambulatory assessment data collection involving the recording of large amounts of private data (Meter et al., 2019).

Recommendations for Working with IRBs

One lesson that can be garnered from the medical literature is the advantage of speaking with IRB representatives early. In a study of HIV treatment for minor men who have sex with men, investigators reported discussing the research with IRBs early so that the board could ask for supporting documentation to educate IRB members where necessary. These strategies included providing journal articles, sharing previous experience, and encouraging board members to attend talks on the subject. In the case of the specific problem of wanting self-consent of minors without parental consent, providing state law information to the board was common. It is important to note that in some cases, due to state law or IRB decisions, the research was not approved (Gilbert et al., 2015); even well-designed projects with the goal of helping youth achieve their optimum development may not be approved due to certain design concerns.

References

Bagley, S. J., Reynolds, W. W., & Nelson, R. M. (2007). Is a "wage-payment" model for research participation appropriate for children?. *Pediatrics, 119*, 46–51. doi:10.1542/peds.2006-1813

boyd, d., & Crawford, K. (2012). Critical questions for big data. *Information, Communication & Society, 15*, 662–679. doi:10.1080/1369118X.2012.678878

Bruzzese, J. M., & Fisher, C. B. (2003). Assessing and enhancing the research consent capacity of children and youth. *Applied Developmental Science, 7*, 13–26. doi:10.1207/S1532480XADS0701_2

Burke, T. M., Abramovitch, R., & Zlotkin, S. (2005). Children's understanding of the risks and benefits associated with research. *Journal of Medical Ethics, 31*, 715–720. doi:10.1136/jme.2003.003228

Calvin, A. J., Bellmore, A., Xu, J. M., & Zhu, X. (2015). #bully: uses of hashtags in posts about bullying on Twitter. *Journal of School Violence, 14*, 133–153. doi:10.1080/15388220.2014.966828

Chu, A. T., DePrince, A. P., & Weinzierl, K. M. (2008). Children's perception of research participation: examining trauma exposure and distress. *Journal of Empirical Research on Human Research Ethics, 3*, 49–58. doi:10.1525/jer.2008.3.1.49.

Crane, S., & Broome, M. E. (2017). Understanding ethical issues of research participation from the perspective of participating children and adolescents: a systematic review. *Worldviews on Evidence-Based Nursing, 14*, 200–209. doi:10.1111/wvn.12209.

Fisher, C. B. (2004). Informed consent and clinical research involving children and adolescents: implications of the revised APA ethics code and HIPAA. *Journal of Clinical Child and Adolescent Psychology, 33*, 832–839. doi:10.1207/s15374424jccp3304_18.

Fisher, C. B., Arbeit, M. R., Dumont, M. S., Macapagal, K., & Mustanski, B. (2016). Self-consent for HIV prevention research involving sexual and gender minority youth: reducing barriers through evidence-based ethics. *Journal of Empirical Research on Human Research Ethics, 11*, 3–14. doi:10.1177/1556264616633963.

Friedman, M. S., Chiu, C. J., Croft, C., Guadamuz, T. E., Stall, R., & Marshal, M. P. (2016). Ethics of online assent: comparing strategies to ensure informed assent among youth. *Journal of Empirical Research on Human Research Ethics, 11*, 15–20. doi:10.1177/1556264615624809

Gilbert, A. L., Knopf, A. S., Fortenberry, J. D., Hosek, S. G., Kapogiannis, B. G., & Zimet, G. D. (2015). Adolescent self-consent for biomedical human immunodeficiency virus prevention research. *Journal of Adolescent Health, 57*, 113–119. doi:10.1016/j.jadohealth.2015.03.017.

Grant, R. W., & Sugarman, J. (2004). Ethics in human subjects research: do incentives matter? *Journal of Medicine and Philosophy, 29*, 717–738. doi:10.1080/03605310490883046

Hurley, J. C., & Underwood, M. K. (2002). Children's understanding of their research rights before and after debriefing: Informed assent, confidentiality, and stopping participation. *Child Development, 73*, 132–143. doi:10.1111/1467-8624.00396.

Mayeux, L., Underwood, M. K., & Risser, S. D. (2007). Perspectives on the ethics of sociometric research with children: how children, peers, and teachers help to inform the debate. *Merrill-Palmer Quarterly, 53*, 53–78.

Meade, M. A., & Slesnick, N. (2002). Ethical considerations for research and treatment with runaway and homeless adolescents. *The Journal of Psychology, 136*(4), 449–463. doi:10.1080/00223980209604171.

Meter, D. J., Ehrenreich, S. E., Carker, C., Flynn, E., & Underwood, M. K. (2019). Adolescents' understanding of their participant rights in a longitudinal study using smartphones for ambulatory assessment. *Journal of Research on Adolescence, 29*, 662–674. doi:10.111/jora.12461.

Miller, V. A., Drotar, D., & Kodish, E. (2004). Children's competence for assent and consent: a review of empirical findings. *Ethics & Behavior, 14*, 255–295. doi:10.1207/s15327019eb1403_3.

Moreno, M. A., Fost, N. C., & Christakis, D. A. (2008). Research ethics in the MySpace era. *Pediatrics, 121*, 157–161.

Moreno, M. A., Grant, A., Kacvinsky, L., Moreno, P., & Fleming, M. (2012). Older adolescents' views regarding participation in Facebook research. *Journal of Adolescent Health, 51*, 439–444. doi:10.1016/j.jadohealth.2012.02.001.

Newcomb, M. E., Clifford, A., Greene, G. J., & Mustanski, B. (2016). Parent perspectives about sexual minority adolescent participation in research and requirements of parental permission. *Journal of Adolescent Health, 59*, 443–449. doi:10.1016/j.jadohealth.2016.05.014.

Office for Human Research Protections, Department of Health and Human Services (2009). Code of federal regulations. Title 45, Public Welfare, PART 46.

Rice, M., & Broome, M. E. (2004). Incentives for children in research. *Journal of Nursing Scholarship, 36*, 167–172. doi:10.1111/j.1547-5069.2004.04030.x

Scherer, D. G., Annett, R. D., & Brody, J. L. (2007). Ethical issues in adolescent and parent informed consent for pediatric asthma research participation. *Journal of Asthma, 44*, 489–496. doi:10.1080/02770900701247137

Stanley, B. H., & Guido, J. R. (1996). Informed consent: psychological and empirical issues. In: Stanley B. H., Sieber J. E., Melton G. B., editors. *Research ethics: A psychological approach*. University of Nebraska Press, Lincoln, pp. 105–128.

Tait, A. R., Voepel-Lewis, T., & Malviya, S. (2003). Do they understand? (Part II): assent of children participating in clinical anesthesia and surgery research. *Anesthesiology, 98*, 609–614. doi:10.1097/00000542-200303000-00006.

Thompson, R. A. (1990). Vulnerability in research: a developmental perspective on research risk. *Child Development, 61*, 1–16. doi:10.2307/1131043.

Tudor, M. (1939). *An experimental study of the effect of evaluative labeling on speech fluency* (Unpublished doctoral dissertation). University of Iowa, Iowa City, IA.

Underwood, M. K., Rosen, L. H., More, D., Ehrenreich, S. E., & Gentsch, J. K. (2012). The BlackBerry project: Capturing the content of adolescents' text messaging. *Developmental Psychology, 48*, 295–302. doi:10.1037/a0025914.

Vitiello, B., Kratochvil, C. J., Silva, S., Curry, J., Reinecke, M., Pathak, S., Waslick, B., Hughes, C. W., Prentice, E. D., May, D. E., & March, J. S. (2007). Research knowledge among the participants in the Treatment for Adolescents With Depression Study (TADS). *Journal of the American Academy of Child & Adolescent Psychiatry, 46*, 1642–1650. doi:10.1097/chi.0b013e318153f8c7.

Zimmer, M. (2010). "But the data is already public": on the ethics of research in Facebook. *Ethics and Information Technology, 12*, 313–325. doi:10.1007/s10676-010-9227-5.

4 Prenatal Animal Models of Behavioral Development

Gale A. Kleven and Seanceray A. Bellinger

Prenatal Animal Models of Behavioral Development

Animal models used in the study of behavioral development permit experimental research methods that would be impossible or unethical to do with humans. More importantly, animal models are central in the study of the fetus because at no other time in development are animals virtually indistinguishable from humans.

Charles Darwin observed that all vertebrate embryos went through nearly identical sequences of change during early development (Darwin, 1859). This similarity between species applies to behavioral development as well, with researchers reporting a nearly identical repertoire of behavior in both animals and humans before birth (Table 4.1). Although humans eventually surpass all species in cognitive and social functioning, behavioral differences between humans and animals are not seen before birth. These similarities make for a stronger argument for the use of animal models in studying behavior during the prenatal period than at any other time in development.

Although all human behaviors are observed prenatally in animals, there are several important differences. The first difference is the frequency of each of the behaviors. Standard research models, such as mice, rats, guinea pigs, and chick embryos are much smaller than humans and have substantially shorter lifespans (Hubrecht & Kirkwood, 2010). Consequently, they have higher metabolic rates and correspondingly higher frequencies of movements. Despite differences in raw frequency rates of behaviors, the proportion of various behaviors remains the same between humans and comparative species (Bekoff, 1995; Bellinger, Lucas, & Kleven, 2015; Kleven & Ronca, 2009; Robinson & Smotherman, 1992b). For example, behaviors that occur with high frequency in the human fetus, such as individual limb movements and mouthing behaviors, are seen in proportional numbers in fetal animals relative to low-frequency behaviors such as head movments or yawning (de Vries, Visser, & Prechtl, 1985; Kleven & Ronca, 2009).

The second difference between animal and human prenatal development is the timing of events relative to birth. All vertebrate species share a common sequence of developmental events known as ontogeny. For each species, however, birth is aligned at a different time point in this sequence (Figure 4.1). For example, mice and rats are born in a rather immature (altricial) state relative to humans. Their eyes and ear canals are not open at birth. In contrast, guinea pigs and chickens are well developed at birth (precocial) relative to humans and can stand on their own and locomote almost immediately (Hubrecht & Kirkwood, 2010). Therefore, birth itself is not a developmental milestone, but merely a point in development when the offspring emerges into the postnatal environment.

Table 4.1 Fetal behaviors observed through ultrasound visualization

High Frequency Behaviors
    Limb movements
    Whole body startles
    Hiccups
    Mouthing movements
    Hand (paw) to face contact
    Trunk movements (bend, twist, curl)
Low Frequency Behaviors
    Head movements
    Jaw opening
    Stretches
    Yawns
    Breathing movements

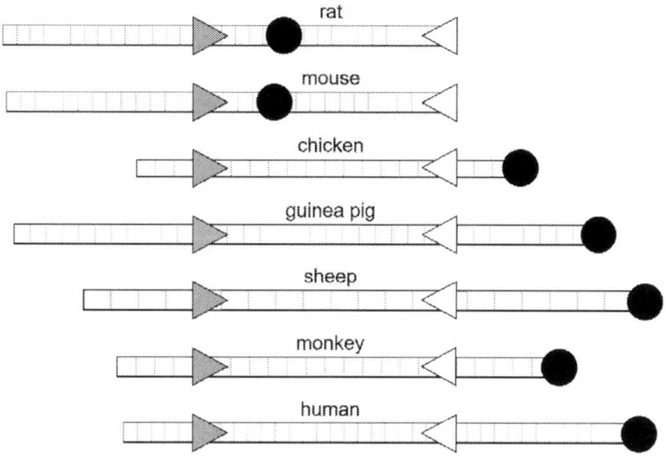

Figure 4.1 Comparative development of common animal models. Each bar depicts gestation scaled relative to milestones in sensori-motor development. Bar hatch marks represent 1 day (rat, mouse, and chicken), 2 days (guinea pig), or 7 days (sheep, monkey, and human). Gestations are aligned by 1st movements (grey arrow) and eye opening (white arrow). Alignment and scaling permit comparisons between species in the timing of birth (black circle), relative to the ontogeny of early emerging behavioral systems.

Precocial species such as guinea pigs, chickens, and sheep are often chosen for prenatal studies, because the equivalent of the entirety of human gestation can be observed before birth/hatching. Guinea pigs, for example, have a 10-week gestation, the first 9 weeks of which correspond roughly 1 week to each of the 9 months of human gestation (Bellinger et al., 2015).

In order to gain direct access to a period of development hidden from casual observation, several innovative models and methods have been developed. There are three main categories of species for which researchers developed these direct observation techniques: birds, rodents, and sheep. Although there are other species that have been investigated occasionally in the past, for example cats (Brown, 1915; Coghill, 1929; Windle & Griffin, 1931) or marsupials (Cassidy, Boudrias, Pflieger, & Cabana, 1994), birds, rodents, and sheep comprise the vast majority of developmental models still used for early behavior research.

Avian Models

Birds, typically chick or quail embryos, can be accessed for direct observation through the use of both *in ovo* and *ex ovo* techniques. *In ovo* methodologies require opening a portion of the eggshell to gain direct access to the embryo. Eggshell windowing requires the removal of a small piece of eggshell and the inner membrane, while the surrogate eggshell technique provides more accessibility and better survivability rates by transferring the embryo to successively bigger eggshells (Farzaneh, Attari, Khoshnam, & Mozdziak, 2018). Observations or manipulations can be made through the opening, which enables developmental monitoring, gene manipulation, and early stimulation modifications. These methods permit longitudinal designs and do not interfere with embryological development. *Ex ovo* culture methodologies require the embryo to be removed from its eggshell and placed in a nutritional medium. This technique allows for the highest amount of embryo accessibility and is often employed in cell labeling and *in vivo* imaging studies on embryogenesis, gastrulation, and cell differentiation and migration (Kulesa, McKinney, & McLennan, 2013). Unfortunately, these designs require a shorter timescale as embryo growth rate is restricted and survivability limited.

Rodent Models

Direct access of the rodent fetus involves surgical techniques to externalize the uterus or fetus into a water bath for behavioral observation. Early methods removed the fetal subject from the uterine environment, severing placenta/umbilical connections to the pregnant female (Carmichael, 1934). Because immature offspring cannot survive long outside the uterus, only a limited amount of quality data could be collected with this method. In recent decades new methods were developed, administering spinal anesthesia to the pregnant female (Smotherman, Richards, & Robinson, 1984; Smotherman & Robinson, 1986, 1991). These techniques allowed the fetal subjects to remain attached to the pregnant female and in good health for several hours. During observations, fetal subjects can then be directly presented with stimuli such as a non-nutritive nipple, or von Frey hair to measure response to a tactile stimulus (Robinson et al., 1992; Smotherman & Robinson, 1988). Due to the invasive nature of the surgical techniques, these studies must be cross-sectional in design.

Ovine (Sheep) Models

Fetal sheep have long been the species of choice in the study of obstetrics and gynecology. Similar to the rodent models, presentation of chemosensory stimuli such as milk or lemon solution is possible through intra-oral cannula placement (Robinson, Wong, Robertson, Nathanielsz, & Smotherman, 1995). Although early externalization methods were similar to those employed by rodent researchers (Barcroft & Barron,

1939), more recent techniques have combined fetal surgery with implantation of electromyograph (EMG) electrodes to reveal fetal behavior continuously across development (Cooke, Brodecky, & Berger, 1990). In contrast to the rodent models which must use a cross-sectional experimental design, after attachment of the EMG leads, the sheep fetus is returned to the maternal uterus to continue developing for the remainder of gestation. Data of muscle contractions are then collected continuously in this longitudinal microgenetic design which is essential for studying state organization and sleep/wake transitions (Karlsson, Arnardóttir, Robinson, & Blumberg, 2011).

In addition to direct fetal access, animal models provide a means to alter the developmental process. For example, animal models can be used to study fetal behavior during hypoxia (Robinson & Smotherman, 1992a; Smotherman & Robinson, 1987) or to measure the immediate effects when alcohol or cocaine is administered directly to the fetus (Chotro, Cordoba, & Molina, 1991; Simonik, Robinson, & Smotherman, 1994; Smotherman, Woodruff, et al., 1986). Taken together, animal models provide a powerful tool to study both typical and atypical development using experimental method.

Altering Prenatal Development

The methods used to alter prenatal development fall into three categories: genetically altered animals, environmental exposures (teratogens), and direct manipulations of the embryo/fetal subject.

Genetically Altered Animals

Genetic contributions to prenatal brain development and behavior can be studied with genetically altered mice. For example, researchers determined changes in fetal behavior were caused by mutations in the Pitx3^{ak}/2J mouse (Kleven, Joshi, Voogd, & Ronca, 2013). This genetically altered mouse is a model of Parkinson's disease in which over 50% of the dopaminergic (DA) neurons in the *substantia nigra* fail to differentiate during prenatal development (Hwang, Ardayfio, Kang, Semina, & Kim, 2003; Smidt et al., 2004). The DA system plays an important role in the development of early behaviors, most notably movement (Robinson & Kleven, 2005; Varlinskaya, Petrov, Robinson, & Smotherman, 1994, 1995), and the suckling response (Robinson, Moody, Spear, & Smotherman, 1993; Smotherman, Moody, Spear, & Robinson, 1993; Smotherman & Robinson, 1995). Researchers were also able to reverse behavioral deficits in the fetus with the DA precursor L-Dopa, confirming the connection between genetics, behavior, and brain functioning (Kleven, Booth, Voogd, & Ronca, 2014).

Environmental Exposures

Similar to genetically altered animals, models of environmental exposure can determine cause and effect between exposures and outcomes. Environmental exposures include any substance or environment capable of altering development: pharmaceutical drugs, drugs of abuse (heroin, cocaine, cannabis, alcohol, tobacco products, etc.) maternal stress, hormones, heavy metals (lead, mercury), poor nutrition, radiation, fever, and even excessive vitamin intake (Acuff-Smith & Vorhees, 1999). In general, any substance that has the potential to change nervous system functioning has the potential to be a behavioral teratogen. General methods of prenatal environmental exposure in animals are the same as those used in standard developmental toxicology and behavioral teratology studies (Acuff-Smith & Vorhees, 1999; Spear & File, 1996; Vorhees, 1986; Wilson, 1965). In keeping with these methods, fetal subjects are exposed to the teratogen indirectly through the pregnant female, rather than direct administration to the fetus. What differs from most prenatal exposure/postnatal testing methods is the inclusion of prenatal measurements of fetal behavior. The inclusion of behavioral observations in close temporal proximity to the prenatal insult results in highly sensitive measures, capable of detecting deficits and abnormalities in behavior that are not always revealed in postnatal assessments (Kleven, Queral, & Robinson, 2004). This heightened level of sensitivity may result from the fetus having little ability to compensate for damage during early development (Kleven & Bellinger, 2015).

Direct Manipulation

Unlike teratological studies in rodent models, environmental exposures in avian models are delivered directly to the egg or developing embryo. One of the advantages of using birds is that the self-contained nature of the egg allows for controllable experimental manipulations of the embryo while bypassing maternal metabolic contributions (Smith, Flentke, & Garic, 2012). Hormones are maternally derived and can vary in concentration depending on factors such as laying order (Lessells, Ruuskanen, & Schwabl, 2016) or maternal environmental factors such as stress, social instability, and availability of resources at the time of egg formation (Bertin et al., 2015). During egg formation, hormones are produced in three different cell layers surrounding the oocyte (Groothuis & Schwabl, 2008), and the yolk is deposited in three layers of varying hormone concentrations (Moore & Johnston, 2008). After laying, the egg contains all of the hormones required for development to begin. This natural process enables researchers to easily manipulate "maternally derived" yolk hormone concentrations before incubation and mimics typical delivery. Testosterone, estrogen, progesterone, and corticosterone are the most common maternally derived hormones investigated, and hormone levels are usually increased to the higher end of a naturalistic range to assess ecologically relevant variations and their impact on offspring behavior.

The two most common exposure methods are *in ovo* yolk injections and *in ovo* slow release microbead implants (Smith et al., 2012). For yolk injections, researchers bore a small hole into the eggshell (above the air space) with a needle and inject a small amount of hormone (usually suspended in a medium of saline, ethanol, or oil) directly into the yolk through the bored hole. The hole is later covered with a small piece of eggshell, paraffin wax, or cellophane tape and eggs can be set to incubate. The injection method is the easiest way to manipulate hormone concentrations and is minimally invasive without interfering with embryological development. The microbead implant method is more invasive and can lead to developmental delays, but it can be done at different time points in embryological development and can target specific tissues (Smith et al., 2012). Hormone concentrations naturally fluctuate throughout embryological development as maternal hormones are utilized and endogenous ones are created (Qasimi, Mohibbi, Nagaoka, & Watanabe, 2018). One advantage of the microbead implant method is that hormones can be manipulated at later stages of development corresponding to natural fluctuations at that time point; however, this may affect hatchability. This method is better suited for measures of toxin and drug exposure on prenatal development.

A common developmental method utilized in avian models to examine the formation of species-typical behaviors involves altering prenatal sensory stimuli. Some species-typical behaviors, which may be considered "innate," may actually be due to a complex interaction between genes and necessary embryological experiences. Eggshell windowing techniques, which involve removing a small portion of the eggshell (above the air space), are used to gain access to the embryos; thereby, permitting researchers to either introduce early sensory experiences, such as light or sound (Foushée & Lickliter, 2002; Honeycutt & Lickliter, 2002; Lickliter & Hellewell, 1992), or deprive them of typically occurring sensory stimuli via devocalization procedures (Gottlieb, 1971, 1978). This procedure does not interfere with hatchability and embryological development (Lickliter, 1990), but altered prenatal sensory experiences can change species-typical behaviors observed post-natally. For example, immediately after hatching, mallard ducklings demonstrate a strong preference for a conspecific (own species) maternal call over a similar call from a different bird species (Gottlieb, 1971). Gilbert Gottlieb developed a technique to isolate and temporarily devocalize embryos in the later stages of incubation (see Gottlieb, 1971 for procedure details). Bird embryos start to produce vocalizations shortly before hatching. He found that hearing and producing these vocalizations in the later stages of development are necessary to develop the species-typical preference for a conspecific call (Gottlieb, 1971), as devocalized ducklings have no preference for a mallard maternal call over a chicken maternal call 48 hrs after hatching (Gottlieb, 1978). These minimally invasive techniques permit longitudinal analyses of embryological and early postnatal behavior in response to altered prenatal experiences.

Observing Prenatal Behavior

The majority of studies observing prenatal behavior use either avian embryos (chickens and quail) or fetal rodents (rats, mice, and guinea pigs). These two groups require vastly different methodology, because of the differences in developmental environments: ovum (egg) versus uterus.

Avian Methods

The lateral eggshell windowing technique (Figure 4.2) has been used extensively in the field of embryological development, especially in studies designed to observe spontaneous limb movement and motor system development. This method involves removing a 2 cm^2 piece of eggshell and inner shell membrane from the side of the egg rather than the top. In prenatal limb coordination studies, this technique is used to gain access to the embryo for kinematic recording (Sharp & Bekoff, 2015; Sharp, Ma, & Bekoff, 1999). Once the right side of the embryo is exposed, it is adhered to a rigid support to prevent hip and leg rotation during movement, and the hip, knee, and ankle joints are marked with a small dot of nail polish for the recording of joint angle kinematic measurements. The same technique is used in prenatal muscle development research (Bradley, Ryu, & Yeseta, 2014; Ryu & Bradley, 2009), in conjunction with implanting small electrodes into the muscle of the exposed embryo to record synchronized EMG of muscle movement and force. The recordings are automatically digitized using software that creates a 2-D rendering of x and y coordinates. These procedures can be done at multiple time points to examine changes in movement behavior over development.

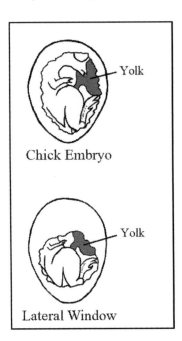

Figure 4.2 Lateral eggshell windowing technique in a chicken embryo. Representation of a chick embryo position inside the eggshell (top). Lateral eggshell window view of above embryo (bottom).

Rodent Direct Observation Methods

In contrast to the relatively noninvasive methods for observing avian embryos, direct access to the rodent embryo/fetus requires surgery. On the day of observation, time-mated females are prepared for fetal observation by administering a chemomyelotomy (a form of spinal anesthesia) under brief general anesthesia (Kleven & Ronca, 2009; Smotherman & Robinson, 1991). This procedure will render the female rat or mouse insensate on the lower half of the body but will not affect the fetus. The pregnant female is secured in a holding apparatus, and a drape is often placed over the female so that she is not affected by the presence of the investigator (Kleven & Ronca, 2009). The female is then lowered into a body temperature bath of Locke's solution (buffered saline for embryos), and the uterine horns externalized into the bath through a small abdominal incision. Female rodents have two uterine horns instead of a single uterus, as in humans and other non-human primates. After a 15-min recovery from general anesthesia, fetal subjects can be observed through the semi-transparent wall of the uterus, or externalized into the bath for direct manipulation (Robinson & Smotherman, 1988).

Rodent Ultrasound Observation Methods

In the last decade, noninvasive methods of prenatal observation became available for animal models. Using either high-resolution sonography (mice and rats) or clinical quality ultrasound (guinea pigs), fetal subjects can be visualized noninvasively in real time. Rats and mice, like most animals, are averse to restraint. Consequently, they require the spinal anesthesia preparation detailed in the last paragraph, and a cross-sectional experimental design. However, guinea pigs are docile and can be acclimated to a wide range of laboratory procedures without restraint, making them an excellent choice for noninvasive ultrasound visualization of fetal behavior (Wagner & Manning, 1976).

Although nearly any strain of guinea pig could be acclimated to the ultrasound procedures, the Institute Armande Frappier (IAF) hairless strain (Charles River Laboratory, Kingston, NY) possesses the greatest utility, because no shaving of the abdomen is necessary. Consequently, the stressors of exposure to noisy clippers and noxious-smelling depilatories are avoided. Guinea pig acclimation to personnel and procedures begins at an early age (before weaning, or before 28 days of age), in order to take full advantage of the docile nature of the guinea pig. Infants are handled on a daily basis and given reinforcement in the form of vitamin treats (BioServe, Flemington, NJ). They are also permanently housed in stable same-sex pairs or triads because guinea pigs are highly social and dependent on social groups (Hennessy & Morris, 2005; Hennessy, Young, O'Leary, & Maken, 2003). Acclimation to the ultrasound, and any other experimental procedures, begins as females approach maturity (~600g).

Acclimation includes performing sham versions of procedures that are done during the experimental phase. These sham procedures typically involve an optional collection of a saliva sample (e.g., to measure cortisol, hormones, drug exposure), and situation of the female on a cushioned examination surface maintained by thermostatic control at body temperature ($38 \pm 0.5°C$). A wheel of Timothy hay (*Phleum pratense L.*) is placed in front of the female for enrichment, and also acts as a distractor during procedures. Females consume hay undisturbed for 10 min before starting any procedures. Guinea pigs are then exposed to the ultrasound sham procedure but are otherwise not handled except to gently chaperone them in front of the hay wheel. During the ultrasound procedure, body temperature ($38 \pm 0.5°C$) Aquasonic 100 ultrasound transmission gel (Parker Labs, Fairfield, NJ) is applied to either the right or left flank and back of the guinea pig. The side chosen is randomized for each female. Sham scanning procedures involve gently placing a transducer probe against the flank of the guinea pig and lightly counterbalancing with a hand on the opposite side. At no time is counterbalancing used to restrain the female. Sham procedures are continued for 20 minutes unless the female becomes uncooperative or agitated (e.g., kicking, vocalizing). If a female is uncooperative, she is returned to the home cage for the day. Females who successfully complete a session of ultrasound acclimation are given a vitamin treat before returning them to the colony room.

Once acclimated, females are outbred to NIH multicolored Hartley males (Elm Hill Labs, Chelmsford, MA). This breeding arrangement produces offspring that are robust, and with each pup having unique multicolored markings on the fur, allows for easy identification of individuals without tattoos or tags (Russell, 1939; Wright, 1927). Females are left undisturbed during the first 2 weeks of gestation, with ultrasound observation commencing on the 3rd week. During the first ultrasound scan, both flanks of the pregnant female are scanned, in order to determine the number and placement of offspring. A subject fetus is then chosen for behavioral observations from each pregnancy. The uterine placement of the chosen fetal subject (e.g., right horn, left horn, and closer to the cervical or ovarian end of the horn) is randomized across the study. Knowing the exact location of the chosen fetus during prenatal development also allows identification at birth, permitting a true longitudinal design where the same

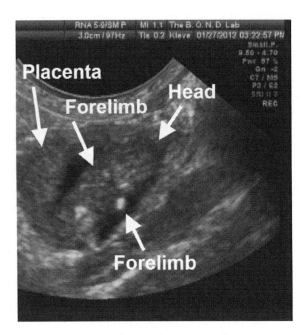

Figure 4.3 Guinea pig ultrasound visualization. Screen capture of a guinea pig fetus at 4 weeks gestation. The fetal subject is engaging in paw-to-face contact.

subjects can be followed across the lifespan. Ultrasound observations of fetal behavior are performed each week at the same time and day throughout pregnancy, with identical procedures as used in the sham acclimation. Observations (Figure 4.3) are recorded in digital format for coding and analysis.

Measuring Behavior

Prenatal Behavior

Prenatal behaviors fall into three basic categories: spontaneous movement, state organization, and evoked behaviors. Spontaneous movement can be measured with either direct observation techniques (Robinson & Smotherman, 1987) or ultrasound visualization (Bellinger et al., 2015; Sekulić et al., 2009; van Kan, de Vries, Luchinger, Mulder, & Taverne, 2009). Spontaneous fetal movements are those endogenously created and not the result of external stimulation. Measurements may emphasize the quantification of any body part movement, limbs for example, in great detail (Robinson, Blumberg, Lane, & Kreber, 2000). Such is the case for a sensitive measure of spontaneous movement, Interlimb Movement Synchrony (Kleven, Lane, & Robinson, 2004). Interlimb Movement Synchrony (IMS) is a measure of interlimb coordination between two limbs. Each fetal limb is scored in successive passes of the same archival video segment, and synchronous movements between the limbs quantified to 0.1 s. Coders must reach a Kappa adjusted intra-rater reliability of 0.90 and inter-rater reliability of 0.80.

Coding involves using an event recorder program such as JWatcher Video (Blumstein, Daniel, & Evans, 2006). Movement events are timestamped by the program when the coder presses a keycode. The resulting data files are then combined in a pairwise manner (right and left forelimbs, right and left hind limbs, contralateral limbs, and ipsilateral limbs) to quantify synchronous movements from the timestamps. These quantifications are typically performed with automated spreadsheets or software written for the task (Kleven et al., 2013, 2004; Kleven & Ronca, 2009). The resulting frequencies that occur for each 0.1 s interval delay between movements within a limb pair are then plotted as a profile of IMS (Figure 4.4, top). These profiles can be further refined by dividing movements into behavioral state categories (Corner & Schenck, 2015; Kleven & Ronca, 2009). When analyzing profiles of IMS by movement type, a clear pattern of the state differences in interlimb coordination emerges (Figure 4.4 middle). More importantly, IMS can be used to measure behavioral deficits caused by a genetic mutation (Kleven et al., 2013), maternal toxin exposure (Bellinger et al., 2015), or even the rescue or reversal of neural damage as depicted in the bottom of Figure 4.4 (Kleven et al., 2014).

Although quantifications of spontaneous movements, such as IMS, are sensitive measures of behavioral function, they are not nearly as powerful as evoked measures. Common evoked measures of prenatal behavior include: (a) nipple attachment, a measure of the suckling response (Robinson, Arnold, Spear, & Smotherman, 1993; Robinson et al., 1992), (b) facial wiping, a defensive or reactive response (Robinson et al., 1993; Robinson & Smotherman, 1991; Smotherman & Robinson, 1988), and (c) conjugate movement, used to measure fetal learning (Robinson & Kleven, 2005; Robinson, Kleven, & Brumley, 2008). All evoked measures require direct access to the fetus, and therefore necessitate surgical preparation as described in the Observing Prenatal Behavior section (Kleven & Ronca, 2009; Smotherman et al., 1984; Smotherman & Robinson, 1991; Smotherman, Robinson, & Miller, 1986). Once prepared, fetal subjects are video recorded for a baseline period and then presented with stimuli such as a non-nutritive nipple (nipple attachment), a von Frey hair (tactile stimulation), or an infusion of solution (e.g., lemon) into the mouth (facial wiping), or fitted with an interlimb yoke (training of conjugate movements). Video recording continues for the duration of the manipulation, to be coded later from playback (Figure 4.5).

Behaviors are coded typically as frequencies and durations for the various behaviors. For example, during a nipple attachment manipulation, grasp attempts, oral grasps and mouthing of the non-nutritive nipple, aversive head turns, forelimb pedalling, and hindlimb movements are quantified both as frequencies and durations for each behavior.

Postnatal Measures

Most avian researchers utilize postnatal behavioral and/or physiological outcome measures. Physiological measures include mass, temperature, heart rate, and hatching success. They can be used as a design check to ensure that group differences are isolated to the primary outcome of interest. For example, in hormone manipulation studies, it is important to have a vehicle-only sham control group to ensure that observed group differences are not attributed to injection procedures. Other times, manipulations are known to cause physiological differences between groups, and it is important to track these differences. For example, elevated yolk testosterone is known to produce differences in body mass (Bertin, Richard-Yris, Möstl, & Lickliter, 2009; Schweitzer, Goldstein, Place, & Adkins-Regan, 2013).

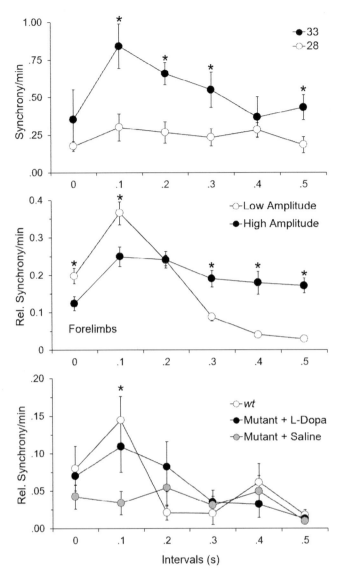

Figure 4.4 Interlimb Movement Synchrony. Points depict the mean IMS per min at 0.1 s intervals for preterm human infants born between 26 and 28 weeks gestation (top), behavioral state organization for fetal rats (middle), and the reversal of behavioral deficits in Pitx3^{ak}/2J genetically altered mice (bottom). IMS profiles (top) compare interlimb coordination between the right and left leg of preterm human infants at 28 weeks (white) and 33 weeks (black) gestational age. The profile for 28-week infants (white) is not different from random, while by week 33 (black) the profile takes on the characteristic shape of tightly coupled movement coordination (Key et al., 2002; Kleven, Hynes, & Robinson, 2003). State organization in the E20 rat fetus forelimbs (middle) is portrayed with IMS profiles of Low Amplitude movements (twitch-like movements similar to active sleep, white) and High Amplitude movements (awake-like and coordinated in appearance, black). State IMS profiles are standardized by movement rates, creating relative synchrony/min profiles. IMS is also used to determine deficit reversals (bottom). For example, the prenatal dopaminergic behavioral deficits in the genetically altered mouse Pitx3^{ak}/6J (bottom, grey) can be reversed by direct administration of 25 mg/kg of L-Dopa to the fetus (bottom, black). IMS profiles for the Pitx3 fetal mice are shown in comparison to the wildtype background C57 mouse fetus (*wt*, white). Both *wt* and L-Dopa treated fetal subjects have IMS profiles that are tightly coupled at the 0.1 s interval. In all panels, error bars depict the *SEM*.

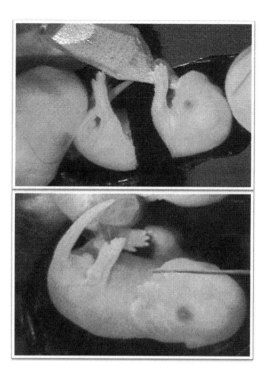

Figure 4.5 Evoked behaviors during direct observation of the mouse fetus. A Day 18 mouse fetus grasps a non-nutritive nipple while gently secured in a holding apparatus with a Velcro strap (top, reprinted from Kleven et al., 2014 with permission). A von Frey hair is used to gently stroke the perioral area of a Day 18 mouse fetus (bottom). The species-typical response to this tactile stimulation is for the fetus to brush away the stimulus instrument with the forepaws (Golani & Fentress, 1985).

There are numerous paradigms and outcome measures used to quantify behavioral changes in both birds and rodents including fear/emotion regulation, social motivation, and perceptual discrimination tasks. However, typical behaviors vary between species in these tasks. For example, rats and mice readily exhibit object novelty preference as a baseline behavior (Antunes & Biala, 2012). Conversely, birds exhibit object neophobia as a baseline behavior and avoid novel objects. In domestic chicks treated with elevated yolk hormones (progesterone, testosterone, and estradiol), displaying enhanced novel object exploration would be indicative of a dampened fear response (Bertin et al., 2015) and altered species-typical behavior. Therefore, it is important to consider both the desired outcome measure and what would be considered species-typical behaviors when designing a study. Common fear or emotion regulation tasks used in birds include tonic immobility, open field exploration, distress call analyses (Daisley, Bromundt, Möstl, & Kotrschal, 2005; Pittet, Houdelier, & Lumineau, 2014), object neophobia (Bertin et al., 2015; Daisley et al., 2005), or emergence tests (Pittet et al., 2014). Typical social tasks include isolation tests, social reinstatement (Pittet et al., 2014), and looking time or approach tests (Schweitzer et al., 2013).

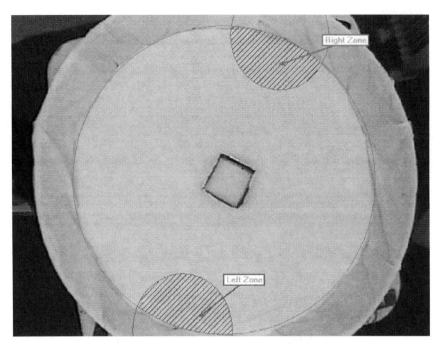

Figure 4.6 Auditory choice preference task arena with demarcated approach zones. Noldus EthoVision XT 8.5 software (Wageningen, The Netherlands) is used to track subjects in arena and time spent in zones.

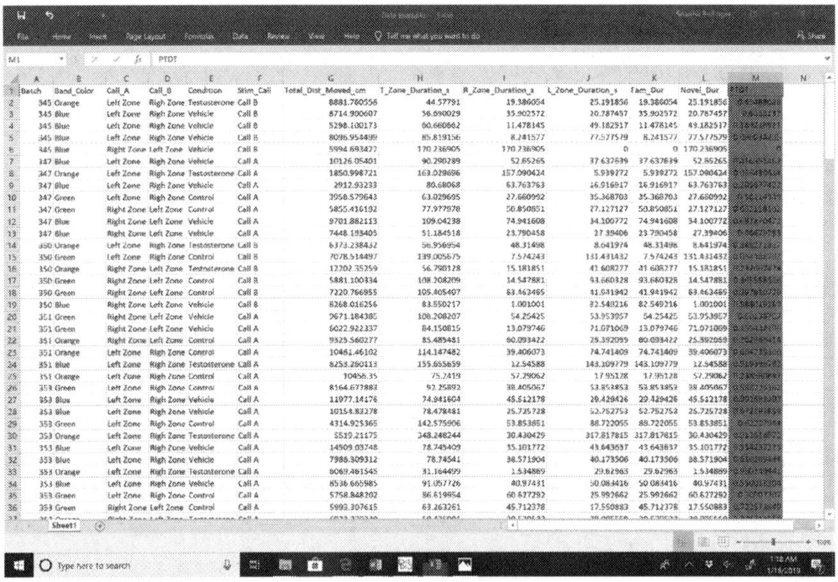

Figure 4.7 Elevated hormone data output from an auditory choice preference task recorded using Noldus EthoVision XT 8.5 software (Wageningen, The Netherlands). The highlighted column corresponds to a proportion of total duration time (PTDT) score that can be calculated from outcome measures provided by EthoVision. Duration of time spent in approach zones are not independent measures, therefore, a PTDT is calculated to obtain a proportion of time spent in the zone playing the familiar maternal call.

$$PTDT = \frac{\text{Familiar zone duration}}{\text{Total time spent in both zones}}$$

A simultaneous choice preference task can be used as a measure of auditory learning and memory in quail neonates (Figure 4.6). In this task, birds are prenatally exposed in the last day of incubation to one of two variants of a conspecific maternal call (Call A or Call B; Heaton, Miller, & Goodwin, 1978). After hatching (24, 48, 72, or 96 hrs of age), chicks are placed individually in an arena, which has two small concealed speakers at opposite ends playing the two maternal call variants (Call A and Call B) simultaneously. After an acclimation period, subjects are allowed to freely roam the arena, while experimenters track the amount of time they spend in each zone (demarcated approach area in front of each speaker). This method allows researchers to investigate how alterations in the type and timing of prenatal sensory experiences interfere with early perceptual learning and memory (Honeycutt & Lickliter, 2002; Lickliter & Hellewell, 1992).

Either manual scoring or the use of a video tracking program such as Noldus EthoVision XT 8.5 software (Wageningen, The Netherlands) is often used to measure behaviors. EthoVision will track subjects and provide specified outcome measures such as total distance moved (cm^2), velocity, duration spent in zones (s), frequencies, and latency to enter zones (s). It will also output the data into an Excel file (Figure 4.7) for statistical analysis purposes (Noldus, Spink, & Tegelenbosch, 2001).

Innovations and Future Direction

The avian embryo is one of the primary models used for embryogenesis, gastrulation, cell differentiation, and organogenesis studies due to its remarkable similarity to human embryological development and the accessibility of the egg to a multitude of experimental techniques (Kulesa et al., 2013). More recent advances in cell fluorescence labeling and *in vivo* imaging have allowed researchers to understand how molecular mechanisms interact in cell formation and migration to form functional embryonic structures. Cell labeling techniques have provided noninvasive methods for visualizing complex cell morphologies and accurately labeling small groups of cells for *in vivo* cell tracking, while imaging techniques have enabled researchers to study neural tube closure, cardiovascular development, and peripheral nervous system development. Genetic research in birds is also becoming more prominent. The majority of genetically altered animal models are rodents. However, recent advances in sperm transfection assisted gene editing (STAGE) and direct injection, have enabled scientists to make more precise genome edits in a wider range of avian species (Cooper, Doran, Challagulla, Tizard, & Jenkins, 2018). These new techniques could be effective in the creation of more knock-out models in avian species. Additionally, the complete avian genome sequencing of chickens and zebra finches has opened research opportunities into cross-species gene comparisons and the identification of genomic features involved in avian development and behavior (Mello & Clayton, 2015). Continued advances in molecular approaches will elucidate and enhance our understanding of the neurobiological mechanisms involved in typical and atypical development.

In rodent models of prenatal development, some of the latest innovations have arrived as a result of changing sensibilities about animal research. A move toward greater use of noninvasive methodologies, such as ultrasound visualization of fetal behavior, creates a more humane set of methods. Where previously an investigator may have used an anti-proliferative toxin or drug to create specific neural damage during development, now a noninvasive temperature manipulation can be used to achieve the same results without harm to the pregnant animal (Argumedo et al., 2016,

2018). These new noninvasive methods are more humane and often more relevant to humans as well. For example, elevations in fetal brain temperature cause rapidly dividing cells to undergo apoptosis, or cell death (Upfold, Smith, & Edwards, 1989). By raising the maternal body temperature by a few degrees in a water bath, selective damage in the fetal brain will result when only dividing cells die, and other cell types are not affected (Hinoue, Fushiki, Nishimura, & Shiota, 2001). This type of manipulation is more relevant to humans than exposure to a rare toxin because it creates a temporary low-grade fever in the pregnant animal, which is common in humans. Additionally, the use of noninvasive longitudinal methods, instead of cross-sectional designs, means fewer animals will be used. These noninvasive methods, when combined with thoughtful species-relevant enrichment (Brewer, Bellinger, Joshi, & Kleven, 2014), create a more humane research environment while serving to advance the body of developmental science.

References

Acuff-Smith, K. D. & Vorhees, C. D. (1999). Neurobehavioral teratology. In R. J. M. Niesink, R. M. A. Jaspers, L. M. W. Kornet, J. M. van Ree, & H. A. Tilson (Eds.), *Introduction to Neurobehavioral Toxicology* (pp. 27–69). Boca Raton, FL: CRC Press.

Antunes, M. & Biala, G. (2012). The novel object recognition memory: neurobiology, test procedure, and its modifications. *Cognitive Processing*, 13(2), 93–110. doi:10.1007/s10339-011-0430-z.

Argumedo, Y. M., Henshaw, K., Bailey, B., Bishop, T. J., Austin, T., & Kleven, G. A. (2016). Mild maternal hyperthermia as a noninvasive antiproliferative teratogen in guinea pigs (*Cavia porcellus*). *Developmental Psychobiology*, 58, S3.

Argumedo, Y. M., Henshaw, K., Bailey, B., Bishop, T. J., Austin, T., & Kleven, G. A. (2018). Mild maternal hyperthermia during mid-gestation causes both fetaland juvenile behavioral deficits in guinea pigs. *Developmental Psychobiology*, 60, S4. doi:10.1002/dev.21598.

Barcroft, J. & Barron, D. H. (1939). The development of behavior in foetal sheep. *Journal of Comparative Neurology*, 70, 477–502.

Bekoff, A. (1995). Development of motor behavior in chick embryos. In J. P. Lecanuet, W. P. Fifer, N. A. Krasnegor, & W. P. Smotherman (Eds.), *Fetal development: a psychobiological perspective* (pp. 191–204). Hillsdale, MI: Lawrence Erlbaum Associates Inc.

Bellinger, S. A., Lucas, D., & Kleven, G. A. (2015). An ecologically relevant guinea pig model of fetal behavior. *Behavioural Brain Research*, 283, 175–183. doi:10.1016/j.bbr.2015.01.047.

Bertin, A., Arnould, C., Moussu, C., Meurisse, M., Constantin, P., Leterrier, C., & Calandreau, L. (2015). Artificially increased yolk hormone levels and neophobia in domestic chicks. *Animals*, 5 (4), 1220–1232. doi:10.3390/ani5040408.

Bertin, A., Richard-Yris, M.-A., Möstl, E., & Lickliter, R. (2009). Increased yolk testosterone facilitates prenatal perceptual learning in northern bobwhite quail (*Colinus virginianus*). *Hormones and Behavior*, 56(4), 416–422. doi:10.1016/j.yhbeh.2009.07.008.

Blumstein, D. T., Daniel, J. C., & Evans, C. S. (2006). JWatcher video (Version 1.0). Australia: Animal Behavior Laboratory, Maquarie University. Retrieved from www.jwatcher.ucla.edu/

Bradley, N. S., Ryu, Y. U., & Yeseta, M. C. (2014). Spontaneous locomotor activity in late-stage chicken embryos is modified by stretch of leg muscles. *The Journal of Experimental Biology*, 217 (6), 896–907. doi:10.1242/jeb.093567.

Brewer, J. S., Bellinger, S. A., Joshi, P., & Kleven, G. A. (2014). Enriched open field facilitates exercise and social interaction in two strains of guinea pig (*Cavia porcellus*). *Journal of the American Association for Laboratory Animal Science*, 53(4), 344–355.

Brown, T. G. (1915). On the activities of the central nervous system of the unborn foetus of the cat; with a discussion of the question whether progression (walking, etc.) is a "learnt" complex. *Journal of Physiology*, 49, 208–215.

Carmichael, L. (1934). An experimental study in the prenatal guinea-pig of the origin and development of reflexes and patterns of behavior in relation to the stimulation of specific receptor areas during the period of active fetal life. *Genetic Psychology Monographs*, 16, 338–491.

Cassidy, G., Boudrias, D., Pflieger, J. F., & Cabana, T. (1994). The development of sensorimotor reflexes in the Brazilian opossum Monodelphis domestica. *Brain, Behavior and Evolution*, 43 (4–5), 244–253.

Chotro, M. G., Cordoba, N. E., & Molina, J. C. (1991). Acute prenatal experience with alcohol in the amniotic fluid: interactions with aversive and appetitive alcohol orosensory learning in the rat pup. *Developmental Psychobiology*, 24(6), 431–451.

Coghill, G. E. (1929). *Anatomy and the Problem of Behavior*. Cambridge, UK: Cambridge University Press.

Cooke, I. R., Brodecky, V., & Berger, P. J. (1990). Easily-implantable electrodes for chronic recording of electromyogram activity in small fetuses. *Journal of Neuroscience Methods*, 33(1), 51–54.

Cooper, C. A., Doran, T. J., Challagulla, A., Tizard, M. L. V., & Jenkins, K. A. (2018). Innovative approaches to genome editing in avian species. *Journal of Animal Science and Biotechnology*, 9, 1–7. doi:10.1186/s40104-018-0231-7.

Corner, M. A. & Schenck, C. H. (2015). Perchance to dream? Primordial motor activity patterns in vertebrates from fish to mammals: their prenatal origin, postnatal persistence during sleep, and pathological reemergence during REM sleep behavior disorder. *Neuroscience Bulletin*, 31(6), 649–662. doi:10.1007/s12264-015-1557-1.

Daisley, J. N., Bromundt, V., Möstl, E., & Kotrschal, K. (2005). Enhanced yolk testosterone influences behavioral phenotype independent of sex in Japanese quail chicks (Coturnix japonica). *Hormones and Behavior*, 47(2), 185–194.

Darwin, C. (1859). *The Origin of Species by Means of Natural Selection, or the Preservation of Favored Races in the Struggle for Life*. New York and London: Merrill and Baker.

de Vries, J. I., Visser, G. H., & Prechtl, H. F. (1985). The emergence of fetal behaviour. II. Quantitative aspects. *Early Human Development*, 12(2), 99–120.

Farzaneh, M., Attari, F., Khoshnam, S. E., & Mozdziak, P. E. (2018). The method of chicken whole embryo culture using the eggshell windowing, surrogate eggshell and *ex ovo* culture system. *British Poultry Science*, 59(2), 240–244. doi:10.1080/00071668.2017.1413234.

Foushée, R. D. & Lickliter, R. (2002). Early visual experience affects postnatal auditory responsiveness in bobwhite quail (*Colinus virginianus*). *Journal of Comparative Psychology*, 116(4), 369–380.

Golani, I. & Fentress, J. C. (1985). Early ontogeny of face grooming in mice. *Developmental Psychobiology*, 18(6), 529–544.

Gottlieb, G. (1971). *Development of species identification in birds: an inquiry into the prenatal determinants of perception*. Chicago, IL: University of Chicago Press.

Gottlieb, G. (1978). Development of species identification in ducklings: IV. Change in species-specific perception caused by auditory deprivation. *Journal of Comparative and Physiological Psychology*, 92(3), 375–387.

Groothuis, T. G. G. & Schwabl, H. (2008). Hormone-mediated maternal effects in birds: mechanisms matter but what do we know of them? *Philosophical Transactions of the Royal Society of London. Series B*, 363, 1647–1661.

Heaton, M. B., Miller, D. B., & Goodwin, D. G. (1978). Species-specific auditory discrimination in bobtail quail neonates. *Developmental Psychobiology*, 11(1), 13–21.

Hennessy, M. B. & Morris, A. (2005). Passive responses of young guinea pigs during exposure to a novel environment: influences of social partners and age. *Developmental Psychobiology*, 46(2), 86–96.

Hennessy, M. B., Young, T. L., O'Leary, S. K., & Maken, D. S. (2003). Social preferences of developing guinea pigs (*Cavia porcellus*) from the preweaning to the periadolescent periods. *Journal of Comparative Psychology*, 117(4), 406–413.

Hinoue, A., Fushiki, S., Nishimura, Y., & Shiota, K. (2001). In utero exposure to brief hyperthermia interferes with the production and migration of neocortical neurons and induces apoptotic neuronal death in the fetal mouse brain. *Brain Research. Developmental Brain Research*, 132(1), 59–67.

Honeycutt, H. & Lickliter, R. (2002). Prenatal experience and postnatal perceptual preferences: evidence for attentional-bias in bobwhite quail embryos (*Colinus virginianus*). *Journal of Comparative Psychology*, 116(3), 270–276.

Hubrecht, R. & Kirkwood, J. K. (2010). *The UFAW Handbook on the Care and Management of Laboratory and Other Research Animals* (8th ed.). Ames, IA: Wiley-Blackwell.

Hwang, D. Y., Ardayfio, P., Kang, U. J., Semina, E. V., & Kim, K. S. (2003). Selective loss of dopaminergic neurons in the *substantia nigra* of Pitx3-deficient aphakia mice. *Molecular Brain Research*, 114, 123–131.

Karlsson, K. A. E., Arnardóttir, H., Robinson, S. R., & Blumberg, M. S. (2011). Dynamics of sleep-wake cyclicity across the fetal period in sheep (*Ovis aries*). *Developmental Psychobiology*, 53(1), 89–95. doi:10.1002/dev.20495

Key, L. J., Kleven, G. A., Lane, M. S., Lauer, K., Gregory, D., & Robinson, S. R. (2002). Development of interlimb movement synchrony in preterm human infants. *Developmental Psychobiology*, 41(1), 82.

Kleven, G. A. & Bellinger, S. A. (2015). Developmental pathways of motor dysfunction. *Developmental Psychobiology*, 57(4), 435–446. doi:10.1002/dev.21304.

Kleven, G. A., Booth, H. M., Voogd, M., & Ronca, A. E. (2014). L-Dopa reverses behavioral deficits in the Pitx3 mouse fetus. *Behavioral Neuroscience*, 128(6), 749–759. doi:10.1037/bne0000016.

Kleven, G. A., Hynes, S. M., & Robinson, S. R. (2003). Temporal patterning of spontaneous motor activity in altricial and precocial rodent fetuses and preterm human infants: a comparative study of bout organization and interlimb movement synchrony. *Society for Neuroscience Abstracts*, 29, program number 40.41.

Kleven, G. A., Joshi, P., Voogd, M., & Ronca, A. E. (2013). Prenatal ontogeny of the dopamine-dependent neurobehavioral phenotype in Pitx3-deficient mice. *European Journal of Neuroscience*, 37(10), 1564–1572. doi:10.1111/ejn.12184.

Kleven, G. A., Lane, M. S., & Robinson, S. R. (2004). Development of interlimb movement synchrony in the rat fetus. *Behavioral Neuroscience*, 118(4), 835–844. doi:10.1037/0735-7044.118.4.835.

Kleven, G. A., Queral, L., & Robinson, S. R. (2004). Prenatal methylazoxymethanol exposure alters evoked responses in fetal rats. *Neurotoxicology and Teratology*, 26(5), 663–671. doi:10.1016/j.ntt.2004.06.003.

Kleven, G. A. & Ronca, A. E. (2007). Comparison of qualitative and quantitative behavioral assessments in fetal mice through both direct and ultrasound observational techniques. *Developmental Psychobiology*, 49(7), 731.

Kleven, G. A. & Ronca, A. E. (2009). Prenatal behavior of the C57BL/6J mouse: a promising model for human fetal movement during early to mid-gestation. *Developmental Psychobiology*, 51(51), 84–94. doi:10.1002/dev.20348

Kulesa, P. M., McKinney, M. C., & McLennan, R. (2013). Developmental imaging: the avian embryo hatches to the challenge. *Birth Defects Research. Part C*, 99(2), 121–133. doi:10.1002/bdrc.21036.

Lessells, C. M., Ruuskanen, S., & Schwabl, H. (2016). Yolk steroids in great tit *Parus major* eggs: variation and covariation between hormones and with environmental and parental factors. *Behavioral Ecology and Sociobiology*, 70, 843–856.

Lickliter, R. (1990). Premature visual stimulation accelerates intersensory functioning in bobwhite quail neonates. *Developmental Psychobiology*, 23(1), 15–27.

Lickliter, R. & Hellewell, T. B. (1992). Contextual determinants of auditory learning in bobwhite quail embryos and hatchlings. *Developmental Psychobiology, 25*(1), 17–31.

Mello, C. V. & Clayton, D. F. (2015). The opportunities and challenges of large-scale molecular approaches to songbird neurobiology. *Neuroscience and Biobehavioral Reviews, 50,* 70–76. doi:10.1016/j.neubiorev.2014.09.017.

Moore, M. C. & Johnston, G. I. H. (2008). Toward a dynamic model of deposition and utilization of yolk steroids. *Integrative and Comparative Biology, 48*(3), 411–418. doi:10.1093/icb/icn079.

Noldus, P. J. J., Spink, A. J., & Tegelenbosch, A. J. (2001). EthoVision: a versatile video tracking system for automation of behavioral experiments. *Behavior Research Methods, 33*(3), 398–414.

Pittet, F., Houdelier, C., & Lumineau, S. (2014). Precocial bird mothers shape sex differences in the behavior of their chicks. *Journal of Experimental Zoology. Part A, 321*(5), 265–275. doi:10.1002/jez.1858.

Qasimi, M. I., Mohibbi, H., Nagaoka, K., & Watanabe, G. (2018). Accumulation of steroid hormones in the eggshells of Japanese quail (*Coturnix japonica*). *General and Comparative Endocrinology, 259,* 161–164. doi:10.1016/j.ygcen.2017.11.020.

Robinson, S. R., Arnold, H. M., Spear, N. E., & Smotherman, W. P. (1993). Experience with milk and an artificial nipple promotes conditioned opioid activity in the rat fetus. *Developmental Psychobiology, 26*(7), 375–387.

Robinson, S. R., Blumberg, M. S., Lane, M. S., & Kreber, L. A. (2000). Spontaneous motor activity in fetal and infant rats is organized into discrete multilimb bouts. *Behavioral Neuroscience, 114* (2), 328–336.

Robinson, S. R., Hoeltzel, T. C., Cooke, K. M., Umphress, S. M., Smotherman, W. P., & Murrish, D. E. (1992). Oral capture and grasping of an artificial nipple by rat fetuses. *Developmental Psychobiology, 25*(8), 543–555.

Robinson, S. R. & Kleven, G. A. (2005). Learning to move before birth. In B. Hopkins & S. Johnson (Eds.), *Advances in Infancy Research: Prenatal Development of Postnatal Functions* (Vol. 2, pp. 131–175). Norwood, NJ: Ablex.

Robinson, S. R., Kleven, G. A., & Brumley, M. R. (2008). Prenatal development of interlimb motor learning in the rat fetus. *Infancy, 13*(3), 204–228. doi:10.1080/15250000802004288.

Robinson, S. R., Moody, C. A., Spear, L. P., & Smotherman, W. P. (1993). Effects of dopamine and kappa opioid receptors on fetal responsiveness to perioral stimuli. *Developmental Psychobiology, 26,* 37–50.

Robinson, S. R. & Smotherman, W. P. (1987). Environmental determinants of behavior in the rat fetus. II. The emergence of synchronous movement. *Animal Behaviour, 35,* 1652–1662.

Robinson, S. R. & Smotherman, W. P. (1988). Chance and chunks in the ontogeny of fetal behavior. In W. P. Smotherman & S. R. Robinson (Eds.), *Behavior of the Fetus* (pp. 95–115). Caldwell, NJ: Telford Press.

Robinson, S. R. & Smotherman, W. P. (1991). The amniotic sac as scaffolding: prenatal ontogeny of an action pattern. *Developmental Psychobiology, 24*(7), 463–485.

Robinson, S. R. & Smotherman, W. P. (1992a). Behavioral response of altricial and precocial rodent fetuses to acute umbilical cord compression. *Behavioral & Neural Biology, 57*(2), 93–102.

Robinson, S. R. & Smotherman, W. P. (1992b). Fundamental motor patterns of the mammalian fetus. *Journal of Neurobiology, 23*(10), 1574–1600.

Robinson, S. R., Wong, C. H., Robertson, S. S., Nathanielsz, P. W., & Smotherman, W. P. (1995). Behavioral responses of the chronically instrumented sheep fetus to chemosensory stimuli presented in utero. *Behavioral Neuroscience, 109*(3), 551–562.

Russell, E. S. (1939). A quantitative study of genetic effects on guinea-pig coat colors. *Genetics, 24,* 332–355.

Ryu, Y. U. & Bradley, N. S. (2009). Precocious locomotor behavior begins in the egg: development of leg muscle patterns for stepping in the chick. *PLoS ONE, 4*(7), 6111. doi:10.1371/journal.pone.0006111.

Schweitzer, C., Goldstein, M. H., Place, N. J., & Adkins-Regan, E. (2013). Long-lasting and sex-specific consequences of elevated egg yolk testosterone for social behavior in Japanese quail. *Hormones and Behavior, 63*(1), 80–87. doi:10.1016/j.yhbeh.2012.10.011.

Sekulić, S. R., Lukac, D., Drapsin, M., Capo, I., Lalosevic, D., & Novakov-Mikic, A. (2009). Ultrasonographic observations of the maturation of basic movements in guinea pig fetuses. *Central European Journal of Biology, 4*(1), 58–61. doi:10.2478/s11535-008-0054-1.

Sharp, A. A. & Bekoff, A. (2015). Pyridoxine treatment alters embryonic motility in chicks: implications for the role of proprioception. *Developmental Psychobiology, 57*(2), 271–277. doi:10.1002/dev.21282.

Sharp, A. A., Ma, E., & Bekoff, A. (1999). Developmental changes in leg coordination of the chick at embryonic days 9, 11, and 13: uncoupling of ankle movements. *Journal of Neurophysiology, 82*(5), 2406–2414.

Simonik, D. K., Robinson, S. R., & Smotherman, W. P. (1994). Central administration of cocaine produces age-dependent effects on behavior in the fetal rat. *Behavioral Neuroscience, 108*(6), 1179–1187.

Smidt, M. P., Smits, S. M., Bouwmeester, H., Hamers, F. P., van der Linden, A. J., Hellemons, A. J., ... Burbach, J. P. (2004). Early developmental failure of *substantia nigra* dopamine neurons in mice lacking the homeodomain gene Pitx3. *Development, 131*(5), 1145–1155.

Smith, S. M., Flentke, G. R., & Garic, A. (2012). Avian models in teratology and developmental toxicology. *Methods in Molecular Biology, 889*, 85–103. doi:10.1007/978-1-61779-867-2_7.

Smotherman, W. P., Moody, C. A., Spear, L. P., & Robinson, S. R. (1993). Fetal behavior and the endogenous opioid system: D1 dopamine receptor interactions with the kappa opioid system. *Physiology & Behavior, 53*(1), 191–197.

Smotherman, W. P., Richards, L. S., & Robinson, S. R. (1984). Techniques for observing fetal behavior in utero: a comparison of chemomyelotomy and spinal transection. *Developmental Psychobiology, 17*(6), 661–674.

Smotherman, W. P. & Robinson, S. R. (1986). A method for endoscopic visualization of rat fetuses in situ. *Physiology & Behavior, 37*(4), 663–665.

Smotherman, W. P. & Robinson, S. R. (1987). Stereotypic behavioral response of rat fetuses to acute hypoxia is altered by maternal alcohol consumption. *American Journal of Obstetrics & Gynecology, 157*(4 Pt 1), 982–986.

Smotherman, W. P. & Robinson, S. R. (1988). Behavior of rat fetuses following chemical or tactile stimulation. *Behavioral Neuroscience, 102*(1), 24–34.

Smotherman, W. P. & Robinson, S. R. (1991). Accessibility of the rat fetus for psychobiological investigation. In H. N. Shair, G. A. Barr, & M. A. Hofer (Eds.), *Developmental Psychobiology: New Methods and Changing Concepts* (pp. 148–163). New York: Oxford University Press.

Smotherman, W. P. & Robinson, S. R. (1995). Dopamine D-sub-1 and D-sub-2 effects on fetal mouthing responses to milk. *Physiology & Behavior, 57*(1), 15–19.

Smotherman, W. P., Robinson, S. R., & Miller, B. J. (1986). A reversible preparation for observing the behavior of fetal rats in utero: spinal anesthesia with lidocaine. *Physiology & Behavior, 37*(1), 57–60.

Smotherman, W. P., Woodruff, K. S., Robinson, S. R., Del Real, C., Barron, S., & Riley, E. P. (1986). Spontaneous fetal behavior after maternal exposure to ethanol. *Pharmacology, Biochemistry & Behavior, 24*(2), 165–170.

Spear, L. P. & File, S. E. (1996). Methodological considerations in neurobehavioral teratology. *Pharmacology, Biochemistry & Behavior, 55*(4), 455–457.

Upfold, J. B., Smith, M. S., & Edwards, M. J. (1989). Quantitative study of the effects of maternal hyperthermia on cell death and proliferation in the guinea pig brain on day 21 of pregnancy. *Teratology, 39*(2), 173–179.

van Kan, C. M., de Vries, J. I. P., Luchinger, A. B., Mulder, E. J. H., & Taverne, M. A. M. (2009). Ontogeny of fetal movements in the guinea pig. *Physiology & Behavior, 98*, 338–344. doi:10.1016/j.physbeh.2009.06.011.

Varlinskaya, E. I., Petrov, E. S., Robinson, S. R., & Smotherman, W. P. (1994). Intracisternal administration of SKF-38393 and SCH-23390: behavioral effects in the rat fetus. *Pharmacology, Biochemistry & Behavior*, 48(3), 741–748.

Varlinskaya, E. I., Petrov, E. S., Robinson, S. R., & Smotherman, W. P. (1995). Asymmetrical development of the dopamine system in the fetal rat as indicated by lateralized administration of SKF-38393 and SCH-23390. *Pharmacology, Biochemistry & Behavior*, 50(3), 359–367.

Vorhees, C. V. (1986). Principles of behavioral teratology. In E. P. Riley & C. V. Vorhees (Eds.), *Handbook of Behavioral Teratology* (pp. 23–46). New York: Plenum Press.

Wagner, J. E. & Manning, P. J. (Eds.). (1976). *The Biology of the Guinea Pig*. New York: Academic Press.

Wilson, J. G. (1965). Embryological considerations in teratology. In J. G. Wilson & J. Warkany (Eds.), *Teratology: Principles and Techniques* (pp. 251–260). Chicago, IL: University of Chicago Press.

Windle, W. F. & Griffin, A. M. (1931). Observations on embryonic and fetal movements of the cat. *Journal of Comparative Neurology*, 52, 149–188.

Wright, S. (1927). The effects in combination of the major color-factors of the guinea pig. *Genetics*, 12, 530–569.

5 Physiological and Behavioral Research Methods across Prenatal and Infant Periods

Nancy Aaron Jones and Krystal D. Mize

Introduction

What role do infants have in their own developmental course? This question has intrigued theorists and researchers alike. Despite the undeniable influence of the environment on an individual and their potential developmental trajectory, there are still questions about the infant's repertoire of capabilities and how deprived and enriched contexts influence the maturational unfolding of the infant. Measures of the role of the fetus in its own development are also limited. However, recognizing that genetic expression and biological maturation are continuing to evolve from prenatal to postnatal periods, researchers have developed several unique measures, utilized to study fetal and infant development. Theoretical accounts place physiology and biology (Michel, 2013) at the heart of the individual's own development, with acknowledgement of the interactive influences of temperament, neurophysiology, evolved emotional and cognitive characteristics, as well as social context impacting the types of outcomes that set the trajectory for later stages of development (Jones & Sloan, 2018). We conceptualize the course of development as a continuum with the starting point encompassing the environment within the womb and the person–environment interaction impacting complex patterns of normative and risk outcomes.

Our goal is to emphasize the importance of this early period for developmental change, as no other time offers the same opportunity to enrich (or inhibit) the individual's peak potential (Monk & Hane, 2014). Creating and utilizing methods that are valid and reliable is of utmost importance if developmental scientists truly strive to conceptualize normative developmental patterns versus those that are at risk. Although interventions can be introduced postnatally, the window for alterations in key components of development are believed to be more plastic or sensitive to change in the womb due to the pre- to postnatal development sequence. Ultimately, the longevity of fetal programming (Sandman, Davis, Buss, & Glynn, 2012) of infant behaviors and neurophysiology should be investigated in order to tailor effective interventions, if appropriate, to ultimately create a beneficial and maximally lasting outcome.

Summary of the Topic

Historical (Kennard, 1944; Kennard & Fulton, 1942) and contemporary theories (Calkins, 2015; Fox & Rutter, 2010) have noted the paramount importance of understanding individual variation during ontogeny and its effect on development, including the view that age (even gestational age) has a qualitative impact on the brain processes that are of importance during specific developmental moments in time. Moreover the type of experiences that a fetus or an infant is exposed to can potentially change the trajectory of growth, with many family systems providing optimal environmental contexts. Conversely, differential susceptibility of infants in families with stress, anxiety, and depression or those that experience the detrimental effects of poverty (Belsky & Pluess, 2009) can also change the trajectory and can alter the view that scientists must take to assess developmental milestones. An ambitious undertaking across all these contexts is for the scientist to choose the appropriate method and measures that can be utilized to understand the dynamics of the developmental system as well as the trajectory of development for the individual. The challenge is to measure direct individual experiences and how those occurrences affect other developmental systems, in particular the emerging cascade of cognitions and emotions in the individual, as well as the plethora of social encounters and social ecology that are ubiquitous in the infant's experiences.

Fetal and infant growth are vulnerable periods; therefore, while the scientist seeks to understand the intricacies of this stage, they must respect the unique measurement challenges that limit the timing and detail of the information obtained. Studies in psychobiological and neurophysiological development historically utilized animal models (Michel, 2013). However, recent advances in technology have made studying fetus-to-infant development in *humans* non-invasive and thus feasible (Reissland & Kisilevsky, 2016) with the proper training. Although this chapter is not exhaustive of all the approaches to studying fetal and infant development, here we will review recent methods in neurophysiology, neurobiology and the behavioral procedures that are employed to understand the important emotional and cognitive changes that occur from the fetal period and into the first year of life.

The origins of the brain structures that are formed during fetal development have been elucidated recently by Monk and Hane (2014) and Reissland and Kisilevsky (2016). The task moving forward is to examine functional variation in normative samples as well as those groups that experience advantageous or risky outcomes. In infant research, the methods utilized to examine variation in development of the brain has become a primary source of information for understanding functioning and changes across time. Researchers place increasingly more importance on developmental neurophysiology as it provides great insights into both normal and abnormal behavior. Further, it allows for examining the experience-dependent plasticity (Greenough, Black, & Wallace, 1987) of the brain and for uncovering the optimal periods for setting a trajectory toward typical development or promoting interventions that can reduce or eliminate risk. Understanding the timing of effective interventions and the parameters of impacting risk during development can link brain research during development to the transactional models that are efficacious across scientific domains, especially those that have been hypothesized to meaningfully affect fetuses and infants and their development.

Possible Measurement and Designs in Fetal and Infant Research

A number of traditional scientific methods and designs are used to study change across development, including cross-sectional, longitudinal and cross-sequential designs, standardized assessments, structured and unstructured observations, as well studies of physiological and neuro-developmental functioning. Fetuses and infants are typically assessed with correlational or naturalistic designs as manipulations may be ethically questionable.

There are several unique features of fetal/infant research including the fact that infants are studied with their parents (in fetuses primarily their mothers) and consideration of state (arousal and sleep-wake state) looms larger than with other samples. When the performance/competences of fetuses and infants are meaningfully evaluated they are, in many instances, found to be qualitatively different than at other ages. Ultimately, the current state of the field is to examine interactive designs and designs that cut across disciplines. For example, Calkins (2015) brings together the work of developmentalists that study genetics and biology as well as family systems and socialization theories of infant development. Moreover, Michel's (2013) primary thesis statement is that developmental psychobiology brings together various fields (e.g. psychology, education, biology, social ecology and others) to form a unifying construct of development. Given the convergence of these disparate areas of study, the methods utilized also cut across fields.

Fetuses and infants are studied individually with measures of physical health (growth, nutrition, sleep-wake cycles and elimination) as the overriding concern. Psychological aspects of fetal and infant functioning are more often downplayed (e.g., the NIH (National Institutes of Health) toolbox begins at 3 years of age; see Gershon et al., 2013); although there are scientists and programs that recognize the value of investigating neurocognitive measures, infant mental health or applied programming as a consequence of fetal programming (Beebe et al., 2011; Brito et al., 2019; Kaplan, Evans, & Monk, 2008). In addition, in early stages of development there is the potential for the interactive and social measures to be discussed primarily as advantageous or risky.

Fetuses and infants tend to be defined by their context and this is especially the case for when the topic of risk is investigated. In other words, it is typically not the forming individual that is responsible for the majority of the outcomes; rather it is the mother, the family or the context that confers problems (or advantages) to the child. For example, in infant attachment studies, the infant is developing their attachment relationship but the mother's sensitivity is studied as the primary source of the quality of that relationship (Grossmann, Grossmann, & Waters, 2005). This context issue is true even if it is physiological or neurological risk studies. While this problem is unavoidable during early development, there should be a recognition of this as a confound across the field.

Fetal Studies

Studies in the area of human fetal development are sparse yet emerging due to the ability to "see" the infant through an ultrasound lens. Technical advances plus the recognition that the prenatal environment may impact capacities that unfold after birth have led to an upsurge in interest in this topic (Reissland & Kisilevsky, 2016). Moreover, seminal work by Lickliter and Honeycutt (2003) suggests that prenatal experience is a topic for developmental sciences in understanding the formation of many cognitive and social outcomes. Further, novel work in epigenetics and maternal stress behaviors has produced similar outcomes with notable impacts of parental genes and stress on their offspring's stress regulation (Meaney, 2010). While their work focuses on animal models, the links between these and human experiences are evident, documenting a novel conceptualization of hormones, genes, and social interaction patterns across development. In particular, the knowledge that prenatal hormones and potentially modifying prenatal hormones affect social interaction and outcomes in future stress patterns has demonstrated the importance of these measures during fetal development. Researchers have examined both behavioral and physiological characteristics and functioning at these two age periods in humans. For fetal studies, the topics have included behavioral qualities, like motor behaviors, activity levels, and sleep-wake cycles; but the primary interest has been physiological and clinical aspects of health (see Chapters 5, 6, 9, 12, and 16 in Reissland & Kisilevsky, 2016 for reviews of these topics). In some of the first studies utilizing ultrasounds as well as the concordance between heart rate variability and behavior, DiPietro and her colleagues demonstrated the predictive validity of fetal measures (movement and cardiac physiology) for understanding development of infant temperament (DiPietro, Hodgson, Costigan, & Hilton, 1996). Their series of studies not only showed relationships between fetal behaviors *in utero* and temperament postnatally, these studies were precise and novel in their methods. They made significant strides in understanding arousal, links between cardiac function and neurodevelopment as well as individual differences in the continuum between the environment of the fetus and the postnatal environment of the infant (DiPietro et al., 2010). Ultimately the point here is that fetal development informs later periods of development including measures of individual differences.

In order to understand the challenges for researchers and the methods of data collection in humans during the fetal period, it is necessary to recount the limits that scientists encounter at this time of life. Notably, a fetus is not independent of their mother's body. Thus, collection of data during pregnancy requires the direct involvement of the parents in general and the mother in particular. As expected, reliability and validity concerns can arise and be problematic for understanding the fetus themselves since assessment is only directly possible of the mother. Obtaining parent participation is also an issue in infancy and it is even more challenging to get parental cooperation during the fetal period when parents may view the fetus as fragile in nature. Despite these limitations, researchers are beginning to report promising results on fetal development and its impact across development.

With recent technological advances, studies have begun to examine structural brain development in fetuses (MRI and MEG; Muenssinger et al., 2013; Rousseau et al., 2006); however, the reliability and validity of these fetal measures are not well established and the data collection is very involved and time consuming. Other measures that are examined to understand fetal well-being and viability outside the womb are the biophysical profile (an assessment of stress responsivity), cardiac activity and maternal exposure to or use of toxic or illicit substances and their association with fetal health (Mulder & Visser, 2016). The latter measure is indirect but it is assumed that fetuses ingest the substances that their mothers do. Questions about resiliency of the fetus have been undertaken when there is evidence that fetuses are sheltered from negative outcomes via the protection of the placenta and the placental barrier which has been shown to filter out some (but not all) toxins. In our own studies, we and others (Diego et al., 2006; Feldman, Weller, Zagoory-Sharon, & Levine, 2007; Jones & Sloan, 2018) have attempted to describe brain development in fetuses of depressed mothers by examining the mothers' neurohormones *in utero* and then again postnatally to examine the links between maternal levels and infant levels and outcomes. These

Infant Studies

Infants definitely have an active and functioning intra- and inter-psychic life and many behavioral studies have uncovered amazing developmental processes that occur during the early days and months of postnatal life. Unique findings during infancy have been unearthed through behavioral studies, including the understanding of how infants acquire and utilize information, how infants develop sensory and motor skills, and finally how they integrate social cognition to form an understanding of relationships. Yet as Bell (2015) notes, "cute baby tricks" should not be used for extended and explosive interpretation. In other words, researchers must be cautious of over-interpretation and glamorizing findings without rational and reliable results that have been subjected to replication across labs. A challenge for infant researchers is to "think like an infant", to understand the preverbal infant from their perspective, while using scientific methods to test their skills and abilities. Integrating measures seems to be the key. For example, behavioral researchers have demonstrated that expressive behaviors alone do not invariably predict underlying affective states (Halbestadt, 1986). Yet, physiological measures combined with behavioral indications of affective intensity can potentially illustrate a more detailed and complete picture of what is known about an infant's expressive capacities. In our own work we have utilized behavior observations, EEG, and, more recently, salivary cortisol measures in the context of a mother–infant and social-rival paradigm. Including physiological measures to the study has provided a more thorough understanding of attachment and the mother–infant emotional relationship during threats of usurpation than with behavioral measures alone (Mize & Jones, 2012; Platt & Jones, 2018).

Physiological measures have been fruitful to measure in infancy as they are viewed as less subjective than behavioral studies and unlikely to provide spurious outcomes. This is evident in that studies on the association between physiology and temperament as well as measures of variations in individual characteristics have provided a wealth of findings that have been replicated in various labs and have even been integrated into clinical psychology (Hane & Fox, 2016; Leung et al., 2010). Across development, researchers have employed various measures of brain activity (e.g. MRI, fMRI and PET), yet collecting valid and reliable data in infants is difficult due to movement, toxicity, and state regulation issues. Newer technologies such as fNIRS (Wilcox & Biondi, 2015) suggest promise but are still subject to validation. Additionally, research on the links between more tried and true brain activity patterns (EEG and ERPs) and neurohormonal responding are beginning to shed light on various issues in infant development. Regardless of the physiological measure incorporated into behavioral research, the ultimate goal is to understand the bio-behavioral relationships that infants experience and to unearth reliable measures of infant capacities.

As we have noted in previous work (Jones & Sloan, 2018), there are likely more than 15 different hormones that interact with fetal and infant development and many of these hormones influence early brain development patterns. Scientists, however, have tended to uncover dysregulatory patterns and thus studies of normative neurodevelopment are less prominent. In our first studies with fetal participants, we demonstrated that patterns of dopamine, norepinephrine, and cortisol of infants of depressed mothers mirrored the patterns of their depressed mothers (Lundy et al., 1999). Subsequent studies on serotonin and other stress hormones have supported and extended these early reports (Diego et al., 2004). A number of other studies have also shown that, though difficult to measure and sometimes unreliable, cortisol reactivity provides important information about the variation in stress regulation (Jansen, Beijers, Riksen-Walraven, & de Weerth, 2010) even in infancy.

One neuropeptide that has received less attention until recently is oxytocin. However, normative levels of oxytocin in infants have been related to birth, affection, breastfeeding, and touch as well as levels of maternal protective behaviors. Recent reviews of the literature suggest that oxytocin, in particular, may influence the development of the areas of the brain that inhibit social inhibitions and fear responses (Hammock, 2015), suggesting that lack of oxytocin may limit the ability to regulate fear. Yet further studies need to be conducted to support this supposition as well as to examine potential associations between brain development and neurohormone levels during fetal and infant development.

Core Methodologies in Fetal and Infant Neurodevelopment Research

Incorporation of physiological and neurohormones into research designs requires intensive training and expensive, specialized equipment. EEG technology and training is more accessible in the typical behavioral science department than is the training and equipment necessary to analyze hormone data. Therefore, more attention to EEG analysis is presented in this chapter relative to hormone analyses. Given the specialized laboratory equipment and training needed for the latter, students/researchers are encouraged to send their samples off for analysis at biological laboratories.

Electroencephalograms (EEGs) in Infant Research

EEG research in infancy, though different in form in today's world with advanced computing techniques available, dates back to the 1930s when Lindsley measured the EEG across the lifespan (Lindsley, 1939, 1944). Although several acquisition and analysis methods have been developed over the years, the basic principles behind recording the EEG remain the same (Stern, Ray, & Quigley, 2001). Data is acquired by placing sensors/electrodes on the scalp that are attached to electric circuitry that amplifies the EEG signal. This signal is filtered to remove excessive noise and then outputted to a medium where the signal can be viewed and subsequently analyzed. With the exception of some clinical applications that use a paper tracing to visually inspect the EEG signal, virtually all current EEG research conducted utilizes quantitative (qEEG) procedures to reduce and analyze the EEG signal.

The usage of EEG in infants allows for the study and assessment of the origins of early emotional and cognitive processes without the need of an overt display of behavior nor verbal skills that infant may not have acquired yet. In fact, EEG is among the select few tools that enables researchers to track brain functioning beginning neonatally and continuing throughout the lifespan with no foreseeable negative consequences to the study participants. Although very useful, EEG studies pose a number of unique challenges in infancy ranging from the actual acquisition of the signal to the generalizability of findings across age groups.

EEG Acquisition

The first step in collecting EEG recordings is placing electrodes on to the scalp over areas of interest. The 10–20 system (Jasper, 1958) is the most commonly used system to determine electrode sites and is the most reliable method of representing/illuminating the exact electrode placements (e.g. midfrontal is F3 (left hemisphere) and F4 (right hemisphere)). Collection of multiple locations is possible; however, in infant studies, the number of sites recorded may be more limited and thus specific to theoretical questions for logistical and practical reasons. The scalp is cleaned and abraded before applying a conductive medium (Electrode Gel) between the scalp and the electrode to obtain a strong and clear EEG signal. Electrodes can be applied individually or the infant can be fitted with a lycra-stretchable cap. Electrode caps are commonly used in infant EEG research as they bypass the need to make time-consuming measurements of the scalp and are relatively non-invasive. A recent development in electrode array technology involves the use of a net of pedestals containing electrolyte sponges with up to 256 embedded electrodes. This netting is first submerged in an electrolyte substance and then placed over the head and adjusted in a short period of time, eliminating the need to abrade the skin or apply a conductive substance to each individual electrode. This is an advantage in infant research as it effectively avoids irritating the skin during the abrasion process and it allows for the application of a large array of electrodes quickly, but it is expensive. Additionally, due to the fact the sensors are not fixed, movement artifact is common with the nets and when used with infants, the nets can be easily displaced or damaged (de Haan, 2013). Each method has its challenges and the use of the preferred method is up to the researcher selecting the best design for their theoretical questions.

In all cases, however, a minimum of at least two electrodes is necessary as recording techniques require the difference in electrical potential between two sites. In ERP work, bipolar recordings are used in which the researcher does not separate the two electrodes. However, in unipolar techniques, the researcher must choose a reference site. Several referencing techniques have been developed to record the EEG signal and while grand average montage (Bertrand, Perrin, & Pernier, 1985) is preferred, researchers of infancy studies have utilized the central vertez (Cz) as a relatively non-active site because it is easily accessible and can be converted to an average reference if needed and if a sufficient number of leads are collected. The amount of time required to position the large number of electrodes needed to use the grand average montage is a challenge when recording from infants, and further, the spatial area of the infant's head is limited. Another commonly used referencing scheme utilized in EEG research is the linked ears or mastoids referencing method. These two methods have been successfully applied in a number of infant EEG studies (e.g. Dawson et al., 2001; Stroganova, Orekova, & Posikera, 1999) yet the vertex is the least invasive location for infant participants. In addition, the vertex reference has been shown to have excellent reliability (r= .85-.98; Hagemann, Naumann, & Thayer, 2001) yet these studies have been on adults, therefore studies with infants are called for to support the construct and convergent validity of EEG power/asymmetries derived using this montage.

The microvolt brain electrical activity sensed by the electrodes is subsequently amplified (usually 20,000 times) before it can be digitized or displayed. As the EEG signal is buried in a myriad of unwanted signals, analogue and/or digital filters are used to minimize the signal-to-noise ratio of the EEG, with digital filters offering more stability and flexibility in programming. Notably, EEG artifact or noise related to environmental interference is also filtered out via various manual or software programs. Artifact can arise from extraneous electromagnetic signals from computer monitors, overhead lighting and power cables, radio waves, cellular phones, and the movement of objects and people in the vicinity of the recording room. While potentially problematic, artifact can be decreased through the use of 60Hz notch filters, room shielding, and differential amplifiers with common mode rejection as well as by reducing electrode impedances and keeping equipment maintained (likely reducing electrode slippage, the build-up of corrosion on the surface, and movement of dangling wires). For infant EEG data collection and analysis, eye (EOG), muscle (EMG), and motor movements are a concern because the loss of data can be exorbitant. Some high-frequency signals like EMG can be eliminated by the use of low-pass filters; however, reducing movement is the best way to collect quality data. Techniques for reducing infant movement during the EEG recording procedure include: recording the EEG only while the infant is in an alert, non-distressed state; using attention-eliciting stimuli (i.e. soap bubbles or shaking a rattle in front of the baby); and for very young infants, wrapping them in a blanket. The simplest and most common post-hoc method used to eliminate artifact is visually examining the EEG and manually omitting artifact from further analyses. Notes, event markers, and video recordings of infant behaviors can greatly aid in discerning artifacts. Because the EEG record has to be carefully screened by trained observers, this manual artifact elimination is time consuming and expensive. A contemporary method for eliminating artifacts may involve the use of computer algorithms to detect artifacts, remove them from the signal via regression, or eliminate them using regression or principal component analyses. These techniques have the advantage of salvaging sections from the EEG record that would have otherwise been eliminated. Regardless of the artifact rejection technique used, it is important to implement reliability checks across visual EEG editors and/or across methods to ensure consistency.

EEG Analysis

EEG data can be analyzed in a number of ways depending on what the researcher is interested in learning from the infant's brain activity. Developmental EEG studies have looked at the presence and quantity of spectral peaks along with their frequency location as an index of EEG/brain maturation (Diego, Jones, & Field, 2010). Saby and Marshall (2012) reviewed the utility of frequency band analysis to elucidate the complex relation between EEG frequency components associated with development. Power values for specific frequency bands are thought to be inversely related to activity. Yet it is unknown whether power values in specific areas increase or decrease in quantity during development or during the maturation of unique and specific tasks; this includes questions related to other areas of the brain like temporal, parietal, and occipital regions. Perhaps the most widely studied component of the EEG signal in infant EEG studies is the resting bands. Unlike the bands that are used in adult studies, 1) delta (1–3 Hz); 2) theta (4–7 Hz); 3) alpha (8–13 Hz); and 4) beta (14–30Hz)), in infancy, frequency bands are less definitive. Bell and her colleagues (Bell, 2002; Cuevas, Bell, Marcovitch, & Calkins, 2012) have established that 6–9 Hz activity is related to the cognitive functions of 6–12-month-old infants; however, it is unclear if this is also true for younger infants. Spectral properties of the EEG undergo extensive development during the first years of life; a given behavior or physiological state is likely to manifest different spectral properties at different stages of development. Pivik et al. (1993) have suggested that EEG should be analyzed using a wide frequency bandwidth in infancy, which encompasses any frequency with evidence of power (i.e. 3–12Hz). Yet another technique put forth is that individual spectra should be examined, followed by determination of more narrow frequency bands, as they are centered around the peaks. Infant studies assessing cognition and emotions have applied this approach (Diego, Jones, & Field, 2010).

Three types of frequency data outcomes are obtained by researchers in EEG studies. Power allows for examination of the frequency range at which most activity for the given band(s) of interest occurs and is then used as the main quantitative metric that is compared with power values from other frequency bands, scalp locations, and/or conditions across subjects using statistical methods. Because power values are not normally distributed, EEG power values are commonly log-transformed in order to normalize their distribution. Asymmetry scores are computed as the difference in the power values of a given right-hemisphere site minus the power value for its homologous electrode site at the left hemisphere (i.e. F4-F3 power). This value has been shown to be stable across short and long time periods in infancy (Brooker, Caen, Davidson, & Goldsmith, 2017). Research has shown relationships between frontal EEG asymmetry and other physiological factors. For example, Buss et al. (2003) examined EEG asymmetry and both basal and reactive cortisol levels in 6-month-old infants. Infants with extreme right frontal EEG asymmetry levels demonstrated higher levels of stress cortisol.

Coherence analysis can also be used in studies with a focus on brain maturation. Coherence is a measure of the interrelational dependency between two processes; or their synchrony. In EEG research, coherence is usually conducted to estimate the similarity between the EEG signals acquired from two different locations within the scalp at exactly the same time. High coherence values between two recording sites suggest a high degree of anatomical and or functional interconnection between electrode sites and possibly cortical regions (Thatcher, Krause, & Hrybyk, 1986). Furthermore, EEG coherence between the left and right hemisphere might reflect the amount of information being processed (Surwillo, 1971). These ideas are compatible with recent research that found an increase in coherence values from 5 months to 4 years of age, suggesting brain maturation (Thatcher, North, & Biver, 2008). Recent studies have also linked coherence to working memory both within infancy and into childhood. The findings suggest that coherence between different regions of the brain become more localized to the task at older ages; however, coherence is linked to working memory by 10 months (Cuevas et al., 2012).

Neurohormone Data Collection and Analysis

Cortisol as Reactivity and Regulation

Understanding the brain development of infants is a worthwhile endeavor and EEGs offer insight into the activity of the brain. However, examining the correspondence between EEG and neurohormone measures provides a richer view of neurodevelopmental patterns. While we've given a lot of detail as to the analysis of EEG data, less is necessary for neurohormone collection and measurement. This is because unless the student/researcher has access to the proper training and equipment readily available, we suggest sending off samples for analysis at biological laboratories that specialize in the type of analysis required. Salimetrics can provide salivary cortisol analysis kits if the lab personnel are adequately trained and the lab has access to the appropriate freezer, hoods, pipettes, centrifuges, plate washers, shakers, and plate readers, in addition to the computer programs (e.g., Biotek) and printer used to evaluate and understand the outcomes. Otherwise, cortisol can be sent to Salimetrics for analysis. Sending off the samples eliminates the need for the expense of the equipment and additional wet lab spaced needed to analyze the samples. Regardless, samples should be collected with an age-appropriate Salivette sampling device (Sarstedt Inc., Rommelsdorf, Germany) and, if appropriate, the cotton rolls pretreated with citric acid in order to facilitate a salivary response from participants. With younger infants, researchers may want to use passive drool as infants may not be exposed to other foods besides breast milk. Samples should be labeled and frozen within 30 minutes of collection, then stored at -20°C for future assay.

Oxytocin Levels

Similarly for oxytocin and other measures of urinary neurohormones, collection of infant samples can be done with a pediatric urine bag, which is then frozen at -70°C for future assay. The assays are done via ELISA (enzyme-linked immunosorbent assay) analysis and therefore require a biological lab including a solid phase extractor, plate reader, a safety hood or cabinet, a shaker, etc. Steps and methods for doing these analyses are specific to the type outputs that are required and therefore require extensive training. We ship the samples in dry ice to another lab that developed the specific technique for assessing tonic oxytocin values. While it is necessary to understand the type of data collect, i.e., the amount and the manner of collection and storage, working with a specialized lab eliminates the need for expensive equipment that is typically standard in biology/chemistry or biomedical labs and allows us to focus on other important aspects of the research. While expertise in biological sample analysis can be obtained, our opinion is that it is more efficient and sometimes prudent to send the samples to the experts in the field.

Innovations in Infant Development Research

There are two fundamental methodological ideas that have revolutionized developmental scientists' study of pre- and postnatal development. First is the idea that prenatal experiences influence and interact with postnatal development and that the fetus transitions smoothly into postnatal life. Early work in this realm utilized rudimentary ultrasounds to understand fetal state development, physiological regulation, and the effects on infant temperament (DiPietro et al., 1996, 2005). The notion that fetuses had environmental experiences and this impacted their development was new and scientists used this as a springboard for producing reliable ways of assessing fetus-to-infant capacities, individual differences, and physiology. In our studies, we use mother–infant neurohormones to understand the developmental influences of fetal characteristics on the mother–infant relationship. Our work is based on merging developmental risk and protective factors present during these early periods of development that could impact outcomes associated with forming relationships across childhood. While not all neuro-hormones can be independently studied, inasmuch as maternal hormones are involved in pregnancy, childbirth, and postnatal feeding, the investigation of neurohormonal impact on infants has been informative.

The second idea that has changed methodologies used in developmental science is the adherence to the presence of neural plasticity, a process that cuts across fetal and infant development. The human brain emerges as a functioning organ during prenatal development and continues to develop after birth, undergoing extensive neuronal myelination, differentiation, and synaptogenesis throughout infancy (Kandel, Schwartz, & Jessell, 2000). Neural plasticity occurs and while generally neural activity is relatively stable, infant EEG patterns are affected by experiential factors across age. So while infancy may impact life-long emotional and cognitive processes and development, through plasticity those developmental patterns can be altered by enriched or deprived environments. This idea sets the stage for mapping the person-by-environment interaction that occurs, not only in studies on genes and DNA (i.e., epigenetics) but to elucidate behavioral and physiological functioning of fetal and infant development.

Conclusion

Describing and explaining growth during the fetal and infant periods is challenging but modern technology and innovative methodologies have made it feasible. Behavioral methods alone are useful but limited by their subjective nature, especially when applied to non-verbal participants. Infancy and early childhood are both times of dynamic changes in the state of the system, and the biological and anatomical variances in cortical structures are in turn reflected in EEG and neurohormonal outputs. EEG has the sensitivity needed to examine immediate changes in excitement, emotional stress, muscle tension, and even cognitive processes. The specific characteristics of the fetus/infant and the changing properties of the EEG over development can complicate interpretation of research results across age groups but ultimately these measures inform developmental science in significant ways. Research, though, will also benefit from integrated designs and analyses as well as newer methods, like fNIRS. Similarly, neurohormonal levels can be used to measure tonic and stimulus-linked changes in stress-based arousal, affection, and other characteristics of biological functioning of the infant. This makes these neurological measures ideal for fetal/infant studies because it reveals the relatively stable and genetically based temperamental qualities of infants (Brooker et al., 2017). These measures also have the potential to provide insight on brain plasticity and typical and atypical development as a function of environmental influences (e.g. in context of maternal depression (Jones, Platt & Mize, 2016). Used collectively, the various physiological measures in concert with behavioral methods can provide developmental researchers with a strong tool-kit with which to study early developmental phenomena.

References

Beebe, B., Steele, M., Jaffe, J., Buck, K. A., Chen, H., Cohen, P., et al. (2011). Maternal anxiety symptoms and mother–infant self- and interactive contingency. *Infant Mental Health Journal, 32 (2)*, 174–206.

Bell, M. A. (2002). Power changes in infant EEG frequency bands during a spatial working memory task. *Psychophysiology, 39*, 450–458.

Bell, M. A. (2015). Bringing the field of infant cognition and perception toward a biopsychosocial perspective. In S. D. Calkins (Ed.), *Handbook of Infant Biopsychosocial Development* (pp. 27–37). New York: The Guilford Press.

Belsky, J. & Pluess, M. (2009). Beyond diathesis stress: differential susceptibility to environmental influences. *Psychological Bulletin, 135*, 885–908.

Bertrand, O., Perrin, F., & Pernier, J. (1985). A theoretical justification of the average reference in topographic evoked potential studies. *Electroencephalography and Clinical Neurophysiology/Evoked Potentials Section, 62*(6), 462–464.

Brito, N. H., Fifer, W. P., Amso, D., Barr, R., Bell, M. A., Calkins, S., et al. (2019). Beyond the Bayley: neurocognitive assessments of development during infancy and toddlerhood. *Developmental Neuropsychology, 44(2)*, 220–247. doi:10.1080/87565641.2018.1564310.

Brooker, R., Canen, M. J., Davidson, R. J., & Goldsmith, H. H. (2017). Short- and long-term stability of alpha asymmetry in infants: baseline and affective measures. *Psychophysiology, 54*, 1100–1109.

Buss, K. A., Schmacher, J. R. M., Dolski, I., Kalin, N. H., Goldsmith, H. H., & Davidson, R. J. (2003). Right frontal brain activity, cortisol, and withdrawal behavior in 6-month-old infants. *Behavioral Neuroscience, 117(1)*, 11–20.

Calkins, S. D. (2015). *Handbook of Infant Biopsychosocial Development*. New York: The Guilford Press.

Cuevas, K., Bell, M. A., Marcovitch, S., & Calkins, S. D. (2012). EEG and ECG from 5 to 10 months of age: developmental changes in baseline activation and cognitive processing during a working memory task. *International Journal of Psychophysiology, 80*, 119–128.

Dawson, G., Ashman, S. B., Hessel, D., Spieker, S., Frey, K., Panagiotides, H., et al. (2001). Autonomic and brain electrical activity in securely- and insecurely-attached infants of depressed mothers. *Infant Behavior & Development, 24*, 135–149.

de Haan, M. (2013). Introduction. In M. de Haan (Ed.), *Infant EEG and Event-related Potentials: Studies in Developmental Psychology* (pp. 1–4). UK: Psychology Press.

Diego, M. A., Field, T., Cullen, C., Hernandez-Reif, M., Schanberg, S., & Kuhn, C. (2004). Prepartum, postpartum and chronic depression effects on infants. *Psychiatry, 67*, 63–80.

Diego, M. A., Jones, N. A., & Field, T. (2010). EEG in 1-week, 1-month and 3-month-old infants of depressed and non-depressed mothers. *Biological Psychology, 83(1)*, 7–14.

Diego, M. A., Jones, N. A., Field, T., Hernandez-Reif, M., Schanberg, S., Kuhn, C., et al. (2006). Maternal psychological distress, prenatal cortisol, and fetal weight. *Psychosomatic Medicine, 68*, 747–753.

DiPietro, J. A., Hodgson, D. M., Costigan, K. A., & Hilton, S. C. (1996). Fetal neurobehavioral development. *Child Development, 67*, 2553–2567.

DiPietro, J. A., Kivlighan, K. T., Costigan, K. A., Rubin, S. E., Shiffler, D. E., Henderson, J. L., et al. (2010). Prenatal antecedents of newborn neurological maturation. *Child Development, 81(1)*, 115–130. doi:10.1111/j.1467-8624.2009.01384.x.

Feldman, R., Weller, A., Zagoory-Sharon, O., & Levine, A. (2007). Evidence for a neuroendocrinological foundation of human affiliation: plasma oxytocin levels across pregnancy and the postpartum period predict mother–infant bonding. *Psychological Science, 18(11)*, 965–970.

Fox, N. A. & Rutter, M. (2010). Introduction to the special section on the effects of early experience on development. *Child Development, 81*, 23–27. doi:10.1111/j.1467-8624.2009.01379.x.

Gershon, R. C., Wagster, M. V., Hendrie, H. C., Fox, N. A., Cook, K. F., & Nowinski, C. J. (2013). NIH toolbox for assessment of neurological and behavioral function. *Neurology, 80(11 Supplement 3)*, S2–S6. doi:10.1212/WNL.0b013e3182872e5f.

Greenough, W. T., Black, J. E., & Wallace, C. S. (1987). Experience and brain development. *Child Development, 58(3)*, 539–559. doi:10.2307/1130197.

Grossmann, K. E., Grossmann, K., & Waters, E. (2005). *Attachment from Infancy to Adulthood: the Major Longitudinal Studies*. New York: NY: Guilford.

Hagemann, D., Naumann, E., & Thayer, J. F. (2001). The quest for the EEG reference revisited: a glance from brain asymmetry research. *Psychophysiology, 38*, 847–857.

Halbestadt, A. (1986). Family socialization of emotional expression and nonverbal communication styles and skills. *Journal of Personality and Social Psychology, 51*, 827–836.

Hammock, E. A. D. (2015). Developmental perspectives on oxytocin and vasopressin. *Neuropsychopharmacology Review, 40*, 24–42.

Hane, A. A. & Fox, N. A. (2016). Early caregiving and human biobehavioral development: a comparative physiology approach. *Current Opinion in Behavioral Science, 7*, 82–90.

Jansen, J., Beijers, R., Riksen-Walraven, M., & de Weerth, C. (2010). Cortisol reactivity in young infants. *Psychoneuroendocrinology, 35(3)*, 329–338.

Jasper, H. H. (1958). The ten-twenty electrode system of the international federation. *Electroencephalography and Neurophysiology, 10*, 371–375.

Jones, N. A. & Sloan, A. (2018). Neuro-hormones and temperament interact during infant development. *Philosophical Transactions of Royal Society, B, 18(54)*. doi:10.1098/rstb.2017.0159

Jones, N. A., Platt, M., & Mize, K. D. (2016). Breastfeeding impacts brain activation and interaction patterns in infants of depressed mothers. In J. Worobey (Ed.) *Infant Feeding: Parental Perceptions, Behaviors and Health Effects* (pp. 61–76). New York: NOVA Science Publishers, Inc.

Kandel, E. R., Schwartz, J. H., & Jessell, T. M. (2000). *Principles of Neural Science* (4th ed.). New York: McGraw-Hill.

Kaplan, L. A., Evans, L., & Monk, C. (2008). Effects of mothers' prenatal psychiatric status and postnatal caregiving on infant biobehavioral regulation: can prenatal programming be modified? *Early Human Development, 84(4)*, 249–256. doi:10.1016/j.earlhumdev.2007.06.004.

Kennard, M. A. (1944). Reactions of monkeys of various ages to partial and complete decortication. *Journal of Neurophysiology and Experimental Neurology, 3*, 289–310.

Kennard, M. A. & Fulton, J. F. (1942). Age and reorganization of central nervous system. *Journal of the Mount Sinai Hospital, 9*, 594–606.

Leung, E., Tasker, S. L., Atkinson, L., Vaillancourt, T., Schulkin, J., & Schmidt, L. A. (2010). Perceived maternal stress during pregnancy and its relation to infant stress reactivity at 2 days and 10 months of postnatal life. *Clinical Pediatrics, 49(2)*, 158–165.

Lickliter, R. & Honeycutt, H. (2003). A developmental evolutionary framework for psychology. *Review of General Psychology, 17*, 184–189.

Lindsley, D. B. (1939). A longitudinal study of the occipital alpha rhythm in normal children: frequency and amplitude standards. *Journal of Genetic Psychology, 55*, 197–213.

Lindsley, D. B. (1944). *Electroencephalography*. Oxford, England: Ronald Press.

Lundy, B. L., Jones, N. A., Field, T., Nearing, G., Davalos, M., Pietro, P. A., et al. (1999). Prenatal depression effects on neonates. *Infant Behavior and Development, 22(1)*, 119–129.

Meaney, M. (2010). Epigenetics and the biological definition of gene X environment interactions. *Child Development, 79*, 1378–1395.

Michel, G. F. (2013). The role of developmental psychobiology in the unification of psychology. *Review of General Psychology, 17(2)*, 210–215. doi:10.1037/a0032936.

Mize, K. D. & Jones, N. A. (2012). Infant physiological and behavioral responses to loss of maternal attention to a social-rival. *International Journal of Psychophysiology, 83(1)*, 16–23.

Monk, C. & Hane, A. A. (2014). Fetal and infant neurobehavioral development: basic processes and environmental influences. In A. Wenzel (Ed.), *The Oxford Handbook of Perinatal Psychology* (pp. 1–41). New York: Oxford University Press. doi:10.1093/oxfordhb/9780199778072.013.20.

Muenssinger, J., Matuz, T., Schleger, F., Kiefer-Schmidt, I., Goelz, R., Waker-Gussmann, A., et al. (2013). Auditory habituation in the fetus and neonate: a fMEG study. *Developmental Science, 16(2)*, 287–295.

Mulder, E. J. H. & Visser, G. H. A. (2016). Fetal behavior: clinical and experimental research in the human. In N. J. Reissland & B. S. Kisilevsky (Eds.), *Fetal Development: Research on Brain and Behavior, Environmental Influences and Emerging Technologies* (pp. 87–105). Switzerland: Springer International Publishing.

Pivik, R. T., Broughton, R. J., Coppola, R., Davidson, R. J., Fox, N., & Nuwer, M. R. (1993). Guidelines for the recording and quantitative analysis of electroencephalographic activity in research contexts. *Psychophysiology, 30,* 547–558.

Platt, M. & Jones, N. A. (2018). The physiology of rivalry in infancy. In S. Hart & N. A. Jones (Eds.), *The Psychology of Rivalry* (pp. 35–47). New York: Nova Science Publishers.

Reissland, N. J. & Kisilevsky, B. S. (2016). *Fetal Development: Research on Brain and Behavior, Environmental Influences and Emerging Technologies.* Switzerland: Springer International Publishing.

Rousseau, F., Glenn, O. A., Iordanova, B., Rodriguez-Carranza, C., Vigneron, D. B., Barkovich, A. J., et al. (2006). Registration-based approach for reconstruction of high resolution in utero fetal MR brain images. *Academic Radiology, 13(9),* 1072–1081.

Saby, J. N. & Marshall, P. J. (2012). The Utility of EEG Band Power Analysis in the Study of Infancy and Early Childhood. *Developmental Neuropsychology, 37(3),* 253–273. doi:10.1080/87565641.2011.614663

Sandman, C. A., Davis, E. P., Buss, C., & Glynn, L. M. (2012). Exposure to prenatal psychobiological stress exerts programming influences on the mother and her fetus. *Neuroendocrinology, 95,* 8–21.

Stern, R. M., Ray, W. J., & Quigley, K. S. (2001). *Psychophysiological Recording,* (2nd ed.). New York: Oxford University Press.

Stroganova, T. A., Orekova, E. V., & Posikera, I. N. (1999). EEG alpha rhythm in infants. *Clinical Neurophysiology, 110,* 997–1012.

Surwillo, W. W. (1971). Digit span and EEG frequency in normal children. *Electroencephalography and Clinical Neurophysiology, 31(1),* 93–95.

Thatcher, R. W., Krause, P. J., & Hrybyk, M. (1986). Cortico-cortical associations and EEG coherence: a two-compartmental model. *Electroencephalography and Clinical Neurophysiology, 64(2),* 123–143.

Thatcher, R. W., North, D. M., & Biver, C. J. (2008). Development of cortical connections as measured by EEG coherence and phase. *Human Brain Mapping, 29(12),* 1400–1415.

Wilcox, T., & Biondi, M. (2015). fNIRS in the developmental sciences. *Wiley Interdisciplinary Review of Cognitive Sciences, 6,* 263–283.

6 Studying Perceptual Development in Infancy

Fabrice Damon, Nicholas J. Minar[1,2], and Anne Hillairet de Boisferon

Introduction

The world is filled with numerous sights, sounds, textures, tastes, and smells. As adults, we seamlessly perceive and combine these various sensory inputs in order to successfully navigate through our surroundings. For example, when we see a dog opening and closing its mouth in a rhythmic fashion, we have no trouble concluding that the "bark-bark" that we hear belongs to and originates from the dog. While it seems obvious that the barking sound would originate from a dog, that is only because we, as adults, have a lifetime of sensory experience seeing dogs and hearing barking noises together. A question posed by a developmental psychologist might be: how do young infants, who have little to no perceptual experience of the world, begin to perceive and integrate sensory inputs early in life? This chapter will serve as an introduction to the methods used and the questions asked by developmental psychologists studying unisensory and multisensory perceptual development in infancy.

One might ask: "why is it important to study perceptual development in infancy?" One reason is that by better understanding how our perceptual systems develop, we can better understand both the impact of sensory experience on our biology as well as the impact of our biology on our sensory experience. There are many complex and bidirectional interactions between the organization of our nervous system and our life experiences; by studying perceptual development and the impact of sensory experience early in life, we can better understand these interactions and discover what is typical during normal development (Lewkowicz, 2011; Oyama, 2000). A second reason to study perceptual development is not only to understand what is typical, but also to identify what is atypical. For example, in order to identify children with sensory processing deficits – as is common in children diagnosed with autistic spectrum disorders (ASDs) – we must first identify the typical developmental trajectory of our perceptual systems. Such knowledge of what is typical may improve early clinical interventions and foster positive long-term health outcomes, which is only possible after typical perceptual development has been established (Guiraud et al., 2012; Stevenson et al., 2015). Finally, many aspects of our social lives are built on sensory perception, such as language processing, face recognition, and distinguishing objects in our environment from one another. By investigating perceptual development, we gain a better understanding of what makes humans as varied and complex as we are.

In this chapter, you will learn about various research methods developmental psychologists use to study perceptual development in infancy, along with the types of questions these research methods can answer. We hope that you will gain a more nuanced understanding of developmental research methodologies, becoming familiar not only with what young infants can perceive, but how their perception is studied. This chapter will focus primarily on research examining infants aged 1–18 months, but will discuss other research focusing on infants of other ages when relevant.

The Importance of Looking Behavior in the Study of Infant Perception

Since young infants do not possess extensive vocabularies like adults, developmental psychologists cannot ask them directly what they are thinking and perceiving. Instead, developmental psychologists must rely on other measures to *infer* what infants perceive. The primary measure of infant behavior that developmental psychologists utilize when inferring infants' perception and cognition is looking behavior. Since the human visual system is online immediately after birth, infants begin to use vision to learn about their surroundings within the first days of life (Farroni et al., 2005; Haith, 1980; Lewis, Maurer, & Kay, 1978). For example, nine-minute-old newborn infants will visually follow a moving stimulus, especially when that stimulus resembles a human face (Goren, Sarty, & Wu, 1975). While it is unlikely that these nine-minute-old infants "know" that the object they are looking at is another individual's face, their systematic behavior suggests that preferences for certain objects begin to emerge early in life. Even though the visual system at birth is not as developed as an adult's visual system, infants' systematic looking behavior is studied by developmental psychologists and can be used to answer a wide array of research questions. Additionally, when one considers that inputs from the visual system can be combined with inputs from the auditory system immediately after birth, the amount of research questions to be asked grows exponentially (Coulon, Guellai, & Streri, 2011; Lewkowicz, Leo, & Simion, 2010; Morrongiello, Fenwick, & Chance, 1998; Sai, 2005). As you will learn, many experimental methods in this chapter take advantage of infants' systematic looking behavior to answer questions about perceptual development, such as the visual paired comparison and habituation/dishabituation procedures. This chapter will also discuss experimental techniques that examine infants' neural activation patterns to answer questions regarding perceptual development, such as electroencephalography (EEG), event-related potentials (ERPs), and functional near-infrared spectroscopy (fNIRS).

Visual Paired Comparison Procedure

The first method we will describe is perhaps the oldest looking-time measure still used to study infants' perceptual abilities. The visual paired comparison procedure was developed by Robert Fantz in the late 1950s/early 1960s and was designed to test whether infants could discriminate, or tell the difference between, two stimuli. Robert Fantz utilized this procedure by placing 2–3-month-old infants in a chamber where they could simultaneously view two pictures side by side. This procedure was used by Fantz to examine whether infants could discriminate a picture of a human face from a picture of a bullseye pattern.

In the visual paired comparison procedure, infants' looking behavior to two pictures was observed by a researcher and compared after the experiment. You can imagine that if an infant could not tell the difference between a picture of a face and a picture of a bullseye pattern, or had no preference for one over the other, they would split their looking time to each picture equally. However, if infants could tell that these two

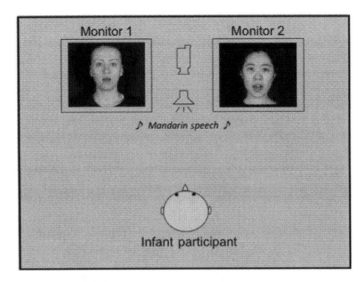

Figure 6.1 Schematic representation of the modern visual paired comparison procedure. As can be seen, the infant is presented with two talking faces. Each face articulates a monologue in a different language (one in English and one in Mandarin). The speaker between the two monitors plays the auditory speech that matches only one of these faces; in this case, the Mandarin speaker. Infants' looking time to each screen is recorded and if infants prefer the matching stimulus, it is predicted that they will look longer to the face articulating Mandarin. Image generated by the authors.

pictures were different and instead preferred, for example, the picture of the face over the bullseye, they would look longer to the picture of the face. In fact, this is exactly what Fantz found (Fantz, 1958, 1961). This procedure, the visual paired comparison, gathers data on infants' *preference* for one stimulus over another by presenting two stimuli at the same time. It does not examine whether infants know "what" they are looking at. Thus, Fantz could only state that the infants in his experiment preferred a face stimulus over a non-face pattern and could not draw conclusions on *why* this was the case. This is an important characteristic of most infant research, mainly that the majority of studies only *describe* infants' behavior and that careful consideration must be given before inferring *why* a particular behavior is present.

A common multisensory variation of Fantz's procedure exists today and has infants sit in front of two computer screens where they simultaneously view two video clips. Other than using computer technology to present videos, this procedure can also present sound in conjunction with one of the videos. In this procedure infants view two different videos, video 1 on a monitor situated in infants' left visual field and video 2 on a monitor situated in their right visual field. A critical aspect of this procedure is that while the videos are both playing, infants hear sound from a speaker located between the two monitors that only corresponds to one of the videos. You can think of this procedure as a vision and hearing matching task, where infants are viewing two different videos on two different screens simultaneously but only one screen matches what the infant is hearing. This procedure allows developmental psychologists to examine if infants prefer a visual stimulus that matches an auditory input. This procedure, and other variants of it, have been used extensively in language development research to examine if, when, and how infants match auditory speech to its corresponding talking face (Barker & Tomblin, 2004; Bebko, Weiss, Demark, & Gomez, 2006; Kubicek et al., 2014; Lewkowicz, Minar, Tift, & Brandon, 2015). An example of this type of procedure can be seen in the schematic below in Figure 6.1.

Thus, the multisensory visual paired comparison procedure is used to ask the question: "do infants' match what they are hearing with what they are seeing and how might this change over development?" As one can imagine, this procedure can serve many functions and can present infants with a whole range of stimuli, from moving/sounding objects (Lewkowicz, 1992; Lewkowicz & Minar, 2014) to pictures of animals and their corresponding calls (Vouloumanos, Druhen, Hauser, & Huizink, 2009). Developmental psychologists must interpret infants' preferences for one stimulus over another with care, as it is difficult to interpret a lack of a preference for one stimulus over another, also known as a null preference (Aslin, 2007). In other words, if an infant does not prefer the matching audiovisual stimulus to the non-matching one, does this mean that the infant cannot tell the difference between the two or is there truly no preference for one over the other? This is one weakness of the visual paired comparison procedure and is addressed by the next procedure to be discussed, the infant habituation/dishabituation procedure.

Infant Habituation/Dishabituation

The visual paired comparison procedure can be used to indicate whether infants can tell the difference (discriminate) between two stimuli, but it is hard to determine this if no preference for one stimulus over another is shown. Thus, the question now becomes: "how do we truly know if infants can tell one stimulus from another?" Imagine a scenario where you are sitting in front of a computer watching a slideshow of pictures. If you were presented with the same picture over and over, you would grow bored and lose interest in the slideshow quickly. If, however, all of a sudden a different, new picture appeared, your interest in the slide show might temporarily increase. Developmental psychologists use a similar concept to determine whether infants can discriminate two stimuli from one another by using a procedure called infant habituation/dishabituation. This technique rests on the assumption that a stimulus elicits some behavioral response and that repeated presentation of the same stimulus will yield a decreased behavioral response (habituation). Subsequently, the presentation of another (different) stimulus will result in a recovery of attention (dishabituation) (Thompson, 2009).

The concept of habituation was first used with infants in the 1960s/1970s and was discovered to be a robust indicator in infant discrimination (Cohen, 1969, 1972; Lewis, Goldberg, & Campbell, 1969; McCall & Kagan, 1967). In practice, two approaches to habituation are possible: an infant-controlled version and a familiarization version. Both procedures are composed of a habituation phase where infants habituate to a repeated stimulus, and a test phase where infants' looking behavior is expected to recover if discrimination occurs.

In the infant-controlled version, the presentation of stimulus material depends on how long infants attend to the stimulus. Unless eye-tracking technology is utilized (discussed in next section) infants' looking behavior is coded by an experimenter observing the infant via a video camera in another room. This experimenter presents stimulus material on a computer screen directly in front of the infant, but only when the infant is attending to the screen. Conversely, when the infant looks away from the computer screen for a period of one second (or in some experiments two seconds) the experimenter advances to the next trial. Put simply, this procedure is "infant-controlled" because trials begin when the infant attends to the computer screen and end when the infant disengages their attention from the screen. This procedure begins by presenting infants with a repeated stimulus over an unspecified number of trials and infants view the repeated stimulus until their looking time has decreased by 50%. Once this occurs, infants have "habituated" to the repeated stimulus. Following habituation, test trials are presented that differ from the repeated habituation trials in some critical way and infants' looking time during the test trials is measured. The fundamental aspect of this test procedure is that once infants reach habituation, new stimuli are presented. If infants notice (discriminate) that the new stimulus is indeed new (or different in some way), this will be reflected by an increase in looking time. An example illustration of two different infants' looking behaviors, one that discriminated a novel stimulus and one that did not, can be seen in Figure 6.2.

In the familiarization version of this procedure, the habituation phase consists of a fixed number of trials and is not infant-controlled. For example, the infant might be presented with four fixed trials, each of which are 10 seconds, and a stimulus is displayed on the screen whether the infant is looking or not. Once these familiarization trials have been presented, it is *assumed* that infants have habituated to the stimulus. The test phase once again compares the habituated stimulus to a novel stimulus. One difference between this version and the infant-controlled version is that typically two stimuli are presented side by side. This procedure allows developmental psychologists to investigate infants' classification abilities, or whether an object belongs with a set of other objects (for a review see, Quinn, 2011). For example, if an infant is presented

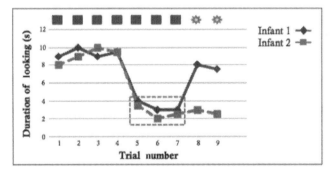

Figure 6.2 Illustration of two infants' looking times during the process of habituation. For this example, the shape at the top of the figure indicates the stimulus being presented on a computer screen during each trial (purple square or a green star). Both infants exhibit high levels of attention to the purple square initially, but it is clear that their attention drops as the trials continue. The red dotted box indicates when their attention has decreased by 50% of its initial levels, signaling that habituation has occurred. At this point, the novel stimulus is presented (the green star). It is clear by the upward spike in looking time (attention) that Infant 1 successfully discriminates the change in stimulus, whereas Infant 2 does not because there was no change in looking behavior.

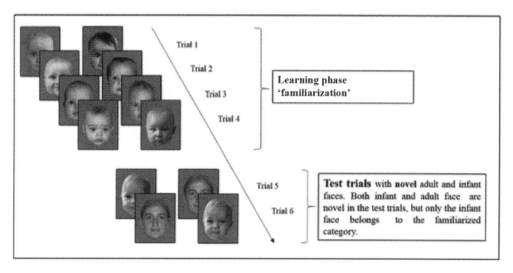

Figure 6.3 A schematic of the infant habituation/dishabituation procedure using a familiarization procedure. This particular example illustrates how researchers use this procedure to examine category formation in infants, specifically testing the categories of adult vs. infant faces. Faces are presented at the rate of two per trial, side by side, for four 10-second trials (Adapted from Damon, Quinn, Heron-Delaney, Lee, & Pascalis, 2016). Once the infant has become familiar with infant faces (infant-face category) novel trials are shown that include adult faces. If infants discriminate faces belonging to the novel category they should look longer to the adult faces.

with a series of different infant faces, he/she would eventually habituate to them. During the test phase, the infant could then be shown both infant and adult faces. Because the infant was shown a "category" of only infant faces during habituation, the presence of an adult face (a new category of faces) would investigate whether infants had learned when faces belong to infant and adult categories (see Figure 6.3). If infants are sensitive to the differences between faces belonging to the infant category vs. the adult category, they should look longer to the novel exemplar from the adult category.

As you can imagine, developmental psychologists can investigate whether infants can discriminate all kinds of stimuli using these habituation techniques. Furthermore, changes in stimuli between habituation and test trials do not need to be only visual, but can be auditory or audiovisual as well. To give you an idea of the range of topics being investigated with this technique, developmental psychologists have investigated whether infants can discriminate between: faces of different races (Kelly et al., 2007; Minar & Lewkowicz, 2017), objects moving at different speeds (Möhring, Liu, & Libertus, 2017), and linguistic vs. non-linguistic vocal expressions (Soderstrom, Reimchen, Sauter, & Morgan, 2017).

The Development of Automated Corneal-Reflection Eye Tracking

The advance of technology has allowed developmental psychologists to ask even more precise questions regarding infants' perceptual development and attention. As previously mentioned, infants' looking behavior is typically measured by examining either

90 *Fabrice Damon et al.*

the direction of their gaze to one stimulus over another or their attention to a screen during an experimental session. However, the development of eye-tracking systems allows developmental psychologists to automatically monitor eye movements without human bias or interference. Eye-tracking methods have been around since the early 1970s and are now regularly used with infants (Haith, 1969; Maurer, 1975; Salapatek, 1968). The basis for this method is simple; a point of infrared light is reflected off the cornea – which is the transparent layer of tissue covering the pupil, iris, and anterior chamber of the eyeball – and can be used to estimate the direction and position of one's eye gaze on a monitor. Infrared light is invisible to the human eye, making this method ideal when examining perceptual development in infants.

Modern eye-trackers contain infrared light illuminators, a camera that captures the light as it is reflected off the cornea. This reflection of infrared light is automatically processed via a computer to produce a gaze location at a specific point in time within a coordinate system corresponding to the presentation monitor. The use of eye-trackers allows developmental psychologists to ask the question: "where are infants specifically allocating their attention when viewing a stimulus?" Because modern eye-trackers have a sampling rate up to 2000 times per second (2000 Hz) this allows for precise temporal and spatial resolution of infants' eye gaze (depending on the accuracy of the calibration). Eye-tracking data consist of eye coordinates sampled over time and can be separated into fixations (a focused point of attention) or saccades (a period of movement between fixations). When using an eye-tracker, developmental psychologists typically present infants with a video and simply observe where their attention is or is not focused throughout the video. This is done by identifying areas of interest (AOIs) that represent specific portions of the stimulus. For example, if an infant is watching a video of a talking face, three AOIs developmental psychologists might be interested in are the eyes, mouth, and nose (see Figure 6.4).

Each fixation that falls within an AOI may only last fractions of a second, but are summed and totaled over the whole experimental session. Developmental psychologists can then see the number of fixations and the total amount of looking time spent focusing to each AOI. These methods have been used to demonstrate that the manner in which young infants scan and attend to human faces changes over the course of the first year of development. Specifically, Lewkowicz and Hansen-Tift (2012) examined

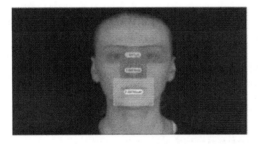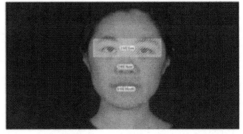

Figure 6.4 Eye, nose, and mouth AOIs used when conducting an eye-tracking experiment with 4–6 and 10–12-month-olds by Minar & Lewkowicz, 2017. Note the colored boxes were not visible during the experimental session and are only present here for illustrative purposes. Image generated by the authors.

where infants allocated their attention when viewing a talking face speaking either the infant's native or a non-native language. When seeing and hearing a talking face at 4 months, infants tended to focus their attention on the speaker's eyes. However, by 6 months their attention began to shift away from the eyes and by 8–10 months, infants were focusing more on the mouth. Attention then shifted away from the speaker's mouth by 12 months, but only if the talking face was presented in the infant's native language (Lewkowicz & Hansen-Tift, 2012). The authors concluded that infants attended more to the mouth between 8–10 months in order to access audiovisual speech cues, which are important at this stage in development because it coincides with the onset of infant babbling and likely facilitates the acquisition of language. By contrast, the shift back to the eyes in older infants suggests that infants had acquired sufficient expertise with their native language and could allocate their attention to other social cues provided by the eyes (Figure 6.5).

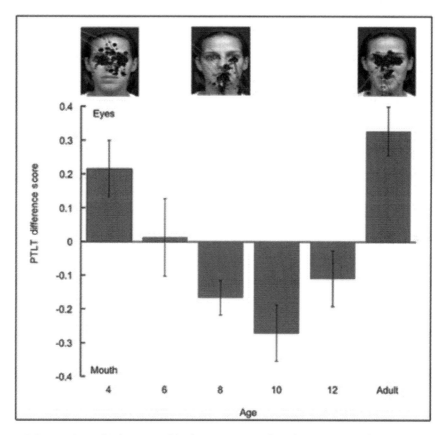

Figure 6.5 Proportion of infants' total looking time to either the eye or mouth regions across the first year of life (and in healthy adults). The images at the top show representative scan patterns infants exhibited when viewing the talking face at 4 and 8 months of age (along with an adult's scan patterns). The x-axis indicates infants' age. A proportion of total looking time (PTLT) score greater than 0 on the y-axis indicates greater looking to the eyes, whereas a score below 0 indicates greater looking to the mouth. Only findings from the native language condition are shown here. Figure taken from Lewkowicz and Hansen-Tift (2012).

Eye-tracking technology has been particularly useful in studying the origins of social cognition, especially when investigating attentional biases towards faces as a marker of social development (Leppänen, 2016; Peltola, Yrttiaho, & Leppänen, 2018). Other topics in infant research that have used eye-tracking technology include face detection among a set of objects (Jakobsen, Umstead, & Simpson, 2016), markers of ASDs (Jones & Klin, 2013; Norbury et al., 2009; Smith & Bennetto, 2007; Tenenbaum, Amso, Abar & Sheinkopf, 2014), and the anticipation of future events (see for review Gredebäck, Johnson, & von Hofsten, 2010). Eye-trackers can even calculate variations in pupil size throughout an experimental session, which have been used as a measure of memory and emotional response (for review see Hepach & Westermann, 2016).

Eye-tracking methods do, however, have some drawbacks. They are expensive compared to traditional looking-time measures, such as the visual paired comparison and habituation/dishabituation procedures. Furthermore, if an eye-tracker fails to measure corneal reflection, as can be the case if an infant moves around too much during the experimental session, missing data can be a significant issue. Overall, the benefits tend to outweigh the negatives because eye movement measures provide rich, precise, and objective data regarding where infants focus their attention. Moreover, the ability to sample eye fixations over time and to time-lock those fixations with the appearance of a stimulus gives valuable insight to infants' cognitive and perceptual abilities. The rapid advancement of both eye-tracking technology and analyses hold great promise and have led to highly innovative findings regarding early perception and cognition.

Electrophysiological Recording in Infants

We will now shift from discussing procedures that utilize infants' overt behavior to procedures that examine infants' underlying brain activation while viewing stimuli. Similar to procedures measuring infants' overt behaviors (looking time), procedures measuring their underlying brain activation must still be carefully interpreted by developmental psychologists. These procedures usually have infants watch a stimulus, or a series of events, while simultaneously measuring their brain-activation dynamics. The purpose of these procedures is to elucidate the relationship between a presented stimulus and the neural activation underlying infants' perception/cognition related to that stimulus. This is only possible because in 1875 Richard Caton discovered that systematic electrical currents in the brain could be measured (Caton, 1875). More than 50 years later, Edgar Adrian and Sir Bryan Harold Cabot Matthews recorded the electrical activity of the brain through the human scalp and were able to identify regular oscillations in the cortex, or "brain waves", by using a technique developed by Hans Berger in 1929 (Adrian & Matthews, 1934a, 1934b). Since then, the technique of recording human brain electrical activation, or electroencephalography (EEG), has undergone significant advances (Barlow, 1997; Teplan, 2002). A detailed overview of how EEGs are recorded and analyzed is beyond the scope of this chapter, but the basic principles of this technique remain the same across a wide variety of research studies. Specifically, EEG is a noninvasive brain-imaging technique that continuously measures the electrical activity of neurons through an array of electrodes placed over the scalp (see Figure 6.6). It is important to note that this procedure does not measure individual neuronal responses, but rather measures the activation of groups of neurons that are responding in a systematic fashion to an experimental stimulation (de Haan, 2015). This allows for a rough picture of infants' overall neural activation during the presentation of a stimulus.

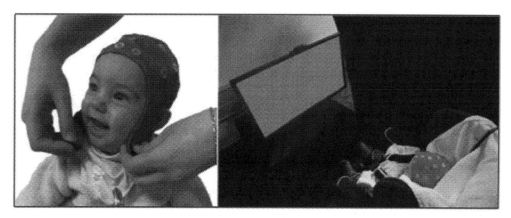

Figure 6.6 Infant (Irène, 4 months of age) wearing an ANT 32-channel headcap (left). Electrodes are sewn in and experimenters only have to insert conductive gel around the electrode–scalp interface to measure underlying brain activation. EEGs are typically measured with an infant seated in a padded infant car chair in front of the computer screen while wearing the EEG headcap (right).

One issue with EEG data is that they are composed of a mixture of both neuronal activity related to the experimental session as well as extraneous artifacts due to body movements (e.g., eye movements, muscular activities, etc.). EEG data can even be influenced by fluctuations in the power cables used with the equipment. The electrical activation due to body and eye movements can result in much larger electrical signals than those caused by stimulus-related brain activity, making results difficult to interpret. This issue is compounded in infant research because young infants rarely sit still and can exhibit poor motor control. These issues combined make the collection of "clean" EEG data quite problematic. Developmental psychologists, however, have had success when measuring infants' EEGs by using age-appropriate stimuli and by setting up infant-friendly lab environments (Hoehl & Wahl, 2012).

More commonly utilized in infant research are ERPs, which are another measurement of brain activation. Although EEGs and ERPs are both collected in a similar manner, they differ in the brain functions they measure. For the purposes of this chapter, we can conceptualize EEGs as recordings of the ongoing electrical activity that correspond to different mental states (e.g., the "alpha" rhythm tends to be between 8 and 13 Hz and is associated to a relaxed state). ERPs instead reflect changes in brain activation in *response* to a specific event (hence the name "event-related potential") and can be linked to a stimulus, a response, or a cognitive process. In other words, the regular change in EEG activity following the presentation of a stimulus event can be averaged over many trials to reveal an ERP. In this way, ERPs differ from EEGs because they measure brain activity that is precisely time-locked to a stimulus event (de Haan, 2015), but are a subset of the brain's global EEG response.

Composite ERP waveforms have been decomposed into components that reflect the activation of certain dedicated neural networks (Luck, 2005). Standard, or common, neural activation patterns have been discovered through many research studies and the development of these activation patterns is of interest to developmental psychologists. In adults, for example, the presentation of a human face elicits a standard neural reaction, namely a negatively sloped activation pattern called N170. Activation of the N170 wave peaks roughly 170 ms after stimulus onset and is located in the posterior and lateral areas of the brain, indicating increased activation of the fusiform and inferior-temporal gyri (Bentin, Allison, Puce, Perez, & McCarthy, 1996). This response of the N170, however, is not present in young infants. Because infants have not had the same amount of perceptual experience with faces as adults, their brains do not respond to this stimulus in the same way. As a result, ERPs have been used to demonstrate that the dynamics of the N170 wave change over early development (Batty & Taylor, 2006). This demonstrates that researchers must be careful when generalizing ERP findings from adults to children and infants; not only does the latency and topography of brain-activation change during development, but experience with certain stimuli also changes the brain's neuronal response to them. To drive this point home, the infant equivalent of the adult N170 is called the N290, which is an activation pattern in response to faces that is more globally distributed in the infant brain. The N290 peaks in activation around 350 ms in 3-month-olds and 290 ms in 12-month-olds, thus changing over early development as experience with faces increases (de Haan, Johnson, & Halit, 2003).

ERPs and EEGs have been extensively applied to many areas of infant research and have informed us of underlying neural mechanisms related to attention, memory, emotions, speech, and face processing (for a review, see Nelson & McCleery, 2008). For example, infant researchers have used EEG signals to determine that 5-month-old infants perceive social actions (eye contact and infant-directed speech) with dedicated, but separate, neuronal activation patterns (Parise & Csibra, 2013). Other researchers have used EEGs to investigate neuronal activation patterns in 6- to 9-month-old infants when presented with simple arithmetic scenarios, indicating that different neuronal activation patterns occur when arithmetic scenarios are possible vs. impossible (Berger, Tzur, & Posner, 2006).

Fast Visual Periodic Stimulation: A Recent Development from an Old Technique

The ERPs described previously can be challenging to collect with infants because they have a very low signal-to-noise ratio (SNR), which means that a large number of trials are needed to collect good results. This highlights one challenge of using ERPs in infant research, which can often lead to attrition rates of 25–75% (Hoehl & Wahl, 2012). However, all measures of brain functioning do not suffer from this limitation. While we have only discussed ERPs and EEGs as a response to isolated stimulus events, it is also possible to record neural activation in response to stimuli that are presented in sequences at a fixed rate. When a stimulus is repeatedly presented at a fixed rate, evoked neural responses also occur at the same rate as the stimulus, providing regularly spaced, robust EEG responses. This is called steady-state visual evoked potentials (SSVEPs) (Regan, 1966; for a review see Norcia, Appelbaum, Ales, Cottereau, & Rossion, 2015).

Discovered in the very early days of EEG (Adrian & Matthews, 1934a), SSVEP techniques have recently seen a significant surge in interest and have been adapted to investigate high-level visual processes, such as face processing in adults and infants (de Heering & Rossion, 2015; Rossion, Torfs, Jacques, & Liu-Shuang, 2015). This technique is used to examine neural responses in infants using what is called the fast periodic visual stimulation (FPVS) or "periodic oddball paradigm". In this paradigm, an infrequent stimulus of one type (the "oddball") is embedded *periodically* within a stream of frequent stimuli of a different type (Heinrich, Mell, & Bach, 2009). The key point in this procedure is the periodicity of the stimulus of interest. Any stimulus presented at a fixed rate will elicit a robust brain response at the same rate. Using this method, de Heering and Rossion (2015) investigated the developmental course of face categorization in 4- to 6-month-old infants. Specifically, infants were presented with a series of images (various objects) on a computer screen at a rate of 6 images per second (i.e., 6 Hz). Face images were embedded as every 5th stimulus in this fast series of objects (see Figure 6.7).

In this study, the EEG responses that occurred at a rate of 6 Hz reflect the synchronization of infants' visual system to the stimulus presentation rate (i.e., the "base" response to the visual stimulation). By contrast, the EEG responses that occurred at a frequency of 1.2 Hz (every 5th stimulus) reflect the face-sensitive response (i.e., the oddball). Using this method, de Heering and Rossion (2015) found that faces elicited a distinct pattern of neural activation compared to images of animals and objects; this distinct pattern was mostly located in the right hemisphere of the brain (see Figure 6.8). Since EEG signals at time-locked frequencies are intrinsically meaningful and distinguishable from noise, this affords developmental psychologists a quantifiable signature of the neural process associated with a stimulus of interest (in this case faces). In short, developmental psychologists are able to infer the discrimination abilities of young infants as a measure of response magnitude to the control and oddball stimuli.

Overall, both transient (ERPs) and periodic (FPVS) EEG measures can be obtained implicitly and noninvasively in young infants, allowing developmental psychologists to study infants' neural responses to stimuli even though they may not yet be mature

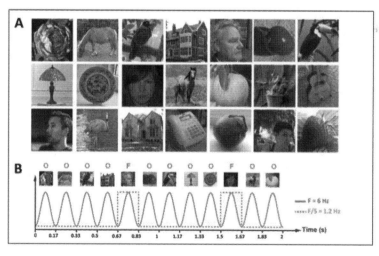

Figure 6.7 A) Examples of face (F) and object (O) stimuli presented during a 20-second sequence at 6 Hz (i.e., 120 images). Face stimuli varied in size, viewpoint, expression, gender, etc. and were presented every fifth image within sequence of object images. (B) Part B illustrates the frequency (1.2Hz) at which the face stimuli were presented within the series of other objects. From: de Heering and Rossion (2015).

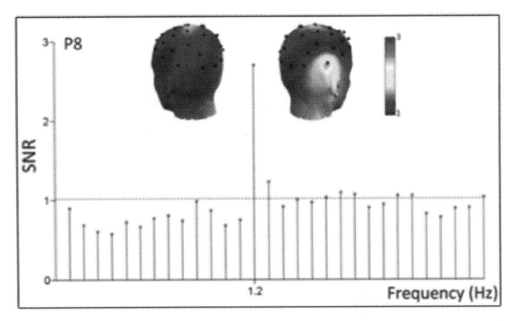

Figure 6.8 Grand-average of EEG SNR spectrum of 15 infants recorded at the occipito-temporal channel P8 (right hemisphere). The results indicate a distinct peak corresponding to exactly when the face stimuli were presented (1.2 Hz). Warm colors indicate greater neural activation. Adapted from de Heering and Rossion (2015).

enough to provide explicit discrimination responses (motor or linguistic responses). This makes FPVS approaches the procedure of choice when studying the developmental course of neural underpinnings related to perceptual and sensory processing in infants.

Neuro-Imaging Method for Infants: Hemodynamic Correlates of Cognition

Another technology used to study infants' perceptual capabilities is functional near-infrared spectroscopy (fNIRS) (Aslin, Shukla, & Emberson, 2015). Although the principles of fNIRS were demonstrated more than 30 years ago (Jobsis, 1977), this method is relatively new to the developmental field and allows developmental psychologists to measure precise brain areas that become active in response to a stimulus. Functional near-infrared spectroscopy is much more spatially precise than EEG/ERP, but is an *indirect* measure of neural activity that is based on the correlation between blood oxygenation and metabolic demand. Because the firing of neurons consumes blood oxygen, the activation of a specific group of neurons creates a local increase of deoxygenated hemoglobin. These hemodynamic responses unfold rather slowly, and typically lag a few seconds behind the stimulus being presented (approximately 8–10 s after stimulus presentation). This technique measures the neural activity associated with changes in blood oxygen levels by using optical fibers embedded in a cap attached to the head of the infant. Near-infrared light is emitted from an optical fiber (emitter) at the surface of the scalp and is surrounded by optical fibers (detectors) that measure how much light is returned to the surface of the scalp (see Figure 6.9).

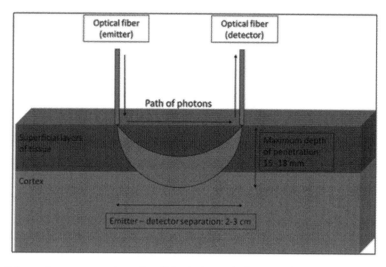

Figure 6.9 Schematic representation of an fNIRS channel, showing the banana-shaped pathway of light photons leaving the emitter and reaching the detector. Photons dip into the superficial layers of the cortex (i.e., gray matter) after passing through several layers of tissue (i.e., skin, skull, cerebral-spinal fluid, and surface vasculature) and allow researchers to quantify neural activation.

The distance between an emitter and a detector (an emitter–detector pair is referred as an "fNIRS channel") determines the depth of penetration possible by the emitted light, with greater distance leading to deeper penetration. Unfortunately, the size of an fNIRS channel is intrinsically limited to ± 3 cm because a larger fNIRS channel leads to stronger signal reduction and would require higher laser-light intensities, which might cause damage to brain tissue. Current fNIRS devices possess a maximum light penetration of 15–18 mm from the scalp surface, leaving brain regions deeper than 2 cm from the surface outside the range of recording. Despite this constraint, fNIRS has proven an excellent tool to study infant neural responses because it has a very high tolerance to head and body movements.

Face processing, specifically the development of whole-face processing (also known as holistic processing), is one of the various domains investigated using fNIRS (for a review see Aslin et al., 2015). Holistic face perception is the process of combining facial features (eyes, nose, mouth) into a unified perception of a face, as opposed to seeing faces as disjointed features (Taubert, Apthorp, Aagten-Murphy, & Alais, 2011). This process is viewed as an automatic aspect of normal face processing and it has been demonstrated that its development is critically linked with the amount of face exposure infants experience during the first year of life (Le Grand, Mondloch, Maurer, & Brent, 2004; Rossion, 2009). To examine the development of holistic processing, Kobayashi et al. (2012) presented 5- to 8-month-old infants with images from the 16th-century painter Giuseppe Arcimboldo. These images depict faces that are comprised of non-face elements (i.e., fruits and vegetables, flowers, etc.) rather than elementary facial features. Arcimboldo images are known to induce a holistic face perception because of their global face-like configuration, even when the face contains non-face elements.

98 *Fabrice Damon et al.*

Perceiving faces within the non-face Arcimboldo images is taken as evidence of holistic processing. When the paintings are inverted, however, the non-face Arcimboldo images are not perceived as faces (see Figure 6.10). Kobayashi et al. (2012) measured the hemodynamic responses of 7- to 8-month-olds when shown regular and inverted Arcimboldo faces.

Kobayashi et al. (2012) found that the concentration of oxyhemoglobin increased in 7–8-month-olds' left temporal area during the presentation of the upright Arcimboldo images, but not for inverted images. Thus, 7- and 8-month-olds exhibited a neural response indicative of holistic face perception when shown the upright images, even though the "perceived" faces were composed of non-facial features. These findings supported earlier holistic face-processing results obtained using traditional looking-time procedures (Schwarzer, Zauner, & Jovanovic, 2007).

Surprisingly, Kobayashi et al. (2012) found that 7- and 8-month-olds exhibited a left-hemispheric dominance in the processing of upright Arcimboldo images, whereas de Heering and Rossion (2015) reported that face categorization in 4-month-olds elicited a right-hemispheric dominance. Such inconsistencies are unfortunately common in infancy research, especially given substantial developmental differences in task difficulty, procedures, and dependent variables. Overall, neuroimaging methods and electrophysiological techniques are constantly improving and provide powerful tools in the search for a better understanding of cognitive development. However, both the fNIRS and EEG systems require a great deal of care when interpreting and comparing results across experiments.

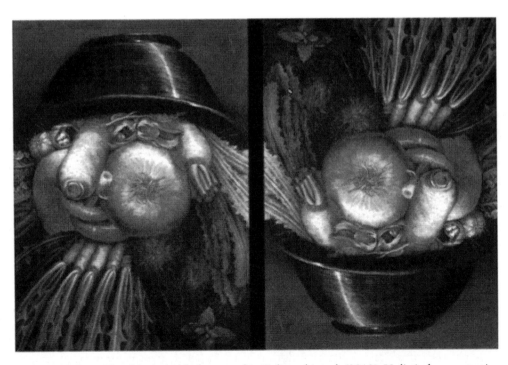

Figure 6.10 Example of Arcimboldo faces used in Kobayashi et al. (2012). Holistic face perception is typically reported when viewing the painting on the left, but not when viewing the painting on the right (inverted face image). Adapted from Aslin (2012).

Conclusion

We have seen various methods used in infancy research, from behavior (e.g., looking time, visual scanning) to neural correlates of cognition (e.g., EEG, fNIRS). Each method has contributed to our understanding of infants' perceptual, cognitive, and social abilities at different, but complementary, levels of analysis. Because developmental psychologists typically work with preverbal research subjects, these methods highlight how it is necessity to develop and refine paradigms with implicit measurement methods that do not rely on verbal communication. We did not mention any examples in this chapter, but because infant procedures do not rely on verbal communication, researchers can often use these methods when studying non-human, animal species (e.g., infant macaque monkeys), allowing for comparative developmental approaches (Damon et al., 2017; Simpson et al., 2017).

We hope this chapter demonstrated that different experimental procedures are used to answer different infant-related research questions. It is important to consider, when examining both adult and infant research findings, whether the method used was appropriate to answer the proposed research question. Irrespective of the method used, it is incumbent on developmental psychologists to keep in mind that there is a certain level of fundamental uncertainty linking an obtained measurement of infant behavior, or neural response, to the underlying perception or cognition that produced it. Whether analyzing infant looking time or neural activation, there are a wide variety of possible mechanisms (e.g., sensory, motor, perceptual, physiological, etc.) that may explain the observed behavior. As a result, we challenge you, the reader, to always thoroughly examine and reflect on what is actually measured during an experimental study and to pay close attention to how such results are interpreted and conveyed; not only when reviewing infant literature, but all empirical studies. This will not only improve your critical-thinking skills going forward, but will also help guard against unwarranted causal inferences.

Notes

1 The majority of this work was done when the author was affiliated with the Institute for the Study of Child Development – Rutgers Robert Wood Johnson Medical School, New Brunswick, NJ, 08901, USA.
2 Denotes corresponding author.

References

Adrian, E. D. & Matthews, B. H. C. (1934a). The berger rhythm: potential changes from the occipital lobes in man. *Brain, 57,* 355–385.

Adrian, E. D. & Matthews, B. H. C. (1934b). The interpretation of potential waves in the cortex. *The Journal of Physiology, 81,* 440–471. doi:10.1113/jphysiol.1934.sp003147.

Aslin, R. N. (2007). What's in a look? *Developmental Science, 10,* 48–53. doi:10.1111/j.1467-7687.2007.00563.x.

Aslin, R. N. (2012). Questioning the questions that have been asked about the infant brain using near-infrared spectroscopy. *Cognitive Neuropsychology, 29*(1–2), 7–33. doi:10.1080/02643294.2012.654773.

Aslin, R. N., Shukla, M., & Emberson, L. L. (2015). Hemodynamic correlates of cognition in human infants. *Annual Review of Psychology, 66,* 349–379. doi:10.1146/annurev-psych-010213-115108.

Barker, B. A. & Tomblin, J. B. (2004). Bimodal speech perception in infant hearing aid and cochlear implant users. *Archives of Otolaryngology – Head & Neck Surgery*, 130(5), 582–586. doi:10.1001/archotol.130.5.582.

Barlow, J. S. (1997). The early history of EEG data-processing at the Massachusetts Institute of Technology and the Massachusetts General Hospital. *International Journal of Psychophysiology*, 26(1–3), 443–454. doi:10.1016/S0167-8760(97)00781-2.

Batty, M. & Taylor, M. J. (2006). The development of emotional face processing during childhood. *Developmental Science*, 9(2), 207–220. doi:10.1111/j.1467-7687.2006.00480.x.

Bebko, J. M., Weiss, J. A., Demark, J. L., & Gomez, P. (2006). Discrimination of temporal synchrony in intermodal events by children with autism and children with developmental disabilities without autism. *Journal of Child Psychology and Psychiatry*, 47(1), 88–98. doi:10.1111/j.1469-7610.2005.01443.x.

Bentin, S., Allison, T., Puce, A., Perez, E., & McCarthy, G. (1996). Electrophysiological studies of face perception in humans. *Journal of Cognitive Neuroscience*, 8, 551–565. doi:10.1162/jocn.1996.8.6.551.Electrophysiological.

Berger, A., Tzur, G., & Posner, M. I. (2006). Infant brains detect arithmetic errors. *Proceedings of the National Academy of Sciences*, 103(33), 12649–12653. doi:10.1073/pnas.0605350103.

Caton, R. (1875). Electrical currents of the brain. *The Journal of Nervous and Mental Disease*, 2 (4), 610.

Cohen, L. B. (1969). Observing responses, visual preferences, and habituation to visual stimuli in infants. *Journal of Experimental Child Psychology*, 7(3), 419–433.

Cohen, L. B. (1972). Attention-getting and attention-holding processes of infant visual preferences. *Child Development*, 43, 869–879.

Constantino, J. N., Kennon-McGill, S., Weichselbaum, C., Marrus, N., Haider, A., Glowinski, A. L., Gillespie, S., Klaiman, C., Klin, A., & Jones, W. (2017). Infant viewing of social scenes is under genetic control and is atypical in autism. *Nature*, 547, 340–344. doi:10.1038/nature22999.

Coulon, M., Guellai, B., & Streri, A. (2011). Recognition of unfamiliar talking faces at birth. *International Journal of Behavioral Development*, 35(3), 282–287. doi:10.1177/0165025410396765.

Damon, F., Méary, D., Quinn, P. C., Lee, K., Simpson, E. A., Paukner, A., Suomi, S. J., & Pascalis, O. (2017). Preference for facial averageness: evidence for a common mechanism in human and macaque infants. *Scientific Reports*, 7, 46303. doi:10.1038/srep46303.

Damon, F., Quinn, P. C., Heron-Delaney, M., Lee, K., & Pascalis, O. (2016). Development of category formation for faces differing by age in 9- to 12-month-olds: an effect of experience with infant faces. *The British Journal of Developmental Psychology*, 34, 582–597. doi:10.1111/bjdp.12152.

de Haan, M. (2015). Neuroscientific methods with children. In R. M. Lerner, W. F. Overton, & P. C. M. Molenaar (Eds.), *Handbook of Child Psychology and Developmental Science* (7th ed., pp. 683–712). New York, NY: Wiley.

de Haan, M., Johnson, M. H., & Halit, H. (2003). Development of face-sensitive event-related potentials during infancy: a review. *International Journal of Psychophysiology*, 51, 45–58. doi:10.1016/S0167-8760(03)00152-1.

de Heering, A. & Rossion, B. (2015). Rapid categorization of natural face images in the infant right hemisphere. *Elife*, 4, e06564. doi:10.7554/eLife.06564.

Fantz, R. L. (1958). Pattern vision in young infants. *The Psychological Record*, 8, 43–47.

Fantz, R. L. (1961). The origin of form perception. *Scientific American*, 204(5), 66–73. doi:10.1038/scientificamerican0561-66.

Farroni, T., Johnson, M. H., Menon, E., Zulian, L., Faraguna, D., & Csibra, G. (2005). Newborns' preference for face-relevant stimuli: effects of contrast polarity. *Proceedings of the National Academy of Sciences*, 102(47), 17245–17250. doi:10.1073/pnas.0502205102.

Goren, C. C., Sarty, M., & Wu, P. Y. (1975). Visual following and pattern discrimination of face-like stimuli by newborn infants. *Pediatrics*, *56*(4), 544–549.

Gredebäck, G., Johnson, S. P., & von Hofsten, C. (2010). Eye tracking in infancy research. *Developmental Neuropsychology*, *35*, 1–19. doi:10.1080/87565640903325758.

Guiraud, J. A., Tomalski, P., Kushnerenko, E., Ribeiro, H., Davies, K., Charman, T., Elsabbagh, M., Johnson, M., & the BASIS Team. (2012). Atypical audiovisual speech integration in infants at risk for autism. *PLoS One*, *7*(5), e36428. doi:10.1371/journal.pone.0036428.

Haith, M. M. (1969). Infrared television recording and measurement of ocular behavior in the human infant. *The American Psychologist*, *24*, 279–283. doi:10.1037/h0028419.

Haith, M. M. (1980). *Rules That Babies Look By: the Organization of Newborn Visual Activity*. Hillsdale, NJ: Lawrence Erlbaum.

Heinrich, S. P., Mell, D., & Bach, M. (2009). Frequency-domain analysis of fast oddball responses to visual stimuli: a feasibility study. *International Journal of Psychophysiology*, *73*, 287–293. doi:10.1016/j.ijpsycho.2009.04.011.

Hepach, R., & Westermann, G. (2016). Pupillometry in infancy research. *Journal of Cognition and Development*, *17*, 359–377. doi:10.1080/15248372.2015.1135801.

Hoehl, S. & Wahl, S. (2012). Recording infant ERP data for cognitive research. *Developmental Neuropsychology*, *37*, 187–209. doi:10.1080/87565641.2011.627958.

Jakobsen, K. V., Umstead, L., & Simpson, E. A. (2016). Efficient human face detection in infancy. *Developmental Psychobiology*, *58*, 129–136. doi:10.1002/dev.21338.

Jobsis, F. (1977). Noninvasive, infrared monitoring of cerebral and myocardial oxygen sufficiency and circulatory parameters. *Science*, *198*, 1264–1267. doi:10.1126/science.929199.

Jones, W. & Klin, A. (2013). Attention to eyes is present but in decline in 2–6-month-old infants later diagnosed with autism. *Nature*, *504*, 427–431. doi:10.1038/nature12715.

Kelly, D. J., Quinn, P. C., Slater, A. M., Lee, K., Ge, L., & Pascalis, O. (2007). The other-race effect develops during infancy evidence of perceptual narrowing. *Psychological Science*, *18*(12), 1084–1089.

Kobayashi, M., Otsuka, Y., Nakato, E., Kanazawa, S., Yamaguchi, M. K., & Kakigi, R. (2012). Do infants recognize the Arcimboldo images as faces? Behavioral and near-infrared spectroscopic study. *Journal of Experimental Child Psychology*, *111*, 22–36. doi:10.1016/j.jecp.2011.07.008.

Kubicek, C., De Boisferon, A. H., Dupierrix, E., Pascalis, O., Lœvenbruck, H., Gervain, J., & Schwarzer, G. (2014). Cross-modal matching of audio-visual German and French fluent speech in infancy. *PLoS One*, *9*(2), e89275. doi:10.1371/journal.pone.0089275.

Le Grand, R., Mondloch, C. J., Maurer, D., & Brent, H. P. (2004). Impairment in holistic face processing following early visual deprivation. *Psychological Science*, *15*, 762–768. doi:10.1111/j.0956-7976.2004.00753.x.

Leppänen, J. M. (2016). Using eye tracking to understand infants' attentional bias for faces. *Child Development Perspectives*, *10*, 161–165. doi:10.1111/cdep.12180.

Lewis, M., Goldberg, S., & Campbell, H. (1969). A developmental study of information processing within the first three years of life: response decrement to a redundant signal. *Monographs of the Society for Research in Child Development*, *34*(9), iii-41.

Lewis, T. L., Maurer, D., & Kay, D. (1978). Newborns' central vision: whole or hole? *Journal of Experimental Child Psychology*, *26*(1), 193–203.

Lewkowicz, D. J. (1992). Infants' response to temporally based intersensory equivalence: the effect of synchronous sounds on visual preferences for moving stimuli. *Infant Behavior and Development*, *15*(3), 297–324.

Lewkowicz, D. J. (2011). The biological implausibility of the nature–nurture dichotomy and what it means for the study of infancy. *Infancy*, *16*(4), 331–367. doi:10.1111/j.1532-7078.2011.00079.x.

Lewkowicz, D. J. & Hansen-Tift, A. M. (2012). Infants deploy selective attention to the mouth of a talking face when learning speech. *Proceedings of the National Academy of Sciences*, *109*(5), 1431–1436.

Lewkowicz, D. J., Leo, I., & Simion, F. (2010). Intersensory perception at birth: newborns match nonhuman primate faces and voices. *Infancy*, 15(1), 46–60. doi:10.1111/j.1532-7078.2009.00005.x.

Lewkowicz, D. J. & Minar, N. J. (2014). Infants are not sensitive to synesthetic cross-modality correspondences: A comment on Walker et al.(2010). *Psychological science*, 25(3), 832–834.

Lewkowicz, D. J., Minar, N. J., Tift, A. H., & Brandon, M. (2015). Perception of the multisensory coherence of fluent audiovisual speech in infancy: its emergence and the role of experience. *Journal of Experimental Child Psychology*, 130, 147–162. doi:10.1016/j.jecp.2014.10.006.

Luck, S. J. (2005). *An Introduction to the Event Related Potential Technique*. Cambridge, MA: MIT Press.

Maurer, D. (1975). Infant visual perception: methods of study. In L. B. Cohen & P. Salapatek (Eds.), *Infant Perception: from Sensation to Cognition* (pp. 1–76). London: Academic Press.

McCall, R. B. & Kagan, J. (1967). Stimulus-schema discrepancy and attention in the infant. *Journal of Experimental Child Psychology*, 5(3), 381–390.

Minar, N. J. & Lewkowicz, D. J. (2017). Overcoming the other-race effect in infancy with multisensory redundancy: 10–12-month-olds discriminate dynamic other-race faces producing speech. *Developmental Science*, 21(4). doi:10.1111/desc.12604.

Möhring, W., Liu, R., & Libertus, M. E. (2017). Infants' speed discrimination: effects of different ratios and spatial orientations. *Infancy*, 22(6), 762–777. doi:10.1111/infa.12196.

Morrongiello, B. A., Fenwick, K. D., & Chance, G. (1998). Crossmodal learning in newborn infants: inferences about properties of auditory-visual events. *Infant Behavior and Development*, 21(4), 543–553. doi:10.1016/S0163-6383(98)90028-5.

Nelson, C. A. & McCleery, J. P. (2008). Use of event-related potentials in the study of typical and atypical development. *Journal of the American Academy of Child and Adolescent Psychiatry*, 47, 1252–1261. doi:10.1097/CHI.0b013e318185a6d8.

Norbury, C. F., Brock, J., Cragg, L., Einav, S., Griffiths, H., & Nation, K. (2009). Eye-movement patterns are associated with communicative competence in autistic spectrum disorders. *Journal of Child Psychology and Psychiatry*, 50(7), 834–842.

Norcia, A. M., Appelbaum, L. G., Ales, J. M., Cottereau, B. R., & Rossion, B. (2015). The steady-state visual evoked potential in vision research: a review. *Journal of Vision*, 15, 4. doi:10.1167/15.6.4.doi.

Oyama, S. (2000). *The Ontogeny of Information: Developmental Systems and Evolution*. Durham, NC: Duke University Press.

Parise, E. & Csibra, G. (2013). Neural responses to multimodal ostensive signals in 5-month-old infants. *PloS One*, 8(8), e72360. doi:10.1371/journal.pone.0072360.

Peltola, M. J., Yrttiaho, S., & Leppänen, J. M. (2018). Infants' attention bias to faces as an early marker of social development. *Developmental Science*, 1–14. doi:10.1111/desc.12687.

Quinn, P. C. (2011). Born to categorize. In U. Goswami (Ed.), *The Wiley-Blackwell Handbook of Childhood Cognitive Development* (2nd ed., pp. 129–152). Oxford, UK: Wiley-Blackwell.

Regan, D. (1966). Some characteristics of average steady-state and transient responses evoked by modulated light. *Electroencephalography and Clinical Neurophysiology*, 20, 238–248. doi:10.1016/0013-4694(66)90088-5.

Rossion, B. (2009). Distinguishing the cause and consequence of face inversion: the perceptual field hypothesis. *Acta Psychologica*, 132, 300–312. doi:10.1016/j.actpsy.2009.08.002.

Rossion, B., Torfs, K., Jacques, C., & Liu-Shuang, J. (2015). Fast periodic presentation of natural images reveals a robust face-selective electrophysiological response in the human brain. *Journal of Vision*, 15, 1–18. doi:10.1167/15.1.18.

Sai, F. Z. (2005). The role of the mother's voice in developing mother's face preference: evidence for intermodal perception at birth. *Infant and Child Development*, 14, 29–50. doi:10.1002/icd.376.

Salapatek, P. (1968). Visual scanning of geometric figures by the human newborn. *Journal of Comparative and Physiological Psychology*, 66, 247–258. doi:10.1037/h0026376.

Schwarzer, G., Zauner, N., & Jovanovic, B. (2007). Evidence of a shift from featural to configural face processing in infancy. *Developmental Science*, 10, 452–463. doi:10.1111/j.1467-7687.2007.00599.x.

Simpson, E. A., Jakobsen, K. V., Damon, F., Suomi, S. J., Ferrari, P. F., & Paukner, A. (2017). Face detection and the development of own-species bias in infant macaques. *Child Development*, 88, 103–113. doi:10.1111/cdev.12565.

Smith, E. G. & Bennetto, L. (2007). Audiovisual speech integration and lipreading in autism. *Journal of Child Psychology and Psychiatry*, 48(8), 813–821.

Soderstrom, M., Reimchen, M., Sauter, D., & Morgan, J. L. (2017). Do infants discriminate non-linguistic vocal expressions of positive emotions?. *Cognition and Emotion*, 31(2), 298–311. doi:10.1080/02699931.2015.1108904.

Stevenson, R. A., Segers, M., Ferber, S., Barense, M. D., Camarata, S., & Wallace, M. T. (2015). Keeping time in the brain: autism spectrum disorder and audiovisual temporal processing. *Autism Research*, 9(7), 720–738. doi:10.1002/aur.1566.

Taubert, J., Apthorp, D., Aagten-Murphy, D., & Alais, D. (2011). The role of holistic processing in face perception: evidence from the face inversion effect. *Vision Research*, 51(11), 1273–1278. doi:10.1016/j.visres.2011.04.002.

Tenenbaum, E., Amso, D., Abar, B. W., & Sheinkopf, S. J. (2014). Attention and word learning in autistic, language delayed and typically developing children. *Frontiers in Psychology*, 5, 490.

Teplan, M. (2002). Fundamentals of EEG measurement. *Measurement Science Review*, 2(2), 1–11.

Thompson, R. F. (2009). Habituation: a history. *Neurobiology of Learning and Memory*, 92, 127–134. doi:10.1016/j.nlm.2008.07.011.

Vouloumanos, A., Druhen, M. J., Hauser, M. D., & Huizink, A. T. (2009). Five-month-old infants' identification of the sources of vocalizations. *Proceedings of the National Academy of Sciences*, 106(44), 18867–18872. doi:10.1073/pnas.09060491065-385.

7 Studying Children's Verb Learning across Development

Jane B. Childers, Sneh Lalani, Blaire Porter, Sophia Arriazola, Priscilla Tovar-Perez, and Bibiana Cutilletta

Introduction

A critical developmental task for young children is acquiring one (or more) native language(s). This is a difficult feat that children usually accomplish with little direct instruction by the age of 4 or 5 years. An important component of language development is the process of learning the verbs in a language. Given that verbs refer to dynamic events, infants and young children must learn to separate the ongoing stream of action that surrounds them into meaningful events (e.g., Baldwin & Baird, 2001; Hespos, Saylor, & Grossman, 2009) and understand how caregivers use language to describe events. Verbs (action words) differ from nouns (names for objects) as verbs often refer to interactions between multiple objects (e.g., Gentner, 1982). Verbs also vary by language. Every language has nouns, but the verb category is not universal (instead all languages have predicates). Also, caregivers speaking different languages may use different verbs to refer to different events or parts of events (e.g., Talmy, 1975). Thus, learning a new verb has been described as solving a "packaging problem" (e.g., Gleitman & Gleitman, 1992) because it involves conceptually packaging dynamic and transient events that fit a particular verb in a language (Gentner, 1982; Gentner & Boroditsky, 2001). This complexity of verb acquisition highlights the challenges that learning a new verb can present for young children.

Summary of Current Knowledge about Children's Verb Learning

An examination of the current literature reveals that research has mostly been focused on the acquisition of nouns rather than verbs. Researchers have demonstrated that children use a combination of cognitive tools during noun acquisition. These tools include 1) a "shape bias," the expectation that nouns extend to objects similar in shape (e.g., Landau, Smith, & Jones, 1988, 1998), 2) "representational insight," or the expectation that all objects have a name, and 3) "fast mapping," the rapid connection of new nouns with objects after only a few exposures (Carey & Bartlett, 1978). Perhaps fewer studies have focused on the acquisition of verbs because, when compared to nouns, children produce more nouns than verbs in their early vocabularies (e.g., Gentner, 1982). This "noun bias" is evident across languages.

For verbs, there is evidence that children are able to use the syntax or grammar in sentences to direct their attention to certain parts of events (e.g., Gleitman, 1990). Studies show that 2-year-old children correctly distinguish transitive sentences (or sentences with a direct object) from intransitive sentences (or sentences without a direct object). Transitive sentences (e.g., *The duck is gorping the bunny*) are often associated with a causative action (e.g., *the duck pushes the bunny down*), while intransitive sentences (e.g., *The duck and bunny are gorping*) are associated with non-causative actions (e.g., *the duck and bunny wave their arms*) (Fisher, 2002; Naigles, 1990). Taken together, the studies suggest that young children have some key knowledge about the syntax of their native language that they can use to form an initial link between a new verb and an event by the time they are 2 years old.

Other studies suggest young children often have trouble extending verbs to new objects, situations, or sentences. Children can be highly conservative in their use of new verbs, tending to use newly acquired verbs in ways previously heard (Huttenlocher, Smiley, & Charney, 1983; Tomasello, 1992, 2000). In fact, a study of Japanese-speaking children found that while 3-year-old children could extend newly learned nouns, they did not extend new verbs to include new objects until 5 years (Imai, Haryu, & Okada, 2005). Similarly, Kersten and Smith (2002) found that English-speaking 3-year-olds have difficulty extending new verbs when the objects in the new events are novel (e.g., bug-like creatures), but do not have a similar difficulty extending nouns. In sum, children's ability to use newly acquired verbs may develop gradually between 2 and 4 years of age (Forbes & Farrar, 1993; Imai, Haryu, & Okada, 2005; Kersten & Smith, 2002). This is important as using a word productively and creatively is an important component of language development.

Possible Measurements and Designs

Studies of verb learning with preschool-aged children usually use proximal methods with individual child participants. Typically, sessions include the child and 1–2 experimenters, and are conducted either in an on-campus laboratory, off-campus child care center, or home setting. In our lab, we collect most of our data from children in local child care centers. We use a cross-sectional developmental design, meaning we typically include a group of children from 2–3 different age groups (typically 2 ½, 3 ½ and 4 ½ years) in each study.

Assembling a Research Team

Before describing the specific procedures we use to test verb acquisition in young children, we will first describe our general approach to conducting research with undergraduate research assistants. Our lab typically includes 8–10 undergraduate students each semester. These students have completed a written application and in-person interview, and the Principal Investigator (PI) selects students who have experience with young children along with skills that would be useful in the lab (e.g., organization, initiative). Set working hours are assigned every week, which works well as students know when they are expected to work and can work in pairs while collecting data off campus. Students are trained to be an experimenter, coder, and data analyst. Even though it may be beneficial to have each student performing a specific task, it is good for student researchers to be trained on a variety of tasks and to be encouraged to take on different responsibilities in the lab.

Core Methodologies: Overview

Several methods are used to study verb learning in young children. In the next section of the chapter, we will focus on three key procedures used in this area and describe how we have used these procedures to collect data from young children. We start by describing how we recruit participants, and then describe studies that have made use of "live" events with concrete objects, studies that have included iPads or tablets to present stimuli, and finally, as an example of innovative procedures in this area, we will discuss studies that use an eye tracker. As finding child participants can be difficult, our strategy is to run multiple studies with the same participant. These studies of course need to be independent of each other to avoid carryover or practice effects. These three key procedures demonstrate the range of research designs that can be carried out with undergraduate research assistants.

Recruiting Participants

Recruiting children for research studies of any type can prove to be challenging. Child participation depends on parental consent, availability, and the collaboration between child care centers and researchers. If a study includes specific age constraints, recruitment can be more difficult. When considering experimental research, families may choose to not have their children participate due to privacy concerns such as video recording, home visits, scheduling conflicts, and mistrust of researchers. In order to recruit participants, these concerns must be acknowledged and addressed in a parent letter and/or the consent form. Children provide assent at this age (2–5 years) by showing willingness to participate in procedures. If they begin to ask to stop interacting with us, either explicitly (using language) or implicitly (by failing to comply with our directions), ethically their actions must be taken seriously and the procedure is stopped, even if it is incomplete.

Child care centers are useful research sites as these centers may allow researchers to conduct studies as long as researchers maintain flexible scheduling, communicate with center administrators frequently, and respect the participants as well as the center. Each child care facility can present its own set of challenges; however, it is the researchers' responsibility to build positive rapport and adjust to the needs of the center. Often, each child care facility will require a background check from research assistants and require that one staff member accompany the research assistant and child at all times. After these checks are completed, the center provides a quiet room in which to conduct the study, minimizing background noise (a teacher is often present). The center administrators allow the research assistants into the classrooms in order to build a rapport with the children before running the study.

When conducting research with children outside of the child care center, it can be difficult to find ways to recruit parents who would be willing to allow their children to participate in the study. Oftentimes researchers recruit participants using a shared database, through social media or personal contacts, and/or by attending local child fairs.

Method 1: Using Live Events in Studies

A "live event" or "behavioral enactment" study involves an experimenter demonstrating something to the participant using concrete objects. At the time of testing, an experimenter shows a participant a series of objects or events and follows a script in order to standardize presentations across participants.

An example of using live events in research studies is evident in a study by Childers and Paik (2009), which investigated whether children could compare three events to each other to learn a new verb. In this study, the experimenter used a specific movement or set of movements with objects to create a change to an affected object. Children then either saw a set of close comparisons (3 events with similar objects) or far comparisons (3 events with dissimilar objects, different numbers of objects, and different movements). Each set demonstrated the same target action. During the testing phase of the study, children were given the target object (from the first example), an object similar to the target object (close extension), and an object dissimilar from the target object (far extension). They were then asked to perform the verb. Results showed that children more often performed the target action. In the close condition and the far condition, participants performed more close extension actions.

Using live events as opposed to recorded events in research with children has both advantages and disadvantages. One of the key advantages to using live stimuli as opposed to recordings is that younger children (e.g., 2-year-olds) can show better attention to live events than recorded events (Diener, Pierroutsakos, Troseth, & Roberts, 2008). This ability to process stimuli and maintain attention is important when collecting data with child participants because their short attention spans can affect the results. In addition, if children are able to point to an object or enact an event at test, this active behavior can provide especially compelling evidence of learning.

A disadvantage of using live events is the variability that can arise across experimenters. Because the event is being performed for every child, variation can arise in how the experimenter presents the stimuli and/or in how he or she produces the sentences during each trial. One way to reduce this variability is to create a script for the experimenter to follow every time he or she presents the stimuli to a child, as well as to carefully train experimenters on using scripts and presenting the objects or events. Another option is to record each experimental session and then have multiple coders code each experimental session from digital video recordings. This process helps us to identify any important inconsistencies across experimenters that we can consider, as well as ensures that we can watch children's behavior more carefully as it is coded.

It can be difficult to code or categorize children's responses at test. We start by creating a list or table of possible responses, and a code that would fit those enactments. This list can be added to as data is collected and unanticipated responses are seen. Usually, test items are designed with specific responses in mind, and this can be used to create the first list (e.g., responses that would preserve the action shown vs. ones that would be irrelevant). During the experimental session, one research assistant codes the participant's responses as they unfold, but the session is also digitally recorded. Back at the lab, two more people each code the participant from the video without looking at what was previously coded and if disagreements arise, they are discussed (usually at a lab meeting).

Method 2: Using iPads to Present Stimuli in Studies

It is difficult to maintain a toddler's interest when conducting research on language acquisition due to their short attention span. Thus, it is important to use methods that are age-appropriate and engaging. In our studies, iPads are used for several reasons, including their portability, their appeal to children, and their audio-visual capabilities. According to Holloway, Green, and Livingstone (2013), more and more children are using electronics such as their parents' iPhones, laptops, video gaming systems, and televisions, and children in our studies have been eager to engage in our studies using iPads (or tablets) (2013). As an example, Rattanasone et al. (2016) provides evidence of the usefulness of iPads as a research tool for studying language acquisition in children aged 3- to 4-years-old.

Our researchers travel between the lab and different local child care centers, and thus we have found that iPads are easy to take with us from place to place. Our lab has two iPads; one is used to present dynamic video stimuli for a study, while the other is used as a camera to record the participant and their reactions during the study. We use colorful cases to hold each iPad to remind us which iPad is used for which function and to appeal to the child.

In one of our current studies, we use iPads to ask whether children's verb learning is affected when events that can be compared to each other are separated in time. This is an important question because in everyday life, children often hear a verb at different times during the day. Our specific research question is whether having experience with two very similar events before two more varied events helps children learn how to compare events to each other. This "progressive alignment" or similar first condition is compared to a condition in which children see all varied events.

In this study, to start the experimental session, children are taken to a quiet room in their child care center. They are first shown four warm-up trials to give them practice at pointing to one of two familiar objects or events on an iPad. Then, in the progressive alignment (PA) condition, they see four similar events depicting the verb "koobing," which is the action of using an object to make an impression in another malleable object (see Figure 7.1). Between each event, there is a one-minute delay (we play one minute of a *Mickey Mouse Clubhouse* episode). Children are then shown two tests trials, each showing a pair of actions on a split screen, and they are asked to find "koobing" (point to one event). A second set is then shown to the child who also hears the verb "pilking," which is the act of using one object to squish another sponge-like object (see Figure 7.2). We always ask the child to learn more than one verb, or be exposed to more than one set of stimuli, to be sure that our results are not only reflective of an individual set of events or objects. Children are again asked to point to one of two events, repeated in two test trials, at test. The side of the correct answer is varied across trials.

To run the study, an experimenter controls an iPad and uses a script to present the stimulus sentences. A second experimenter during the session codes which side of the screen the child points to, and records the session using a second iPad as a camera for later coding from a third experimenter who is not present during the original session. When used effectively, we have found that iPads are a great way to present video stimuli to preschoolers.

Method 3: Using an Eye Tracker to Better Understand Children's Verb Learning

A key innovation arising in the past 10–15 years in studies of child development is the inclusion of eye tracking devices. Eye tracking is used in various fields, and across various age ranges. Specifically, eye trackers are devices that emit near infrared light invisible to the naked eye. The device emits this light which bounces off (is reflected from) the participant's corneas as she gazes at a stimulus (see Figure 7.3). Eye tracking has been used with adults (e.g., Papafragou, Hulbert, & Trueswell, 2008), infants, and

 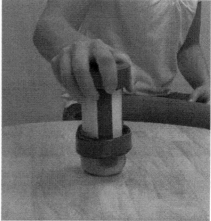

Figure 7.1 & Figure 7.2 The picture on the left (A) refers to "koobing" (using an object to make an impression in another malleable object); the picture on the right (B) refers to "pilking" (using one object to squish another sponge-like object).

young children (Childers et al., 2016; Fernald, Zangl, Portillo, & Marchman, 2008). An eye tracker records the participant's eye movements throughout the presentation; however, it also provides other useful information. Eye tracking can tell you the duration of the participant's first fixation on an area of interest (AOI), as well as how long they attended to an AOI. An AOI is an analytical tool used to define both static and dynamic (moving or transforming) areas in videos, in order to extract descriptive statistics based on eye-tracking metrics for the area defined. They are drawn through Tobii Studio using a drawing tool to click and drag until the shape is covering the area of the video you want to analyze.

In labs that use eye tracking, it is important to have a checklist and protocol available to the researcher when preparing and conducting a session. Eye trackers can be sensitive equipment and it is important to turn on the equipment properly and make sure all cords are connected, especially for mobile eye trackers. Having a pre-session check list and a protocol near the eye-tracking equipment ensures continuity and reduces mistakes during the data collection process.

Eye tracking requires a participant to sit relatively still in front of a monitor and maintain their gaze on a screen. For most adults this is not a difficult task; even if adults do shift their gaze away from the screen, it is fairly easy to redirect their attention in a timely manner. One way to make an eye-tracking session more enjoyable for a child is by referring to the chair in front of the eye tracker as a spaceship seat or a royal throne. Verbal encouragement is also helpful, such as saying, "Look what's happening now!" We find that using a live experimenter who uses a script while the events are shown helps preschoolers attend during the task and engage (with adults, they likely could hear audio stimuli that is prerecorded). If the child is going to be allotted a prize at the end of the experiment, it is also good to remind them that when they are done, they will get to pick out a toy to take home.

Different age groups might also call for different types of seating arrangements in front of the eye tracker. Adults will be able to use a regular desk chair; however, young

Figure 7.3 Photo shows a child pointing at a test during an experimental session with an eye tracker, with an undergraduate experimenter. Photo credit: Trinity University.

children or infants might require a booster seat or may need to be held by their parent, so their eyes are level with the monitor. If held by a parent, it is important that the parent's eyes not be in line with the monitor so the eye tracking is only picking up the infant's eye movements.

Once seated in from the TV monitor and eye tracker (see Figure 7.3), each experimental session starts with a calibration phase. Calibration is a step in the eye-tracking procedure that allows the eye tracker to adjust to a specific participant's eye movements. In the Tobii eye tracker that we use, different age groups use different versions of calibration stimuli. For example, adults might simply follow a small black dot around a screen in a 9-point calibration test. However, young children would more likely use a 5-point calibration test that features an animation of a jumping kitten. It is important to choose the appropriate calibration setting for the age range so that the eye tracker can properly track the participant's eye movements. After calibration is completed (which only takes a few minutes), the experimental session can begin. In that session, in our lab, children are shown a set of events during a learning phase and then a split-screen test trial (see e.g., Childers et al., 2016).

Conclusion

Successfully acquiring at least one language is critical to the development of young children. Our lab focuses on studying how children learn verbs in order to test whether a specific theory about how observers compare examples (the theory of structural alignment) could apply to verb learning. Many developmental word-learning studies have tested children's ability to learn new nouns, with fewer studies asking which mechanisms underlie their ability to learn new verbs. However, learning a new verb can be especially difficult for young children as verbs are used to describe dynamic, transient events rather than concrete objects. In order to understand the cognitive processes that go into learning verbs, it is important to study children's cognition to gain further insight into the way they process events as they learn verbs.

In our research, we use three key procedures to study verb learning, including the use of live events, using iPads to present video stimuli, and including eye tracking to gather quantitative data about where on a screen a child is attending. These three procedures are useful to know about as they can be readily implemented and adapted to other topics in development. They also allow easy data collection through the portability of the iPads, as well as accurate data through the use of both live events and videotaped ones. The live events allow for observed behavior (explicit task), while the eye tracker allows the researcher more insight into where and how long the participant is looking at the stimuli (indirect, implicit measure). Using these methods, developmental researchers can gain insight into the mental processes young children use when learning a new verb.

References

Baldwin, D. A. & Baird, J. A. (2001). Discerning intentions in dynamic human action. *Trends in Cognitive Sciences*, 5(4), 171–178.
Carey, S. & Bartlett, E. (1978). Acquiring a single new word. *Papers and Reports on Child Language Development*, 15, 17–29.
Childers, J. B. & Paik, J. H. (2009). Korean-and English-speaking children use cross-situational information to learn novel predicate terms. *Journal of Child Language*, 36(1), 201–224.
Childers, J. B., Parrish, R., Olson, C. V., Burch, C., Fung, G., & McIntyre, K. P. (2016). Early verb learning: How do children learn how to compare events? *Journal of Cognition and Development*, 17(1), 41–66.
Diener, M. L., Pierroutsakos, S. L., Troseth, G. L., & Roberts, A. (2008). Video versus reality: Infants' attention and affective responses to video and live presentations. *Media Psychology*, 11(3), 418–441.
Fernald, A., Zangl, R., Portillo, A. L., & Marchman, V. A. (2008). Looking while listening: Using eye movements to monitor spoken language. *Developmental Psycholinguistics: On-line Methods in Children's Language Processing*, 44, 97.
Fisher, C. (2002). Structural limits on verb mapping: The role of abstract structure in 2.5-year-olds' interpretations of novel verbs. *Developmental Science*, 5(1), 55–64.
Forbes, J. N. & Farrar, M. J. (1993). Children's initial assumptions about the meaning of novel motion verbs: Biased and conservative? *Cognitive Development*, 8(3), 273–290.
Gentner, D. (1982). Why nouns are learned before verbs: Linguistic relativity versus natural partitioning. In S. A. Kuczaj (Ed.), *Language development* Vol. 2., *Language, Thought and Culture* (pp. 301–334). Hillsdale, NJ: Lawrence Erlbaum Associates.
Gentner, D. & Boroditsky, L. (2001). Individuation, relativity, and early word learning. *Language Acquisition and Conceptual Development*, 3, 215–256.
Gleitman, L. R. (1990). The structural sources of verb meanings. *Language Acquisition*, 1(1), 3–55.
Gleitman, L. R. & Gleitman, H. (1992). A picture is worth a thousand words, but that's the problem: The role of syntax in vocabulary acquisition. *Current Directions in Psychological Science*, 1(1), 31–35.

Hespos, S. J., Saylor, M. M., & Grossman, S. R. (2009). Infants' ability to parse continuous actions. *Developmental Psychology, 45*(2), 575–585.

Holloway, D., Green, L., & Livingstone, S. (2013). Zero to eight: Young children and their internet use. *EU Kids*.

Huttenlocher, J., Smiley, P., & Charney, R. (1983). Emergence of action categories in the child: Evidence from verb meanings. *Psychological Review, 90*(1), 72–93.

Imai, M., Haryu, E., & Okada, H. (2005). Mapping novel nouns and verbs onto dynamic action events: Are verb meanings easier to learn than noun meanings for Japanese children? *Child Development, 76*(2), 340–355.

Kersten, A. W. & Smith, L. B. (2002). Attention to novel objects during verb learning. *Child Development, 73*(1), 93–109.

Landau, B., Smith, L. B., & Jones, S. S. (1988). The importance of shape in early lexical learning. *Cognitive Development, 3*(3), 299–321.

Landau, B., Smith, L. B., & Jones, S. S. (1998). Object shape, object function, and object name. *Journal of Memory and Language, 38*(1), 1–27.

Naigles, L. (1990). Children use syntax to learn verb meanings. *Journal of Child Language, 17*(2), 357–374.

Papafragou, A., Hulbert, J., & Trueswell, J. (2008). Does language guide event perception? Evidence from eye movements. *Cognition, 108*(1), 155–184.

Rattanasone, X. N., Davies, B., Schembri, T., Andronos, F., & Demuth, K. (2016). The iPad as a research tool for the understanding of English plurals by English, Chinese, and other L1 seaking 3- and 4-year-olds. *Frontiers in Psychology, 7*, 1–11. ArticleID: 1773.

Talmy, L. (1975). Semantics and syntax of motion. *Syntax and Semantics, 4*, 181–238.

Tomasello, M. (1992). *First Verbs: A Case Study of Early Grammatical Development*. Cambridge, UK: Cambridge University Press.

Tomasello, M. (2000). Do young children have adult syntactic competence? *Cognition, 74*(3), 209–253.

8 Developmental Robotics for Language Learning

Angelo Cangelosi and Matthew Schlesinger

> Instead of trying to produce a programme to simulate the adult mind, why not rather try to produce one which simulates the child's? If this were then subjected to an appropriate course of education one would obtain the adult brain.
>
> Turing (1950:440)

Introduction to Developmental Robotics

Interdisciplinary approaches to the study of cognitive development benefit from the integration of child psychology experiments with computational and robotics models. Using either simulation models of development in cognitive agents, or robotics models and experiments on the acquisition of specific cognitive functions, it is possible to examine developmental theories. These computational models permit the test and validation of psychology theories by forcing the operationalization of general, and sometimes loosely defined, theoretical concepts into detailed operations which must run on a computer program (Cangelosi & Parisi, 2002). Models capable of replicating known behavioral and cognitive phenomena, including the reproduction of errors and impaired performance, can also be used to make further predictions to revise and refine psychological theories (Pezzulo et al., 2013).

Recent developments in artificial intelligence and cognitive robotics have led to the novel approach of developmental robotics. Developmental robotics is the "interdisciplinary approach to the autonomous design of behavioral and cognitive capabilities in artificial agents (robots) that takes direct inspiration from the developmental principles and mechanisms observed in natural cognitive systems (children)." (Cangelosi & Schlesinger, 2015:4). This approach puts a strong emphasis on the value of constraining the robot's cognitive architecture, and its behavioral and learning performance, into known child psychology theories and data. This then permits the modeling of the developmental succession of qualitative and quantitative stages leading to the acquisition of adult-like cognitive skills.

Developmental robotics has been used for the modeling of a variety of cognitive phenomena, such as intrinsic motivation, motor and perceptual development, social learning, language acquisition, and the learning of abstract knowledge (see Cangelosi & Schlesinger, 2015 for a recent and comprehensive review of the state of the art in this field). Most of these robotics models put a strong emphasis on the interaction between the developing robot and its physical and social environment. Thus, developmental robotics is naturally suited to model embodied and situated cognition for the grounding of cognition (Pezzulo et al., 2013).

This chapter will first introduce some of the methods used in developmental robotics models of cognitive and sensorimotor processes. It describes some of the main robot platforms and simulation tools used for developmental models, and some of the cognitive architectures used to implement the robot's learning and interaction processes. It will then analyze some examples of developmental models of cognition. This will include models of the embodiment strategies in early word learning and models of the role of finger counting and gesture in number learning. These different examples will give an idea of the breadth of the language acquisition processes that can be modelled, and the importance of exploiting the embodied and situated bases of interaction in development. To conclude, some of the application areas of robotics in developmental research and clinical contexts will be considered.

Methods

Baby Robot Platforms and Simulators

The birth of developmental robotics research in the early 2000s has led to the design and production of a variety of platforms for research on baby humanoid robots. Guizzo (2010) and Cangelosi and Schlesinger (2018; Chapter 2) provide a systematic assessment of various "baby" robot platforms, e.g. comparing them along the dimensions of robot appearance and behavioral complexity. Here we will briefly describe two of the most commonly used developmental robotics platforms: iCub and NAO.

The iCub humanoid baby robot (Metta et al., 2010; www.icub.org) is one of the most widely used platforms for developmental robotics research (Figure 8.1). This robot was built with the explicit purpose of supporting cross-laboratory collaborations through the open source licensing model. This has allowed various laboratories working on the iCub to replicate and validate results and integrate existing software modules

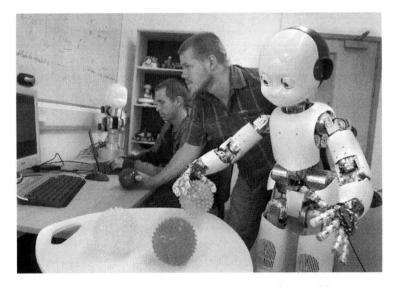

Figure 8.1 The iCub robot in a human–robot interaction setting for word-learning experiments.

and cognitive models for more complex cognitive capabilities. The iCub is 105 cm tall and weighs approximately 22 kilograms. Its body was designed to model that of a 3.5-year-old child. The robot has a total of 53 Degrees of Freedom (DOF), which is a high number of actuators in comparison with related humanoid platforms of similar size. As the robot was designed with the primary aim of studying manipulation and mobility, it has a high number of DOF in the hands and upper torso. The total of 53 DOFs consist of 6 for the head, 14 for the two arms, 18 for the two hands, 3 for the torso, and 12 for the two legs. This platform is one of the most frequently used in developmental robotics research.

The humanoid robot NAO (Gouaillier et al., 2008), originally produced by the French company Aldebaran Robotics (now SoftBank Robotics: www.softbankrobotics.com), is another one of the main humanoid platforms increasingly used in developmental robotics. The widespread use of the NAO is the result of the affordable price for research purposes (approximately $6000 in 2018), but also for its selection since 2008 as the "Standard Platform" for the RobotCup robot soccer competition (robotcup.org). This made the NAO available for research, as well as to prepare for the RobotCup competition, in numerous university labs worldwide. The first NAO (AL-01) was produced in 2005, with subsequent academic editions available for research purposes since 2009. The NAO is a small humanoid robot, 58 cm tall, with a weight of 4.8 kg. The Academic Edition, which is most commonly used in developmental robotics, has a total of 25 DOF. These consist of 2 DOF for the head, 10 for the two arms, 1 for the pelvis, 10 for the two legs and 2 for the two hands. In the version used for the RoboCup standard competition, the robot only has 23 DOF, as the hands are not actuated.

For both the iCub and the NAO, various simulation software packages exist. These permit the carrying out of studies for fast prototyping of the model, or can be used when the access to the physical robot is not possible. More recent development of commercial robot platforms used in cognitive and developmental robotics include the Pepper robot by SoftBank Robotics (a scaled-up version of the NAO robot) and the MIRo robot by Consequential Robotics, an animal-like social robot.

Cognitive Architectures

The term cognitive architecture refers to a general-purpose computational model which captures the essential structure and process of the mind and which can be used as the control architecture in cognitive agents (Sun, 2007). Such a type of architecture would typically include a knowledge-representation system, different memory stores (long-term and short term), knowledge-manipulation processes, and in some cases learning methods. This broad modeling framework and the simultaneous use of the same processes to simulate a variety of cognitive capabilities can lead to the unification of many findings into a single theoretical framework, which can then be subject to further testing and validation (Langley et al, 2009).

Vernon and colleagues (2010) analyze three paradigms for cognitive modeling, each with a set of general cognitive architectures: (i) cognitivist; (ii) emergentist; and (iii) hybrid. The cognitivist paradigm, also known as the symbolic paradigm, is based on the classical view of artificial intelligence (GOFAI: Good Old fashion Artificial Intelligence) and on the information-processing approach in psychology. Such a paradigm states that cognition fundamentally consists of symbolic knowledge representations and of symbol-manipulation phenomena. Computationally, this approach is based on formal logic- and rule-based representation systems and, more recently, on statistical machine learning and probabilistic Bayesian modeling methods. The emergentist paradigm, on the contrary, views cognition as the resulting, emergent self-organizing phenomenon stemming from the interaction of the individual with its physical environment and social world. The emergentist approach is based on a varying family of paradigms, which include connectionist neural networks, dynamical systems, and evolutionary and adaptive behavior systems. Hybrid paradigms try to integrate mechanisms from both cognitivist and emergentist approaches. For example, the CLARION architecture (Sun et al., 2001) combines emergentist neural network modules to represent implicit knowledge, and symbolic production rules to model explicit symbol-manipulation processes.

Cognitive architectures are increasingly being proposed and developed within the field of cognitive and developmental robotics. Here we will focus on a developmental cognitive architecture designed on purpose to model the role of embodiment in word learning: the Epigenetic Robotic Architecture (ERA) (Morse et al., 2010). This cognitive architecture is based on an ensemble of artificial neural networks used to implement learning from multimodal stimuli (visual, speech, postural) and to control the robot's behavior. The architecture consists of multiple maps, each realized via a Self-Organizing Map (SOM; also called Kohonen Map). A SOM is an artificial neural network where the output layer consists of a two-dimensional grid of neurons, called a map. After training, the output neurons self-organize to create a similarity map. The SOMs used in the ERA architecture (color map, shape map, postural map) can be pre-trained respectively to build a categorical similarity representation of color stimuli, of object shapes, and of the robot's own body posture. Another map (speech map) can be used to encode word representations, and this can, for example, be linked to an automatic speech-recognition system which activates the recognized word. The map-to-map links are constituted by Hebbian connections. These connections implement the associative learning between the most active node in each map, activated by visual, postural, and speech stimuli.

The organization and properties of such a robot architecture can be used to operationalize the key developmental principles and mechanisms needed for language development (Morse & Cangelosi, 2017). The SOMs constitute the building blocks of a hierarchical set of interconnected cortical brain areas. Specifically, the use of pre-trained SOMs has the purpose to endow the robot with the pre-linguistic capability to recognize and categorize objects' colors and shapes. The Hebbian connections between the active nodes in each map implement the principle of multimodal associate learning needed to link the name of an object to its visual features (color and/or shape category).

Examples of Developmental Robotics Models

Language Learning

Developmental robotics is especially suited for the modeling of the embodied basis of language learning, as it can exploit the properties of the physical (i.e. body-mediated) interaction with the environment. Experiments with developmental baby robots can simulate the acquisition of the names of objects they see and interact with, and of the names of actions they perform or observe. These words are used to communicate with other robots and human participants.

A prototypical example of a developmental robotics model of child psychology phenomena in language learning is that of Morse et al. (2015). This model directly addresses the issue of embodiment factors, that is, how spatial locations, and their corresponding postural changes, play a key role in infants' word learning. The iCub robot is used for these experiments. The robot is controlled by the ERA cognitive architecture, with the Hebbian associative connections trained online during the experiment. This implements the developmental principle that word–object associations are the direct result of the robot's interaction with its tutor and its physical environment.

The robot experimental procedure follows exactly the one used in child psychology experiments on early word learning, i.e. the Baldwin Task of Samuelson et al. (2011). In this study, the experimenter sits in front of the robot (or the child), with a table where objects are shown and labeled. Every time an object is shown, the robot (as the child) shifts its posture (torso, arms, and gaze) to look at the object, and learns to categorize it according to its visual features such as color and shape. The experimenter starts by showing two novel objects to the robot: (i) the target object, whose name has to be learned, and (ii) the foil object acting as distractor. These objects are shown one at a time, respectively on the left and right location of the table. The experimenter then hides the objects and directs the participant's attention towards the right side where the first (target) object was shown, and says: "This is a Modi". The two objects are shown again, one at a time, as in the initial steps. Finally, both objects are presented simultaneously in a new location at the center of the table, and the robot is asked "Find the Modi". The robot experiments use the ERA cognitive architecture to model the shape- and color-categorization capabilities, via the SOM maps; the posture representation skills, via the poster map; and the associative Hebbian learning between these modalities.

In the combined experimental and robot modeling study of Morse et al. (2015), a set of five experiments with robot participants and four with children are carried out. These use either the default Baldwin object–label mapping tasks (in which names are encountered in the absence of their target) or an Interference task (i.e. when their target is present, but in a location previously associated with a foil). The robot experiments first replicated existing infant tasks and data. Two extra, novel robot experiments were used to test the effects of a second postural change (sitting/standing) in addition to the left/right posture change of the previous experiments. The results of these novel robot experiments show that in the Interference Posture Change Task, when the posture shift is implemented via the sitting/standing dimension during the naming event of the final step, the robot learns and maintains the association between the target object and its "Modi" name. Thus the novel robot experiments predicted that a sitting/standing posture change in the Interference task will allow the child to learn the object–label association.

The results of the follow-up experiments with children replicated the same pattern of results as from the robot studies. In particular, the child data validated the novel robot modeling predictions of both the tasks with posture change and with Interference. This showed that despite spatial location being task-irrelevant in the Interference with Posture Change Task, infants (as predicted with robots) use body-centric spatial contingency over temporal contingency to map the name to the object. Both infants and robots remember the name–object mapping even in new spatial locations. In addition, the analyses of the robot's neural control architecture showed how this memory can emerge. This iCub study demonstrates an exquisite coupling of the body's momentary spatial orientation and internal cognitive operations.

This cognitive architecture has been subsequently applied to other robot and child language-development phenomena. This, for example, includes robot models of the study of mutual exclusivity (Twomey et al., 2016). An extended version of this architecture, which includes a model of the development of a theory of mind in robots, has been tested to model the trust in human–robot interaction (Vinanzi et al., in press).

Number Learning

Number cognition is another key example of the contribution of embodied cognition to the acquisition of abstract, symbol-like manipulation capabilities. Various embodied strategies, such as pointing gestures and object touching, have been shown to facilitate the development of number cognition skills (e.g. Alibali & DiRusso, 1999). Moreover, neurocognitive and psychological data with children and adults show that finger-counting strategies and finger-based representations play an important role in the development of numerical and arithmetical skills and in the learning of number words (e.g. Moeller et al., 2011).

One developmental robotics model of number cognition has focused the contribution of the counting gestures to learning to count (Rucinski et al., 2012), taking direct inspiration from Alibali and DiRusso's (1999) child psychology experiments. The robot's cognitive architecture consists of a simple recurrent network called the Elman Network. The counting task was simulated by requiring the network to output the number words corresponding to the sequential counting of the objects shown in the visual input layer. The robot was trained and tested in several experimental conditions, such as counting with vision only, with natural counting gestures, and with artificial rhythmic gestures. These experiments showed that supplying the network with proprioceptive information on the pointing gestures allowed it to significantly improve the counting accuracy, as compared with the condition of counting using only visual information. Furthermore, contrasting the effects of natural spatio-temporal counting gestures with those of artificial rhythmic ones revealed that it is important that counting gestures are characterized by a spatial correspondence to the counted items.

The developmental robotics paradigm was also used to investigate whether finger counting and the association of number words to each finger can bootstrap the representation of numbers in a developmental robot. This model uses a recurrent artificial neural network to model the learning of associations between finger counting and sequences of numbers (De La Cruz et al., 2014; Di Nuovo et al., 2015). These studies manipulate the coupling between different modalities, as with (i) the Auditory-Only condition, i.e. when the robot solely learns to repeat the sequence of number words ("one", "two", ... up to "ten"), (ii) the Finger-Only condition on learning to open the fingers of the hands in a fixed sequence, and (iii) the Finger+Auditory condition, i.e. with the robot's simultaneously learning of the sequence of acoustic number words and the sequence of moving fingers. Experiments with both the simulated and the physical iCub robot show that learning the number-word sequences together with finger sequencing helps the fast building of the initial representation of numbers in the robot. Robots that only learn the auditor sequences achieve worst performances. Moreover, the neural network's internal representations for these two counting conditions result in qualitatively different patterns of the similarity between numbers. Only the Finger+Auditory sequence learning the neural network represents the relative distance between numbers, which corresponds to the quantitative difference between numbers.

Conclusions

The robotics cognitive architectures and experiments presented in this chapter show the potential of the developmental robotics approach to model a variety of phenomena linking embodiment and symbol-manipulation skills. They range from the modeling of embodiment cues in learning the names of objects to the embodiment strategies of pointing gestures and finger counting in the acquisition of number cognition skills.

The direct link between developmental robotics models and child psychology experiments and data shows the fruitful scientific and technological benefits of a highly interdisciplinary approach to the understanding and modeling of cognition in natural cognitive agents (Cangelosi & Schlesinger, 2018). This also helps the design and implementation of sensorimotor mechanisms in the development of language- and symbol-manipulation skills in robots, for potential use in robotics applications such as robot tutors for children or assistive robotics for autism therapy.

Several pioneering investigations have looked at the translation of robot modeling research, especially those on social interaction, into applications of assistive robotics for children with autism spectrum disorder (ASD) (e.g. Dautenhahn, 1999; Scassellati et al., 2012). These studies show that the use of robots as autism therapy tools provides increased social engagement, spontaneous imitation and turn-taking with another child, and initiation of physical contact with the experimenter (Scassellati et al., 2012). Similar approaches have been applied to other disabilities, such as in the treatment of children with diabetes (Belpaeme et al., 2012) and with motor disabilities (Sarabia & Demiris, 2013). Finally, a key area of application for baby robots is education (Karim et al., 2015). These studies on robot tutors for teaching of disciplines such as mathematics, science, and language have their roots in classical psychology socio-constructivist theories (e.g. Vygotsky, 1980).

References

Alibali, M. W. & DiRusso, A. A. (1999). The function of gesture in learning to count: More than keeping track. *Cognitive Development*, 14(1), 37–56.

Belpaeme, T., Baxter, P., Read, R., Wood, R., Cuayáhuitl, H., et al. (2012). Multimodal child-robot interaction: Building social bonds. *Journal of Human–Robot Interaction*, 1(2), 33–53.

Cangelosi A., Parisi, D. (2002). Computer simulation: A new scientific approach to the study of language evolution. In A. Cangelosi & D. Parisi (Eds.), *Simulating the Evolution of Language*, London: Springer, 3–28.

Cangelosi, A. & Schlesinger, M. (2015). *Developmental Robotics: From Babies to Robots*, Cambridge, MA: MIT Press.

Cangelosi, A., Schlesinger, M. (2018). From babies to robots: The contribution of developmental robotics to developmental psychology. *Child Development Perspectives*, 12(3), 183–188.

Dautenhahn, K. (1999). Robots as social actors: Aurora and the case of Autism. In Proc. CT99, The Third International Cognitive Technology Conference, August, San Francisco.

De La Cruz V. M, Di Nuovo, A., Di Nuovo, S., & Cangelosi A. (2014). Making fingers and words count in a cognitive robot. *Frontiers in Behavioral Neuroscience*, 8, 13.

Di Nuovo, A., De La Cruz, V., & Cangelosi, A. (2015). A deep learning neural network for number cognition: A bi-cultural study with the iCub. In Proceedings of the 2015 Joint IEEE International Conference on Development and Learning and Epigenetic Robotics (ICDL-EpiRob).

Gouaillier, D., Hugel, V., Blazevic, P., Kilner, C., Monceaux, J., Lafourcade, P., Marnier, B., Serre, J., & Maisonnier, B.. (2008). The Nao humanoid: A combination of performance and affordability. *CoRR*: 1.

Guizzo, E. (2010). The robot baby reality matrix. *IEEE Spectrum*, 47(7), 16.

Karim, M. E., Lemaignan, S., & Mondada, F. (2015). A review: Can robots reshape K-12 STEM education? In Advanced Robotics and its Social Impacts (ARSO), 2015 IEEE International Workshop on (pp. 1–8). IEEE.

Langley, P., Laird, J. E., & Rogers, S. (2009). Cognitive architectures: Research issues and challenges. *Cognitive Systems Research*, 10(2), 141–160.

Metta, G., Natale, L., Nori, F., Sandini, G., Vernon, D., Fadiga, L. von Hofsten, C., Rosander, K., Lopes, M., Santos-Victor, J., Bernardino, A., & Montesano, L. (2010). The iCub humanoid robot: An open-systems platform for research in cognitive development. *Neural Networks*, 23(8), 1125–1134.

Moeller, K., Martignon, L., Wessolowski, S., Engel, J., & Nuerk, H.C. (2011). Effects of finger counting on numerical development – the opposing views of neurocognition and mathematics education. *Frontiers in Psychology*, 2(328). 10.3389/fpsyg.2011.00328.

Morse, A., Benitez, V., Belpaeme, T., Smith, L., & Cangelosi, A. (2015). Posture affects how robots and infants map words to objects. *PLoS ONE*, 10, 3. 10.1371/journal.pone.0116012.

Morse, A. & Cangelosi, A. (2017). Why are there developmental stages in language learning? A developmental robotics model of language development. *Cognitive Science*, 7(1), 32–51. 10.1111/cogs.12390.

Morse, A. F., DeGreeff, J., Belpaeme, T., & Cangelosi, A. (2010). Epigenetic Robotics Architecture (ERA). *IEEE Transactions on Autonomous Mental Development*, 2(4), 325–339.

Pezzulo, G., Barsalou, L. W., Cangelosi, A., Fischer, M.H., McRae, K., & Spivey, M. (2013). Computational grounded cognition: A new alliance between grounded cognition and computational modelling. *Frontiers in Psychology*, 6(612), 1–11.

Rucinski, M., Cangelosi, A. & Belpaeme, T. (2012) Robotic model of the contribution of gesture to learning to count. In Proceedings of the IEEE International Conference on Development and Learning and Epigenetic Robotics (ICDL-Epirob 2012) (pp. 1–6).

Samuelson, L. K., Smith, L. B., Perry, L. K., & Spencer, J. P. (2011). Grounding word learning in space. *PLoS ONE*, 6, e28095.

Sarabia, M. & Demiris, Y. (2013). A humanoid robot companion for wheelchair users. In G. Herrmann et al. Ed., *Social robotics: Lecture Notes in Computer Science*. Berlin, Germany: Springer, 432–441.

Scassellati, B., Admoni, H., & Matarić, M. (2012). Robots for use in autism research. *Annual Review of Biomedical Engineering*, 14, 275–294.

Sun, R. (2007). The importance of cognitive architectures: An analysis based on clarion. *Journal of Experimental & Theoretical Artificial Intelligence*, 19(2), 159–193.

Sun, R., Merrill, E., & Peterson, T.. (2001). From implicit skills to explicit knowledge: A bottom-up model of skill learning. *Cognitive Science*, 25(2), 203–244.

Turing, A. M. (1950). Computing machinery and intelligence. *Mind*, 59(236), 433–460.

Twomey, K. E., Morse, A. F., Cangelosi, A., & Horst, J. (2016). Children's referent selection and word learning: Insights from a developmental robotic system. *Interaction Studies*, 17(1), 101–127.

Vernon, D., von Hofsten, C., & Fadiga, L. (2010). *A Roadmap for Cognitive Development in Humanoid Robots: Cognitive Systems Monographs (COSMOS)*, Vol 11, Berlin, Germany: Springer-Verlag Berlin.

Vinanzi, S., Patacchiola, M., Chella, A., & Cangelosi, A. (in press). Would a robot trust you? Developmental robotics model of trust and theory of mind. *Philosophical Transactions of the Royal Society B*.

Vygotsky, L. S. (1980). *Mind in Society: The Development of Higher Psychological Processes*, Cambridge, MA: Harvard University Press.

9 Attachment Theory and Research in a Developmental Framework

Patricia Crittenden and Susan Spieker

Introduction

Attachment theory is at a crossroads. Bowlby proposed attachment as a universal theory of specific enduring protective relationships that promoted survival (Bowlby, 1944, 1969/1982, 1973) whereas Ainsworth described individual differences in attachment relationships (Ainsworth, Blehar, Waters, & Wall, 1978). Bowlby introduced new ways to develop attachment theory and Ainsworth added new methods of testing hypotheses drawn from it. Both generated a series of controversies that explored the parameters of the field and resulted in disputes that led to different approaches to attachment theory. By the end of the twentieth century, two predominant approaches to attachment theory had emerged, each with a theory of attachment and individual differences in attachment. The two approaches used many of the same assessments but with different coding guidelines. Currently, one group is questioning the clinical relevance and reach of attachment, and there is a lively debate regarding individual differences in attachment. This is an excellent time to review the accomplishments and consider the future of attachment theory, research methodology, and clinical applications.

Attachment as a Universal Human Process

Bowlby's Attachment Theory

Possibly, John Bowlby's most important contribution was his method for generating attachment theory. In his clinical work, Bowlby discovered continuities among the life histories of his patients. For example, he observed that many troubled adults had experienced separations from their parents during childhood (Bowlby, 1944) and that, far from being self-generated fantasies, many troubled adults had experienced danger in their early years (Bowlby, 1973). Bowlby sought explanations for such observations in other theories and empirical findings from diverse fields of inquiry. For Bowlby, the theories were psychoanalysis, general systems theory, and ethology; later he added cognitive psychology in the form of information processing (Bowlby, 1980). His central ideas were that (1) attachment was selected through evolution because it increases the probability of survival, (2) behavior is based on representation, and (3) external reality can be represented in more than one way (as opposed to being known directly in a unified manner). Although not a developmental psychologist, Bowlby introduced the notion of developmental 'pathways' to adaptation and maladaptation (as opposed to linear 'trajectories' or the absence of developmental influence on adult outcomes). The crucial methodological takeaway from Bowlby is the importance of integrating ideas from other fields.

Ainsworth's Individual Differences in the Quality of Attachment Relationships

Mary Ainsworth gathered the empirical data that gave credence to attachment theory. Her observations revealed three patterns of attachment relationships; these became the ABC individual differences in infant–mother attachment. Ainsworth's (1967) early work in Uganda used anthropological observation and introduced the concept of the mother as a secure base for her infant. Ainsworth replicated this finding in Baltimore, using periodic home observations across the first year of life. Developmentally, Ainsworth tracked infant and mother behavior across the first year of life; methodologically, she transformed home observations into rating scales of central constructs and created a culminating laboratory assessment, the Strange Situation Procedure (SSP). The SSP became the 'gold standard' for validating most future assessments of attachment. Ainsworth's work established the link between maternal sensitive responsiveness and secure attachment (Ainsworth et al., 1978). Later studies of brief bouts of mother–infant interaction found a weaker than expected association (Bakermans-Kranenburg, van IJzendoorn, & Juffer, 2003; De Wolff & van IJzendoorn, 1997). Possibly, single brief dyadic interactions did not capture the essence of repeated long home observations, specifically, mothers' responses when infants felt anxious. Although Ainsworth's research used normative samples, she noted that mothers must not themselves feel endangered if they were to promote secure attachment in their infants. Ainsworth's work initiated a half-century of research, mostly by developmental psychologists, on individual differences in attachment relationships, especially in infancy and adulthood.

Comparing Two Expanded Approaches to Individual Difference: DMM and ABC+D

The Dynamic-Maturational Model of Attachment and Adaptation (DMM, Crittenden, 1995, 2016) and the ABC+D model (Main, Kaplan, & Cassidy, 1985; Main & Solomon, 1986, 1990) both expand Ainsworth's SSP ABC groups at 11 months to later ages and to a broader range of behavior.[1] Both approaches began in the early 1980s, but Crittenden based the DMM on Ainsworth's participation in the Social Ecology and Development program at the University of Virginia, whereas Main grounded the ABC+D method on Ainsworth's earlier, more behavioral thinking at Johns Hopkins University. Further, the theory around 'D' (disorganization) was completed by the 1990s, whereas the DMM continued to be refined and evolves even now. See Figure 9.1.

Main's ABC+D samples were normative to advantaged socioeconomic status, whereas the first DMM samples had low socioeconomic status and high rates of child abuse and neglect. The DMM focus on adaptation as compared to the ABC+D focus on security may reflect the differences in the development samples.

A debate on the relevance of the DMM and ABC+D approaches to theory, assessment, and application appeared in a series of published articles (in order of publication: van IJzendoorn, Bakermans-Kranenburg, Steele, & Granqvist, 2018; Crittenden & Spieker, 2018; Spieker & Crittenden, 2018; van IJzendoorn, Steele, & Granqvist, 2018). The issues that differentiate the two approaches include theory, methodology, empirical findings, and applications. See Table 9.1.

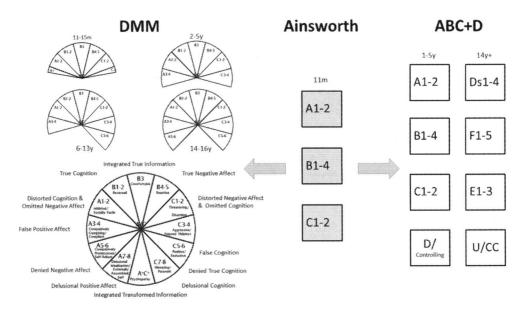

Figure 9.1 Ainsworth's original model of individual differences in attachment and the DMM and ABC+D expansions. (Used with permission)

Table 9.1 Comparing DMM and ABC+D theories on theory, development, structure of the models, assessment, empirical results, and applications

Attributes	DMM	ABC+D
Theory		
Set-goal of attachment	Adaptation, including reproduction in adulthood	Security
Emphasis	Coping with danger	Benefits of security
Focus/applications	Mental health, child protection, criminality	Child–mother security
Development		
Infancy	Strategy for safety with caregiver	Security
2–5 years	Strategies for safety & hierarchy with caregivers	Security
6–Puberty	Recognition of own strategy & motivations (self)	6 years: security
Adolescence	Integration of sexual desire with attachment	Not articulated
Adulthood	Management of multiple attachment relationships	Transmission to next generation
Structure of model		
Categories or dimensions	2-dimensional array yielding 3 gradated categories	4 discrete categories

(Continued)

Table 9.1 (Cont.)

Attributes	DMM	ABC+D
Number of categories: infancy	6, plus depression modifier	4 or 2: usually analyzed as secure/anxious
Number of categories: older	Up to 21, + trauma & arousal; unique to each person	4 or 2 (with new labels) analyzed as secure/anxious
Cross-generation continuity	Interaction of maturation, birth order, & events	Continuity
Assessment methods[*]		
SSP (enacted): assess	Child's self-protective strategy	Infant/child pattern of attachment
SSP (enacted): film	Parent & child, alternating wide-angle and close-up	Infant/child in close-up perspective
SSP (enacted): classify	Parent & child patterns	Infant/child rating scales
School-age–puberty	SAA: enacted, imaged, discourse	6-Year Reunion: enacted
School-age – puberty		CAI: rated discourse
AAI (discourse): interview	More danger questions	Wishes for child
AAI (discourse): classify	6 coded memory systems	Rating scales like SSP
Empirical results		
Specificity of risk	~1–6% security in risk group	12–30% 'false secures' in risk group
Breadth of security	~1/3 of normative sample	~2/3 of normative sample
Clinical findings	Diagnostic sub-patterns (ABC, trauma, arousal)	Risk has higher D (& unresolved D)
Cross-classification: normative	50% agreement in normative samples	50% agreement in normative samples
Cross-classification: risk/clinical	~30% agreement in risk samples – more risk	~30% in risk samples – more secure
Applications		
Person-specific clinical use	Mental health & forensic use (SSP & AAI)	SSP 'disorganization' is not suitable
Diagnostic model	General & Family Functional Formulations	Frightened/frightening → Disorganized
Treatment programs	Prefer individual formulation for treatment	Suitable for treatment programs
Research	Programmatic: danger → strategies → treatment	Risk conditions, transmission & treatment

[*] Limited to methods with 5+ validating studies and 3 or more categorical outcomes.

Core Methodologies Used by Attachment Researchers

Attachment researchers have relied on four primary methods to study attachment: *anthropological observation* (Ainsworth, 1967; Ainsworth et al., 1978), *structured observation with increasing threat* (SSP, Ainsworth, et al., 1978), *picture cards of increasing threat* (Klagsbrun & Bowlby, 1976), and *interviews with increasingly threatening questions* (Adult Attachment Interview (AAI), George, Kaplan, & Main 1984, 1996).

Anthropological observation best promotes the discovery of new experiences and processes; in this case, Ainsworth's discovery of the ABC patterns of individual differences in attachment. We found only three other studies with similar home observations (DiLalla & Crittenden, 1990; Grossmann, Grossmann, Spangler, Suess, & Unzner, 1985; Waters & Deane, 1985); such observation is labor-intensive, and its interpretation requires the researcher to extract meaning from an extremely cluttered field (as opposed to testing focused hypotheses). For Waters and Deane's Attachment Q-Sort (ASQ, 1985), the necessary observation period was approximately 6–8 hours on two separate days, thus greatly exceeding the 20-minute SSP. The lengthy observation time probably reflects the time needed for a threat to occur spontaneously in children's homes. The result was a continuum of security that was only modestly related to SSP outcomes (van IJzendoorn, Vereijken, Bakermans-Kranenburg, & Riksen-Walraven, 2004).

Classifying SSPs involved writing a narrative of the procedure before applying several rating scales (which were developed *from* the narratives *after* the first sample was classified). Such narratives formed the basis of the DMM and ABC+D expansions of Ainsworth's ABC model. Again, unstructured observation led to discoveries. The Six-Year Reunion (Main & Cassidy, 1988), which has declined in use, illustrates the developmental limits of using separation to elicit protective strategies in middle childhood.

Picture card assessment lacked a method for interpretation (e.g., Klagsbrun & Bowlby, 1976); the School-aged Assessment of Attachment (SAA, Crittenden, 1997–2005) used a specified combination of narrative and discourse techniques to develop a procedure suited to the skills and concerns of children in middle childhood. The discovery from the first set of transcribed SAAs involved identifying how children imbedded 'forbidden' information about danger in stories about *other* children. These clues demonstrated children's use of connotative language to represent and communicate unacceptable thoughts. Crittenden's training and experience as a teacher for children in middle childhood probably informed her recognition of what children experienced as threatening and how they expressed their understanding.

The Adult Attachment Interview (AAI, George et al., 1984, 1996) was used by both the ABC+D and DMM approaches. The ABC+D 'Berkeley' method for classifying AAIs operationalized the hypothesis of mother-to-infant continuity of the same pattern of attachment and used rating scales that were analogous to those in the SSP (Main & Goldwyn, 1984; Main, Goldwyn, & Hesse, 2003). By limiting the outcomes in adulthood to those of infancy, the Berkeley method sometimes created dilemmas, e.g., 'derogation' being defined as Type A whereas factor analyses found it to be indicative of Type C (Roisman, Fraley, & Belsky, 2007). The ABC+D classifications of the AAI lost power for differentiating among adults by constraining the outcome classifications to those shown by infants, rather than exploring the range of responses.

The DMM used a different approach. Crittenden and her colleagues focused on high-risk adults, annotating anything unusual in the discourse, and then seeking evidence of a difference in the actual history of the speakers (known from outside the AAI). When coders found similar discourse markers in several transcripts, Crittenden added them to the set of Berkeley discourse markers and clustered them by memory systems (Schacter & Tulving, 1994) rather than through rating scales (Crittenden & Landini, 2011). It is probably relevant to the DMM discourse analysis that Crittenden's original training was in literature, including the study of grammar and connotative language. Although one outcome was the uncertainty of an ever-emergent method, the advantage was an increasing fit of the DMM assessments to people with the maladaptation of child protection, mental health treatment, and prison populations.

Our takeaway ideas from this review of attachment methods include:

1. Use of the same assessment procedures facilitated comparison of alternate approaches.
2. Observational methods are most productive when used in an open-ended manner.
3. Threat is needed to elicit attachment patterns/strategies.
4. The assumption of mother-to-infant matches in the pattern of attachment eliminates a developmental perspective.
5. Exclusive use of rating scales to condense data reduces the possibility of discovering new patterns.
6. Expertise from outside of attachment or even psychology may improve the understanding of developmental processes (cf. Bowlby).

As we look to the future of research in attachment, we keep these conclusions in mind and seek new methods to expand our knowledge.

Moving Forward: Hot Topics and New Methodologies for the Future

Based on the breadth and depth of DMM theory, as shown in Table 9.1, we use the DMM as we look to the future of attachment theory and methodology in a developmental context. The focus is on adaptation (with less emphasis on security), protective relationships (rather than individual functioning), assessing which strategy(ies) individuals use (rather than categorizing people by attachment type), and the contribution of context to an individual's selection of adaptive strategies (rather than implicitly assuming safe contexts). We note that DMM theory is inherently developmental, with attachment changing in response to maturation (a bio-genetic contribution to development) and to the different dangers around which attachment strategies become organized at different ages (a sociocultural contribution to development). To illustrate the potential of attachment theory to address current problems, we suggest applications within several domains.

Theory represents reality; its constructs represent aspects of reality. We address representations clustered as five levels of complexity: genes, biological structures, psychological processes, interpersonal processes, and sociocultural processes. Although scientists usually train in one of these (or, more accurately, a subspecialty within one of these), none functions independently of the others. Genes define the biochemical means of development, but without biological organs, their potential cannot be realized. The biological organs exist in an environment (of nutrition, caregiving, etc.) that shapes the genetic influence on the development of the organs, yielding individual differences even when the genes are identical copies of one another. The organs, then, also represent reality albeit at a more complex level. If one considers the brain as one such organ, it represents both the body of which it is part and also the external environment. One can say that the brain represents the intersection of self and non-self in the form of activated neural networks and, further, that the networks are in a constant process of change. These neural networks, in each individual, become the psychology of that person's disposed behavior. Behavior, however, rarely occurs in isolation; instead, it affects other humans at the relational level and, reciprocally, is affected by the behavior of other humans. Thus, relationships are another level of representation of adaptation.

Finally, in this condensed representational model, the outer context of cultural groupings represents the opportunities and limitations placed on the development and adaptation of groups of people (ranging from basic biological resources such as climate to human resources such as education and laws). See Figure 9.2. Research is needed that expands attachment theory in each of these representational domains using modern technology.

Genetic Contributions to Attachment and Individual Differences in Attachment

Attachment in birds and mammals has a genetic basis. Identifying the genes would be useful. Many have hypothesized that individual differences in attachment are also genetically based, in the form of temperament or differential susceptibility to environmental influences (Bakermans-Kranenburg & van IJzendoorn, 2007; Klein Velderman, Bakermans-Kranenburg, Juffer, & van IJzendoorn, 2006). Again, specifying the genes and eliminating other explanations would be useful.

Neurological Evidence of Individual Differences in Attachment

Both functional neurological imaging and assays of neurotransmitters have demonstrated differences between secure and insecure individuals (Strathearn, Fonagy, Amico, & Montague, 2009) and those with and without psychological trauma (Kim, Fonagy, Allen, & Strathearn, 2014). Research needs to elucidate the indicators of the types of insecurity, together with how much variance in functioning the categories account for. Having this information might augment the accuracy of psychological assessments of attachment and have implications for identifying which individuals need similar treatment approaches.

Psychological Representation of Individual Differences in Attachment

Twenty-five years ago, Crittenden identified exposure to danger as the basis for children developing self-protective attachment strategies (Crittenden, 1992). Later ACEs (adverse childhood events) were associated with child and adult dysfunction (Felitti, 2009). The

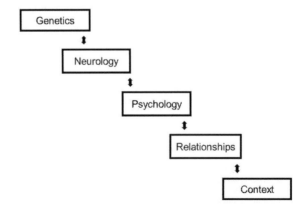

Figure 9.2 Multiple forms of representation of the relation of self to context (used with permission).

crucial difference in these two conceptualizations is that Crittenden proposed that dangers were most likely to lead to psychological trauma *when* children were neither protected nor comforted by an attachment figure during the event and, later, not guided to reconsider and reorganize their representation of the event as they matured. That is, as children's zone of proximal development changed and when they received support from their attachment figures, children should be able to accommodate the traumatizing event more adaptively (Crittenden, 1997). Further, successful representation of danger should predispose more adaptive responses to future threats that were similar to the early threat (Crittenden, 1992, 2016).

Relational Representations of Individual Differences in Attachment

Attachment is specific to relationships, not individuals. For example, children have different attachments to their fathers and mothers (Main & Weston, 1981) and siblings have different attachments to the same parent (Farnfield, 2017; Kozlowska & Elliott, 2016; Ward, Vaughn, & Robb, 1988). More work is needed on variation within families and on individuals' potential to acquire new strategies in new relationships or at developmentally sensitive periods (for example, the preoperational shift, entry to school, puberty, and the transition to adulthood.) Knowing the conditions that facilitate change could be of great use to clinicians hoping to reduce maladaptive behavior.

Context-based Variation in the Distribution of Individual Differences in Attachment Strategies

Nations and population groups within nations differ in exposure to danger and their history of such exposure. Comparison of distributions of protective strategies within groupings that have experienced similar dangers could clarify the adaptive value of different strategies in different contexts (Pleshkova & Muhamedrahimov, 2010; True, Pisani, & Oumar, 2001; Valenzuela, 1997). Understanding context-based variations could help to focus treatment on reducing the danger or changing perceptions of danger as best fit each troubled person's situation.

Conclusion: Multiple Methodologies Suited to Multiple Domains of Analysis

As work in attachment moves from its 'secure base' in methodologies based on Ainsworth's SSP, there is a temptation to move toward biological methods, as if they provided the most accurate information. Our understanding is that methods in each domain reveal some aspects of human behavior while being silent or even misleading regarding others. Methods provide the clearest understanding when gathered together and integrated to correct misinformation. The yield from a broadly based integrative process will be a clearer understanding – that awaits the next input of new information.

Specifically, genetic information defines the range of human possibility; nevertheless, there are too many layers of influence beyond genes for genetic information to predict behavior. Neurological information indicates which genetic possibilities were actualized, but today's technology cannot predict the enactment of particular behaviors at particular moments. Moreover, with today's technology, individual differences are extracted by humans who identify patterns within the precise technological output – thus gaining meaning while losing precision. Researchers infer psychological information from behavior or self-reports; psychological information is more precise about probable future behavior than genetic or neurological information, but less clear about the processes leading to responses. Interpersonal relational information adds greatly to our ability to predict actual behavior but is vulnerable to a misunderstanding regarding the nature of relationships. Again, there seems to be a trade-off between precision and meaningfulness. Contextual/cultural methods describe populations, but at the cost of omitting individual differences. Considerable work exists on socioeconomic status, but other cultural conditions could prove informative.

Researchers in attachment would be well advised to use a greater variety of linked methodologies, seeking a confluence of meaning among the streams of input. Doing so will likely result in discarding of misguided ideas and clarification of what is known and not known. This clarification, in turn, will promote the application of knowledge to people who suffer from the effects of unprotected and uncomforted exposure to danger.

We conclude that attachment research could benefit from an infusion of varied methodologies, but should not assume that any one or two could replace the others. Further, the omission of many assessments from Table 9.1 for lack of five published validation studies suggests the need for more systematic validation, through many methods and different laboratories, before trained experts apply assessments in forensic and clinical settings. Longitudinal studies are needed to chart developmental pathways; existing longitudinal studies classified with the ABC+D method might benefit from reclassifications with DMM methods. In addition to testing precise hypotheses and refining existing assessments, researchers should consider hypotheses and methods that yield evidence beyond the boundaries of existing theory.

Rethinking the Development of Theory

Kuhn and Popper created a paradigm shift in how we think about theory development (Notturno, 1984). A central notion was that theory could not be proved, but its hypotheses can be disproven. This idea seems to assume a static form of theory, one that can be elucidated in the form of constructs and untestable postulates that lead to hypotheses that can be tested. That works well for mathematically structured experimental sciences but is uncomfortable for the life sciences, particularly human science.

Two unique aspects of the life sciences are that they are never static and change is always systemic. Life unfolds according to principles, but the more complex the life form is, the less predefined are the myriad unique outcomes. Because the evolutionary process has not stopped, its description cannot be complete.

For theories of individual differences in human adaptation, of which the DMM is one, this has two important implications. First, the theory itself is part of a systemic process of observation and description of events in which each iteration opens new vistas, changing both what can be observed and the description of what was observed. In this sense, *theories* of individual differences are always evolving. When they cease to evolve, they accumulate error, until they reach the point of no longer being useful (e.g., Granqvist et al., 2017). Second, hypotheses and the testing of hypotheses become comparative rather than definitive. One hypothesis is not supported and another rejected. Instead, a hypothesis is supported by accounting for relatively more of the evidence compared to another hypothesis or by proving relatively more useful for a particular application than another hypothesis, or both.

Crossroads mark moments when a pathway can change. We propose that another shift in understanding theory development is needed to describe individual differences in ontology, including the development of attachment across the lifespan. The DMM holds the potential to generate hypotheses about universal developmental processes that promote the adaptation of individuals, families, and cultural groups and about processes to ameliorate cases of maladaptation. Richer theory, together with a range of methodologies, can return work in the field of attachment to its roots in seeking to understand and help people in troubled relationships.

Note

1 We excluded social psychology self-report approaches because they focus primarily on adulthood and do not usually address development. For a discussion, see Pace and Bufford (2018).

References

Ainsworth, M. D. S. (1967). *Infancy in Uganda: Infant Care and the Growth of Love*. Baltimore: Johns Hopkins University Press.

Ainsworth, M. D. S., Blehar, M. C., Waters, E., & Wall, S. (1978). *Patterns of Attachment: A Psychological Study of the Strange Situation*. Hillsdale, NJ: Lawrence Erlbaum Associates, Inc.

Bakermans-Kranenburg, M. J. & van Ijzendoorn, M. H. (2007). Research Review: genetic vulnerability or differential susceptibility in child development: The case of attachment. *Journal of Child Psychology and Psychiatry*, 48(12), 1160–1173. doi:10.1111/j.1469-7610.2007.01801.x.

Bakermans-Kranenburg, M. J., van IJzendoorn, M. H., & Juffer, F. (2003). Less is more: Meta-analyses of sensitivity and attachment interventions in early childhood. *Psychological Bulletin*, 129(2), 195–215. doi: 10.1037/0033-2909.129.2.195.

Bowlby, J. (1944). Forty-four juvenile thieves: Their characters and homelife. *International Journal of Psycho-Analysis*, 25, 19–52.

Bowlby, J. (1969/1982). *Attachment and Loss: Vol 1. Attachment*. New York: Basic Books.

Bowlby, J. (1973). *Attachment and Loss: Vol 2. Separation: Anxiety and Anger*. New York: Basic Books.

Bowlby, J. (1980). *Attachment and Loss: Vol 3. Loss: Sadness and Depression*. New York: Basic Books.

Crittenden, P. M. (1992). Children's strategies for coping with adverse home environments. *International Journal of Child Abuse and Neglect*, 16, 329–343.

Crittenden, P. M. (1995). Attachment and psychopathology. In S. Goldberg, R. Muir, & J. Kerr (Eds.), *John Bowlby's Attachment Theory: Historical, Clinical, and* social significance (pp. 367–406). New York: The Analytic Press.

Crittenden, P. M. (1997). Toward an integrative theory of trauma: A dynamic maturation approach. In D. Cicchetti & S. Toth (Eds.), *The Rochester Symposium on Developmental Psychopathology* (pp. 33–84). Rochester, NY: University of Rochester Press.

Crittenden, P. M. (1997–2005). School-age Assessment of Attachment Coding Manual. Unpublished manuscript, Miami, FL, available from the author.

Crittenden, P. M. (2016). *Raising Parents: Attachment, Representation, and Treatment* (2nd ed.). London: Routledge.

Crittenden, P. M. & Landini, A. (2011). *Assessing Adult Attachment: A Dynamic-Maturational Approach to Discourse Analysis*. New York: W.W. Norton.

Crittenden, P. M. & Spieker, S. J. (2018). Dynamic-Maturational Model of Attachment and Adaptation versus ABC+D assessments of attachment in child protection and treatment: Reply to van IJzendoorn, Bakermans, Steele, & Granqvist (2018). *Infant Mental Health Journal*, 39(6), 647–651. doi: 10.1002/imhj.21750.

De Wolff, M. S. & van IJzendoorn, M. H. (1997). Sensitivity and attachment: A meta-analysis on parental antecedents of infant attachment. *Child Development*, 68(4), 571–591. doi: 10.1111/j.1467-8624.1997.tb04218.x.

DiLalla, D. L. & Crittenden, P. M. (1990). Dimensions in maltreated children's behavior: A factor analytic approach. *Infant Behavior and Development*, 13, 439–460.

Farnfield, S. (2017). Fix my child: The importance of including siblings in clinical assessments. *Clinical Child Psychology and Psychiatry*, 22, 421–435. doi: 10.1177/1359104517707995.

Felitti, V. J. (2009). Adverse childhood experiences and adult health. *Academy of Pediatrics*, 9(3), 131–132. doi: 10.1016/j.acap.2009.03.001.

George, C., Kaplan, N., & Main, M. (1984). *Adult Attachment Interview Protocol*. Berkeley, CA: University of California at Berkeley.

George, C., Kaplan, N., & Main, M. (1996). *Adult Attachment Interview Protocol* (3rd ed.). Berkeley, CA: University of California at Berkeley.

Granqvist, P., Sroufe, L. A., Dozier, M., Hesse, E., Steele, M., van IJzendoorn, M., ... Duschinsky, R. (2017). Disorganized attachment in infancy: A review of the phenomenon and its implications for clinicians and policy-makers. *Attachment & Human Development*, 19(6), 534–558. doi: 10.1080/14616734.2017.1354040.

Grossmann, K., Grossmann, K. E., Spangler, G., Suess, G., & Unzner, L. (1985). Maternal sensitivity and newborns' orientation responses as related to quality of attachment in northern Germany. *Monographs of the Society for Research in Child Development*, 50(1–2), 233–256.

Kim, S., Fonagy, P., Allen, J., & Strathearn, L. (2014). Mothers' unresolved trauma blunts amygdala response to infant distress. *Social Neuroscience*, 9, 352.

Klagsbrun, M. & Bowlby, J. (1976). Responses to separation from parents: A clinical test for young children. *British Journal of Projective Psychology & Personality Study*, 21, 7–27.

Klein Velderman, M., Bakermans-Kranenburg, M. J., Juffer, F., & van IJzendoorn, M. H. (2006). Effects of attachment-based interventions on maternal sensitivity and infant attachment: Differential susceptibility of highly reactive infants. *Journal of Family Psychology*, 20(2), 266–274. doi: 10.1037/0893-3200.20.2.266.

Kozlowska, K. & Elliott, B. (2016). Don't forget the siblings: School-aged siblings of children presenting to mental health services show at-risk patterns of attachment. *Clinical Child Psychology and Psychiatry*, 1–15. doi: 10.1177/1359104516653993.

Main, M. & Cassidy, J. (1988). Categories of response to reunion with the parent at age 6: Predictable from infant attachment classifications and stable over a 1-month period. *Developmental Psychology*, 24(3), 415–426. doi: 0.1037/0012-1649.24.3.415.

Main, M. & Goldwyn, R. (1984). *Adult Attachment Scoring and Classification System*. Berkeley, CA: University of California at Berkeley.

Main, M., Goldwyn, R., & Hesse, E. (2003). *Adult attachment Scoring and Classification System*. Version 7.2. Berkeley, CA: University of California at Berkeley.

Main, M., Kaplan, N., & Cassidy, J. (1985). Security in infancy, childhood, and adulthood: A move to the level of representation. In I. Bretherton & E. Waters (Eds.) Growing points in attachment theory and research. *Monographs of the Society for Research in Child Development*, 50(51–52, Serial No. 209), 66–104.

Main, M. & Solomon, J. (1986). Discovery of a new, insecure disorganized/disoriented attachment pattern. In T. B. Brazelton & M. Yogman (Eds.), *Affective Development in Infancy* (pp. 95–124). Norwood, NJ: Ablex.

Main, M. & Solomon, J. (1990). Procedures for identifying infants as disorganized/disoriented during the Ainsworth strange situation. In M. T. Greenberg (Ed.), *Attachment in the Preschool Years: Theory, Research, and Intervention* (pp. 121–160). Chicago, IL: University of Chicago Press.

Main, M. & Weston, D. R. (1981). The quality of the toddler's relationship to mother and to father: Related to conflict behavior and the readiness to establish new relationships. *Child Development*, 52(3), 932–940.

Notturno, M. A. (1984). The Popper/Kuhn debate: Truth and two faces of relativism. *Psychological Medicine*, 14(2), 273–289.

Pace, A. L. & Bufford, R. K. (2018). Assessing adult attachment: Relation and validity of two Dynamic-Maturational approaches. *Interpersona*, 12(3), 232–252.

Pleshkova, N. L. & Muhamedrahimov, R. J. (2010). Quality of attachment in St Petersburg (Russian Federation): A sample of family-reared infants. *Clinical Child Psychology and Psychiatry*, 15(3), 355–362. doi: 10.1177/1359104510365453.

Roisman, G. I., Fraley, R. C., & Belsky, J. (2007). A taxometric study of the Adult Attachment Interview. *Developmental Psychology*, 43(3), 675–686. doi: 10.1037/0012-1649.43.3.675.

Schacter, D. L. & Tulving, E. (Eds.) (1994). *Memory systems*. Cambridge, MA: The MIT Press.

Spieker, S. J. & Crittenden, P. M. (2018). Can attachment inform decision-making in child protection and forensic settings? *Infant Mental Health Journal*, 39(6), 625–641. doi: 10.1002/imhj.21746.

Strathearn, L., Fonagy, P., Amico, J. A., & Montague, P. R. (2009). Adult attachment predicts maternal brain and peripheral oxytocin response to infant cues. *Neuropsychopharmacology*, 34, 2655–2666. doi: 10.1038/np.2009.103.

True, M. M., Pisani, L., & Oumar, F. (2001). Infant–mother attachment among the Dogon of Mali. *Child Development*, 72(5), 1451–1466. doi.org/10.1111/1467-8624.00359.

Valenzuela, M. (1997). Maternal sensitivity in a developing society: The context of urban poverty and infant chronic undernutrition. *Developmental Psychology*, 33(5), 845–855. doi:org/10.1037/0012-1649.33.5.845.

van IJzendoorn, M. H., Bakermans, J. J. W., Steele, M., & Granqvist, P. (2018). Diagnostic use of crittenden's attachment measures in family court is not beyond a reasonable doubt. *Infant Mental Health Journal*, 39(6), 642–646. doi: 10.1002/imhj.21747.

van IJzendoorn, M. H., Steele, M., & Granqvist, P. (2018). On exactitude in science: A map of the empire the size of the empire. *Infant Mental Health Journal*, 39(6), 652–655. doi: 10.1002/imhj.21751.

van IJzendoorn, M. H., Vereijken, C. M., Bakermans-Kranenburg, M. J., & Riksen-Walraven, J. M. (2004). Assessing attachment security with the Attachment Q Sort: Meta-analytic evidence for the validity of the observer AQS. *Child Development*, 75(4), 1188–1213. doi: 10.1111/j.1467-8624.2004.00733.x.

Ward, M. J., Vaughn, B. E., & Robb, M. D. (1988). Social-emotional adaptation and infant-mother attachment in siblings: Role of the mother in cross-sibling consistency. *Child Development*, 59(3), 643–651. doi: 10.2307/1130564.

Waters, E. & Deane, K. (1985). Defining and assessing individual differences in attachment relationships: Q-methodology and the organization of behavior in infancy and early childhood. In I. Bretherton & E. Waters (Eds.), Growing points of attachment theory and research. *Monographs of the Society for Research in Child Development*, 50(Serial No. 209), 41–65.

10 Social Ecological Influences

The Role of Residential Neighborhoods in the Development of Children and Youth

Margaret O'Brien Caughy

Introduction

A cornerstone of developmental theory is recognition of the importance of ecological contexts in shaping the development of children and youth. Bronfenbrenner's bioecological model posits that development occurs as a result of "progressively more complex reciprocal interactions between an active, evolving biopsychological human organism and the persons, objects, and symbols in its immediate environment" (Bronfenbrenner & Ceci, 1994) (p. 572) and that these interactions are influenced by both proximal factors, such as parents and peers, and more distal factors such as school and community contexts and broader societal norms. Bronfenbrenner's focus on the role of ecological context in development has stimulated decades of research focusing on a range of contexts including families, schools, and communities. In this chapter, we focus specifically on neighborhood influences on children. Research on neighborhood influences has increased exponentially in recent years; the number of publications in developmental science in the last three years that included a focus on neighborhoods increased approximately 700% compared to a similar period 20 years ago.

Advancing our understanding of how neighborhood contexts affect development requires scientists to employ appropriate measurement and design approaches. However, recent advances in assessing neighborhood influences are not often represented in developmental science research. In this chapter, we briefly review the extant literature on how neighborhood context influences developmental outcomes, with an emphasis on how neighborhood effects differ across developmental periods. Methods for assessing neighborhood characteristics are described including secondary data sources, observational methods, and survey methods, and we highlight recent innovations in neighborhood assessment methods such as the use of mobile technology and Google Earth. Design and data analysis challenges for studying ecological influences are discussed in depth. The chapter concludes with recommendations for how developmental scientists can incorporate innovative measurement and design approaches into their research to further knowledge of ecological influences on the development of children and youth.

Summary of Neighborhood Influences on Development

The unique influence of neighborhood context on the development and well-being of children and youth is documented for a wide range of domains as well as across developmental periods. Although researchers have documented poorer cognitive and academic outcomes related to higher levels of neighborhood risk (Caughy, Hayslett-McCall, & O'Campo, 2007; Duncan, Brooks-Gunn, & Klebanov, 1994; Entwisle, Alexander, & Olson, 1994; Leventhal & Brooks-Gunn, 2004), the majority of research has focused on socioemotional and physical outcomes. Living in neighborhoods characterized by higher levels of concentrated economic disadvantage and negative social climate is associated with higher level of behavior problems including internalizing problems, externalizing problems, and conduct disorders for both preschool-aged children (Caughy, Nettles, O'Campo, & Lohrfink, 2006; Caughy, O'Campo, & Nettles, 2008; Flouri & Sarmadi, 2016; Kohen, Brooks-Gunn, Leventhal, & Hertzmann, 2002; Lima, Caughy, Nettles, & O'Campo, 2010) and school-aged children (Attar, Guerra, & Tolan, 1994; Beyers, Bates, Pettit, & Dodge, 2003; Boyle & Lipman, 2002; Schwartz & Gorman, 2003). Research on neighborhood effects in adolescence is dominated by a focus on risk-taking and delinquency outcomes (Ge, Brody, Conger, Simons, & Murry, 2002; Ray, Thornton, Frick, Steinberg, & Cauffman, 2016; Reardon, Brennan, & Buka, 2002; Roche, Ensminger, & Cherlin, 2007; Roche & Leventhal, 2009; Tolan, Gorman-Smith, & Henry, 2003; Vries, Peter, Graaf, & Nikken, 2016).

Mechanisms of Neighborhood Effects

Early research on neighborhoods focused on parenting (Furstenberg, 1993; Klebanov, Brooks-Gunn, & Duncan, 1994; Simons, Johnson, Conger, & Lorenz, 1997) as well as peer relationships (for adolescents) (Crane, 1991; Kupersmidt, Griesler, DeRosier, Patterson, & Davis, 1995; Simons, Johnson, Beaman, Conger, & Whitbeck, 1996) as the mediating mechanism of neighborhood effects on children and youth. For example, it was hypothesized that risky neighborhoods were associated with higher levels of harsh and inconsistent parenting, which in turn put children and youth at risk for poor behavioral and academic outcomes. With regards to peers, it was suggested risky neighborhoods increased the exposure of adolescents to deviant peer influences, thereby increasing the likelihood of youth involvement in risky behavior. However, as neighborhood research accumulated, it became evident these more proximal factors did not predominantly play a mediating role for neighborhood effects but rather that the role of parenting and peers often differed depending on neighborhood conditions. Roche and Leventhal (2009) suggested three ways in which neighborhoods could interact with more proximal relationships: amplified disadvantages (the impact of poor parenting or exposure to deviant peers is magnified in risky neighborhoods); amplified advantages (the impact of positive parenting is magnified in low risk neighborhoods); and family compensatory effects (supportive parenting has a larger effect on youth outcomes in the context of risky neighborhood conditions).

By and large, empirical evidence supports both an "amplified disadvantages" perspective and a "family compensatory effects" model. For example, parenting characterized by high levels of nurturance, support, and engagement is more strongly associated with positive child outcomes in risky neighborhoods (Roche, Ellen, & Astone, 2005; Roy, McCoy, & Raver, 2014), and harsh, inconsistent parenting is associated with worse outcomes in risky neighborhoods relative to less risky neighborhoods (Roche & Leventhal, 2009; Simons et al., 2002). Similar compensatory relations have been found for peer influences, with the salutatory impact of positive peer relations magnified in disadvantaged neighborhoods (Mason et al., 2017).

Recent neighborhood research has focused on the role of child self-regulation ability as both a mediator and potential moderator of neighborhood effects on development. Roy et al. (2014) reported that moving from a low poverty to a high poverty neighborhood was associated with increased dysregulation among 5th grade children. Exposure to neighborhood crime and violence, specifically, has been associated with disruptions in attentional processes and self-regulation (McCoy, Raver, & Sharkey, 2015; Sharkey, Tirado-Strayer, Papachristos, & Raver, 2012). These findings align with earlier research that neighborhood violence is associated with higher levels of externalizing problems (Attar et al., 1994; Schwartz & Gorman, 2003) as these behavior problems reflect a fundamental deficit in self-regulation. Poor self-regulation also appears to magnify the impact of family and community risk factors (King & Mrug, 2018) as well as limiting the benefits of positive family and community supports (Fine, Mahler, Steinberg, Frick, & Cauffman, 2017).

Neighborhoods and Child Physical Health

Research on the impact of neighborhood conditions on child physical health, particularly child physical activity and child overweight/obesity, is considerably more extensive and well-developed than corresponding research on behavioral and academic outcomes. There are several reasons for this disparity. First, research on determinants of child overweight/obesity originates primarily in the field of public health, and neighborhood context has been studied for a longer period of time in the public health discipline. Second, identifying how neighborhoods affect child physical health, be it through the impact of the built environment on children's outdoor play opportunities or on the access to affordable healthy food, is more straightforward to conceptualize than for other domains of child well-being.

Two systematic reviews of the literature on neighborhood built environment and child obesity conducted about 10 years ago reported mixed findings (Dunton, Kaplan, Wolch, Jerrett, & Reynolds, 2009; Papas et al., 2007). However, a more recent review by Casey (2014) reported more consistent findings, specifically with regards to a positive association between neighborhood walkability and higher levels of physical activity and lower weight for children. One of the limitations of early research in this area was that most was cross-sectional in nature. More recent research has employed longitudinal designs and has supported the link between neighborhoods that are favorable to physical activity, healthy nutrition, higher levels of physical activity, and lower levels of overweight/obesity among both school-age children and adolescents (Saelens et al., 2018; Sallis et al., 2018).

Measurement and Design Approaches for the Study of Neighborhood Influences

Identifying the Unit of Measurement

The first task in designing a research study focused on neighborhood effects and the well-being of children and youth is to decide how to define the neighborhood itself. This decision has both pragmatic and conceptual implications. The pragmatic issues are related to the types of data one may want to utilize to characterize the neighborhood, described more fully below. Most researchers utilize census data to characterize the economic status and population characteristics of a neighborhood, and those data can be captured at the census block group, census tract, or zip code (with some manipulation) levels. Research suggests census block groups are the best approximation of physical neighborhoods, at least in urban areas, although census tracts can be decent approximations (Huie, 2001; O'Campo, 2003). Regardless, it will be more of a challenge to use census data if one defines neighborhood boundaries in a way that is inconsistent with census boundaries.

Pragmatic issues related to defining the neighborhood boundaries also differ depending on study location. For example, the concept of a neighborhood is very different in densely populated urban areas such as New York or Chicago compared to rural communities in Georgia and North Carolina. Heterogeneity in both rural and urban areas also needs to be recognized. Cities with well-developed transportation systems such as New York and San Francisco will have a different neighborhood dynamic than cities without such extensive public transportation such as Dallas or Denver. In rural areas, physical geography can make a difference, such as with the mountainous areas of West Virginia and the bayous of coastal Louisiana. Sparsely populated locations, such as the "frontier" counties of west Texas and significant portions of the western United States also challenge our conventional definitions of "neighborhood".

Let Theory Be Your Guide

Ultimately, researchers should consider carefully their conceptual framework and the mechanisms by which neighborhood effects are believed to operate when defining neighborhood boundaries. For example, if the focus is on the physical environment, such as in studies of neighborhood walkability and child physical activity, one should consider neighborhood boundaries that reasonably bound the range of child physical activity on a day-to-day basis. If it is the social aspects of a neighborhood that are thought to be important, such as in considerations of neighborhood social capital or neighborhood peer influences, the researcher should consider what neighborhood boundaries best capture patterns of social interaction in the community. Researchers should also consider carefully the developmental stage of the children under study. The neighborhood of influence will be different for children who are very young who cannot navigate the neighborhood on their own compared to adolescents who have a much larger range of mobility.

Approaches to Measuring Neighborhoods

Once a researcher has defined neighborhood boundaries, the next step is to identify sources of data for characterizing the neighborhood. Again, as with neighborhood boundaries, the selection of specific measures should be based on the theoretical framework guiding the study. Neighborhoods are generally characterized in terms of their *structural* characteristics (economic status, physical conditions, crime) and *social* characteristics (social cohesion, informal social control, social climate) (Caughy et al., 2012). Furthermore, neighborhood measures include both *objective* measures, such as census data, as well as *subjective* measures, such as the perceptions of neighborhood residents of neighborhood conditions (O'Campo & Caughy, 2007). Measures of the same domain of neighborhood characteristics can include both objective and subjective measures. For example, physical conditions can be assessed using systematic social observation, an objective measure, or perceptions of neighborhood conditions as reported by residents, a subjective measure. In the following sections, we provide an overview of the most common methods for assessing neighborhoods.

Secondary Data Sources

By far, the most widely used data on neighborhoods come from the U.S. Census, which can provide a wide range of not only economic characteristics (poverty levels, employment status) but also population characteristics (race/ethnicity, population mobility, language use) and housing characteristics (rooms per household, ownership status). Census data can be downloaded directly from the U.S. government website or obtained from commercial sources. One advantage of a commercial source of census data is that some provide projections of census variables, which can be useful if it is late in the decade, and the census data are out of date.

Several steps are needed before one can integrate census data into a study. First, study participants need to be linked to the correct geographic unit, be it census block group, census tract, or zip code. With the exception of zip code, this will require one to geocode the addresses of study participants, a procedure available through all major geographic information system (GIS) software packages. At the most granular, the GIS program will provide the latitude and longitude of a participant's address, which can then be linked to census geography.

However, even after linking participants with their census geography, decisions remain regarding how census data will be utilized. The census provides counts of individuals, so proportions need to be calculated (proportion of each race/ethnic group, proportion employed, etc.). Likewise, the creation of composite variables should be considered. Most commonly, researchers create indices of concentrated economic disadvantage. Common measures include one created by Sampson (Sampson, Morenoff, & Earls, 1999; Sampson, Raudenbush, & Earls, 1997) and a similar measure created by Coulton (Coulton, 1995), each of which standardizes individual census variables at the neighborhood level (census block group or census tract) against a larger geographic unit such as the city or state and then averages them. These composite measures both demonstrate high levels of internal reliability as well as predictive validity (Caughy et al., 2008; Lima et al., 2010).

However, there are a number of other, less frequently used secondary data to consider in neighborhood research. For example, crime data can be obtained from local jurisdictions or from the U.S. Department of Justice. As with census data, decisions need to be made regarding how crime data will be utilized. For example, one can create summary measures for the entire neighborhood such as violent crimes per capita or total crimes per square mile. Alternatively, one can retain the specific location of the crime and examine how proximity to crime affects children and youth. As summarized above, recent research indicates living close to a violent crime incident is associated with dysregulation in children (McCoy et al., 2015; Sharkey et al., 2012).

Direct Observational Methods

Observational measures of neighborhoods are referred to as *systematic social observation* (SSO) methods and involve sending groups of individuals into neighborhoods to rate their structure and physical conditions. SSO data have been collected by rating videos of neighborhoods recorded by cameras positioned in vehicles driving slowly through them (Raudenbush & Sampson, 1999), by individuals rating items from a vehicle while another person drives through the neighborhood (so called "windshield" surveys, Burchinal, Vernon-Feagans, & Cox, 2008), or by pairs of individuals walking through the neighborhood (Caughy, O'Campo, & Patterson, 2001).

Typically, SSO raters evaluate the physical condition of buildings and public spaces and document the types of buildings, size of streets and amount of traffic, and the presence and activity of individuals observed in the neighborhood. Decisions regarding what to observe should be based on the researcher's theory of neighborhood effects and the specific outcome being examined. For example, if one is interested in how neighborhood walkability is related to child physical activity, then SSO raters might gather information regarding the presence and condition of sidewalks and busyness of streets in the neighborhood. In contrast, if one is interested in the relation between neighborhood conditions and adolescent drug use, SSO raters might gather information related to the presence of loitering groups of adults and youth, signs of gang activity, and/or the presence of discarded drug paraphernalia.

Regardless of the specific observational data gathered, practical considerations must be addressed before systematic social observation can commence. Specifically, researchers must decide what time of day neighborhoods will be observed, and this time should be standardized across neighborhoods. The time of day chosen should be consistent with what the researcher hopes to observe. Burton and Jarrett's (2000) in-depth observation of a neighborhood with high rates of crime and drug trafficking found that families with children utilized public spaces in the neighborhood during the morning and early afternoon because drug dealers were prevalent in outdoor areas in the late afternoon/evening. Time of observation is important in low crime neighborhoods as well. For example, if one is interested in observing neighborhood social interaction, then observations should be scheduled after school/work hours. Finally, time of year can be important, as there will be less outdoor activity during the coldest time of the year in northern areas and during the hottest time of the year in the south.

Finally, similar to other observational methods, SSO raters need to be trained to an appropriate level of interrater reliability. Training begins with classroom sessions during which observational items are reviewed and slides representative of the neighborhoods to be rated are viewed and rated. In-class sessions are followed by traveling to selected "pilot" neighborhoods and conducting group ratings until interrater reliability is achieved. Official data collection is usually conducted by pairs of individuals for safety reasons, and ratings are arrived at by consensus. Throughout data collection, a subset of observations should be rated by a second pair of raters to monitor interrater reliability and to prevent rater drift.

Perceptions of Neighborhoods

Many neighborhood researchers are interested in the social characteristics of neighborhoods such as collective efficacy, or the degree to which neighbors come together to solve neighborhood problems (Sampson et al., 1997). Other social features of neighborhoods that have been assessed include neighborhood climate, or how one feels about the neighborhood's atmosphere (Caughy & O'Campo, 2006), and collective socialization, or the degree to which neighbors intervene with children in the neighborhood other than their own (Caughy, Nettles, & O'Campo, 2007). It is through the personal contact between neighborhood residents that many feel the most important neighborhood effects are mediated, and the extant research supports these social aspects of neighborhoods as important for the well-being of children and youth in a range of domains (Brody et al., 2001; Caughy, O'Campo, & Muntaner, 2003; Dorsey & Forehand, 2003; Xue, Leventhal, Brooks-Gunn, & Earls, 2005).

However, these characteristics of neighborhoods can only be measured via report by residents. There are a number of survey measures of neighborhood social characteristics including one developed by Sampson and colleagues for the Project on Human Development in Chicago Neighborhoods (PHDCN; Earls, 1999) and the Neighborhood Environment for Children Rating Scales (NECRS) developed by Claudia Coulton and her colleagues (Coulton, Korbin, & Su, 1996). These survey tools are among the most comprehensive, tapping a wide range of social characteristics of neighborhoods. In addition, these measures include scales that assess the perception of residents of the physical conditions of neighborhoods, including the condition of buildings and public spaces and the presence of trash and/or graffiti.

Several factors should be considered when choosing a self-report measure of residents' perceptions. Optimally, reports are obtained from a sample of neighborhood residents separate from the sample of study participants, as was done in the PHDCN. However, this option is often too costly, thereby limiting its feasibility. Most commonly, researchers gather neighborhood perceptions data from the same study participants who are providing data for the outcome of interest. Caution must be taken to avoid issues of "same source bias" which would result in artificially inflating the correlation between neighborhood perceptions measures and the outcome because both were reported by the same person (Duncan & Raudenbush, 1999). For example, consider a researcher who is interested in how neighborhood social cohesion is related to adult depression and gathers data regarding both neighborhood cohesion and depression from the same individual. An individual's depressive symptomatology could affect his/her perceptions of the degree of community cohesion in the neighborhood, thereby biasing any relation between these two factors. In studies of children and adolescents, the problem of same source bias can be mitigated by obtaining data on youth outcomes from a source different than the parent or child such as by teacher report or by direct assessment of the child.

Analytic Approaches for Studying Neighborhoods

The most common data analysis approach used in the study of neighborhood effects is the "multilevel" model, so called because the analytic model separates effects related to individuals from effects related to higher orders of organization, in this case, the neighborhood (Snijders & Bosker, 1999). These methods are important because they take into account the correlation between individuals who live in the same neighborhood. Specifically, if two study participants live in the same census block group, for example, then any variables characterizing the census block group will be the same for those two individuals, violating the assumption of independence of observations for ordinary least squared regression analysis.

There are several statistical packages specifically designed to analyze multilevel data such as MLwiN (www.bristol.ac.uk/cmm/software/mlwin/; Goldstein, 1995) and HLM (www.ssicentral.com/hlm/; Bryk & Raudenbush, 2002). In addition, statistical software packages such MPlus can be used to test multilevel models (Muthen, 1997), and modules for analyzing multilevel models are included in standard statistical packages such as SAS (Singer, 1998), SPSS (Peugh & Enders, 2005), and STATA (Rabe-Hesketh & Skrondal, 2008). Each approach has its own strengths and weaknesses, a full discussion of which is beyond the scope of this chapter.

Innovations in the Study of Neighborhood Influences on Development

Although studies of neighborhood effects in developmental science are not new, there are a number of more recent advances in approaches for studying neighborhoods that have not consistently penetrated the developmental science literature. Here, we will consider a few of these innovations including the use of spatial analytic methods, using remote sensing technology to conduct systematic social observations of neighborhoods, and the use of mobile technology.

Using Spatial Analytic Methods

One of the pervasive limitations of most research on neighborhoods in developmental science is a failure to capture the spatial nature of communities (Sharkey & Faber, 2014). The neighborhood unit, whether it be a census block group, a census tract, or a zip code, is treated as a homogeneous, autonomous unit. For example, if one thinks that the physical conditions of a neighborhood are important, then the normal way we treat neighborhoods as census tracts or census block groups assumes that physical conditions are similar across the neighborhood and that any effects of the physical environment of a particular neighborhood are independent of the physical environment of the surrounding neighborhoods. These assumptions may mask important within-neighborhood variation and also fail to capture effects of neighborhood conditions most proximal to the child.

Moving beyond our static, homogeneous views of neighborhoods requires using more sophisticated spatial analysis methods, an approach rarely, if ever, seen in the developmental science literature. I had an opportunity to utilize spatial analysis in a study of neighborhood effects by collaborating with scholars with expertise in these methods, and the results supported the importance of a spatial analytic approach. For example, we found that the effects of neighborhood poverty in Baltimore on child cognitive outcomes are conditioned on the poverty level of surrounding neighborhoods (Caughy et al., 2007).

In a study of a low-income neighborhood in Dallas, I collaborated with scholars in spatial analysis in the design, collection, and analysis of neighborhood data for a study of neighborhood change. Neighborhood observational data were maintained at the parcel level (e.g., the property upon which a single house or building sits), providing us with the flexibility of defining the neighborhood in a way not dictated by census geography. An analysis of these observational data indicated that census block group summaries masked important variations in neighborhood conditions within the block group as well as relations between neighborhood conditions and health outcomes (Leonard, Caughy, Mays, & Murdoch, 2011). In an analysis of effects of neighborhood conditions on child behavior problems, we examined the relation of conditions for a range of concentric areas around the child's residence and found the neighborhood physical conditions within 400 and 800 meters of the child's residence (an area between about .19 and .78 square miles) were most strongly related to child behavior problems

(Caughy, Leonard, Beron, & Murdoch, 2013). This area is slightly larger than the average census block group size in the neighborhood (.10 to .20 square miles) but smaller than the census tract size (1.4 square miles), indicating that neither census geography is an accurate measure of the neighborhood of influence for child behavior problems. Furthermore, our approach was a more accurate approach of the child's proximal neighborhood because it was constructed in a way that crossed census boundaries if, for example, a child lived at the edge of a census block group.

Emerging Technological Approaches for Measuring Neighborhood Contexts

Technological advances in recent years have opened up a number of innovative approaches to measuring neighborhood contexts and assessing their effects on children and youth. For example, remote sensing using such services as Google Street View or Bing Maps is being used to assess neighborhood physical conditions rather than researchers directly conducting the observations (Odgers, Caspi, Bates, Sampson, & Moffitt, 2012; Rundle, Bader, Richards, Neckerman, & Teitler, 2011; Schootman et al., 2016). Little of this research has focused on children, however, and what research there is has centered on assessing the neighborhood built environment in relation to child physical activity (Carson & Janssen, 2012; Schootman et al., 2016).

Another significant advance in neighborhood research has been the use of mobile technology to collect data from both study participants as well as data about the geographic spaces where children are spending time. *Ecological momentary assessment*, or EMA, is most often used as a way of gathering "real time" data on an individual's experience at a specific point in time by administering multiple brief surveys during the data collection period using mobile phones. Most research using EMA in child and adolescent populations has focused on the study of mood disorders such as depression and anxiety as a way of capturing the dynamic nature of the youth's well-being in relation to contextual demands (aan het Rot, Hogenelst, & Schoevers, 2012; Tan et al., 2012). More recently, Kirchner and Shiffman (2016) proposed the term *geographically explicit ecological momentary assessment* to describe "an explicitly geographic measurement framework that can be leveraged to study the way people and places reciprocally determine each other over time" (p. 1212). Although the utilization of such frameworks in developmental science is exceedingly rare, the potential of such methods is significant. For example, Mason et al. (2016) used EMA methods to integrate data on adolescents' moods and behaviors, their interactions and peers, and the economic characteristics of their "activity space", or the physical area in which the adolescent was engaging in his/her day-to-day activities. Results indicated that risky peer networks increased the incidence of substance use among youth with conflictual parent relationships but only for youth whose daily activity space was also characterized as risky.

Conclusion

Methodological advances in both measurement and analysis have supported a boon in the study of how neighborhood contexts shape the lives of families and children. These advances have moved the field of developmental science closer to the ideal of Bronfenbrenner's bioecological model, which states that developmental science should "[emphasize] the dynamic interplay of processes across time frames, levels of analysis, and contexts" (Bronfenbrenner & Evans, 2000) (p. 115). A substantial body of research now documents meaningful differences in the health and well-being of children and youth associated with factors beyond individual differences in children and families that lies in differences in the communities in which they live. It is no longer sufficient, however, to document *if* neighborhoods matter but *how*, *why*, and *for whom* they matter. Future advances in the field of neighborhood research depend on developmental scientists' embrace of more sophisticated methods of data collection and analysis. Only by pushing neighborhood research to the next level will we yield results that can be leveraged for meaningful change and to improve the lives of children and youth.

References

aan het Rot, M., Hogenelst, K., & Schoevers, R. A. (2012). Mood disorders in everyday life: A systematic review of experience sampling and ecological momentary assessment studies. *Clinical Psychology Review*, 32, 510–523. doi:10.1016/j.cpr.2012.05.007.

Attar, B. K., Guerra, N. G., & Tolan, P. (1994). Neighborhood disadvantage, stressful life events, and adjustment in urban elementary-school children. *Journal of Clinical Child Psychology*, 23, 391–400. doi:10.1207/s15374424jccp2304_5.

Beyers, J. M., Bates, J. E., Pettit, G. S., & Dodge, K. A. (2003). Neighborhood structure, parenting processes, and the development of youths' externalizing behaviors: A multilevel analysis. *American Journal of Community Psychology*, 31, 35–53. doi:10.1023/A:1023018502759.

Boyle, M. H. & Lipman, E. L. (2002). Do places matter? Socioeconomic disadvantage and behavioral problems of children in Canada. *Journal of Consulting and Clinical Psychology*, 70, 378–389. doi:10.1037/0022-006X.70.2.378.

Brody, G. H., Ge, X., Conger, R., Gibbons, F. X., Murry, V. M., Gerrard, M., & Simons, R. L. (2001). The influence of neighborhood disadvantage, collective socialization, and parenting on African American children's affiliation with deviant peers. *Child Development*, 72, 1231–1246. doi:10.1111/1467-8624.00344.

Bronfenbrenner, U. & Ceci, S. J. (1994). Nature-nurture reconceptualized in developmental perspective: A bioecological model. *Psychological Review*, 101, 568–586. http://dx.doi.org.proxy-remote.galib.uga.edu/10.1037/0033-295X.101.4.568.

Bronfenbrenner, U. & Evans, G. W. (2000). Developmental science in the 21st century: Emerging theoretical models, research designs, and empirical findings. *Social Development*, 9, 115–125. doi:10.1111/1467-9507.00114.

Bryk, A. S. & Raudenbush, S. W. (2002). *Hierarchical Linear Models: Application and Data Analysis Methods* (2nd ed., Vol. 1). Newbury Park, CA: Sage Publications.

Burchinal, M., Vernon-Feagans, L., & Cox, M. (2008). Cumulative social risk, parenting, and infant development in rural low-income communities. *Parenting: Science & Practice*, 8, 41–69. doi:10.1080/15295190701830672.

Burton, L. M. & Jarrett, R. L. (2000). In the mix, yet on the margins: The place of families in urban neighborhood and child development research. *Journal of Marriage & the Family*, 62, 1114–1135. doi:10.1111/j.1741-3737.2000.01114.x.

Carson, V. & Janssen, I. (2012). Neighborhood disorder and screen time among 10–16 year old Canadian youth: A cross-sectional study. *International Journal of Behavioral Nutrition and Physical Activity*, 9, 66. doi:10.1186/1479-5868-9-66.

Casey, R., Oppert, J.-M., Weber, C., Charreire, H., Salze, P., Badariotti, D., ... Simon, C. (2014). Determinants of childhood obesity: What can we learn from built environment studies? *Food Quality and Preference*, 31, 164–172. doi:10.1016/j.foodqual.2011.06.003.

Caughy, M. O., Franzini, L., Windle, M., Dittus, P., Cuccaro, P., Elliott, M. N., & Schuster, M. A. (2012). Social competence in late elementary school: Relationships to parenting and neighborhood context. *Journal of Youth and Adolescence*, 41, 1613–1627. doi:10.1007/s10964-012-9779-2.

Caughy, M. O., Hayslett-McCall, K. L., & O'Campo, P. J. (2007). No neighborhood is an island: Incorporating distal neighborhood effects into multilevel studies of child developmental competence. *Health & Place, 13*, 788–798. doi:10.1016/j.healthplace.2007.01.006.

Caughy, M. O., Leonard, T. C. M., Beron, K., & Murdoch, J. C. (2013). Defining neighborhood boundaries in studies of spatial dependence in child behavior problems. *International Journal of Health Geographics, 12*, 24. www.ij-healthgeographics.com/content/12/1/24.

Caughy, M. O., Nettles, S. M., & O'Campo, P. J. (2007). Community influences on behavioral and academic adjustment in first grade: An examination of an integrated process model. *Journal of Child and Family Studies, 16*, 819–836. doi:10.1007/s10826-006-9128-8.

Caughy, M. O., Nettles, S. M., O'Campo, P. J., & Lohrfink, K. F. (2006). Neighborhood matters: Racial socialization and the development of young African American children. *Child Development, 77*, 1220–1236. doi:10.1111/j.1467-8624.2006.00930.x.

Caughy, M. O. & O'Campo, P. J. (2006). Neighborhood impoverishment, social capital, and the cognitive development of African American preschoolers. *American Journal of Community Psychology, 37*, 141–154. doi:10.1007/s10464-005-9001-8.

Caughy, M. O., O'Campo, P. J., & Muntaner, C. (2003). When being alone might be better: Neighborhood poverty, social capital, and child mental health. *Social Science & Medicine, 57*, 227–237. doi:10.1016/S0277-9536(02)00342-8.

Caughy, M. O., O'Campo, P. J., & Nettles, S. M. (2008). The effect of residential neighborhood on child behavior problems in first grade. *American Journal of Community Psychology, 42*, 39–50. doi:10.1007/s10464-008-9185-9.

Caughy, M. O., O'Campo, P. J., & Patterson, J. (2001). A brief observational measure for urban neighborhoods. *Health & Place, 7*, 225–236. doi:10.1016/S1353-8292(01)00012-0.

Coulton, C. J. (1995). Using community-level indicators of children's well-being in comprehensive community initatives. In J. P. Connell, A. C. Kubisch, L. B. Schorr & C. H. Weiss (Eds.), *New Approaches to Evaluating Community Initiatives: Concepts, Methods, and Contexts* (pp. 173–199). Washington, DC: The Aspen Institute.

Coulton, C. J., Korbin, J. E., & Su, M. (1996). Measuring neighborhood context for young children in an urban area. *American Journal of Community Psychology, 24*, 5–33. http://ejournals.ebsco.com.proxy-remote.galib.uga.edu/direct.asp?ArticleID=42FEB4DF262524A90C4A.

Crane, J. (1991). The epidemic theory of ghettos and neighborhood effects on dropping out and teenage childbearing. *American Journal of Sociology, 96*, 1226–1259. doi:10.1086/229654.

Dorsey, S. & Forehand, R. (2003). The relation of social capital to child psychosocial adjustment difficulties: The role of positive parenting and neighborhood dangerousness. *Journal of Psychopathology and Behavioral Assessment, 25*, 11–23. doi:10.1023/A:1022295802449.

Duncan, G. J., Brooks-Gunn, J., & Klebanov, P. K. (1994). Economic deprivation and early childhood development. *Child Development, 65*, 296–318. doi:10.1111/1467-8624.ep9405315105.

Duncan, G. J. & Raudenbush, S. W. (1999). Assessing the effects of context in studies of child and youth development. *Educational Psychologist, 34*, 29–41. doi:10.1207/s15326985ep3401_3.

Dunton, G. F., Kaplan, J., Wolch, J., Jerrett, M., & Reynolds, K. D. (2009). Physical environmental correlates of childhood obesity: A systematic review. *Obesity Reviews, 10*, 393–402. doi:10.1111/j.1467-789X.2009.00572.x.

Earls, F. (1999). *Project on Human Development in Chicago Neighborhoods: Community Survey* (Vol. 1994–95). Boston, MA: Harvard Medical School.

Entwisle, D. R., Alexander, K. L., & Olson, L. S. (1994). The gender gap in math: Its possible origins in neighborhood effects. *American Sociological Review, 59*, 822–838. doi:10.2307/2096370.

Fine, A., Mahler, A., Steinberg, L., Frick, P. J., & Cauffman, E. (2017). Individual in context: The role of impulse control on the association between the home, school, and neighborhood developmental contexts and adolescent delinquency. *Journal of Youth and Adolescence, 46*, 1488–1502. doi:10.1007/s10964-016-0565-4.

Flouri, E. & Sarmadi, Z. (2016). Prosocial behavior and childhood trajectories of internalizing and externalizing problems: The role of neighborhood and school contexts. *Developmental Psychology, 52*, 253–258. doi:10.1037/dev0000076.

Furstenberg, F. F. (1993). How families manage risk and opportunity in dangerous neighborhoods. In W. J. Wilson (Ed.), *Sociology and the Public Agenda* (pp. 231–258). Newbury Park, CA: Sage Publications.

Ge, X., Brody, G. H., Conger, R. D., Simons, R. L., & Murry, V. M. (2002). Contextual amplification of pubertal transition effects on deviant peer affiliation and externalizing behavior among African American children. *Developmental Psychology, 38*, 42–54. http://dx.doi.org.proxy-remote.galib.uga.edu/10.1037/0012-1649.38.1.42.

Goldstein, H. (1995). *Multilevel Statistical Models*. New York: Halstead Press.

Huie, S. A. B. (2001). The concept of neighborhood in health and mortality research. *Sociological Spectrum, 21*, 341–358. doi:10.1080/027321701300202028.

King, V. L. & Mrug, S. (2018). The relationship between violence exposure and academic achievement in African American adolescents is moderated by emotion regulation. *The Journal of Early Adolescence, 38*, 497–512. doi:10.1177/0272431616675973.

Kirchner, T. R. & Shiffman, S. (2016). Spatio-temporal determinants of mental health and well-being: Advances in geographically-explicit ecological momentary assessment (GEMA). *Social Psychiatry and Psychiatric Epidemiology, 51*, 1211–1223. doi:10.1007/s00127-016-1277-5.

Klebanov, P. K., Brooks-Gunn, J., & Duncan, G. J. (1994). Does neighborhood and family poverty affect mother's parenting, mental health, and social support? *Journal of Marriage and the Family, 56*, 441–455. doi:10.2307/353111.

Kohen, D. E., Brooks-Gunn, J., Leventhal, T., & Hertzmann, C. (2002). Neighborhood income and physical and social disorder in Canada: Associations with young children's competencies. *Child Development, 73*, 1844–1860. doi:10.1111/1467-8624.t01-1-00510.

Kupersmidt, J. B., Griesler, P. C., DeRosier, M. E., Patterson, C. J., & Davis, P. W. (1995). Childhood aggression and peer relations in the context of family and neighborhood. *Child Development, 66*, 360–375. doi:10.1111/j.1467-8624.1995.tb00876.x.

Leonard, T. C. M., Caughy, M. O., Mays, J. K., & Murdoch, J. C. (2011). Systematic neighborhood observations at high spatial resolution: Methodology and assessment of potential benefits. *PLoS One, 6*, e20225. doi:10.1371/journal.pone.0020225.

Leventhal, T. & Brooks-Gunn, J. (2004). A randomized study of neighborhood effects on low-income children's educational outcomes. *Developmental Psychology, 40*, 488–507. http://dx.doi.org.proxy-remote.galib.uga.edu/10.1037/0012-1649.40.4.488.

Lima, J., Caughy, M. O., Nettles, S. M., & O'Campo, P. J. (2010). Effects of cumulative risk and effects on behavioral adjustment in first grade: Moderation by neighborhood context. *Social Science & Medicine, 71*, 1447–1454. doi:10.1016/j.socscimed.2010.06.022.

Mason, M. J., Light, J. M., Mennis, J., Rusby, J. C., Westling, E., Crewe, S., ... Flay, B. R. (2017). Neighborhood disorder, peer network health, and substance use among young urban adolescents. *Drug and Alcohol Dependence, 178*, 208–214. doi:10.1016/j.drugalcdep.2017.05.005.

Mason, M. J., Mennis, J., Light, J., Rusby, J., Westling, E., Crewe, S., ... Zaharakis, N. (2016). Parents, peers, and places: Young urban adolescents' microsystems and substance use involvement. *Journal of Child and Family Studies, 25*, 1441–1450. doi:10.1007/s10826-015-0344-y.

McCoy, D. C., Raver, C. C., & Sharkey, P. (2015). Children's cognitive performance and selective attention following recent community violence. *Journal of Health and Social Behavior, 56*, 19–36. doi:10.1177/0022146514567576.

Muthen, B. (1997). Latent variable modeling of longitudinal and multilevel data. In A. Raftery (Ed.), *Sociological Methodology* (pp. 453–480). Boston, MA: Blackwell Publishers.

O'Campo, P. J. (2003). Invited commentary: Advancing theory and methods for multilevel models of residential neighborhoods and health. *American Journal of Epidemiology, 157*, 9–13. doi:10.1093/aje/kwf171.

O'Campo, P. J. & Caughy, M. O. (2007). Measures of residential community contexts. In J. M. Oakes & J. S. Kaufman (Eds.), *Methods in Social Epidemiology* (pp. 193–208). New York: Jossey-Bass.

Odgers, C. L., Caspi, A., Bates, C. J., Sampson, R. J., & Moffitt, T. E. (2012). Systematic social observation of children's neighborhoods using Google Street View: A reliable and cost-effective method. *Journal of Child Psychology & Psychiatry & Allied Disciplines, 53*, 1009–1017. doi:10.1111/j.1469-7610.2012.02565.x.

Papas, M. A., Alberg, A. J., Ewing, R., Helzlsouer, K. J., Gary, T. L., & Klassen, A. C. (2007). The built environment and obesity. *Epidemiologic Reviews, 29*, 129–143. doi:10.1016/j.socscimed.2010.06.022.

Peugh, J. L. & Enders, C. K. (2005). Using the SPSS Mixed procedure to fit cross-sectional and longitudinal multilevel models. *Educational and Psychological Measurement, 65*, 717–741. doi:10.1177%2F0013164405278558.

Rabe-Hesketh, S. & Skrondal, A. (2008). *Multilevel and Longitudinal Modeling Using Stata*. College Station, TX: STATA Press.

Raudenbush, S. W. & Sampson, R. J. (1999). Ecometrics: Toward a science of assessing ecological settings, with application to the systematic social observation of neighborhoods. *Sociological Methodology, 29*, 1–41. doi:10.1111/0081-1750.00059.

Ray, J. V., Thornton, L. C., Frick, P. J., Steinberg, L., & Cauffman, E. (2016). Impulse control and callous-unemotional traits distinguish patterns of delinquency and substance use in justice involved adolescents: Examining the moderating role of neighborhood context. *Journal of Abnormal Child Psychology, 44*, 599–611. doi:10.1007/s10802-015-0057-0.

Reardon, S., Brennan, R., & Buka, S. (2002). Estimating multi-level discrete-time hazard models using cross-sectional data: Neighborhood effects on the onset of adolescent cigarette use. *Multivariate Behavioral Research, 37*, 297–330. doi:10.1207/S15327906MBR3703_1.

Roche, K. M., Ellen, J., & Astone, N. M. (2005). Effects of out-of-school care on sex initiation among young adolescents in low-income central city neighborhoods. *Archives of Pediatric and Adolescent Medicine, 159*, 68–73. doi:10.1001/archpedi.159.1.68.

Roche, K. M., Ensminger, M. E., & Cherlin, A. (2007). Variations in parenting and adolescent outcomes among African American and Latino families living in low-income, urban areas. *Journal of Family Issues, 28*, 882–909. doi:10.1177%2F0192513X07299617.

Roche, K. M. & Leventhal, T. (2009). Beyond neighborhood poverty: Family management, neighborhood disorder, and early transitions to sex. *Journal of Family Psychology, 23*, 819–827. http://psycnet.apa.org/doi/10.1037/a0016554.

Roy, A. L., McCoy, D. C., & Raver, C. C. (2014). Instability versus quality: Residential mobility, neighborhood poverty, and children's self-regulation. *Developmental Psychology, 50*, 1891–1896. doi:10.1037/a0036984.

Rundle, A. G., Bader, M. D. M., Richards, C. A., Neckerman, K. M., & Teitler, J. O. (2011). Using Google Street View to audit neighborhood environments. *American Journal of Preventive Medicine, 40*, 94–100. doi:10.1016/j.amepre.2010.09.034.

Saelens, B. E., Glanz, K., Frank, L. D., Couch, S. C., Zhou, C., Colburn, T., & Sallis, J. F. (2018). Two-year changes in child weight status, diet, and activity by neighborhood nutrition and physical activity environment. *Obesity, 26*, 1338–1346. doi:10.1002/oby.22247.

Sallis, J. F., Conway, T. L., Cain, K. L., Carlson, J. A., Frank, L. D., Kerr, J., ... Saelens, B. E. (2018). Neighborhood built environment and socioeconomic status in relation to physical activity, sedentary behavior, and weight status of adolescents. *Preventive Medicine, 110*, 47–54. doi:10.1016/j.ypmed.2018.02.009.

Sampson, R. J., Morenoff, J. D., & Earls, F. (1999). Beyond social capital: Spatial dynamics of collective efficacy for children. *American Sociological Review, 64*, 633–660. doi:10.2307/2657367.

Sampson, R. J., Raudenbush, S. W., & Earls, F. (1997). Neighborhoods and violent crime: A multilevel study of collective efficacy. *Science, 277*, 918–924. doi:10.1126/science.277.5328.918.

Schootman, M., Nelson, E. J., Werner, K., Shacham, E., Elliott, M., Ratnapradipa, K., ... McVay, A. (2016). Emerging technologies to measure neighborhood conditions in public health: implications for interventions and next steps. *International Journal of Health Geographics*, *15*, 20. doi:10.1186/s12942-016-0050-z.

Schwartz, D. & Gorman, A. H. (2003). Community violence exposure and children's academic functioning. *Journal of Educational Psychology*, *95*, 163–173. doi:10.1037/0022-0663.95.1.163.

Sharkey, P. T. & Faber, J. W. (2014). Where, when, why, and for whom do residential contexts matter? Moving away from the dichotomous understanding of neighborhood effects. *Annual Review of Sociology*, *40*, 559–579. doi:10.1146/annurev-soc-071913-043350.

Sharkey, P. T., Tirado-Strayer, N., Papachristos, A. V., & Raver, C. C. (2012). The effect of local violence on children's attention and impulse control. *American Journal of Public Health*, *102*, 2287–2293. doi:10.2105/AJPH.2012.300789.

Simons, R. L., Johnson, C., Beaman, J., Conger, R. D., & Whitbeck, L. B. (1996). Parents and peer group as mediators of the effect of community structure on adolescent problem behavior. *American Journal of Community Psychology*, *24*, 145–171. doi:10.1007/BF02511885.

Simons, R. L., Johnson, C., Conger, R. D., & Lorenz, F. O. (1997). Linking community context to quality of parenting: A study of rural families. *Rural Sociology*, *62*, 207–230. doi:10.1111/j.1549-0831.1997.tb00651.x.

Simons, R. L., Lin, K.-H., Gordon, L. C., Brody, G. H., Murry, V., & Conger, R. D. (2002). Community differences in the association between parenting practices and child conduct problems. *Journal of Marriage & the Family*, *64*, 331–345. doi:10.1111/j.1741-3737.2002.00331.x.

Singer, J. D. (1998). Using SAS PROC MIXED to fit multilevel models, hierarchical models, and individual growth models. *Journal of Educational & Behavioral Statistics*, *23*, 323–355. doi:10.3102%2F10769986023004323.

Snijders, T. A. B. & Bosker, R. J. (1999). *Multilevel Analysis: An Introduction to Basic and Advanced Multilevel Modeling*. Newbury Park, CA: Sage Publications.

Tan, P. Z., Forbes, E. E., Dahl, R. E., Ryan, N. D., Siegle, G. J., Ladouceur, C. D., & Silk, J. S. (2012). Emotional reactivity and regulation in anxious and nonanxious youth: A cell-phone ecological momentary assessment study. *Journal of Child Psychology and Psychiatry*, *53*, 197–206. doi:10.1111/j.1469-7610.2011.02469.x.

Tolan, P. H., Gorman-Smith, D., & Henry, D. B. (2003). The developmental ecology of urban males' youth violence. *Developmental Psychology*, *39*, 274–291. doi:10.1037/0012-1649.39.2.274.

Vries, D. A., Peter, J., Graaf, H., & Nikken, P. (2016). The role of immigrant concentration within and beyond residential neighborhoods in adolescent alcohol use. *Journal of Youth and Adolescence*, *45*, 211–224. doi:10.1007/s10964-015-0333-x.

Xue, Y., Leventhal, T., Brooks-Gunn, J., & Earls, F. (2005). Neighborhood of residence and mental health problems of 5- to 11-year-olds. *Archives of General Psychiatry*, *62*, 554–563. doi:10.1001/archpsyc.62.5.554.

11 Measuring Peer Relationships During Childhood
Exploring the Benefits of Using Peer Nominations

Christopher D. Aults

Peers are powerful socializing agents that affect child development on many levels. From the level of the peer group to dyadic interactions, peers shape children's social, emotional, and cognitive well-being in many ways. Furthermore, the powerful influences go far beyond parental, extended family, or community influences in that peer interactions help children construct the understanding of the self, maintain social hierarchies, and enforce social norms. Therefore, to effectively examine children's social development, peers should be utilized as a wellspring of information about the individual. In developmental science, the most widely used method to measure these variables of interest is peer nominations. This technique can provide data on social status, friendship quality, and the reputations of others.

In this chapter, I will highlight the importance of using peer knowledge to assess a wide range of variables that may be relevant for researchers exploring the social development of children. First, central issues in the use of peer nominations are discussed, including a brief history on this method and several considerations to take into account while using these techniques. Second, the use of peer nominations to measure social status and friendships will be discussed. Third, the benefits of using peer nominations to measure certain overt behaviors, such as aggression and victimization, are discussed. Lastly, recent innovations and directions for future research are discussed.

The Peer Nomination Method

There are many *sociometric methods*—quantitative methods for measuring social relationships within a group—that can be used in developmental science. The most widely used method is peer nominations, or more specifically, a peer nomination inventory (PNI). A PNI can include many variables of interest, such as likeability, social dominance, gender nonconformity, victimization, and internalizing and externalizing problems (Aults, Cooper, Pauletti, Jones, & Perry, 2015; Aults, Machluf, Sellers, & Jones, 2018; Egan & Perry, 2001; Pauletti, Cooper, & Perry, 2014). Originally, the PNI was designed to measure overt behavior in children (Wiggins & Winder, 1961). The design assumed that certain overt behaviors, such as aggression, dependency, withdrawal, depression, and likeability, may not be fully disclosed by participants using self-reports (Wiggins & Winder, 1961). The design also assumed that among individuals who were well acquainted, social reputation would be related to social behavior (Winder & Wiggins, 1964). The PNI taps *peer* knowledge of overt behaviors by simply asking others who are familiar with the participants to nominate those who

About my classmates

	Sunny	Julian	Vicki	Kim	Morgan
1. He/She hits and pushes others around.					
2. He/She tries to get along with everyone.					
3. He/She plays by himself most of the time.					
4. He/She makes fun of people and calls them names.					

Figure 11.1 A sample peer nomination inventory. Questions 1 and 4 are examples of aggressive behavior (physical and verbal, respectively). Question 2 is an example of prosocial behavior. Question 3 is an example of internalizing behavior.

engage in a chosen behavior (see Figure 11.1 for an example). Essentially, if there is a larger consensus among the group for a given criterion, it is assumed that the participant is more likely to display the behaviors associated with that given criterion. PNIs have gone through a myriad of changes over the years, but the strength of the core design of this measurement has remained unchanged.

There are several caveats to consider while implementing a PNI. First, every participant should have the opportunity to evaluate every other member of the group on one or more criteria. This is often referred to as a "round-robin" design (Cillessen, 2009). For example, in Figure 11.1, Sunny can evaluate Morgan on all three criteria; aggression (questions 1 and 4), prosocial behavior, and internalizing. In return, Morgan can evaluate Sunny using the same criteria. This process is carried out for every participant in the *reference group*—the collection of participants within which the criteria are determined.

The second consideration is to determine how the reference group will be chosen. Normally, the reference group is chosen by which age appropriate peer group the participants spend time with. For kindergarten- and early elementary school-aged children, it is recommended that the reference group be the individual classrooms that the children are in for the majority of the school day, i.e., their classmates. For middle school-aged children and adolescents, it is recommended that the reference group be the entire grade, i.e., their grade-mates. For high school-aged adolescents, it is recommended that the reference group be the entire grade level, or even all the peers in the school across grades (Cillessen, 2009).

After the reference group is chosen, another consideration for implementing peer nominations should be how restrictive the nominations can be, e.g., limited versus unlimited. In limited nominations, participants are instructed to make a fixed or small number of nominations. For example, in a study examining social status by Coie, Dodge, and Coppotelli (1982), children were instructed to name three other classmates that they liked the most and three classmates that they liked the least;

they were also instructed to name three classmates who best fit a host of behavioral descriptions (more on this study below). A similar study by Newcomb and Bukowski (1983) also asked children to name three same-sex and same-grade peers whom they considered to be their best friends, and three whom they wanted to play with the least. In the unlimited method, participants are not restricted to naming three classmates, but are instructed to nominate as many or as few peers as they wish. Ultimately, the nature of the study may dictate which method is best, but several points should be considered.

First, limited nominations may be best for smaller sample sizes with younger children. Unlimited peer nominations take some time to complete and may be best for larger sample sizes with older children. Older children often want to report more than a fixed number of peers for certain questions and may have more knowledge about a greater number of peers in different classrooms. Second, recent research suggests that limited nominations may serve as a better proxy for measuring questions regarding bullying and victimization, while unlimited nominations may be more suitable for measuring social status such as popularity or preference (Gommans & Cillessen, 2015). This study also highlights many statistical reasons why unlimited nominations may be preferred, such as a reduction in measurement error, higher construct validity, and larger effect sizes.

Scoring the results from peer nominations also warrants additional concern. Adjusting nominated-based sociometric scores for biases due to variations in group size is often a concern while quantifying participant scores. One procedure to obtain a participant's score on a given variable is to create a proportion score by dividing the observed score (the amount of nominations given for a certain criterion) by the number of nominators in the reference group. These corrected scores are then expressed as proportions of the possible maximum (Velasquez, Bukowski, & Saldarriaga, 2013). If multiple classrooms use the same PNI, it is recommended that researchers test the intraclass correlation coefficient (ICC). The ICC will assess the consistency of the measurements made by the different nominators measuring the same quantity (for recommended guidelines, see Cicchetti, 1994; Perisic & Rosner, 1999).

However, there are some disadvantages to obtaining proportion scores. This method is recommended only if the number of participants across the reference groups are relatively equal. If one reference group is larger than the other, participants in the larger group may have inflated scores relative to the scores from smaller groups (Cillessen, 2009). These inflated scores may affect group means on a variable simply based on the likelihood that a child may have a greater opportunity to be nominated on a given measure. Additionally, in larger reference groups, it is much more likely that a child may be overlooked by the nominators and not be nominated for any of the behaviors listed on the PNI. In practice, finding equal-sized classrooms to implement a PNI is usually difficult to do; however, certain procedures, such as using a regression-based method to control for measurement error due to group size variance, have been proposed (see Velasquez et al., 2013).

Regardless of the reference group or the age of the participants, another consideration for implementing peer nominations is to determine the number of questions that will appear on the PNI. For example, in Figure 11.1, due to illustration purposes, only four questions appear that tap into domains in the three behavioral categories (e.g., aggressive, prosocial, and internalizing behaviors). In practice, a wide range of questions should be used to include multiple types of behaviors. This way, researchers can examine multiple types of behaviors with a shortened measure. However, it is recommended that the PNIs do not contain too many questions. Due to time constraints and the possibility of participant fatigue, a PNI should only contain approximately 20–25 questions in total, with at least two questions per behavioral measure. Having at least two questions that measure a certain behavioral characteristic provides researchers the opportunity to test the *internal consistency*—how closely a related set of items are as a group—to provide evidence that the questions measure the same thing.

Although not an exhaustive list, the discussion above provides some general considerations for using peer nominations to gather data. The discussion now turns to which types of peer relationships can be assessed using PNIs. Below, I will discuss a few ways peer nominations can be used to assess some important topics for developmental researchers, such as social status and friendship.

What Is Social Status and How Does It Differ from Friendship?

A growing body of literature suggests that there is considerable consistency in a child's social status (Cantin & Boivin, 2004; Coie & Dodge, 1983) and that social status can predict long term consequences (Kupersmidt & Coie, 1990). Additionally, evidence suggests that friends can buffer or exacerbate adjustment outcomes for children (Hodges, Malone, & Perry, 1997; Hodges & Perry, 1999; Ladd, 1990). Therefore, it is important for developmental psychologists to properly assess these characteristics to determine how they can predict outcomes. Although certain social statuses such as popularity appear to have similar connections to friendship, the two constructs differ in a few main ways. I will first discuss social status as a process to distinguish it from friendship and then describe ways to measure each.

The first distinction between social status and friendship is that social status operates mainly on the group level, whereas friendship operates mainly on an interpersonal level. Social status is thought to be a unilateral construct that measures the group's attitude toward an individual. Thus, social status is a group level process that hinges on setting and is driven by context. Friendship, on the other hand, is a bilateral construct that is based on reciprocity, affect, and voluntary involvement. Mutual affection is a core component to friendship but not necessary for certain social statuses such as popularity. For example, children can be rated as popular but also rated lower on likeability by the group (LaFontana & Cillessen, 2002). Feelings of intimacy and companionship, in the absence of context, are uniquely associated with friendship, whereas popularity is devoid of affect and is specifically context-dependent. Although some arguments about the measurement of social status and friendship blur the line between how we distinguish them, recent work has helped elucidate some of these issues.

Measuring Social Status and Friendship

Studies measuring social status have relied heavily on sociometric measures, such as peer nominations. Coie and colleagues (Coie et al., 1982; Coie & Dodge, 1983) developed a technique to assess social status revolving around two main factors, acceptance and rejection. Simply, acceptance refers to how much a child is liked by his or her peers, while rejection refers to how much a child is disliked by his or her peers (Asher & McDonald, 2009). Peer nominations on these measures are evaluated to produce social preference scores (general likeability) and social impact scores (visibility within the peer group). Five sociometric status categories emerge when using this procedure. *Popular* children are high in impact and high in preference. *Rejected* children are high in impact and low in preference. *Neglected* children are low in impact and average in preference. *Average* children are average in both categories. Lastly, *controversial* children are high in impact and average in preference.

Sociometric measures have been successful in assigning youth into these categories, but the concept of one of these statuses, particularly popularity, has evolved to be more complex and multidimensional than once thought. Sociometric measures of popularity focus mainly on acceptance whereas *perceived popularity* involves the group's perceptions of who is popular (Parkhurst & Hopmeyer, 1998). Perceived popularity also uses peer nominations, but peers are asked "who in their class is popular?" Parkhurst and Hopmeyer (1998) suggest that this method captures the traditional sociometric characteristics of popularity used in previous studies, while also incorporating other categories, e.g., controversial and rejected. As mentioned earlier, the results suggest that not all popular children are rated as well-liked. This may impact their acceptance score but not undermine their popularity status within the group. Studies using perceived popularity measures have found that relational aggression and popularity are highly associated with one another (Cillessen & Mayeux, 2004), which contrasts sociometric measures that found that aggression is usually associated with controversial and rejected statuses (Coie & Dodge, 1988).

Friendship measurement, on the other hand, is much less about the group's perception of the individual or social dominance within context but is more about acknowledgement of mutual liking and respect between dyads. Peer nominations are also used, although there are many methodological caveats depending on the study in question or the outcome expectancies of a research design. Berndt and McCandless (2009) summarize that friendship should be considered on a continuum from the negative extreme, "strangers," to the positive extreme, "the best of friends." Most studies vary in how they ask their participants to name friends. Some ask participants to simply label "who hangs around together a lot" (Cairns, Cairns, Neckerman, Gest, & Gariepy, 1988; Cairns, Perrin, & Cairns, 1985), while others ask participants to label the names of their three very best friends in rank order (Burk & Laursen, 2005). Additionally, some disagreement between reciprocity in naming friends has been brought forth. Some argue that reciprocal nominations will reduce statistical power, while others suggest that reciprocal nominations would adequately describe the quality of the friendship (Berndt & McCandless, 2009).

Aside from being an effective tool for measuring social status and friendships, peer nominations are also very useful in measuring the reputations of others. Specifically, peer nominations can be an effective tool for measuring certain subtypes of aggressive behavior and certain forms of peer victimization. Below, I will discuss the benefits of utilizing peer knowledge to assess the reputations of others.

Aggressive Behavior and Peer Victimization

Children who engage in *aggressive behavior*—any behavior aimed at harming another individual—are at an increased risk for poor psychological adjustment (Anderson & Heusmann, 2003; Crick, Ostrov, & Werner, 2006). Victims of peer aggression are also at risk for poor psychological adjustment, and exposure to peer victimization can happen as early as kindergarten (Kochenderfer & Ladd, 1997; Ladd, Ettekal, & Kochenderfer-Ladd, 2017). Given the magnitude of this problem, it is not surprising that researchers have become increasingly interested in effective ways to measure aggression and peer victimization in children. Self-report measures are often used to measure specific subtypes of aggressive behavior (e.g., reactive, proactive, and relational) and different forms of peer victimization (e.g., physical and verbal). However, certain inherent weaknesses in the design of self-report measures, alongside the sensitivity of the material posed when asking children about their experiences with aggression and victimization, point to peer nominations as a potentially more effective way to assess these variables.

Teacher nominations—nominations provided by the children's teacher—have also been utilized to measure aggression and victimization. Teacher nominations require the teacher to make assessments of the children's behavior in an unbiased and neutral fashion. Many benefits of teacher nominations exist. Teachers spend a lot of time with the children in classrooms, and they have many years of experience interacting with different students and are usually trained in the field of child development. However, in middle school and high school settings, teachers do not spend a lot of time with certain students outside of the classroom, such as in the lunchroom or locker room, where aggressive behavior could also occur. Therefore, teacher nominations on topics such as aggression and victimization may not be a reliable source of information in middle school or high school settings.

Instead of relying solely on self-reports or other methods of self-disclosure such as teacher reports, peer nominations were designed to measure overt behaviors that may not always be fully disclosed by participants. For some children who display aggressive behavior, revealing how frequent or how severe their aggressive behavior is may harm their ability to continue to act aggressively toward their peers due to the fear of repercussions for their actions. Some aggressive children use aggressive behavior to their benefit either to secure rewards or to increase their social standing within the peer group (Barchia & Bussey, 2011; Perry, Perry, & Rasmussen, 1986). Disclosing this information to researchers, teachers, or parents may severely impact their ability to continue to act aggressively. Reluctance to disclose sensitive information may also impact the ability to effectively assess peer victimization as well. Due to the fear of being singled out for intervention by counselors, exacerbating pathology associated with peer victimization, or by retaliation by aggressive peers, some children who are victimized may be reluctant to disclose how often or how severe their experiences with peer victimization are.

Alongside the reluctance to disclose this sensitive information, weaknesses of self-report measures, such as social desirability bias and demand characteristics, also point to peer nominations as a more effective way to measure aggression and peer victimization. *Social desirability bias*—the tendency of respondents to answer questions on a survey in a manner that will be viewed favorably by others—can impact the quality of self-report measures. Social desirability effects can often take the form of over-reporting good behavior or under-reporting bad behavior (Edwards, 1957).

Another issue with self-reporting sensitive information is a phenomenon called *demand characteristics*. Demand characteristics occur when the respondents form an interpretation of the purpose of the survey and change their responses to fit a favorable view of themselves in the eyes of the researchers (Nichols & Maner, 2008). For example, if an aggressive or victimized child interprets the questionnaire that researchers are using to be about behavior problems at their school, he or she may change their answers to not reveal how severe or frequent their behavioral problems are. This behavior would undermine the assessments, which in turn could undermine the entire study.

There are many experimental manipulations or strategies to counteract weaknesses in surveys, so it is not recommended that self-report measures of aggression and victimization be abandoned completely. In fact, most contemporary studies investigating aggression and victimization during childhood and adolescence utilize both peer and teacher nominations in conjunction with self-report measures. Additionally, overuse of just one type of assessment, either peer or teacher nominations, or self-reports, can lead to shared or *common-method variance*—variations in responses that are caused by the instrument rather than the actual predispositions of the respondent (Podsakoff, MacKenzie, Lee, & Podsakoff, 2003).

Peer nominations have certain advantages over other methods of assessing social status, friendship, and aggression and victimization. Recently, innovations in this technique have uncovered additional aspects of these relationships that have expanded the knowledge base of these topics for developmental science researchers. Below, new innovations and additional considerations for future research will be discussed.

Innovations

Several studies investigating methodological modifications of sociometric data have led to innovations in the field. A study by Poulin and Dishion (2008) investigated whether a long roster sorted alphabetically would lead to a *response bias*—any factor that affects the way responses are provided for participants. They found that participants were more likely to rate participants on certain criteria solely on where their names appeared on the list. Thus, more ratings went to those on the top of the list compared to those on the bottom. These data suggest that researchers should instruct the participants to consider all peers who fit the description of the criteria provided before nominating them in a listwise fashion (Poulin & Dishion, 2008).

Innovations in peer-rating techniques for assessing more specific relationships, such as the study of aggressor–victim relationships in the middle school context, have also been presented. Card and Hodges (2010) developed a technique named the Dyadic Aggression and Victimization Inventory, or DAVI, to examine target-specific aggression and source-specific victimization. In this technique, participants are given a roster of all their peers, and are asked to identify the victims of their own aggression (target-specificity) and the aggressors who victimize them (source-specificity). By utilizing this method, researchers can now examine the dyadic nature of aggression by looking at intra- and interpersonal variables that stimulate aggressive behavior in children. For example, a recent study using a similar method found that certain children with an insecure gender identity (an interpersonal variable) specifically targeted their aggressive behavior toward gender nonconforming peers (an intrapersonal variable) (Pauletti et al., 2014).

Conclusions

The richness of knowledge that exists with the peer network should be of interest to developmental researchers. The value of peer nominations is largely derived from the capacity to provide efficient indices of individual differences of functioning within the peer group (Cillessen, 2009; Velasquez, et al., 2013). Although many iterations of peer nomination techniques exist, the elemental design taps into information that could be valuable for many studies and should be considered by developmental researchers.

References

Anderson, C. A. & Heusmann, L. R. (2003). Human aggression: A social-cognitive view. In M. A. Hogg & J. Cooper Eds., *The Sage Handbook of Social Psychology* (pp. 296–323). Thousand Oaks, CA: Sage Publications Inc.

Asher, S. R. & McDonald, K. L. (2009). The behavioral basis of acceptance, rejection, and perceived popularity. In K. H. Rubin, W. M. Bukowski, & B. Laursen (Eds.), *Handbook of Peer Interactions, Relationships and Groups* (pp. 232–248). New York, NY: Guilford.

Aults, C. D., Cooper, P. J., Pauletti, R. E., Jones, N. A., & Perry, D. G. (2015). Child sex and respiratory sinus arrhythmia reactivity as moderators of the relation between internalizing symptoms and aggression. *Applied Psychophysiology and Biofeedback*, 40, 269–276.

Aults, C. D., Machluf, K., Sellers, P. D., & Jones, N. A. (2018). Adolescent girls' biological sensitivity to context: Heart rate reactivity moderates the relationship between peer victimization and internalizing problems. *Evolutionary Psychological Science*, 5, 178–185.

Barchia, K. & Bussey, K. (2011). Individual and collective social cognitive influences on peer aggression: Exploring the contribution of aggression efficacy, moral disengagement, and collective efficacy. *Aggressive Behavior*, 37, 107–120.

Berndt, T. J. & McCandless, M. A. (2009). Methods for investigating children's relationships with friends. In K. H. Rubin, W. M. Bukowski, & B. Laursen (Eds.), *Handbook of Peer Interactions, Relationships and Groups* (pp. 63–81). New York, NY: Guilford.

Burk, W. J. & Laursen, B. (2005). Adolescent perceptions of friendship and their associations with individual adjustment. *International Journal of Behavioral Development*, 29, 156–164.

Cairns, R. B., Cairns, B. D., Neckerman, H. J., Gest, S. D., & Gariepy, J. L. (1988). Social networks and aggressive behavior: Peer support or peer rejection? *Developmental Psychology*, 24, 815–823.

Cairns, R. B., Perrin, J. E., & Cairns, B. D. (1985). Social structure and social cognition in early adolescence: Affiliative patterns. *Journal of Early Adolescence*, 5, 339–355.

Cantin, S. & Boivin, M. (2004). Change and stability in children's social network and self-perceptions during transition from elementary to junior high school. *International Journal of Behavioral Development*, 28, 561–570.

Card, N. A. & Hodges, E. V. E. (2010). It takes two to fight in school, too: A social relations model of the psychometric properties and relative variance of dyadic aggression and victimization in middle school. *Social Development*, 19, 447–469.

Cicchetti, D. V. (1994). Guidelines, criteria, and rules of thumb for evaluating normed and standardized assessment instruments in psychology. *Psychological Assessment*, 6, 284–290.

Cillessen, A. H. N. (2009). Sociometric methods. In K. H. Rubin, W. M. Bukowski, & B. Laursen (Eds.), *Handbook of Peer Interactions, Relationships and Groups* (pp. 82–99). New York, NY: Guilford.

Cillessen, A. H. N. & Mayeux, L. (2004). From censure to reinforcement: Developmental changes in the association between aggression and social status. *Child Development*, 75, 147–163.

Coie, J. D. & Dodge, K. A. (1983). Continuities and changes in children's social status: A five-year longitudinal study. *Merrill-Palmer Quarterly*, 29, 261–282.

Coie, J. D. & Dodge, K. (1988). Multiple sources of data on social behavior and social status in the school: A cross-age comparison. *Child Development*, 59, 815–829.

Coie, J. D., Dodge, K. A., & Coppotelli, H. (1982). Dimensions and types of social status: A cross-age perspective. *Developmental Psychology*, 18, 557–570.

Crick, N. R., Ostrov, J. M., & Werner, N. E. (2006). A longitudinal study of relational aggression, physical aggression, and children's social psychological adjustment. *Journal of Abnormal Child Psychology*, 34, 131–142.

Edwards, A. L. (1957). *The Social Desirability Variable in Personality Assessment and Research*. New York, NY: The Dryden Press.

Egan, S. K. & Perry, D. G. (2001). Gender identity: A multidimensional analysis with implications for psychosocial adjustment. *Developmental Psychology, 37,* 451–463.

Gommans, R. & Cillessen, A. H. N. (2015). Nominating under constraints: A systematic comparison of unlimited and limited peer nomination methodologies in elementary school. *International Journal of Behavioral Development, 39,* 77–86.

Hodges, E. V. E., Malone, M. J., & Perry, D. G. (1997). Individual risk and social risk as interacting determinants of victimization in the peer group. *Developmental Psychology, 33,* 1032–1039.

Hodges, E. V. E. & Perry, D. G. (1999). Personal and interpersonal antecedents and consequences of victimization by peers. *Journal of Personality and Social Psychology, 76,* 677–685.

Kochenderfer, B. J. & Ladd, G. W. (1997). Victimized children's responses to peers' aggression: Behaviors associated with reduced versus continued victimization. *Development and Psychopathology, 9,* 59–73.

Kupersmidt, J. B. & Coie, J. D. (1990). Preadolescent peer status, aggression, and schooladjustment as predictors or externalizing problems in adolescence. *Child Development, 61,* 1350–1362.

Ladd, G. W. (1990). Having friends, keeping friends, making friends, and being liked by peers in the classroom: Predictors of children's early school adjustment? *Child Development, 61,* 1081–1100.

Ladd, G. W., Ettekal, I., & Kochenderfer-Ladd, B. (2017). Peer victimization trajectories from kindergarten through high school: Differential pathways for children's school engagement and achievement? *Journal of Educational Psychology, 109,* 826–841.

LaFontana, K. M. & Cillessen, A. H. N. (2002). Children's perceptions of popular and unpopular peers: A multimethod assessment. *Developmental Psychology, 38,* 635–647.

Newcomb, A. F. & Bukowski, W. M. (1983). Social impact and social preference as determinants of children's peer group status. *Developmental Psychology, 19,* 856–867.

Nichols, A. & Maner, J. (2008). The good subject effect: Investigating participant demand characteristics. *Journal of General Psychology, 135,* 151–166.

Parkhurst, J. T. & Hopmeyer, A. (1998). Sociometric popularity and peer-perceived popularity: Two distinct dimensions of peer status. *Journal of Early Adolescence, 18,* 125–144.

Pauletti, R. E., Cooper, P. J., & Perry, D. G. (2014). Influences of gender identity on children's maltreatment of gender-nonconforming peers: A person x target analysis. *Journal of Personality and Social Psychology, 106,* 843–866.

Perisic, I. & Rosner, B. (1999). Comparisons of measures of interclass correlations: The general case of unequal group size. *Statistics in Medicine, 18,* 1451–1466.

Perry, D. G., Perry, L. C., & Rasmussen, P. (1986). Cognitive social learning mediators of aggression. *Child Development, 57,* 700–711.

Podsakoff, P. M., MacKenzie, S. B., Lee, J., & Podsakoff, N. P. (2003). Common method biases in behavioral research: A critical review of the literature and recommended remedies. *Journal of Applied Psychology, 88,* 879–903.

Poulin, F. & Dishion, T. J. (2008). Methodological issues in the use of peer sociometric nominations with middle school youth. *Social Development, 17,* 908–921.

Velasquez, A. M., Bukowski, W. M., & Saldarriaga, L. M. (2013). Adjusting for group size effects in peer nomination data. *Social Development, 22,* 845–863.

Wiggins, J. S. & Winder, C. L. (1961). The peer nomination inventory: An empirically derived sociometric measure of adjustment in preadolescent boys. *Psychological Reports, 9,* 611–643.

Winder, C. L. & Wiggins, J. S. (1964). Social reputation and behavior: A further validation of the peer nomination inventory. *Journal of Social Psychology, 68,* 681–684.

12 Gender Identity Development

Madhavi Menon and Sara M. Gorman

Introduction to the Topic

Beginning in early childhood, children become aware of their membership in a gender category; at around the same time they also appear to know that persons of each category behave differently from each other. How this knowledge affects their personalities, self-concepts, and social behaviors has been a topic of interest for developmental researchers (Perry, Pauletti, & Cooper, 2019; Zosuls, Andrews, Martin, England, & Field, 2016 etc.). Gender is all-pervasive, and many people tend to view the world along binary lines divided by gender. In fact, gender is oftentimes the first bit of information that parents-to-be receive about their unborn child. Many would-be parents have been known to throw elaborate "gender-reveal" parties where they learn about the sex of their unborn child, often in the presence of friends and well-wishers. "*Is it a girl or a boy?*" is a question everyone wants answered! The ramifications of such gender labels are fairly quick; parents might paint the nursery in blue or pink. Friends and family might buy clothes and toys based on the gender label, and may even ascribe gender stereotypic adjectives to the baby's behavior both *in-utero* and outside (including calling their infant son "big guy" while calling their infant daughter "sweetie"). Thus, even before a child is born, people around the child view gender as an important attribute that often determines how they might respond to the child. And so begins the child's internalization of gendered norms and standards and the eventual development of their gender identity. Developmental psychologists have been particularly interested in how this gender knowledge affects individual personalities, self-concepts, and social behavior. Several prominent theories of gender have emerged as a result of this interest.

Biological theories of gender development propose that the perceivable differences between men and women can be attributed to the biological differences between them. Specifically, biological theories of gender development assert that gender differences between boys/men and girls/women stem from evolutionary adapted predispositions as well as the unique chromosomal (XY or XX) and hormonal differences observed between each sex due to their biological differences. Evolutionary theories of gender development (e.g. Buss & Kenrick, 1998) assert that, because different pressures were placed upon men and women evolutionarily, certain psychological and behavioral dispositions were built into the human species that have led to the natural selection of certain traits for each gender. As a result, evolutionary theories of gender development maintain that children possess evolutionarily evolved tendencies to seek environments that will allow for the expression of their sexually selected dispositions. Other biological theories of gender development place more emphasis on the biological development of boys and girls, beginning at conception, and the corresponding environmental and hormonal differences observed. For example, Money and Ehrhardt's Biosocial Theory (1972) posits that *critical episodes*, which occur throughout development, ultimately influence individuals' preferences for adopting a masculine or feminine gender role.

Social learning theory proponents such as Albert Bandura (1986; Bussey & Bandura, 1999), posit that children develop their gender identities and role preferences via two pathways, namely, *direct tuition* (and differential reinforcement) where children are rewarded and encouraged to endorse gender-appropriate behaviors, and *observational learning* whereby children adopt behaviors of their same-sex models. The social learning theory (Bussey & Bandura, 1999) thus states that all behavior (including gender) is learned from observing others and the reinforcement children receive from their environments (e.g. parents, teachers, peers, media, etc.).

Kohlberg's theory of gender development (1966, 1969) proposed that as children grow older, their understanding of gender becomes more sophisticated and they use their cognitions to make judgments about their gender identities. Kohlberg's theory further posits that gender develops in a sequence of three discrete stages: gender identity, gender stability, and gender constancy, at the end of which the child would have developed gender identity. (See Ruble, Martin, & Berenbaum, 2006, for more details).

Gender Schema Theory. Similar to Kohlberg's theory, Gender Schema Theory (GST) (Martin & Halverson, 1981; Martin, Ruble, & Szkrybalo, 2002) also stresses that children's gender identity motivates the learning and adoption of gender stereotypes; albeit at a faster rate. The GST posits that children develop gender-relevant schemas which are readily accessible, organized mental frameworks of information to categorize themselves and their world by forming an own-sex, an in-group, and an out-group schema. Furthermore, children focus on gender schematic (or "own-sex") information that provides them with a framework for gender-appropriate behaviors, while ignoring or discounting gender non-schematic or "other-sex" information, thereby cementing their own gender identities.

Summary of Topics

The study of gender-typing research has traditionally focused on three separate but interrelated topics (Hines, 2015): development of gender identity or gender concept—that is, the knowledge that one is either a boy or a girl, and that gender is an unchanging attribute; the development of gender-role stereotypes—i.e. the ideas about what males and females are supposed to be like; and development of gender-typed patterns of behavior—i.e. the child's tendency to favor same-sex activities over those normally associated with the other sex.

Researchers have been solicitous to the age-related changes that occur regarding gender-typing in conjunction with age-related changes in gendered behaviors and gendered thinking (Hines, 2015). It is necessary to study gender with both broad and short-term approaches as both are useful in identifying *how* gender development occurs as well as the processes that are essential for *why* such developmental patterns exist. On account of this dynamic approach to studying gender development, researchers have begun to conceptualize the measurement of gender-pertinent, temporal changes (i.e. changes that result due to the passage of time) with more calculated and specified methodologies. The goal of the current section is to highlight key developmental changes that occur regarding the emergence of children's gender identity, gender-typed patterns of behavior, and gender stereotypes/discriminatory beliefs. It is currently undecided if children's gender identities, as proposed by self-socialization theories, motivate and further the development of gendered behaviors, or if children's gender identities have little to do with the development of gendered behaviors, given that many gendered behaviors occur prior to the age of gender-understanding proposed by most prominent theories of gender development.

Emergence of Gender Stereotypes

While infants seem to lack the mental faculties necessary to possess stereotypical beliefs, the development of stereotypes in young children does begin in infancy with the conceptualization and understanding of sex differences (Alexander & Wilcox, 2012). Infants as early as 6 months of age can discern between male and female faces; by 10 months they possess understandings of male and female possessions, faces, roles, and activities (Levy & Haaf, 1994). Beginning at 24 months, the basis of gender stereotypes is present in the minds of young children (Poulin-Dubois, Serbin, & Derbyshire, 1998) and by 36 months they appear to possess basic gender stereotypes—which coincide directly with the emergence of their understanding of their own gender identity (Martin & Ruble, 2004). By 4–5 years, children begin to demonstrate more abstract stereotypical beliefs (Halim & Ruble, 2010).

Gender Self-Socialization Model (GSSM; Perry et al., 2019; Tobin et al., 2010) regards many of the previously delineated perspectives as valid conceptualizations of the gender–self association. The GSSM takes a multidimensional perspective and posits that there are three constructs which are key to understanding the gender self-socialization processes: gender identity, gender stereotypes, and attribute self-perception. *Gender identity* refers to the association individuals make between the self and a gender category, for example, "I am a boy," or, "I am like other boys," or, "I like being a boy." *Gender stereotypes* refer to the association individuals make between a gender group and an attribute, for example, "Boys are aggressive," or, "boys are good at math." *Attribute self-perception* refers to the association individuals make between the self and an attribute that they (or others) believe differentiate the genders, for example, "I am aggressive," or, "I am good at math." The gender self-socialization paradigm uses these three constructs as building blocks and discusses how each of these constructs is also a product of the cognitive interplay between *gender stereotype emulation, gender stereotype construction,* and *gender identity construction.*

The *gender stereotype emulation* perspective of the GSSM posits that gender identity and gender stereotypes collectively affect attribute self-perceptions. Hence, the more children identify with a gender collective (i.e., gender identity), the more likely they will be to perceive in themselves the attributes they view as more typical of (or desirable for) persons of that gender. According to the GSSM, stereotype emulation begins once children attain basic gender identity around the age of 3 (Carter & Levy, 1988; Ruble et al., 2006; Zosuls et al., 2009), an age when children's self-concepts typically consist of gender-normative ideas (Hannover, 2000).

As children get older, however, two important developmental changes occur. First, there is an emergence and stabilization of individual differences in the various aspects of gender identity as children begin to exhibit variations in their profiles for gender typicality, gender contentment, felt pressure, and gender typicality. The second change that occurs is the development of individual differences in descriptive as well as prescriptive ideologies and stereotypes. Eventually, these two sets of cognitions combine to shape a cognitive system that guides children's self-perceptions of specific attributes. While the motivation of children's emulation of internalized stereotypes is the prime role of gender identity, however, due to the individual variations seen in children's stereotypes, the specific attributes influenced by gender identity vary among children of each sex. For instance, gender contentedness might encourage one boy to adopt macho, assertive, risk-taking behaviors, but lead another to pursue math or sports; felt pressure might cause one girl to avoid math and science but another to avoid assertive behavior, perhaps especially when with boys or men. These ideas are consistent with research findings indicating that different children of the same sex may adopt different sex-typed behaviors (Harris, 1995; Maccoby, 1998; Spence, 1985).

The *gender stereotype construction* perspective of the GSSM posits that children project their own attributes onto a gender collective to the extent that they identify with the collective (e.g., "I am friendly and I am a typical boy, so boys are friendly"). This view focuses on the interactive influences of gender identity and self-perceptions of attributes on gender stereotypes. This perspective is consistent with research that indicates that people often project their own socially desirable as well as socially undesirable attributes onto groups to which they belong (Cadinu & Rothbart, 1996; Greenwald et al., 2002; Krueger & Stanke, 2001; Ross, 1977). Similarly, research also suggests that children sometimes use their own behaviors and preferences to form stereotypes. For instance, when children are shown novel items and asked how much they like each item and how much other boys/girls would like them, research findings indicate that children often attribute their own preferences to same-sex others (Martin, Eisenbud, & Rose, 1995), thus, suggesting that both descriptive as well as prescriptive stereotypes may trace their genesis to the self-perceptions of attributes. Further, gender identity should influence the direction and strength of people's tendencies to project their qualities onto gender groups. Although most people would be expected to project primarily onto their same-sex collective, individuals with a weak gender identity may not demonstrate this bias (Liben & Bigler, 2002; Martin, 2000). Similarly, strongly cross-gender-identified individuals would be more inclined to project their attributes onto the other-gender collective. The perspective that children's gender identity might combine with their self-perceived gender-typing to foster gender stereotypes can help explain why children whose parents hold egalitarian attitudes about gender roles may sometimes develop gender ideologies that are widely divergent from the attitudes of their parents. The GSSM's gender stereotype construction perspective specifies that strong same-gender identity encourages people to project an attribute perceived in the self onto the same-gender collective. However, when people perceive a negative quality in a group to which they belong, they tend to project that negative attribute onto another group.

The GSSM's *gender identity construction* perspective specifies that the more children's self-perceived attributes match their stereotypes for a gender, the more likely they would be to identify with that gender. Thus the GSSM considers how stereotypes and attribute self-perceptions come together to influence each of the gender identity components. For instance, the attainment of membership knowledge may be influenced by the perception of a match between one's own attributes and same-gender stereotypes. However, some research suggests that children's ability to assign themselves to a gender category may precede rather than follow gender-typed preferences (Zosuls et al., 2009). Therefore, perhaps it is more likely that children's attainment of the later stages of membership knowledge development (gender stability and gender conservation) are helped if children note that their sex remains unchanged even when they occasionally engage in cross-sex activities. Similarly matching versus failing to match gender stereotypes might also affect felt pressure for gender conformity. For instance, children who believe they are falling short of important and valued gender stereotypes might apply more pressure on themselves to conform. Further, extant research indicates that people often base their perceptions of gender typicality, gender contentment, and gender centrality on the basis of self-evaluations across multiple attributes that are idiosyncratically weighted (Spence, 1985, 1993). Therefore, the more children view themselves as typifying salient and valued same-gender stereotypes, the more gender typical and content they would feel, and these children would also be more likely to consider gender as a vital component of their identity (i.e., gender centrality).

Thus, the GSSM reflects upon three interrelated processes to help explain how children emulate gender stereotypes and incorporate them into their self-concept, how children build a stable gender identity by self-appraising themselves against gender standards that are personally and consensually determined, and how they project their own attributes onto the same-gender collective. The outcomes of each process are determined by the interactive influences of gender identity and gender stereotypes (stereotype emulation), gender stereotypes and attribute self-perceptions (identity construction), and gender identity and attribute self-perceptions (stereotype construction).

Possible Measurements and Designs in Child Development Research

Infants and young children are a difficult population to assess for a variety of reasons, including their lack of attentional and language capabilities due to which they often cannot be studied using the same research methodologies that might be used with adults. As such, there are some key methods that can be used in this work. Some of the most commonly used research methods and designs include *observational methods*, *longitudinal designs*, *cross-sectional designs*, and *case studies*.

Observational Studies

Sometimes referred to as "naturalistic," observational studies are research studies in which a researcher observes behavior in a systematic manner without influencing or interfering with the behavior in any capacity. Observational child study designs are often exploratory or used when there could be ethical concerns if another study design is used. Using this design does not allow for the implication of causality; this is merely a descriptive research design. For example, if a researcher is interested in studying naturally occurring, gendered toy preferences (e.g. preference to play with a race car or a baby doll) in toddlers, they could do so via an observational child study design. Observing participants in their natural environments has many benefits including our ability to observe the "true" behaviors. However, naturalistic observations could potentially be open to the presence of confounding variables that can affect the accuracy of our results. Thus, laboratory observational studies can be conducted where the participants might come in to an artificially created environment that can yield greater control to the researchers (because many confounding variables can be accounted for and controlled).

Longitudinal Child Studies

In a longitudinal design, a group of children is studied across time (i.e. weeks, months, years). This design allows researchers to see changes in certain behaviors across time, to study patterns of development. Because the same children are seen at all of the ages being studied, this study provides the benefit of ensuring that differences are a consequence of the participants aging rather than individual differences between participants/samples.

Cross-sectional Child Studies

Cross-sectional studies occur when comparisons are made regarding the abilities of two (or more) different groups of children. In cross-sectional designs, the groups of children are of different age ranges. For example, a researcher could study a gender-typed behavior in children aged 5 and 9, and then compare results from each group. There are several benefits of using a cross-sectional design over a longitudinal design. Perhaps the most significant advantage is researchers do not have to wait for the children to get older to see age-related changes. Another benefit of using a cross-sectional design is the study takes place at a single point in time rather than at multiple time points. Cross-sectional child designs can also allow for the garnering of information regarding a specific cohort as well as generational views about gendered behaviors.

Child Case Studies

Case studies involve the assessment of one or a few children who are studied regularly over a period. Child case studies typically last at least 6 months or longer. There are two primary advantages to using child case studies. First, this study design can provide a very rich and detailed picture of development because there are so few children involved. The second notable benefit of this design is that it can be used to investigate special populations of children in detail.

Core Methodologies and Innovations in Social Cognitive Methods in Gender Identity Development Research

Typically, child self-reports, teacher reports, parent reports, observations, and interview methods have been used to study gender identity development. The suggestion that children strive to incorporate into their self-concepts (and behavioral repertoires), attributes that they perceive to be appropriate for persons of their gender, is an enduring one that is shared by researchers of diverse theoretical persuasions. Both cognitive-developmental theorists (e.g., Kagan, 1964; Kohlberg, 1966) and cognitive social learning theorists (e.g., Bandura, 1986; Bussey & Bandura, 1999) have advanced the hypothesis, albeit stressing different motivational mechanisms. Over the years, however, the hypothesis has received inconsistent support, owing perhaps to certain conceptual and methodological shortcomings in the ways the hypothesis has been framed and tested.

The perspective that children adopt (or shun) attributes that they perceive to be appropriate (or inappropriate) for an identity as male or female (e.g., Bandura, 1986; Bussey & Perry, 1976; Mehta, 2015) implies that children's gender stereotypes and gender identity interact to predict attribute adoption. However, most studies testing this hypothesis have focused either on the impact of stereotypes on attribute adoption (and neglected the role of gender identity) or on the impact of gender identity on attribute adoption (and neglected the role of stereotypes).

Gender Stereotypes and Attribute Adoption

Gender stereotypes are children's beliefs about how the sexes differ ("descriptive stereotypes") or should differ ("prescriptive stereotypes"). When preschoolers first acquire gender stereotypes, they view them as moral imperatives (i.e., their gender stereotypes are prescriptive as well as descriptive; Huston, 1983). Once children attain gender constancy, around age 6 or 7 years, many (but not all) show decreased rigidity and increased flexibility in their stereotypes, that is, they come to believe that even if an activity is performed more frequently by persons of one sex, it is still permissible for persons of both sexes (Signorella, Bigler, & Liben, 1993). However, a child's gender identity is distinct from gender stereotypic behavior (Tobin et al., 2010).

Do stereotypes predict attribute adoption for specifically gendered behaviors? This question is usually addressed by relating individual differences in stereotype understanding to attribute adoption. In a typical study, researchers begin by compiling lists of male-typed and female-typed attributes; the lists are based either on real differences between the sexes or, more commonly, on people's (either adults' or children's) ratings of the degree to which each attribute is more typical of (or desirable for) one sex than the other. Sometimes the lists mix attributes from different domains of sex-typing (e.g., personality traits, recreational activities) or mix attributes that vary in social desirability, but sometimes more specialized sublists are constructed; for example, the male-typed and the female-typed lists might each be subdivided into occupations, activities, and traits (e.g., Liben & Bigler, 2002), or into desirable versus undesirable attributes (e.g., Aubry, Ruble, & Silverman, 1999). The lists (or sublists) are then presented to new participants, for whom stereotype "knowledge" and "flexibility" scores are calculated (for each list/sublist). Stereotype knowledge is the number of descriptive stereotypes known; participants are asked to indicate whether each attribute is more common to males or females, and the number of "correct" responses is the index of knowledge. Stereotype flexibility is assessed by asking participants to indicate whether each attribute is appropriate for only one sex or is acceptable for both sexes; the number of "both" responses is the index of flexibility.

It is expected that children with greater stereotype knowledge, and children with less stereotype flexibility, will be more likely than other children to adopt same-gender attributes and to shun other-gender ones. It is assumed that gender identity motivates this process, but biological sex is used as a proxy for gender identity, and individual differences in gender identity are not assessed. Several studies have found the expected associations between the stereotype measures and attribute adoption (e.g., Aubry et al., 1999; Liben & Bigler, 2002; Serbin, Powlishta, & Gulko, 1993). However, the associations are often weak and inconsistent (Endendijk, Andrews, England, & Martin, 2019).

One problem with the forgoing approach is that the stereotype measures as well as the adoption measures reflect aggregations across diverse attributes; this practice might mask a link that exists between a stereotype about a specific behavior (e.g., aggression, math) and adoption of that particular behavior (Liben & Bigler, 2002; Ruble & Martin, 2002). Indeed, stronger evidence for the influence of stereotypes on adoption is found in studies in which a specific attribute is predicted from children's stereotypes about that particular attribute. Fairly strong associations are found between (a) the degree to which children achieve in math, want to learn a particular musical instrument, prefer playmates of a particular sex, aspire to a particular occupation, self-report a particular personality trait, or play with a particular toy and (b) the degree to which children believe the behavior is more common or desirable for persons of their own sex than for the other (Endendijk et al., 2019; Liben & Bigler, 2002; Martin, Andrews, England, Zosuls, & Ruble, 2017; Ruble & Martin, 2002). Additional evidence attesting to the power of specific stereotypes on specific behaviors comes from studies in which a stereotype is created experimentally, either through labeling (e.g., telling children that a novel toy is "for girls" or "for boys"; Martin, 2000) or modeling (e.g., showing children that persons of one sex like an object whereas persons of the other sex avoid it; Perry & Bussey, 1979).

The typical strategy used to assess stereotypes also fails to allow for the possibility that some children hold idiosyncratic stereotypes that influence their behavior and development. In the typical study, the attributes studied are usually limited to ones shown in pretest to be sex-typed—observed or judged to vary with gender at the group level. Attributes that do not show a sex difference are called "neutral" and eliminated from study. However, an attribute need not be differentiated by sex at the group level in order to be gender stereotyped by an individual child. Participation in art or music, for example, may not be sex-typed at the group level (in either reality or perception), but individual children may hold a strong belief that the activity is more common or appropriate for one sex than the other and adopt or avoid it on this basis. Even when a behavior is strongly sex-typed at the group level, individual children may not share the stereotype or may even attribute the behavior to the other gender. Communal behavior, agentic behavior, and even physical aggression are sometimes attributed by children to a gender in a way counter to the usual stereotype (Giles & Heyman, 2005; Guimond, Chatard, Martinot, Crisp, & Redersdorff, 2006). That many children's stereotypes are eccentric was also argued by Martin (2000), who pointed out that children's cognitive networks of gender associations are likely to vary as a function of children's unique experiences with family, media, peer groups, teachers and schools, racial/ethnic subculture, and other factors.

Another shortcoming of stereotype assessments has been a lack of attention to contextual cues. Stereotypes may take the form of rules specifying how persons of each sex do or should behave in particular contexts, and these rules can influence behavior within these settings. A trend in the social psychology literature (and, increasingly, the developmental literature) is a growing awareness of the dependence of gendered cognition and conduct on context. Sex differences in social behavior do often hinge on contextual factors (e.g., group size, familiarity of interaction partner, public vs. private setting, mixed-sex vs. single-sex group, male vs. female interaction partner; Hyde, 2005; Leaper & Smith, 2004). For example, a sex difference in assertion is larger in same-sex than in mixed-sex groups of children (Leaper & Smith, 2004). Children may internalize such context–behavior contingencies in the form of context-dependent expectations and scripts specifying how males and females behave under various circumstances (Deaux & LaFrance, 1998).

Another problem arises when researchers try to predict attribute adoption from stereotype flexibility. The flexibility measure cannot be expected to be a strong predictor of children's gender-based adoption because the rules that children hold about the gender conformity of other people are independent of the rules they hold about their own gender conformity (Liben & Bigler, 2002). Children may feel it is wrong to insist that others follow stereotypes yet become quite upset at the thought of violating the stereotypes themselves.

Finally, using biological sex as a proxy for gender identity is problematic. Biological sex is correlated with factors other than identity (e.g., hormones) that may energize the adoption of attributes categorized as appropriate for a gender. Also, letting biological sex stand in for gender identity precludes evaluating the role that within-sex individual differences in gender identity might play in the adoption of attributes perceived as sex-typed.

Gender identity has been conceptualized in diverse ways. Kohlberg (1966) viewed gender identity as knowing that one is a member of one sex rather than the other. Kagan (1964) regarded gender identity as perceiving the self as conforming to cultural stereotypes for one's gender. Bem (1981) saw gender identity as internalized societal pressure for gender conformity. Green (1974), Spence (1985), and Zucker et al. (1993) viewed gender identity as a fundamental sense of acceptance of, and belonging to, one's gender. Building on this work, Egan and Perry (2001) advanced a multidimensional perspective on gender identity. In their model, gender identity has five components: (a) *membership knowledge* (knowledge of one's gender); (b) *gender typicality* (perceived similarity to the same-gender collective); (c) *gender contentedness* (satisfaction with one's gender); (d) *felt pressure* for gender conformity (pressure felt from parents, peers, and the self for conforming to gender stereotypes); and (e) *intergroup bias* (the belief that one's own sex is superior). Thus, Egan and Perry's model incorporates several of the other conceptualizations of gender identity and is consistent with arguments that collective identity is fruitfully conceptualized as multidimensional (Ashmore, Deaux, & McLaughlin-Volpe, 2004).

Conceptualizations of gender identity addressing individual differences beyond early childhood (e.g., Kagan, 1964; Zucker et al., 1993) have rarely been used in tests of the self-socialization hypothesis. One influential conceptualization that has spawned work on the hypothesis, albeit primarily with adults, is that of Bem (1981). However, Bem's assessment approach is problematic. Bem tried to measure people's felt pressure for gender conformity by assessing the degree to which they lacked a balance of agentic and communal traits in the self-concept. Bem assumed that a person who reported having mostly agentic traits (and few communal traits) was male sex-typed, and similarly a person who reported having primarily communal traits was thus female sex-typed. Furthermore, Bem assumed that being male or female sex-typed reflected an imbalance of gender traits due to internalized societal pressure to adhere to one gender role at the expense of the other.

However, overall masculinity and femininity cannot be inferred solely from self-perceived agentic and communal traits because self-perceived sex-typing is multifactorial (e.g., agentic and communal traits are not highly correlated with male-typical or female-typical behavior in other domains of sex-typing, such as toy and activity preferences, relationship partner preferences, academic pursuits, and occupational aspirations), and different people base their overall felt masculinity and femininity on different aspects of sex-typing (Spence & Hall, 1996). It is thus not surprising that people's self-perceptions of agentic and communal traits do not relate strongly to their self-ratings of how "masculine" and "feminine" they are (e.g., Pedhazur & Tetenbaum, 1979). It is also unlikely that people's overall sense of maleness or femaleness is strongly, if at all, correlated with the amount of pressure they feel for conforming to a particular gender role (Egan & Perry, 2001). Lastly, because Bem's scales assess self-perceived adoption of agentic and communal traits, they are more appropriately viewed as tapping attribute adoption (the putative outcome of self-socialization) rather than gender identity (a putative motivator of the process). Despite these problems, Bem's central hypothesis—strong felt pressure for gender conformity straightjackets development by causing people slavishly to adhere to same-gender norms and avoid cross-sex options—remains compelling and viable.

Egan and Perry (2001), Tobin et al. (2010), and more recently Martin et al. (2017) have argued that gender identity should not be inferred from children's self-perceptions of sex-typed attributes but rather should be assessed via questions that directly ask children how they feel about themselves in relation to gender categories. Work with their model has focused mainly on the implications of gender identity for children's social adjustment and mental health. As hypothesized by Egan and Perry, low gender typicality, low gender contentedness, and high felt pressure predict (concurrently and prospectively) less than optimal adjustment (e.g., lower self-esteem, greater internalizing symptoms, peer rejection), at least for White preadolescent children (Carver, Yunger, & Perry, 2003). However, there exist in this work hints that gender identity might also affect children's adoption of attributes perceived as sex-typed—if it is assumed that most children in the studies possessed commonly shared stereotypes.

For example, in these studies, gender typicality was associated with agentic traits for boys but not girls; gender contentedness was associated with low self-efficacy for female-typed activities for boys but not girls; and felt pressure was associated with reduced agentic behavior for girls but not boys (Carver et al., 2003; Egan & Perry, 2001; Pauletti, Cooper, & Perry, 2014). In addition, a negative relation between felt pressure and self-esteem was stronger for girls than for boys (Carver et al., 2003; Egan & Perry, 2001). Perhaps many esteem-enhancing behaviors (e.g., self-assertion, leadership, sports) are viewed by children of both sexes as more typical of boys than of girls, and therefore felt pressure discourages these behaviors and reduces self-esteem primarily for girls. Additional evidence that gender identity works in cahoots with gender stereotypes comes from Corby, Hodges, and Perry (2007), who examined gender identity in Black, Hispanic, and White preadolescents and found several unexpected links to adjustment for minority children. For example, among Hispanic girls, high gender contentment was associated not only with reduced agentic behavior but also with internalizing symptoms (e.g., anxiety, self-deprecation). Perhaps for these girls, gender identity had promoted the adoption of patriarchal stereotypes (i.e., a subservient, helpless role for females).

Thus, children's gender identity probably works in conjunction with their conceptions of what it means to be male or female to affect development. The GSSM (Menon & Menon, 2017; Perry et al., 2019; Tobin et al., 2010) assumes that, starting at an early age, children simultaneously develop components of gender identity and form beliefs about the attributes that embody gender (some idiosyncratic, some shared with others). At some point, these two sets of cognitions come together to form two interlocking cornerstones of a causal cognitive system that affects children's adoption of specific attributes. Gender identity provides the motivational fuel for the adoption (and avoidance) of behaviors perceived by children as sex-typed, but owing to the idiosyncratic nature of children's stereotypes, the specific behaviors influenced by gender identity might vary among children of each sex. For example, gender contentedness might encourage one boy to adopt aggressive, macho, risk-taking behaviors but lead another to pursue science, math, or sports; felt pressure might cause one girl to avoid math and science but another to avoid assertive behavior, perhaps especially with males.

Conclusion

The GSSM is intended as a heuristic for exploring conjoint influences of gender identity and stereotypes on development. It essentially makes a single prediction—the stronger one's gender identity, the more one brings self-perceptions (and behavior) into line with one's stereotypes—but it can be tested using multiple dimensions of gender identity and multiple potentially stereotyped attributes (that exist at varying levels of contextual embeddedness). The GSSM carries implications for the assessment of sex-typing (children's possession or self-perception of sex-typed attributes), particularly with regards to from whose perspective sex-typing defined. The tradition is to define sex-typed attributes as those that are sex-differentiated (in either reality or consensus). This practice has its roots in the sex-differences approach to investigating gender. The GSSM, however, draws attention to the fact that sex-typing can also be defined from the perspective of the individual child. Defining sex-typing from the child's perspective may be necessary when testing theoretical models that accord causal status to the child's personal and unique perspective on gender, as the GSSM does. Focusing on the child's definition of sex-typing also allows for the possibility that some children construe an attribute to be gendered when the attribute is not agreed on by a panel of judges to be sex-typed.

More theory and research on how gender self-socialization operates at crucial developmental junctures would be worthwhile. For example, how might children's gender identity and stereotypes conjointly affect their transition into the dating arena? Does gender identity govern the activation of dating scripts? Is it true, as suggested by Glick and Hilt (2000), that children with negative stereotypes about the other sex transform these attitudes into less overt but still troublesome "ambivalent sexism" (a superficially benign, but essentially disparaging, stance toward the other sex) when they realize they need the other sex for romance? Does gender self-socialization function similarly or differently for children with different sexual orientations (Carver et al., 2003)? Exploring the predictive capacities of the GSSM may help researchers and clinicians alike appreciate the many ways that gender can invade a child's psyche, sometimes for better, but sometimes for worse.

References

Alexander, G. M. & Wilcox, T. (2012). Sex differences in early infancy. *Child Development Perspectives*, 6(4), 400–406.

Ashmore, R. D., Deaux, K., & McLaughlin-Volpe, T. (2004). An organizing framework for collective identity: Articulation and significance of multidimensionality. *Psychological Bulletin*, 130, 80–114.

Aubry, S., Ruble, D. N., & Silverman, L. B. (1999). The role of gender knowledge in children's gender-typed preferences. In L. Balter & C. S. Tamis-LeMonda (Eds.), *Child Psychology: A Handbook of Contemporary Issues* (pp. 363–390). New York: Psychology Press.

Bandura, A. (1986). *Social Foundations of Thought and Action: A social cognitive theory*. Englewood Cliffs, NJ: Prentice-Hall.

Bem, S. L. (1981). Gender schema theory: A cognitive account of sex typing. *Psychological Review*, 88, 354–364.

Buss, D. M. & Kenrick, D. T. (1998). Evolutionary social psychology. In D. T. Gilbert, S. T. Fiske, & G. Lindzey (Eds.), *The Handbook of Social Psychology* (Vol. 2, pp. 982–1026). New York: McGraw-Hill.

Bussey, K. & Bandura, A. (1999). Social cognitive theory of gender development and differentiation. *Psychological Review*, *106*, 676–713.

Bussey, K. & Perry, D. G. (1976). Sharing reinforcement contingencies with a model: A social-earning analysis of similarity effects in imitation research. *Journal of Personality and Social Psychology*, *34*(6), 1168–1176.

Cadinu, M. R. & Rothbart, M. (1996). Self-anchoring and differentiation processes in the minimal group setting. *Journal of Personality and Social Psychology*, *70*, 661–677.

Carter, D. B. & Levy, G. D. (1988). Cognitive aspects of early sex-role development: The influence of gender schemas on preschoolers' memories and preferences for sex-typed toys and activities. *Child Development*, *59*, 782–792.

Carver, P. R., Yunger, J. L., & Perry, D. G. (2003). Gender identity and adjustment in middle childhood. *Sex Roles*, *49*, 95–109.

Corby, B. C., Hodges, E. V. E., & Perry, D. G. (2007). Gender identity and adjustment in Black, Hispanic, and White preadolescents. *Developmental Psychology*, *43*(1), 261–266.

Deaux, K. & LaFrance, M. (1998). Gender. In D. T. Gilbert, S. T. Fiske, & G. Lindzey (Eds.), *Handbook of Social Psychology* (Vol. 1, pp. 788–827). New York: McGraw-Hill.

Egan, S. K. & Perry, D. G. (2001). Gender identity: A multidimensional analysis with implications for psychosocial adjustment. *Developmental Psychology*, *37*, 451–463.

Endendijk, J. J., Andrews, N. C. Z., England, D. E., & Martin, C. L. (2019). Gender-identity typologies are related to gender-typing, friendships, and social-emotional adjustment in Dutch emerging adults. *International Journal of Behavioral Development*, Advance online publication. doi: 10.1177/0165025418820686.

Giles, J. W. & Heyman, G. D. (2005). Young children's beliefs about the relationship between gender and aggressive behavior. *Child Development*, *76*, 107–121.

Glick, P. & Hilt, L. (2000). Combative children to ambivalent adults: The development of gender prejudice. In T. Eckes & H. M. Trautner (Eds.), *The Developmental Social Psychology of Gender* (pp. 243–272). Mahwah, NJ: Lawrence Erlbaum Associates Publishers.

Green, R. (1974). *Sexual Identity Conflict in Children and Adults*. New York: Basic Books.

Greenwald, A. G., Banaji, M. R., Rudman, L. A., Farnham, S. D., Nosek, B. A., & Mellott, D. S. (2002). A unified theory of implicit attitudes, stereotypes, self-esteem, and self-concept. *Psychological Review*, *109*, 3–25.

Guimond, S., Chatard, A., Martinot, D., Crisp, R. J., & Redersdorff, S. (2006). Social comparison, self-stereotyping, and gender differences in self-construals. *Journal of Personality and Social Psychology*, *90*, 221–242.

Halim, M. L. & Ruble, D. (2010). Gender identity and stereotyping in early and middle childhood. In J. C. Chrisler & D. R. McCreary (Eds.), *Handbook of Gender Research in Psychology: Gender Research in General and Experimental Psychology* (pp. 495–525). New York: Springer Science + Business Media.

Hannover, B. (2000). Development of the self in gendered contexts. In T. Eckes & H. M. Trautner (Eds.), *The Developmental Social Psychology of Gender* (pp. 177–206). Mahwah, NJ: Erlbaum Associates Publishers.

Harris, J. R. (1995). Where is the child's environment? A group socialization theory of development. *Psychological Review*, *102*, 458–489.

Hines, M. (2015). Gendered development. In R. M. Lerner & M. E. Lamb (Eds.), *Handbook of Child Psychology and Developmental Science* (Vol. 3, 7th ed., pp. 842–887). Hoboken, NJ: Wiley.

Huston, A. C. (1983). Sex-typing. In E. M. Hetherington (Ed.), *Handbook of Child Psychology: Socialization, Personality, and Social Development* (Vol. 4, pp. 388–467). New York: Wiley.

Hyde, J. S. (2005). The gender similarities hypothesis. *American Psychologist*, *60*, 581–592.

Kagan, J. (1964). Acquisition and significance of sex typing and sex role identity. In M. L. Hoffman & L. W. Hoffman (Eds.), *Review of Child Development Research* (Vol. 1, pp. 137–168). New York: Russell Sage Foundation.

Kohlberg, L. (1966). A cognitive-developmental analysis of children's sex-role concepts and attitudes. In E. E. Maccody (Ed.), *The Development of Sex Differences* (pp. 82–173). Stanford, CA: Stanford University Press.

Kohlberg, L. (1969). Stage and sequence: The cognitive-developmental approach to socialization. In D. A. Goslin (Ed.), *Handbook of Socialization Theory and Research* (pp. 347–480). Chicago, IL: Rand McNally.

Krueger, J. & Stanke, D. (2001). The role of self-referent and other referent knowledge in perceptions of group characteristics. *Personality and Social Psychology Bulletin*, 27, 878–888.

Leaper, C. & Smith, T. E. (2004). A meta-analytic review of gender variations in children's language use: Talkativeness, affiliative speech, and assertive speech. *Developmental Psychology*, 40, 993–1027.

Levy, G. D. & Haaf, R. A. (1994). Detection of gender-related categories by 10-month-old infants. *Infant Behavior and Development*, 17(4), 457–459.

Liben, L. S. & Bigler, R. S. (2002). The developmental course of gender differentiation: Conceptualizing, measuring, and evaluating constructs and pathways. *Monographs of the Society for Research in Child Development*, 67, (2, Serial No. 269).

Maccoby, E. E. (1998). *The Two Sexes: Growing Up Apart, Coming Together*. Cambridge, MA: Harvard University Press.

Martin, C. L. (2000). Cognitive theories of gender development. In T. Eckes & H. M. Trautner (Eds.), *The Developmental Social Psychology of Gender* (pp. 91–122). Mahwah, NJ: Lawrence Erlbaum Associates Publishers.

Martin, C. L., Andrews, N. C. Z., England, D. E., Zosuls, K., & Ruble, D. N. (2017). A dual identity approach for conceptualizing and measuring children's gender identity. *Child Development*, 88(1), 167–182.

Martin, C. L., Eisenbud, L., & Rose, H. (1995). Children's gender-based reasoning about toys. *Child Development*, 66, 1453–1471.

Martin, C. L. & Halverson, C. F., Jr. (1981). A schematic processing model of sex typing and stereotyping in children. *Child Development*, 52, 1119–1134.

Martin, C. L. & Ruble, D. (2004). Children's search for gender cues: Cognitive perspectives on gender development. *Current Directions in Psychological Science*, 13(2), 67–70.

Martin, C. L., Ruble, D. N., & Szkrybalo, J. (2002). Cognitive theories of early gender development. *Psychological Bulletin*, 128(6), 903–933.

Mehta, C. M. (2015). Gender in context: Considering variability in Wood and Eagly's traditions of gender identity. *Sex Roles*, 73, 490–496.

Menon, M. & Menon, M. (2017). Gender self-socialization. In K. L. Nadal (Ed.), *The SAGE Encyclopedia of Psychology and Gender* (pp. 734–736). Thousand Oaks, CA: Sage publications.

Money, J. & Ehrhardt, A. A. (1972). *Man and Woman, Boy and Girl: The Differentiation and Dimorphism of Gender Identity from Conception to Maturity*. Baltimore, MD: Johns Hopkins University Press.

Pauletti, R. E., Cooper, P. J., & Perry, D. G. (2014). Influences of gender identity on children's maltreatment of gender non-conforming peers: A person x target analysis of aggression. *Journal of Personality and Social Psychology*, 106, 843–866.

Pedhazur, E. J. & Tetenbaum, T. J. (1979). Bem sex role inventory: A theoretical methodological critique. *Journal of Personality and Social Psychology*, 37, 996–1016.

Perry, D. G. & Bussey, K. (1979). The social learning theory of sex differences: Imitation is alive and well. *Journal of Personality and Social Psychology*, 37, 1699–1712.

Perry, D. G., Pauletti, R. E., & Cooper, P. J. (2019). Gender identity in childhood: A review of the literature. *International Journal of Behavioral Development*. Advance online publication. doi: 10.1177/0165025418811129.

Poulin-Dubois, D., Serbin, L. A., & Derbyshire, A. (1998). Toddlers' intermodal and verbal knowledge about gender. *Merrill-Palmer Quarterly*, 44, 338–354.

Ross, M. W. (1977). Paradigm lost or paradigm regained? Behaviour therapy and homosexuality. *New Zealand Psychologist*, 6, 42–51.

Ruble, D. N. & Martin, C. L. (2002). Conceptualizing, measuring, and evaluating the developmental course of gender differentiation: Compliments, queries, and quandaries. *Monograph of the Society for Research in Child Development*, 67, 148–166.

Ruble, D. N., Martin, C. L., & Berenbaum, S. A. (2006). Gender development. In N. Eisenberg, W. Damon, & R. M. Lerner (Eds.), *Handbook of Child Psychology: Vol. 3. Social, Emotional, and Personality Development* (pp. 858–932). Hoboken, NJ: Wiley.

Serbin, L. A., Powlishta, K. K., & Gulko, J. (1993). The development of sex-typing in middle childhood. *Monographs of the Society of Research in Child Development*, 58, (Serial No. 232).

Signorella, M. L., Bigler, R. S., & Liben, L. S. (1993). Developmental differences in children's gender schemata about others: A meta-analytic review. *Developmental Review*, 13, 147–183.

Spence, J. T. (1985). Gender identity and implications for concepts of masculinity and femininity. In T. B. Sonderegger (Ed.), *Nebraska Symposium on Motivation: Vol. 32. Psychology and Gender* (pp. 59–96). Lincoln, NE: University of Nebraska Press.

Spence, J. T. (1993). Gender-related traits and gender ideology: Evidence for a multifactorial theory. *Journal of Personality and Social Psychology*, 64, 624–635.

Spence, J. T. & Hall, S. K. (1996). Children's gender-related self-perceptions, activity preferences, and occupational stereotypes: A test of three models of gender constructs. *Sex Roles*, 35, 659–691.

Tobin, D. D., Menon, M., Menon, M., Spatta, B. C., Hodges, E. V. E., & Perry, D. G. (2010). The intrapsychics of gender: A model of self-socialization. *Psychological Review*, 117, 601–622.

Zosuls, K. M., Andrews, N. C. Z., Martin, C., England, D. E., & Field, R. D. (2016). Developmental changes in the link between gender typicality and peer victimization and exclusion. *Sex Roles*, 75(5–6), 243–256.

Zosuls, K. M., Ruble, D. N., Tamis-LeMonda, C. S., Shrout, P. E., Bornstein, M. H., & Greulich, F. K. (2009). The acquisition of gender labels in infancy:Implications for gender-typed play. *Developmental Psychology*, 45, 688–701.

Zucker, K. J., Bradley, S. J., Sullivan, C. B. L., Kuksis, M., Birkenfeld-Adams, A., & Mitchell, J. N. (1993). A gender identity interview for children. *Journal of Personality Assessment*, 61, 443–456.

13 Methodological Issues in Cross-Cultural Research on Prosocial and Moral Development

Gustavo Carlo and Sahitya Maiya

Scholars across many disciplines have a long-standing interest in the study of morality. From the work of early philosophers and theologians to the relatively more recent efforts in the social and behavioral sciences, morality has often been the focus of intense debate and scrutiny. Several reasons exist for this long-standing interest and scrutiny including questions regarding the moral nature of human beings, the biological and evolutionary beginnings of morality, the development and progression of this phenomena, and various expressions and markers of morality. Moreover, understanding moral agency and development has important implications for societal and individual well-being and adaptation. Indeed, most, if not all, individual and societal challenges and problems are founded on or directly related to considerations of justice and welfare. Within the social and behavioral sciences, then, strong conceptual and methodological approaches are needed to more adequately research on justice and welfare domains of morality.

At the same time, however, adequate considerations of, and research on, morality requires the incorporation of culture-related mechanisms and processes. Unfortunately, traditional theories of morality often relegated culture-related mechanisms as secondary or relatively minimal influences (Colby et al., 1987; Kohlberg, 1969). Similarly, socialization, contextual, and biologically based (including emotions) factors were considered minimized in these theories. Instead, such approaches emphasized or expounded cognitive-developmental mechanisms as central to moral development (Kohlberg, 1969; Piaget, 1932; Turiel, 1998). However, in recent years, there has been dramatic shifts in the worldview paradigm applied to moral development research that includes greater attention to culture-related influences (Carlo & de Guzman, 2009; Super & Harkness, 1986; Whiting, 1980). The growing interest in culture-related processes associated with moral development has resulted in greater demands to address a gap in measurement approaches that incorporates cultural considerations. The present chapter summarizes traditional and culture-sensitive approaches that inform moral development theories and recent attempts to integrate such theories. Then, we turn to a brief overview of measurement approaches to integrate culture into measures of moral development and two case studies of such attempts.

Traditional Theories of Prosocial and Moral Development

Although the study of morality had been the focus of scholars across many disciplines, systematic research on moral development began with Piaget's pioneering studies (Piaget, 1932). This ground-breaking work identified reasoning as a central mechanism that changes across time and is linked to children's understanding of fairness and justice. Moreover, advances in moral reasoning directly correspond to children's advances in cognitive development.

Borrowing heavily from Piaget's ideas, Kohlberg extended this early work in several significant ways. According to Kohlberg (1969), moral development occurs in a systematic manner across the life span in a sequential and universal manner across cultures. Kohlberg also posited six basic stages of moral reasoning development that span from authority- and punishment-oriented to universal, principled-level forms (Colby et al., 1987). Moral judgements were conceptualized as strong predictors of moral behavior, especially at higher stages (Kohlberg & Candee, 1984). Moreover, moral emotions (e.g., empathy, guilt, shame) and socialization processes were minimalized or relegated to secondary importance status (Kohlberg, 1963). Newer conceptions of these early theories have emerged that advance notions of distinct social domains that can be distinguished in children across cultures (Smetana, 1999; Turiel, 1998). Although cognitive-developmental theories of morality continue to contribute and evolve (see Turiel, 2015), the emphasis on cognitive processes as central to moral development is still common across these approaches.

Another group of moral developmental scholars were simultaneously developing a somewhat distinct conception of moral development. Moral socialization theorists such as Grusec and Goodnow (1994), Hoffman (2000), and Gilligan (1977) posited socialization agents and processes as central to fostering moral development. These investigators borrowed heavily from notions that children's moral development is linked directly to experiences and practices that expose them to moral beliefs and behaviors that can be acquired. Some of these experiences subject children to rewards and punishers that facilitate or inhibit specific forms of moral behaviors (Hoffman, 2000). For example, caregivers engage in specific disciplining practices such as power assertion (i.e., imposing authority without explanation) that can mitigate moral development. In contrast, inductive practices (i.e., discipline with reasoning and role-taking inducements) are expected to promote children's moral development. In addition, moral emotions are hypothesized to play an important role in predicting moral behaviors. Thus, in contrast to cognitive-developmental researchers, moral socialization researchers focus on moral emotions and behaviors as markers of moral development.

The early work of cognitive-developmental and moral socialization scholars has led to integrative approaches such as social cognitive theories of moral development (Bandura, 1986; Carlo, 2006; Eisenberg, 1986; Staub, 1978). These approaches have several commonalities to cognitive-developmental and moral socialization theories but attempt to incorporate these several mechanisms in order to better understand children's moral development. Thus, in general, advances in cognitive development and exposure to socialization experiences both influence children's moral development. Moreover, moral behaviors are central markers of morality. In particular, there is an emphasis on prosocial and antisocial behaviors. Prosocial behaviors are defined as actions intended to benefit others (Carlo, 2006; Eisenberg & Fabes, 1998). Sharing, comforting, volunteering, donating, and helping are common forms of prosocial behaviors. In contrast, antisocial behaviors reflect actions that cause harm and injury to others. These latter behaviors have been commonly researched and include lying, cheating, stealing, vandalism, and various forms of aggression (including bullying). Perhaps most importantly, these integrative approaches acknowledge the wide variations in moral development across cultures and societies that result from distinct socialization experiences.

Culture-Centered Theories and Perspectives

Despite the acknowledged influence of culture in children's moral development by socialization and social cognitive theorists, most early research grounded in traditional theories of moral development lacked much focus on culture-related mechanisms. In stark contrast, cultural anthropologists and developmental scholars have posited several important culture-related influences of children's development (Super & Harkness, 1986; Whiting & Edwards, 1988). The first of these influences reflects traditional practices, customs, and rituals that children are exposed to that transmit messages regarding skills and characteristics deemed important for offspring to learn. Prominent among these practices are those that parents and caregivers engage in that serve to guide children's development. However, these practices and customs may stem from other significant adults (e.g., extended family members, teachers) and from social institutions (e.g., schools). A second source of cultural influence is the beliefs and values that might guide socialization agents' interactions with children. For example, caregivers in different societies might endorse distinct child-rearing beliefs, which influence practices (e.g., disciplining techniques) that might be frequently exhibited. Finally, cultural scholars also acknowledge the facilitating or inhibiting effect of children's social context and environment. These environments place a limit or the parameters around which specific behaviors can be manifested. For example, in specific contexts that might be somewhat segregated, some children might have limited opportunities to interact with older or younger children or with children from other ethnic or racial groups.

Ecocultural Stress-Based Model of Moral Development

These culture-focused theories delineate important mechanisms and factors that account for culture-group and individual differences in children's development. However, there is a relative lack of culture-focused theories or approaches in the area of children's moral development. Borrowing from several prior theories, Carlo and his colleagues (Carlo & de Guzman, 2009) have posited an ecocultural stress-based theory of moral development (see Figure 13.1). The heuristic theory integrates social ecology (Bronfenbrenner, 1977), acculturative stress (Berry, 2006), stress and coping (Lazarus & Folkman, 1984), and value-based behavior (Knight, Bernal, & Carlo, 1995) theories to help understand culture-group and individual differences in moral behaviors. There are three basic elements to the theory, including background and contextual influences, intrapersonal traits, and moral behaviors. Of particular importance is the notion that sociocultural experiences are interpreted via individuals' cognitive (e.g., appraisals, perspective taking, reasoning) and affective/behavioral (e.g., emotion-regulation, empathy) skills and dispositions. Moreover, there is a constant interplay among and within these factors such that moral outcomes are the product of these multiple processes.

There is growing supportive evidence that these factors are associated with children's moral behaviors. However, a remaining challenge to adequately test the model is well-validated measures of moral processes and behaviors. Importantly, the difficulty is greatest when conducting research in youth samples of non-European or non-European Americans. Because traditional approaches to the study of moral development often minimized or neglected cultural variability and influences, most existing measures of moral development lack adequate tests of the cultural validity to use with

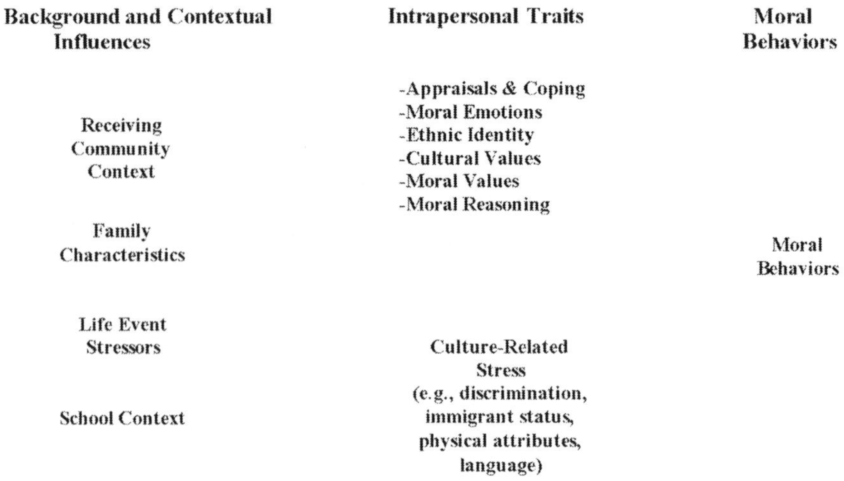

Background and Contextual Influences	Intrapersonal Traits	Moral Behaviors
Receiving Community Context	-Appraisals & Coping -Moral Emotions -Ethnic Identity -Cultural Values -Moral Values -Moral Reasoning	
Family Characteristics		Moral Behaviors
Life Event Stressors		
School Context	Culture-Related Stress (e.g., discrimination, immigrant status, physical attributes, language)	

Figure 13.1 Ecocultural Stress-Based Model of Moral Behaviors (adapted from Carlo & de Guzman, 2009; Raffaelli et al., 2005).

non-European or non-European American samples. Indeed, often, researchers administered moral development measures to culturally diverse samples with minimal and inadequate adaptation (e.g., language translation) and tests (e.g., reports of Cronbach's alphas). Such practices raise the prospects of ethnic and cultural measurement inequivalence and subsequently misleading research findings. Therefore, an important need is for the development and refinement of moral development measures with greater attention to strong ethnic and cultural measurement equivalence in these measures.

Culturally Sensitive Measurement Approaches

Evaluating the measurement properties of a construct is a fundamental prerequisite to asserting the validity and reliability of research findings. Most measures in social sciences are developed with predominantly White, middle-class samples with little consideration regarding whether the developed measure is applicable for other ethnic or cultural groups. Furthermore, the universalist versus relativist debate in the field of moral development can only be adequately addressed by conducting cross-cultural research using strong culturally valid measures. In this section, we will present a brief overview of culturally sensitive measurement approaches in prosocial and moral development, followed by a presentation of two case studies.

Developing and Adapting Measures

Given the focus of this essay, we refer to measurement issues in the context of ethnic and cultural groups. A strong theoretical understanding of the construct of interest is vital because the theory guides in identifying the construct of interest. Considering a clear target ethnic/cultural group offers the advantage of studying culturally relevant ways a construct is experienced in that ethnic/cultural group. Once the construct of interest is identified, then developing and adapting the measure for specific ethnic and cultural groups is the next step in the measurement development process.

There are several steps in developing and refining measures to use with specific cultural groups. Cultural scholars can assemble a series of items that best capture the construct via a comprehensive literature review of theory and previously developed measures (Knight, Roosa, & Umaña-Taylor, 2015). Alternatively, researchers may also rely on qualitative approaches such as semi-structured interviews and focus groups to identify broad themes related to the construct of interest. Based on the identified broad themes, experts can develop specific items and ascertain their face validity. Once a series of items are identified, further refinements could be conducted. Focus groups (as representative as feasible), for example, are a useful tool in refining the items of the newly developed measure. Items that are unclearly worded or that hold different meanings for the studied ethnic/cultural group can then be discarded. Finally, the measure is ready to pilot test with the target ethnic/cultural group sample. Of course, after piloting, it might be necessary to further refine the measure.

Most commonly, measures are administered to other ethnic and cultural groups based on their development with predominantly European American samples (van de Vijver & Leung, 1997a, 1997b). Applying a measure in its original form across different ethnic/cultural groups is advantageous because it allows for straightforward cross-cultural comparisons. However, this approach risks conceptualizing the measure from a European ethnocentric bias, which can lead to misleading findings and inaccurate interpretations. Although this approach is not ideal, there are some adaptations that can be done to improve the cultural adequacy of the measure. For example, researchers can rephrase items in measures to better fit the new culturally relevant language. Items are sometimes added or removed based on a unique cultural significance or insignificance basis. In adapting a measure to use with a new cultural group, careful consideration should be given to procedures surrounding the translation and administration of the measure (see van de Vijver & Leung, 1997a, for a full review). The use of simple sentences, active voice, nouns over pronouns, operational definitions of key concepts, and specific words familiar to translators is encouraged, whereas the use of colloquialisms, subjunctive mood (e.g., could), adverbs (e.g., beyond), possessive forms, and multiple action verbs is discouraged. During the administration process, researchers should also be cognizant of the personal characteristics of the tester or interviewer (e.g., racial differences), interactions between tester and respondents (e.g., minimizing verbal interaction), response procedures (e.g., paper-and-pencil), and instrument stimuli (e.g., stimulus familiarity), wherever applicable. Finally, it is advisable to include collaborators and research assistants who are knowledgeable about the new culture.

Measurement Equivalence

Methodologists have presented a variety of measurement approaches to investigate equivalence across groups such as gender, ethnicity/culture, or socioeconomic status (Hines, 1993; Hui & Triandis, 1985; Little, Preacher, Selig, & Card, 2007; Vandenberg & Lance, 2000). One of the mostly widely used classifications of measurement equivalence includes three types of equivalence: item equivalence, functional equivalence, and scalar equivalence (Hui & Triandis, 1985). Item equivalence is seen when items on a measure have the same meaning across ethnic/cultural groups. An examination of factorial invariance and the similarity of item functioning is useful to examine item equivalence. For instance, the factorial invariance of a prosocial moral reasoning measure can be explored based on correlations among items of the measure or the interrelation between each item to the total scale score of the measure. Thus, item equivalence exists if prosocial moral reasoning items are interrelated in theoretically hypothesized ways, similarly or differently, in various ethnic and cultural groups. Unlike the item-level focus in item equivalence, functional and scalar equivalence focus more on the total scale score. In other words, functional and scalar equivalence are examined based on the association between the total scale score of the construct of interest with the total scale score of other theoretically related constructs. Thus, functional and scalar equivalence exist if prosocial moral reasoning is associated, similarly or differently, with prosocial behavior across ethnic/cultural groups in accord with cultural theories. While functional equivalence is likely when the total scale scores have similar correlates across ethnic and cultural groups, scalar equivalence is likely when the total scale scores have similar magnitudes across ethnic and cultural groups. It is noteworthy that functional equivalence does not require construct meanings to be shared by different groups. Of the three types, scalar equivalence is typically considered the most important to establish for accurate cross-cultural comparisons.

As previously mentioned, factorial invariance tests (or measurement invariance tests) are largely useful in investigating item equivalence and the extent to which psychometric properties of the measure hold for different groups. Empirical tests to assess factorial invariance mainly include factor analyses and item response theory (IRT) analyses (Knight, Tein, Prost, & Gonzales, 2002; McDonald, 1995; Millsap & Kwok, 2004; Widaman, 1995). Factor analysis techniques are based on intercorrelations between items of the measure, whereas IRT techniques are based on the relation between individual items to the total scale score.

Factor analysis techniques can be further classified into exploratory factor analysis (EFA) and confirmatory factor analysis (CFA). Initial studies using a measure may especially benefit from utilizing EFA rather than CFA to ascertain the factor structure of the measure (Worthington & Whittaker, 2006). EFA is a structural equation modeling technique, wherein the underlying structure of a large set of items is uncovered (Fabrigar & Wegener, 2012). Researchers are encouraged go beyond a principal components analysis of their measure and employ a variety of rotation techniques to arrive upon a more stable structure. Rotation techniques should be theoretically grounded, with orthogonal factors specified without intercorrelations between factors and oblique factors specified with intercorrelations between factors. Some common rotation techniques accompanying EFA include varimax, promax, geomin, and oblimin. In contrast, CFA verifies an already established factor structure with different ethnic/cultural groups. CFA is a structural equation modeling technique, wherein each item is represented as a function of one or more factors (Bollen, 1989). A multigroup CFA is particularly useful in establishing factor invariance by fitting a sequence of hierarchically nested models namely, configural invariance (least restrictive), metric invariance, strong factorial invariance, and strict factorial invariance (most restrictive), respectively. Configural invariance exists if a CFA model with the same set of items in each ethnic/cultural group demonstrates good model fit. Metric invariance exists if the factor loadings between individual items and the latent constructs are equivalent across ethnic/cultural groups. Strong invariance exists if the factor loadings and item intercepts are equivalent across ethnic/cultural groups. Lastly, strict invariance exists if factor loadings, item intercepts, and error variances of items are equivalent across ethnic/cultural groups. It is also possible to arrive at partially invariant models for all above categories (Byrne, Shavelson, & Muthén, 1989).

IRT techniques are a more recent alternative to factor analysis techniques for establishing measurement equivalence. IRT models are derived from a monotonically increasing mathematical function termed the item characteristic curve (ICC). ICCs in IRT models are based on item difficulty, item discrimination, and the chance parameter (Camilli & Shepard, 1994; Reise, Widaman, & Pugh, 1993). Item difficulty is defined as the point on the continuum at which respondents have a .5 probability of a given response. Item discrimination pertains to the slope of the ICC at the point on the curve corresponding to the item difficulty. The chance parameter refers to the probability of participants at low levels of the construct responding to the item in hypothesized ways. Thus, measurement invariance can be examined by comparing the ICCs for individual items across ethnic and cultural groups. Similar ICCs suggest invariant items, whereas dissimilar ICCs suggest biased items. Item bias should be explored by comparing the parameters of interest and areas between the ICCs for each ethnic/cultural group (see Camilli & Shepard, 1994 for a full review of methods to assess item bias). While CFA is based on frequentist statistics, IRT is based on more sophisticated probabilistic statistics. However, it is difficult to determine whether a group difference in ICCs is a product of a scale score that is not equivalent across groups or an item that functions differently in different groups in IRT techniques. Therefore, researchers should employ both factor analysis and IRT techniques to establish factorial invariance whenever possible.

In order to assess functional and scalar equivalence, it is recommended that researchers investigate the concordance between empirical and construct validity coefficients across ethnic and cultural groups (Knight, Roosa, & Taylor, 2015). Although empirical validity coefficients measure the relation between the scale score of the target measure and scale scores of different measures of the same construct, construct validity coefficients measure the relation between the scale score of the target measure and scale scores of different theoretically related constructs. Construct validity coefficients are theoretically driven and make unique contributions to cross-cultural research. In the study of prosocial and moral development, construct validity of measures can be established by studying theoretically relevant constructs such as parenting, empathy, or adjustment (Carlo, 2014). Statistically, construct validities can be compared by testing for ethnicity/culture-moderated effects in the associations between the construct of interest and other theoretically related constructs. The above information on culturally sensitive measurement approaches will now be applied to two measurement case studies that exemplify the discussed approaches.

Two Case Studies in Measurement Development of Moral Processes and Outcomes

The history of conducting cultural and cross-cultural research on moral development is long and beyond the scope of the present essay. However, for our purposes, we briefly review work focused on two primary constructs, namely prosocial behaviors and prosocial moral reasoning, to illustrate the application of a culturally sensitive approach in developing and refining measures of moral development to use with culturally diverse populations. The Prosocial Tendencies Measure (PTM) was developed to examine multiple forms of prosocial behaviors (Carlo & Randall, 2002). This measure has been extensively used in studies with culturally diverse populations of youth and adults. The second measure, the Prosocial Reasoning Objective Measure (PROM), assesses individuals' thinking in dilemma situations when faced with an opportunity to help a needy other that conflicts with one's own desires and needs (Carlo, Eisenberg, & Knight, 1992).

Development of the Prosocial Tendencies Measure

The initial items of the PTM were based on an extensive literature review of measures of prosocial behaviors and developed to use with college-aged students of predominantly White, European American heritage. In its original conceptualization, the PTM consisted of only four factors. There were several pilot studies conducted to examine and refine the measure. EFAs were conducted in the first study using the PTM and yielded six factors, which included altruistic, dire, compliant, emotional, anonymous, and public helping (Carlo & Randall, 2002).

The PTM prosocial behavior items are rated on a five-point Likert scale ranging from 1 (*does not describe me at all*) to 5 (*describes me greatly*). Altruistic prosocial behaviors are defined as selflessly motivated prosocial behaviors displayed in the absence of any benefits to the self (e.g., "*One of the best things about doing charity work is that it looks good*" is reverse coded). In contrast, public prosocial behaviors are defined as selfishly motivated prosocial behaviors displayed in the presence of an audience for social rewards and approval (e.g., "*Helping others when I am being watched is when I work best*"). In addition to two prosocial behaviors defined by personal motives, four prosocial behaviors defined by situations were identified. Emotional prosocial behaviors consist of helping in emotionally distressing situations (e.g., "*I usually help others when they are very upset*"). Compliant prosocial behaviors entail helping in response to a specific request for assistance (e.g., "*I never hesitate to help others when they ask for it*"). Dire prosocial behaviors comprise helping in emergencies that typically pose physical danger to another (e.g., "*I tend to help people who are hurt badly*"). Lastly, anonymous prosocial behaviors include helping without the knowledge of the recipient of help (e.g., "*Most of the time, I help others when they do not know who helped them*").

EFAs with varimax rotation also revealed a better-fitting six-factor structure over a four-factor solution. More specifically, emotional and dire prosocial behaviors, theorized as one factor, loaded onto two separate factors. Similarly, anonymous and public prosocial behaviors emerged as two factors instead of one factor. This six-factor structure was supported by subsequent CFAs in future studies (e.g., McGinley & Carlo, 2007). In a more recent examination of the PTM, researchers dropped four items from the measure due to these items loading poorly or loading on more than one factor (two altruistic, one public, and one anonymous; Carlo, Knight, McGinley, Zamboanga, & Jarvis, 2010). Thus, the revised PTM (PTM-R) currently stands as a 21-item, six-factor structure measure.

Of particular importance to the present chapter, several studies have examined the factor structure and measurement equivalence properties of the PTM to use across ethnic and culture groups. The original literature review was followed up by focus groups with both European American and U.S. Mexican (Spanish-speaking and English-speaking) parents of adolescents (Carlo, Hausmann, Christiansen, & Randall, 2003; Carlo & Randall, 2002). Parents were asked about the items and format of the PTM as a valid measure of prosocial behaviors typical of adolescents. Responses were coded and analyzed. In general, the findings showed face validity of the six forms of prosocial behaviors as relevant to U.S. Mexican youth.

Recent research verifies the six-factor structure as the best-fitting factor solution for U.S. Mexican youth (Carlo et al., 2010). Moreover, factorial invariance tests support the item equivalence of the PTM-R across U.S. Mexican and European American adolescents, such that full factorial invariance is attained for the PTM-R across ethnic groups. Construct validity equivalence tests support the functional and scalar equivalence of the PTM-R across these groups. Measurement equivalence of the PTM-R has also been investigated in cultural groups outside the U.S. CFAs suggest that a six-factor solution is a better fit than a one-factor, two-factor, or three-factor alternative for Spanish youth. Additionally, the structure of the PTM-R is equivalent across Spanish boys and girls. Similarly, McGinley and colleagues (2014) found that the factor structure of the PTM-R is equivalent across European American and Argentinian youth. While some research presents a four-factor structure of the PTM-R in Argentinian samples (e.g., Richaud, Mesurado, & Lemos, 2012), McGinley and colleagues (2014) assert that the six-factor structure is better fitting than the four-factor structure alternative. Despite the plausibility of a four-factor solution, the six-factor solution is recommended due to the empirical evidence and the congruency with theory (McGinley, Opal, Richaud, & Mesurado, 2014). Lastly, measurement equivalence of the PTM-R was also explored in a German sample using both factor analysis and item response techniques (Rodrigues, Ulrich, Mussel, Carlo, & Hewig, 2017). A six-factor structure of the PTM-R emerged via EFA, which was corroborated via CFA. Measurement invariance between English- and German-language versions of the PTM-R was demonstrated. Furthermore, item response techniques revealed good item characteristics for all questions, such that each answer category displayed a unique probability peak at the point on the continuum where it was the most probable answer category. Additionally, a good differentiation of item difficulty was demonstrated. Taken together, the factor structure and measurement equivalence of the PTM-R has been established in diverse ethnic and cultural groups.

Reliability

The PTM/PTM-R has demonstrated acceptable to excellent reliabilities across a variety of studies. Carlo and Randall (2002) showed good test-retest reliability over a two-week duration (r = .60-.80). Subsequent studies have confirmed acceptable internal reliability coefficients for the PTM with both ethnic groups within the United States and cultural groups outside the United States. Numerous studies using the PTM have found acceptable internal reliabilities for all six subscales with U.S. Mexican youth (Calderón-Tena, Knight, & Carlo, 2011; Carlo et al., 2010). Other researchers have demonstrated acceptable internal reliabilities for the use of PTM with cultural groups in South America, Europe, and Asia (Lin, Xiaoyi, Li, Liu, & Yang, 2006; McGinley et al., 2014; Tuncel, 2010).

Convergent and Discriminant Validity

Convergent validity of the six types of prosocial behaviors can be verified by comparing them with scores on other measures of prosocial behaviors. Because not all subscales of the PTM are interrelated, a composite using all the subscales is not feasible. For this reason, one would not expect a composite of the PTM to be significantly linked to other global measures of prosocial behaviors. Instead, one would expect specific PTM subscales to be associated with other measures of prosocial behaviors. For example, while public prosocial behavior is related to global prosocial behavior, altruistic prosocial behavior is mostly unrelated (Carlo et al., 2003; Carlo & Randall, 2002). Furthermore, several studies demonstrate significant relations between prosocial behavioral tasks and specific forms of prosocial behaviors (Rodrigues, Ulrich, & Hewig, 2015; Rodrigues et al., 2017). For example, in one study, altruistic prosocial behaviors were associated with dictator game altruistic choices (Rodrigues et al., 2016). In another study, altruistic prosocial tendencies were positively linked to compensation, but not punishment, in a third-party dictator game (Rodrigues, Nagowski, Mussel, & Hewig, 2018). Researchers also reported significantly relations between PTM subscales and volunteering in a sample from Hong Kong (Ngai & Xie, 2018).

Initial evidence for the discriminant validity suggests that the PTM factors tend to be unrelated to participants' self-reports of social desirability and personal distress (Barry, Lui, & Anderson, 2017; Carlo et al., 2003; Carlo & Randall, 2002). Researchers have demonstrated a negative relation between aggression and altruistic prosocial behavior but a positive relation between aggression and public prosocial behavior (Carlo et al., 2003; McGinley & Carlo, 2007). Furthermore, only compliant prosocial behaviors are negatively associated with both aggression and externalizing symptoms (Carlo et al., 2003; Carlo et al., 2010). In recent work, prosocial behaviors have been longitudinally and reciprocally linked to internalizing symptoms (Davis et al., 2016, 2018). Internalizing symptoms are positively related to public but negatively related to altruistic prosocial behaviors, and vice versa.

Construct Validity

Construct validity for the PTM factors has been established in relation to socialization agents, sociocognitive correlates, socioemotive correlates, and adjustment outcomes. The six PTM subscales are typically associated with other constructs in theoretically consistent ways. For instance, socialization researchers hypothesize parental involvement as a key predictor of prosocial behaviors. Parental warmth is predictive of altruistic and compliant prosocial behaviors (Carlo, McGinley, Hayes, Batenhorst, & Wilkinson, 2007). Similarly, parental monitoring, a form of behavioral control, is positively associated with all types of prosocial behavior except for altruistic prosocial behavior (Carlo et al., 2010). Prosocial parenting practices, including social rewards (e.g., praise), experiential prosocial parenting (e.g., parents and children volunteering together), moral conversations (e.g., talking about helping others), and discursive communication (e.g., creating a shared mutual understanding) either directly or indirectly (via sympathy), are positively linked to all types of prosocial behavior (Carlo et al., 2007). Conversely, peer socialization such as affiliation with deviant peers is negatively related to compliant and altruistic prosocial behaviors (Carlo et al., 2014).

In addition to socialization agents, construct validity of the PTM factors is studied with socioemotive and sociocognitive correlates such as empathy, perspective taking, and prosocial moral reasoning. For example, empathy and perspective taking are expected to be positively related to prosocial behavior because they encourage individuals to look beyond their own needs to those of others (Carlo, 2014). Several studies have found robust positive correlations between empathy, perspective taking, and all types of prosocial behaviors excepting public prosocial behavior (Carlo & Randall, 2002; Hardy, 2006). Likewise, advanced levels of prosocial moral reasoning are expected to be positively related to selflessly motivated prosocial behavior, whereas lower levels of prosocial moral reasoning are expected to be positively related to selfishly motivated prosocial behavior. Consistent with these hypotheses, researchers have found that internalized prosocial moral reasoning is related to greater altruistic, emotional, compliant, dire, and anonymous prosocial behaviors, while hedonistic prosocial moral reasoning is related to greater public prosocial behavior (Carlo et al., 2003).

External Validity

Unfortunately, research examining the external validity of PTM is lacking. In one interesting study, investigators successfully used the PTM subscales as a template to examine the forms of prosocial behaviors exhibited in Disney animated films (Padilla-Walker, Coyne, Fraser, & Stockdale, 2013). Altruistic prosocial behaviors were the most commonly portrayed prosocial behaviors in Disney movies, followed by dire, emotional, public, compliant, and anonymous prosocial behaviors. However, other studies that test the external validity of the PTM are needed.

Development of the Prosocial Reasoning Objective Measure (PROM)

Although the PTM is perhaps the most well-validated measure of moral development to use in cross-cultural studies, the PROM is another example of an instrument to use with multiple cultural groups. The PROM was designed to complement the interview measure of prosocial moral reasoning (Eisenberg, 1986). The PROM is a paper-and-pencil measure that can be administered either individually or to groups of children and youth. Both the interview and PROM instruments were originally developed to use based on research from White, European American samples. Moreover, both measures are designed to assess the five levels of prosocial moral reasoning as originally posited by Eisenberg (1986).

The first level of prosocial moral reasoning is termed hedonistic (i.e., concern for self needs and desires). Hedonistic reasoning is evident in preschool and elementary school-age children. Needs-oriented reasoning (second level) refers to a concern for the psychological or physical needs in others and is also evident in early childhood. In elementary and middle school-aged children, approval-oriented reasoning (third level) becomes more frequent and is characterized by an orientation towards gaining the approval of others (e.g., parents, peers, teachers). The fourth level is stereotyped reasoning, which refers to global notions of morality including notions of right and wrong, good and bad, and nice and mean. At the highest level of prosocial moral reasoning is empathic and internalized reasoning. This is reflected in concern for and understanding the plight of others from their perspective and strong internalized care-based principles and beliefs. These latter two levels are more typical in middle and high school-aged youth and are evident in young adults as well. In general, then, one expects a five-factor solution for the PROM.

Participants are expected to read a short story vignette depicting a prosocial behavior opportunity in the context of a dilemma between one's own desires and needs and those of a needy other. After reading the dilemma story, participants choose what the protagonist should do (help or not help) and then rate each provided reason on the importance and relevance to their behavioral choice. Here is a sample story vignette from the PROM.

A young girl named Lucy had a very unusual type of blood. One day, right after Lucy had begun school and was accepted on the baseball team, a doctor called Lucy to ask her to give a large amount of blood to a girl who was very sick and needed more blood of the same kind as Lucy's to get well. Because Lucy was the only person in the town with the sick girl's type of blood, and since this was a rare and serious sickness, the blood would have to be given a number of times over a period of several weeks. So, if Lucy agreed to give her blood, she would have to go into the hospital for several weeks. Being in the hospital would make Lucy feel weak for a while, she would lose her spot on the team, and she would be very far behind in school.

For this story, the following choices are presented: stereotyped reasoning ("*it depends whether Lucy thinks that helping is nice or not*"), approval-oriented reasoning ("*it depends whether Lucy believes her friends and parents will like what she does or not*"), hedonistic ("*it depends whether Lucy feels that losing her spot on the team is important or not*"), empathic/internalized ("*it depends whether Lucy can understand how badly the other girl is feeling*"), and physical needs-oriented ("*it depends how sick the other girl will get*"). Participants are expected to rate the above statements on a seven-point scale ranging from 1 (*not at all*) to 7 (*greatly*).

To a lesser extent, the factor structure and measurement equivalence properties of the PROM have been explored. For instance, Carlo and colleagues (2008) found that the five-factor structure of the PROM displayed adequate model fit for Brazilian and U.S. adolescents. However, combining stereotyped and internalized moral reasoning into one factor (i.e., a four-factor solution) of the PROM and PROM-R fit the best across age, gender, and culture. Similarly, Carlo and colleagues (2013) verified this four-factor structure of the PROM as the best-fitting solution across gender and grade for Spanish adolescents via multiple group CFAs. Using the model comparison approach, the PROM also demonstrated full metric invariance between European American and U.S. Mexican samples and partial metric invariance between European American and Taiwanese samples (Shen, Carlo, & Knight, 2013).

Reliability

The PROM has demonstrated acceptable to excellent reliabilities across a variety of studies. Furthermore, the PROM displayed good test-retest reliability over a two- to three-week period ($r = .70-.79$; Carlo et al., 1992). Multiple studies have verified the internal reliability coefficients for the PROM with different ethnic and cultural groups. Researchers have reported acceptable reliabilities for the PROM with U.S. Mexican youth (Knight, Carlo, Basilio, & Jacobson, 2015). Similar Cronbach alphas have been reported for the PROM with Brazilian, Spanish, Italian, Turkish, and Taiwanese youth (Carlo, Koller, & Eisenberg, 1998; Kumru, Carlo, Mestre, & Samper, 2012; Paciello, Fida, Cerniglia, Tramontano, & Cole, 2013; Shen et al., 2013).

Convergent and Discriminant Validity

Convergent validity of the PROM can be verified by comparing scores on the PROM with scores on the interview measure of prosocial moral reasoning. Carlo et al. (1992)

administered both the PROM and interview measure to middle and high school students and reported positive correlations between PROM and interview scores for internalized and hedonistic reasoning categories. Eisenberg, Carlo, Murphy, and van Court (1995) similarly found a moderate, positive correlation between composite PROM and interview scores concurrently and longitudinally. Initial evidence for the discriminant validity suggests that the PROM subscales are unrelated to verbal intelligence (Carlo et al., 1992). Furthermore, there were no significant zero-order correlations between the PROM subscales and social desirability (Eisenberg et al., 1995).

Construct Validity

Construct validity for the PROM has been established in relation to socialization agents, sociocognitive correlates, socioemotive correlates, and moral outcomes. The PROM category and composite scores are related to other relevant constructs in theoretically consistent ways. In alignment with socialization research, both maternal warmth and strict control positively predict PROM composite scores in Spanish adolescents (Carlo, Mestre, Samper, Tur & Armenta, 2010b). These findings on the predictive roles of warmth and control on the PROM composite are replicated for fathers as well. Similarly, Shen and colleagues (2013) found that parental punitiveness was directly related to the PROM composite score, whereas parental inductions were indirectly related to the PROM composite score via perspective taking and sympathy in a sample of European American, U.S. Mexican, and Taiwanese youth.

In terms of sociocognitive and socioemotive correlates, PROM scores are generally positively related to perspective taking, sympathy, and guilt. For instance, perspective taking is positively related to the PROM composite and internalized reasoning (Carlo et al., 1992) but negatively related to approval-oriented reasoning (Eisenberg et al., 1995). Furthermore, sympathy is positively associated with the PROM composite, internalized and stereotypic forms of reasoning and negatively associated with hedonistic reasoning (Carlo et al., 1992; Eisenberg et al., 1995). Similarly, guilt is positively associated with the PROM composite (Carlo, McGinley, Davis, & Streit, 2012). In one study, Carlo and colleagues (2012) found that the PROM composite mediates the relation between sympathy and prosocial behaviors (i.e., altruistic and compliant) and the relation between guilt and prosocial behaviors (i.e., altruistic and compliant). Interestingly, self-transcendence values are also positively linked to the PROM composite (Paciello et al., 2013).

In terms of moral outcomes, the PROM composite positively predicts individuals' propensity to help and other global prosocial behaviors (Carlo et al., 2010a, 2010b; Paciello et al., 2013) across diverse cultural groups. Global prosocial behaviors are also negatively correlated with hedonistic reasoning (Eisenberg et al., 1995). As previously mentioned, a distinctive pattern of findings emerges when considering the relations between PROM categories and multidimensional prosocial behaviors. In contrast, the PROM composite is negatively associated with adolescent reports of aggression and delinquency (Carlo et al., 2010a; Wyatt & Carlo, 2002).

Conclusions

The research designed to examine the psychometric properties of measures of moral development is sorely lacking, especially for use with culturally diverse populations. In part, the gap stems from decades of theories that posit a universal conception of morality and admonish cultural issues as secondary, or of relatively no, importance. However, the study of moral development necessitates understanding culture-group differences and similarities. To ensure that findings are not confounded by measurement artifact and cultural biases, more research is needed to examine the adequacy of moral development measures to use across distinct cultural groups.

We presented theories that provide guidance on the importance of cultural issues and the ways culture influences children's moral development. Such research grows significantly critical as globalization and diversification increases across the globe. Moreover, globalization has drawn greater attention to and awareness of sociomoral challenges and issues that many societies are facing requiring more evidence-based policies and interventions.

In the last section of the chapter, a summary of attempts to develop and refine a measure of prosocial behaviors (the PTM) to use with U.S. Latino/a youth was presented. Although several psychometric properties have yet to be tested, the measure is, to date, the most well-validated instrument of prosocial behavior used across culturally diverse groups. We also presented a summary of a relatively less-examined measure of moral reasoning (the PROM), whose measurement equivalence properties have been tested to use with Brazilian children and youth. However, much more work is needed on the PTM and the PROM. These measures show promise for advancing our understanding of moral development in across cultures.

Traditional theories have done much to identify moral development processes and outcomes including perspective taking, sympathy, guilt, shame, aggression, and other antisocial behaviors (e.g., delinquency). Of particular concern, however, is the sparse tests of the adequacy of moral development instruments of theoretically relevant constructs to use in culturally diverse populations. For example, there are several measures of prohibition-oriented (Kohlbergian) moral reasoning (e.g., Colby et al., 1987; Gibbs et al., 1984; Rest, 1979) but, to our knowledge, there is no published evidence of measurement equivalence of these measures. This is a concern given the strong interest in testing the cross-cultural universality of Kohlberg's moral stage theory. Indeed, there is substantive evidence that suggests cross-cultural inequivalence in prohibition-oriented moral reasoning (Gibbs, Basinger, Grime, & Snarey, 2007). These and other related findings (see Henrich, Heine, & Norenzayan, 2010) highlight the need for more attention to cross-cultural research in moral development. Given the increasing demands for relevant research to address current global sociomoral challenges, the field would do well to heed the call for research on the measurement properties of measures of moral development to use across culturally diverse populations.

References

Bandura, A. (1986). *Social Foundations of Thought and Action: A Social-Cognitive Theory*. Englewood Cliffs, NJ: Prentice.

Barry, C. T., Lui, J. H. L., & Anderson, A. (2017). Adolescent narcissism, aggression, and prosocial behavior: The relevance of socially desirable responding. *Journal of Personality Assessment, 99*, 46–55. doi:10.1080/00223891.2016.1193812.

Berry, J. W. (2006). Acculturative stress. In P. T. P. Wong & L. C. J. Wong (Eds.), *Handbook of Multicultural Perspectives on Stress and coping: International and Cultural Psychology* (pp. 287–298). Boston, MA: Springer.

Bollen, K. A. (1989). *Structural Equations with Latent Variables*. New York: Wiley.

Bronfenbrenner, U. (1977). Toward an experimental ecology of human development. *American Psychologist*, 32, 513–531.

Byrne, B. M., Shavelson, R. J., & Muthén, B. (1989). Testing for the equivalence of factor covariance and mean structures: The issue of partial measurement invariance. *Psychological Bulletin*, 105, 456–466.

Calderón-Tena, C. O., Knight, G. P., & Carlo, G. (2011). The socialization of prosocial behavioral tendencies among Mexican American adolescents: The role of familism values. *Cultural Diversity and Ethnic Minority Psychology*, 17, 98–106.

Camilli, G. & Shepard, L. A. (1994). *Methods for Identifying Biased Test Items*. Thousand Oaks, CA: Sage.

Carlo, G. (2006). Care-based and altruistically-based morality. In M. Killen & J. G. Smetana (Eds.), *Handbook of Moral Development* (pp. 551–579). Mahwah, NJ: Erlbaum.

Carlo, G. (2014). The development and correlates of prosocial moral behaviors. In M. Killen & J. G. Smetana (Eds.), *Handbook of Moral Development* (2nd ed., pp. 208–234). New York, NY: Psychology Press.

Carlo, G. & de Guzman, M. R. T. (2009). Theories and research on prosocial competencies among U.S. Latinos/as. In F. A. Villarruel, G. Carlo, J. M. Grau, M. Azmitia, N. J. Cabrera, & T. J. Chahin (Eds.), *Handbook of U.S. Latino Psychology: Developmental and Community-Based Perspectives* (pp. 191–212). Thousand Oaks, CA: Sage.

Carlo, G., Eisenberg, N., & Knight, G. P. (1992). An objective measure of adolescents' prosocial moral reasoning. *Journal of Research on Adolescence*, 2, 331–349.

Carlo, G., Hausmann, A., Christiansen, S., & Randall, B. A. (2003). Sociocognitive and behavioral correlates of a measure of prosocial tendencies for adolescents. *Journal of Early Adolescence*, 23, 107–134.

Carlo, G., Knight, G. P., McGinley, M., Zamboanga, B. L., & Jarvis, L. H. (2010). Measurement and functional equivalence in prosocial behaviors among European and Mexican American early adolescents. *Journal of Research on Adolescence*, 20, 334–358.

Carlo, G., Koller, S., & Eisenberg, N. (1998). Prosocial moral reasoning in institutionalized delinquent, orphaned, and noninstitutionalized Brazilian adolescents. *Journal of Adolescent Research*, 13, 363–376.

Carlo, G., McGinley, M., Davis, A., & Streit, C. (2012). Behaving badly or goodly: Is it because I feel guilty, shameful, or sympathetic? Or is it a matter of what I think? *New Directions For Youth Development*, 2012(136), 75–93.

Carlo, G., McGinley, M., Hayes, R., Batenhorst, C., & Wilkinson, J. (2007). Parenting styles or practices? Parenting, sympathy, and prosocial behaviors among adolescents. *The Journal of Genetic Psychology*, 168, 147–176.

Carlo, G., McGinley, M., Roesch, S. C., & Kaminski, J. (2008). Culture group, age, and gender measurement invariance in prosocial moral reasoning among adolescents from Brazil and the United States. *Journal of Moral Education*, 37, 485–502.

Carlo, G., Mestre, M., McGinley, M., Tur-Porcar, A., Samper, P., & Opal, D. (2014). The protective role of prosocial behaviors on antisocial behaviors: The mediating effects of deviant peer affiliation. *Journal of Adolescence*, 37, 359–366.

Carlo, G., Mestre, M., McGinley, M., Tur-Porcar, A., Samper, P., & Streit, C. (2013). The structure and correlates of a measure of prosocial moral reasoning in adolescents from Spain. *European Journal of Developmental Psychology*, 10, 174–189.

Carlo, G., Mestre, M., Samper, P., Tur, A., & Armenta, B. (2010a). Feelings or cognitions? Moral cognitions and emotions as longitudinal predictors of prosocial and aggressive behaviors. *Personality and Individual Differences*, 48, 872–877.

Carlo, G., Mestre, M., Samper, P., Tur, A., & Armenta, B. E. (2010b). The longitudinal relations among dimensions of parenting styles, sympathy, prosocial moral reasoning and prosocial behaviors. *International Journal of Behavioral Development*, 35, 116–124.

Carlo, G. & Randall, B. A. (2002). The development of a measure of prosocial behaviors for late adolescents. *Journal of Youth and Adolescence*, 31, 31–44.

Colby, A., Kohlberg, L., Speicher, B., Hewer, A., Candee, D., Gibbs, J., & Power, C. (1987). *The Measurement of Moral Judgement, Vol. 2: Standard Issue Scoring Manual*. New York: Cambridge Univ. Press.

Davis, A. N., Carlo, G., Schwartz, S. J., Unger, J., Zamboanga, B., Lorenzo-Blanco, E., & Soto, D. (2016). The longitudinal associations between discrimination, depressive symptoms, and prosocial behaviors in U.S. Latino/a recent immigrant adolescents. *Journal of Youth and Adolescence*, 45, 457–470.

Davis, A. N., Carlo, G., Schwartz, S. J., Zamboanga, B. L., Armenta, B., Kim, S. Y., ... Streit, C. (2018). The roles of familism and emotion reappraisal in the relations between acculturative stress and prosocial behaviors in Latino/a college students. *Journal of Latina/o Psychology*, 6, 175–189.

Eisenberg, N. (1986). *Altruistic Emotion, Cognition and Behavior*. Hillsdale, NJ: Lawrence Erlbaum.

Eisenberg, N., Carlo, G., Murphy, B., & van Court, P. (1995). Prosocial development in late adolescence: A longitudinal study. *Child Development*, 66, 1179–1197.

Eisenberg, N. & Fabes, R. A. (1998). Prosocial development. In W. Damon (Series Ed.) & N. Eisenberg (Vol. Ed.), *Handbook of Child Psychology: Vol. 3. Social, Emotional, and Personality Development* (5th ed., pp. 701–778). New York: Wiley.

Fabrigar, L. & Wegener, D. (2012). *Exploratory Factor Analysis*. Oxford: Oxford University Press.

Gibbs, J., Arnold, K. D., Morgan, R. L., Schwartz, E. S., Gavaghan, M. P., & Tappan, M. B. (1984). Construction and validation of a multiple-choice measure of moral reasoning. *Child Development*, 55, 527–536.

Gibbs, J., Basinger, K., Grime, R., & Snarey, J. (2007). Moral judgment development across cultures: Revisiting Kohlberg's universality claims. *Developmental Review*, 27, 443–500.

Gilligan, C. (1977). In a different voice: Women's conceptions of self and of morality. *Harvard Educational Review*, 47, 481–517.

Grusec, J. E. & Goodnow, J. J. (1994). Impact of parental discipline methods on the child's internalization of values: A reconceptualization of current points of view. *Developmental Psychology*, 30, 4–19.

Hardy, S. A. (2006). Identity, reasoning, and emotion: An empirical comparison of three sources of moral motivation. *Motivation and Emotion*, 30, 207–215.

Henrich, J., Heine, S. J., & Norenzayan, A. (2010). The weirdest people in the world? *Behavioral and Brain Sciences*, 33, 62–135.

Hines, A. M. (1993). Linking qualitative and quantitative methods in cross-cultural survey research: Techniques from cognitive science. *American Journal of Community Psychology*, 21, 729–746.

Hoffman, M. L. (2000). *Empathy and Moral Development: Implications for Caring and Justice*. New York: Cambridge University Press.

Hui, C. H. & Triandis, H. C. (1985). Measurement in cross-cultural psychology: A review and comparison of strategies. *Journal of Cross-Cultural Psychology*, 16, 131–152.

Knight, G., Bernal, M., & Carlo, G. (1995). Socialization and the development of cooperative, competitive, and individualistic behaviors among Mexican American children. In E. E. Garcia & B. M. McLaughlin (Eds.), *Meeting the Challenge of Linguistic and Cultural Diversity in Early Childhood Education, Vol. 6: Yearbook in Early Childhood Education* (pp. 85–102). New York: Teachers College Press.

Knight, G. P., Carlo, G., Basilio, C. D., & Jacobson, R. P. (2015). Familism values, perspective taking, and prosocial moral reasoning: predicting prosocial tendencies among Mexican American adolescents. *Journal of Research on Adolescence*, 25, 717–727.

Knight, G. P., Roosa, M., & Umaña-Taylor, A. (2015). *Studying Ethnic Minority and Economically Disadvantaged Populations*. Washington: American Psychological Association.

Knight, G.P., Tein, J.-Y., Prost, J.H., & Gonzales, N.A. (2002). Measurement equivalence and research on Latino children and families: The importance of culturally informed theory. In J. Contreras, K. Kears, & A. Neal-Barnett (Eds.), *Latino Children and Families in the United States: Current Research and Future Directions* (pp. 181–201). Westport, CT: Praeger.

Kohlberg, L. (1963). Moral development and identification. In H. W. Stevenson (Ed.) & J. Kagan, C. Spiker (Collaborators), N. B. Henry & H. G. Richey (Eds.), *Child Psychology: The Sixty-Second Yearbook of the National Society for the Study of Education, Part 1* (pp. 277–332). Chicago, IL: National Society for the Study of Education; Chicago, IL: University of Chicago Press.

Kohlberg, L. (1969). Stage and sequence: The cognitive-developmental approach to socialization. In D. Goslin (Ed.), *Handbook of Socialization Theory and Research* (pp. 347–480). Chicago, IL: Rand-McNally.

Kohlberg, L. & Candee, D. (1984). The relationship of moral judgment to moral action. In W. M. Kurtines & J. L. Gewirtz (Eds.), *Morality, Moral Behavior, and Moral Development* (pp. 52–73). New York: Wiley.

Kumru, A., Carlo, G., Mestre, M., & Samper, P. (2012). Prosocial moral reasoning and prosocial behavior among Turkish and Spanish adolescents. *Social Behavior and Personality: An International Journal, 40*, 205–214.

Lazarus, R. & Folkman, S. (1984). *Stress, Appraisal, and Coping*. New York: Springer.

Lin, H., Xiaoyi, Li, H., Liu, C., & Yang, S. (2006). Yunnan student prosocial tendencies trends and projections for school adjustment. *Psychological Development and Education, 22*, 44–51.

Little, T. D., Preacher, K. J., Selig, J. P., & Card, N. A. (2007). New developments in latentvariable panel analyses of longitudinal data. *International Journal of Behavioral Development, 31*, 357–365.

McDonald, R. P. (1995). Testing for approximate dimensionality. In D. Laveault, B. D. Sumbo, M. E. Gessaroli, & M. W. Boss (Eds.), *Modern Theories of Measurement: Problems and Issues* (pp. 63–85). Ottawa, Ontario, Canada: Edumetric Research Group, University of Ottawa.

McGinley, M. & Carlo, G. (2007). Two sides of the same coin? The relations between prosocial and physically aggressive behaviors. *Journal of Youth and Adolescence, 36*, 337–349.

McGinley, M., Opal, D., Richaud, M. C., & Mesurado, B. (2014). Cross-cultural evidence of multidimensional prosocial behaviors. In L. M. Padilla-Walker, & G. Carlo (Eds.), *Prosocial Development: A Multidimensional Approach* (pp. 258–278). New York, NY: Oxford University Press.

Millsap, R. E. & Kwok, O.-M. (2004). Evaluating the impact of partial factorial invariance onselection in two populations. *Psychological Methods, 9*, 93–115.

Ngai, S. S. & Xie, L. (2018). Toward a validation of the prosocial tendencies measure among Chinese adolescents in Hong Kong. *Child Indicators Research, 11*, 1281–1299.

Paciello, M., Fida, R., Cerniglia, L., Tramontano, C., & Cole, E. (2013). High cost helping scenario: The role of empathy, prosocial reasoning and moral disengagement on helping behavior. *Personality and Individual Differences, 55*, 3–7.

Padilla-Walker, L., Coyne, S., Fraser, A., & Stockdale, L. (2013). Is Disney the nicest place on earth? A content analysis of prosocial behavior in animated Disney films. *Journal of Communication, 63*, 393–412.

Piaget, J. (1932). *The Moral Judgment of the Child*. New York: The Free Press.

Raffaelli, M., Carlo, G., Carranza, M., & Gonzalez-Kruger, G. (2005). Understanding Latino children and adolescents in the mainstream: Placing culture at the center of developmental models. *New Directions for Child and Adolescent Development, 2005*(109), 23–32.

Reise, S. P., Widaman, K. F., & Pugh, R. H. (1993). Confirmatory factor analysis and item response theory: Two approaches for exploring measurement invariance. *Psychological Bulletin, 114*, 552–566.

Rest, J. (1979). *Development in Judging Moral Issues*. Minneapolis: University of Minnesota.

Richaud, M., Mesurado, B., & Cortada, A. (2012). Analysis of dimensions of prosocial behavior in an Argentinean sample of children. *Psychological Reports, 111*, 687–696.

Richaud, M., Mesurado, B., & Lemos, V. (2012). Links between perception of parental actions and prosocial behavior in early adolescence. *Journal of Child and Family Studies, 22*, 637–646.

Rodrigues, J., Nagowski, N., Mussel, P., & Hewig, J. (2018). Altruistic punishment is connected to trait anger, not trait altruism, if compensation is available. *Heliyon, 4*, e00962. ISSN 2405-8440 https://doi.org/10.1016/j.heliyon.2018.e00962.

Rodrigues, J., Ulrich, N., & Hewig, J. (2015). A neural signature of fairness in altruism: A game of theta? *Social Neuroscience, 10*, 192–205.

Rodrigues, J., Ulrich, N., Mussel, P., Carlo, G., & Hewig, J. (2017). Measuring prosocial tendencies in germany: sources of validity and reliablity of the revised prosocial tendency measure. *Frontiers in Psychology, 8*, 1–17.

Shen, Y., Carlo, G., & Knight, G. (2013). Relations between parental discipline, empathy related traits, and prosocial moral reasoning. *The Journal of Early Adolescence, 33*, 994–1021.

Smetana, J. G. (1999). The role of parents in moral development: A social domain analysis. *Journal of Moral Education, 28*, 311–321.

Staub, E. (1978). *Positive Social Behavior and Morality: Vol. 1. Social and Personal Influences*. New York: Academic.

Super, C. & Harkness, S. (1986). The developmental niche: A conceptualization at the interface of child and culture. *International Journal of Behavioral Development, 9*, 545–569.

Tuncel, S. D. (2010). Comparing tendencies of athletes and nonathletes. *Journal of Physical Education and Sport, 29*, 81–85.

Turiel, E. (1998). The development of morality. In W. Damon (Series Ed.) & N. Eisenberg (Vol. Ed.), *Handbook of Child Psychology, Vol. 3: Social, Emotional, and Personality Development* (5th ed., pp. 863–932). New York: Wiley.

Turiel, E. (2015). Moral development. In R. M. Lerner (Editor-in-Chief), W. F. Overton, & P. C. Molenaar (Eds.) *Handbook of Child Psychology and Developmental Science. Vol. 1: Theory and Method* (7th ed., pp. 484–522). Hoboken, NJ: Wiley.

van de Vijver, F. J. R. & Leung, K. (1997a). *Cross-Cultural Psychology Series, Vol. 1. Method and Data Analysis for Cross-Cultural Research*. Thousand Oaks, CA: Sage.

van de Vijver, F. J. R. & Leung, K. (1997b). Methods and data analysis of comparative research. In J. W. Berry, Y. H. Poortinga, & J. Pandey (Eds.), *Handbook of Cross-Cultural Psychology: Theory and Method* (pp. 257–300). Boston: Allyn and Bacon.

Vandenberg, R. J. & Lance, C. E. (2000). A review and synthesis of the measurement invariance literature: Suggestions, practices, and recommendations for organizational research. *Organizational Research Methods, 3*, 4–70.

Whiting, B. B. (1980). Culture and social behavior: A model for the development of social behavior. *Ethos: Journal of the Society for Psychological Anthropology, 8*, 95–115.

Whiting, B. B. & Edwards, C. P. (1988). *Children of Different Worlds: The Formation of Social Behavior*. Cambridge, MA: Harvard University Press.

Widaman, K. F. (1995). On methods for comparing apples and oranges. *Multivariate Behavioral Research, 30*, 101–106.

Worthington, R. & Whittaker, T. (2006). Scale development research. *The Counseling Psychologist, 34*, 806–838.

Wyatt, J. & Carlo, G. (2002). What will my parents think? Relations among adolescents' expected parental reactions, prosocial moral reasoning, and prosocial and antisocial behaviors. *Journal of Adolescent Research, 17*, 646–666.

14 Translational Science
Developmental Psychopathology and Social Policy

Ross A. Thompson

Research in developmental psychopathology and studies on child and family policy address multifaceted questions. Developmental psychopathology concerns the origins and consequences of child psychological disorders and their treatment. Child and family policy studies concern the effects of social conditions on children and interventions to address these consequences. Each field is an example of translational science that bridges basic science and practice. Stated differently, each field brings knowledge on developmental processes into clinical and policy arenas, and also bring insights from practice back to the lab.

These fields also share other characteristics. Both fields, for example, primarily concern the needs of children at risk, either from stresses associated with child maltreatment, child poverty, or other policy-related concerns, or from conditions associated with psychological disorders. Researchers must remain sensitive to these sources of stress, trauma, or vulnerability as they seek to increase understanding that will improve children's well-being. In addition, because many of the difficulties that children encounter are from the social conditions in which they live, researchers in each field enlist an ecological orientation in their design and interpretation of research investigations. This requires understanding the mutual influences of the child and different levels of the social ecology such as the family, neighborhood, and community, as well as government policies. Developmental scientists also recognize that children's functioning is affected by not only by risk factors but also by protective factors that exist within and around the child, such as social support at home or in the neighborhood, and thus research attention to both risk and protective factors is important, especially for informing intervention.

These common characteristics of work in developmental psychopathology and child and family policy make research in these translational fields important and interesting. Methodologically, these characteristics contribute to considerable breadth of approach, but also some distinctive features of how researchers in these fields approach their work.

Introduction to the Topic

Developmental psychopathology is a multidisciplinary field of inquiry into the factors contributing to the development of child psychopathology (Cicchetti, 2013; Lewis & Rudolph, 2014). As the name implies, developmental psychopathologists focus on the internal and external influences that increase the odds that children will develop internalizing disorders (such as depression, anxiety disorders, or trauma- or stress-related disorders) or externalizing disorders (such as conduct disorder, oppositional defiant disorder, or other disorders marked by impulsive, aggressive behavior). This knowledge is then enlisted into the design of interventions that can either prevent psychological problems from developing or contribute to their remediation. Developmental psychopathologists study these influences within a developmental framework, understanding that vulnerable children are also developing persons who face the same age-related challenges and opportunities that more typical children do. Thus a developmental psychopathologist would inquire, for example, how the growth of parent–child attachments and the development of a sense of self in early childhood are affected by child maltreatment, or how the emergence of capacities for emotion regulation are affected by living with a parent who is depressed. They believe that understanding typical developmental processes can inform understanding of children at risk for psychopathology, and that the reverse is also true, and this approach is typical of translational science.

Because a wide range of internal and external influences contribute to the development of psychopathology, researchers in this area attend to the dynamic interaction between multiple levels of development, including genetic, neurobiological, physiological, social, cognitive, emotional, cultural, and institutional influences. This multilevel orientation is complemented by an ecological approach that views developing children as nested within and influenced by multiple levels of the social ecology. Developmental psychopathologists also believe that development is probabilistic rather than deterministic. The same risk factors can be associated with different developmental outcomes (the principle of multifinality) and individuals with the same difficulties may arrive at them through different developmental pathways (the principle of equifinality). Not surprisingly, these principles require careful thought when deriving conclusions concerning the association of risk factors with child outcomes. Taken together, these characteristics of developmental psychopathology contribute to research approaches that enable an integrative analysis of developmental processes over time, and also methods that enable the evaluation of promising interventions.

Developmental scientists who study problems in child and family policy likewise address a broad range of topics, including the consequences of variations in child care quality, the effects of marital conflict and divorce on children, the origins and effects of child abuse or neglect, the developmental consequences of foster care experience, how children are affected by poverty and family economic adversity, and many other issues (Aber, Bishop-Josef, Jones, McLearn, & Phillips, 2007; Zigler & Hall, 2000). Researchers also evaluate the effects of planned interventions to improve children's well-being, such as strategies to improve the early learning of children at risk for educational underachievement, the benefits for children of family programs to help provide emotional or economic support to parents, the effects of interventions to reduce stress and improve well-being for children in foster care and other difficult circumstances, and other concerns.

In the midst of these wide-ranging research investigations relevant to public policy, several characteristics are commonly observed. Developmental scientists in this field adopt a developmental orientation, recognizing that the effects of child care, child maltreatment, poverty, and other concerns are relative in many ways to the developmental capabilities of the child. They also enlist an ecological orientation because of how much the effects of these experiences, and opportunities to change their consequences, depend on understanding and altering the social conditions in which children live. Researchers in this area also use a multilevel approach. When considering the effects of child care quality on children, for example, researchers study its immediate and longer-term consequences for multiple developmental domains, such as learning and academic achievement, social and emotional functioning, self-regulatory ability, and biological stress reactivity and brain development. Finally, researchers whose work is relevant to child and family policy are cautious in deriving direct policy applications from their work, recognizing the value of replication, the possibility that findings may be sample-specific, the potential influence of unmeasured variables, and in general the complexity of translating research findings into sound public policy.

To illustrate how developmental psychologists and social policy researchers approach their research, consider child poverty. Poverty early in life significantly increases the risk of many negative life outcomes, including the development of a range of internalizing and externalizing disorders (Wadsworth, Evans, Grant, Carter, & Duffy, 2016). But not all children in poverty suffer in these ways, leading researchers to examine the influences that can mediate the effects of poverty on development or moderate its impact. These influences include: (a) the effects of poverty on parents and family functioning; (b) how children are affected by neighborhoods in poverty that are sometimes characterized by unsafe play spaces, poor quality child care, and poor schools; (c) the effects of poverty on children's self-perceptions and goals for the future; and (d) how the stresses associated with poverty affect the developing brain and other physiological systems. These mediating and moderating influences are relevant, in turn, to identifying risk factors that contribute to the negative outcomes associated with poverty and the protective factors that can buffer their impact. For example, parents who are depressed and anxious about economic problems are less nurturant and supportive of their children, but the impact of this risk factor is reduced by social safety net programs that ease financial strain, or the availability of social support for children outside the family. Researchers have also realized that poverty affects younger children differently than older children (with greater consequences when poverty is experienced early) because these mediating and moderating factors have different influences at early ages (e.g., Duncan, Ziol-Guest, & Kalil, 2010).

Thus developmental scientists quickly move beyond the conclusion that "poverty is bad for children" to an exploration of the influences that can alter its impact, because doing so helps to identify potential avenues for intervention to support children. Examining these processes requires a developmental orientation (because these processes have different influences at different ages), a multilevel approach (because poverty can influence children biologically, social-cognitively, socially, and academically), and an ecological view (because the effects of poverty relate not just to the child and the family but also to neighborhood and school quality, community resources, public policies and cultural values). And while no single investigation fully encompasses developmental, multilevel, and ecological orientations, researchers must consider how each orientation affects the interpretation of their results and the translational conclusions they can derive from the broader research literature on children and poverty.

Possible Measurement and Designs

As this overview of research in developmental psychopathology and child policy suggests, diverse research methods are used. In fact, most of the research approaches discussed in other chapters of this volume find applications to the fields of developmental psychopathology and studies related to child and family policy. Researchers enlist longitudinal as well as cross-sectional research designs, experimental as well as correlational methods, and measures that range from interviews and surveys to detailed observational ratings to standardized performance measures. Like other fields in developmental psychology, researchers have increasingly enlisted biological measures into their methodological toolkit, recognizing that noninvasive and inexpensive assessments of stress hormones (like cortisol) and parasympathetic regulation (like cardiac measures of vagal tone) can provide valuable convergent measures of variables like emotional coping and self-regulation. Moreover, researchers in this field, like others, have also been drawn to the secondary analysis of large longitudinal datasets that permit greater statistical power for evaluating research questions.

What, then, makes research in developmental psychopathology and child policy methodologically distinctive? Translational science requires that researchers devote more searching attention to several research issues that all researchers must consider, but the lab-to-practice quality of research in these fields compels more complex consideration.

One of the most important is a focus on the reliability and robustness of research findings (Duncan, Engel, Claessens, & Dowsett, 2014). The reliability of research results is a concern for all researchers, of course, and has been the focus of recent debates over whether well-accepted research findings in psychology are replicable. But when research results are relevant to developmental psychopathology and/or public policy, their reliability is especially important because of the potential for mistaken or even harmful applications in translational science. For this reason, researchers in these fields devote particular attention to questions related to the reliability and robustness of the research literature from which clinical or policy applications may be derived. Here are two examples. First, have research findings been replicated in one or more independent samples? If so, do the replication results reveal differences as well as consistency in the results that may be relevant to clinical or policy applications? For example, maltreated children exhibit dysregulated stress reactivity because of how they are treated, but the dysregulation is much different for neglected compared to emotionally abused children (Thompson, 2014). Second, can findings be suitably generalized to other populations who may be different from the study sample (e.g., the rural poor differ in significant ways from the urban poor)? This may be an especially important consideration if the other populations will also be affected by the clinical or policy applications of the research.

A second distinctive concern of researchers in these fields is with the practical as well as the statistical significance of research findings. Stated differently, are research results necessarily meaningful for policy and/or intervention even if they are statistically significant? This is an important question because many research studies (especially with large samples) can yield statistically significant results but with uncertain practical significance if outcomes were not appreciably changed. If three-year-olds who participated for two years in an early intervention program scored only 1 to 2 points higher on standardized tests of cognitive and language development compared to nonparticipating children, for example, does this indicate program success (Love et al., 2005)? Although program administrators and policymakers can make intuitive judgments based on results such as these, researchers who study these issues require less subjective indicators of impact that extend beyond statistical significance. They may use, for example, a measure of effect size that quantifies the magnitude of the difference between two groups in relation to the variability of the measure. Effect size is less influenced by the sample size than are measures of statistical significance, and thus can be a more valuable index of impact. In the illustration above, the effect size of a 1–2 point difference between intervention and control groups was found to be a large effect size, even though it was small in absolute magnitude. It thus lends support to the practical value of the intervention that was being assessed.

Other measures of practical significance are more complex. For example, researchers sometimes calculate a cost–benefit analysis in which the quantified costs of an intervention are compared to the quantified benefits it produces to determine whether the program is an economical investment of public or private resources (see Reynolds, Temple, White, Ou, & Robertson, 2011, for an example). Identifying and quantifying benefits – which can include benefits to the child, family, and society, as well as costs averted by the program benefits to each – is a complex (and sometimes controversial) determination.

A third distinctive concern that characterizes thoughtful researchers in these translational fields is attention to the potential influence of their values on their research. One of the central purposes of the research process is to create unbiased and generalizable knowledge, and many research procedures are designed to prevent the intrusion of the researcher's personal values into the findings that result. Researchers endorse these procedures, but their commitment to the well-being of the children they study and beliefs about the policies and practices that would benefit them can lead naturally to practices that can inadvertently bias the research process. The selection of research variables, the recruitment of a research sample, how responses to measures are interpreted, and the data analytic design all involve decisions in which a researcher's values and beliefs can influence the choices that are made and, as a consequence, the study's results.

The researcher's values can most significantly influence the research process in the interpretation and generalization of research findings. Researchers typically include comments on the limitations of the study in their discussion section, of course, but when the findings address important questions of public policy or clinical intervention, these limitations can be easily overlooked in the conclusions and recommended applications of the findings. Values concerning the benefits of early education or parental leave, for example, can cause researchers to focus attention on findings supporting this view and overlook contrary evidence in the results. Sometimes recommendations for the reform of judicial policies concerning child custody are based on the findings of a small-scale study of children in different custody arrangements; or a therapeutic strategy for children with serious disorders is recommended that has only been successfully implemented with less-troubled samples. These tendencies are inevitable because researchers themselves are passionate about what they study, but they are more problematic in translational science because of the practical applications of research findings. They are curbed when thoughtful researchers have the humility to realize that a single study contributes only a small increment to increasing knowledge, that conclusions must be refined in the context of further research, and that practical applications await a well-established foundation of carefully designed studies.

This leads to a final distinctive concern of research in these fields: the challenges of research ethics. Research in developmental psychopathology and child and family policy confronts distinct ethical challenges that require careful attention throughout the research process. Here are some examples. Research scientists are mandated reporters of suspected child maltreatment. How, therefore, do they study families with heightened likelihood of child abuse and neglect without placing these families at risk of being reported to authorities? How do researchers address the possibility of research findings being used inappropriately to the disadvantage of the population under study, such as in research on the cognitive and motivational consequences of growing up in poverty? When studying politically vulnerable populations, such as children of undocumented parents, how do researchers ensure the confidentiality of research materials that might reveal the family's undocumented status? How do researchers interpret the mandate for consent to research participation (and assent for children) when children are young, are involved in potentially abusive family relationships, or have serious psychological disorders? Can their parents be suitably enlisted to provide consent on their behalf? More generally, how can researchers ensure that the children who participate in their studies, who are already vulnerable because of prior experiences, clinical psychopathology, or the settings in which they live, experience the research process in a manner that does not increase their distress?

All researchers have to address the ethical requirements of the research they undertake, but those who are devoted to translational science have unusual challenges. Researchers' thoughtful engagement with these issues is part of their professional responsibility and increases their sensitivity to the needs of the populations of children they study.

Core Methodologies Used

Developmental psychopathologists and researchers concerned with child and family policy use a variety of methods in their work, but two core methodologies stand out as more common to the translational science of their fields. One is the use of the randomized controlled trial to provide evidence for the impact of a promising intervention. The other is the use of field research to connect developmental science to the contexts in which children live and develop.

Randomized Controlled Trials

One of the fundamental concerns of research in developmental psychopathology and child and family studies is how to substantiate causal associations between an intervention and a child outcome. The intervention may consist of a promising preventive or therapeutic procedure, or a new form of classroom instruction, and the goal of the research is to determine its impact. Because of the importance of deriving well-founded conclusions concerning impact, researchers have developed the randomized controlled trial (RCT) as the optimal research design for program evaluation.

The RCT is often a double-blind design in which research participants are randomly assigned to study conditions – which consist of the treatment condition (i.e., the intervention being tested) and one or more control conditions (which can include a no-treatment control and/or control conditions involving alternative treatments) – in which the researcher has no knowledge of which participants are in which conditions, and nor do participants. Randomization of condition assignment minimizes selection bias and its potential effects on study outcomes. After randomization, people participate in the conditions to which they have been assigned and subsequently outcome measures are collected. These measures can be compared across treatment groups and, if the measures were also collected before treatments, measures of change as the result of the treatments can also be compared.

RCT research designs have been used for many years to evaluate the effects of new practices that can have significant financial or health consequences, such as in businesses and medicine (Manzi, 2012). In government, the Obama administration instituted procedures to require evidence for program effectiveness from RCT studies as the basis for funding decisions for programs in areas such as teen pregnancy prevention, workforce training, and home visitation (Haskins & Margolis, 2014). Partly as a consequence, RCT research has become the gold standard for showing evidence of program effectiveness in developmental psychopathology and child and family policy. The study profiled earlier of the impact of an early intervention program on three-year-olds' cognitive and language development is an example of an RCT design (Love et al., 2005). In another RCT study with a sample of families who had been identified for child maltreatment, Cicchetti, Rogosch, and Toth (2006) reported significant increases in secure attachment in two-year-olds who participated with their mothers in a year of Infant–Parent Psychotherapy, and greater secure attachment than infants who participated with their mothers in two other comparison intervention groups.

Implementing the RCT to evaluate program effectiveness can be expensive and time-consuming, and it can be difficult in some circumstances, such as when the number of qualified participants is small or the nature of the intervention does not permit researchers and/or participants to be blind to their condition. Moreover, there are ethical challenges to conducting RCT research, especially when it involves denying potentially significant health or mental health benefits to participants in control conditions. For these reasons, some researchers suggest broadening the standards for acceptable forms of evidence to demonstrate program effectiveness.

Field Research

Field research is used by scientists in a variety of research areas, including biology, economics, and public health, and it is a central methodology for research in anthropology and sociology. In developmental science, field research is not at all unique to work in developmental psychopathology and child and family policy but, like the RCT, it has an important role in the translational science of these areas. Field research strengthens bridges between developmental science and the contexts and applications of that science to clinical and policy problems. Many (perhaps most) developmental psychopathologists do not venture far from the lab, but field studies of coercive family processes, antisocial peer influences, and the developmental consequences of child maltreatment, along with other topics, have also been seminal to the development of understanding of these areas. Moreover, field research has often been the setting for examining the impact of research-based interventions to address these and other psychological problems. Likewise, field studies relevant to child and family policies include research on child care, schools, foster care families, homeless children, and other topics. The settings for many intervention studies include early education programs, schools, community parks, and other places where children live and develop (see Golinkoff, Hirsh-Pasek, Grob, & Schlesinger, 2017, for examples).

Research conducted in the field has the benefits of informing and sometimes challenging research practices and findings derived from the lab to provide better linkages between science and practice. In one example, researchers were interested in engaging low-income fathers in a parenting program, but only after conducting community interviews with fathers were they able to identify the best practices that would succeed in working successfully with the fathers they sought (Shindler, Fisher, & Shonkoff, 2017). Developmental scientists who conduct field research face the challenges deriving from lack of control over influences on research participants that can affect study outcomes, as well as the inability to bring sophisticated technology (such as neuroimaging capability) into most settings. For these and other reasons, some research programs move fluidly between lab and field environments, conducting foundational research in the lab and then going into community settings to examine the generalizability and robustness of these findings in the lived contexts of children and families.

Innovations

There are at least two innovations that have significantly strengthened research methodology in developmental psychopathology and child and family policy research.

First, researchers are increasingly incorporating biological measures into research in these fields. One reason for doing so is that these measures provide useful convergent data concerning underlying psychological processes that are relevant to developmental psychopathology and the impact of social conditions on children. As noted earlier, for example, maltreated children exhibit dysregulated stress reactivity – in other words, they respond to stressful events in an atypical manner owing to their prior experiences of abuse or neglect (Thompson, 2014). But careful studies using the stress hormone cortisol (which can be assessed noninvasively through saliva samples) have shown that stress dysregulation is different for children who have been neglected compared to those who have been emotionally abused. Neglected children show low cortisol levels that may reflect a stress system that has become overwhelmed, while emotionally maltreated children show high cortisol levels that may reflect their vigilance for further threat at home (Bruce, Gunnar, Pears, & Fisher, 2013). Enlisting a biological measure like cortisol enables important distinctions within the population of maltreated children in the impact of stressful experiences on them, with potential implications for treatment.

Another reason for incorporating biological measures into research is to distinguish biological from environmental sources of risk for developing psychopathology. Although developmental scientists have long recognized that the traditional distinction between nature and nurture is scientifically obsolete because development derives from the complex interweaving of both influences, it can be valuable to distinguish biological from environmental risk factors when studying the origins of psychopathology. To do so, researchers increasingly incorporate methods from molecular genetics into their studies that enable the identification of specific gene alleles from DNA genotyping. Based on these studies, specific genes have been found to be associated with heightened risk for the development of aggression and conduct problems, impulsivity, and some internalizing disorders. Developmental psychopathologists also use brain imaging methods in their studies of topics such as adolescent risk-taking behavior and the development of autism and other conditions. The purpose of using biologically informed methods in these ways is not to portray clinical conditions as biologically determined but rather to better understand the interaction of biological risk factors with risk and protective influences from experience in the environment.

In the child and family policy field, researchers have been slower to incorporate biological methods into their studies, but this is changing. Biological measures can be useful for evaluating the impact of planned interventions on child outcomes. As one illustration, two researchers showed that after three and a half years of participation in a conditional cash-transfer antipoverty program in Mexico, preschool children showed more normal cortisol levels, and children of the most depressed mothers showed the greatest benefit (Fernald & Gunnar, 2009).

Further applications of biologically informed methods can be anticipated in the future because they contribute to a multilevel understanding of developmental influences and outcomes. The challenge in their use in psychological research is that the connection of biological measures with psychological processes is indirect and, at times, complex. Cortisol, for example, can index stress reactivity when it is carefully and appropriately measured, but it also indexes other psychological processes that can make the interpretation of cortisol reactivity more challenging.

Second, researchers are increasingly turning to the secondary analysis of large longitudinal datasets to address important research questions with the statistical power that large datasets offer. There are a remarkable number of datasets that have been made available for other researchers to use, and many include variables of interest to those interested in the origins and consequences of psychological disorders and the effects of public policies on children and their families. Indeed, some of these datasets were originally designed to address issues like these. As one illustration, the National Institutes of Child Health and Human Development Study of Early Child Care and Youth Development (NICHD SECCYD) was inaugurated in 1991 as a large national study of the effects of early child care experience on developmental outcomes. More than 1000 families were recruited when children were born and the children were studied through their early years to understand how their development was affected by the child care choices that families made. The study continued long after the relevant data were gathered, however, with the most recent wave of assessments occurring when the children were young adults, resulting in a treasured dataset with many measures of psychological and behavioral processes assessed longitudinally throughout childhood, adolescence, and early adulthood. In doing so, researchers gathered many assessments of variables relevant not only to public policy issues like child care but also to the emergence of psychopathology and many other concerns. As one example, Burt and Roisman (2010) obtained assessments of children in this study from age 54 months through 15 years to identify a developmental "cascade" of changes for some children that began with externalizing problems in early childhood to impairments in competent behavior at older ages to adolescent internalizing problems, such as depression and anxiety. It is rare to be able to study the longitudinal course of risk for psychopathology in this manner.

Discoveries like these would be impossible without the concerted effort devoted to following a large sample of children and families for many years, and thus datasets like these are a valuable resource for examining developmental questions. The major challenge in conducting secondary analyses of existing datasets is they may not include all the measures needed to address these questions, or the measures that are most pertinent might be poor assessments of the variable a researcher wants to include. In the study by Burt and Roisman (2010) described above, for example, the measures of externalizing and internalizing behavior and most of the measures of children's competence were derived from maternal report. Mothers may not be the most objective reporters of their children's behavior, especially when the child's behavior is troubled. Moreover, it is impossible to ignore the possibility that the developmental cascade identified by the researchers might derive, at least in part, from maternal perceptions of changes in her child over time. These concerns are difficult to resolve, however, because we cannot change the design of the NICHD SECCYD to obtain more direct measures of psychopathology and competence, so researchers using this dataset have to settle for the measures which currently exist.

Conclusion

One of the important missions of developmental science is to improve the welfare of children and youth, and most researchers are committed to this goal in their research programs. Translational science intentionally bridges science and practice to advance this mission, and research in developmental psychopathology and child and family policy studies are examples of translational approaches in developmental science. Although there are not many methodologies that are unique to these fields, researchers have an orientation toward their work that includes serious attention to the reliability and robustness of research findings that might find practical applications to programs and policy, attention to the practical (as well as statistical) significance of research findings, concern with the potential intrusion of personal values into the research process, and unique ethical challenges. Their use of randomized controlled trials and field studies add to the distinctiveness of work in these fields. Taken together, they help to bring the basic science of human development into interventions and policies that can significantly improve the well-being of children.

References

Aber, J. L., Bishop-Josef, S. J., Jones, S. M., McLearn, K. T., & Phillips, D. A. (2007). *Child Development and Social Policy: Knowledge for Action*. Washington, DC: American Psychological Association.

Bruce, J., Gunnar, M. R., Pears, K. C., & Fisher, P. A. (2013). Early adverse care, stress neurobiology, and prevention science: Lessons learned. *Prevention Science, 14*, 247–256. doi:10.1007/s11121-012-0354-6.

Burt, K. B. & Roisman, G. I. (2010). Competence and psychopathology: Cascade effects in the NICHD Study of Early Child Care and Youth Development. *Development and Psychopathology, 22*, 557–567. doi:10.1017/S0954579410000271.

Cicchetti, D. (2013). An overview of developmental psychopathology. In P. D. Zelazo (Ed.), *Oxford Handbook of Developmental Psychology Vol. 2. Self and other* (pp. 455–480). New York: Oxford University Press.

Cicchetti, D., Rogosch, F. A., & Toth, S. L. (2006). Fostering secure attachment in infants in maltreating families through preventive interventions. *Development and Psychopathology, 18*, 623–649. doi:10.10170S0954579406060329.

Duncan, G. J., Engel, M., Claessens, A., & Dowsett, C. J. (2014). Replication and robustness in developmental research. *Developmental Psychology, 50*, 2417–2425. doi:10.1037/a0037996.

Duncan, G. J., Ziol-Guest, K. M., & Kalil, A. (2010). Early-childhood poverty and adult attainment, behavior, and health. *Child Development, 81*, 306–325. doi:10.1111/j.1467-8624.2009.01396.x.

Fernald, L. C. H. & Gunnar, M. R. (2009). Poverty-alleviation program participation and salivary cortisol in very low-income children. *Social Science & Medicine, 68*, 2180–2189. doi:10.1016/j.socscimed.2009.03.032.

Golinkoff, R. M., Hirsh-Pasek, K., Grob, R., & Schlesinger, M. (2017). "Oh, the places you'll go" by bringing developmental science into the world! *Child Development, 88*, 1402–1408. doi:10.1111/cdev.12929.

Haskins, R. & Margolis, G. (2014). *Show Me the Evidence: Obama's Fight for Rigor and Results in Social Policy*. Washington, DC: Brookings.

Lewis, M. & Rudolph, K. D. (2014). *Handbook of Developmental Psychopathology*. New York: Springer.

Love, J. M., Kisker, E. E., Ross, C., Raikes, H., Constantine, J., Boller, K., Brooks-Gunn, J., Chazan-Cohen, R., Tarullo, L. B., Brady-Smith, C., Fuligni, A. S., Schochet, P. Z., Paulsell, D., &

Vogel, C. (2005). The effectiveness of Early Head Start for 3-year-old children and their parents: Lessons for policy and programs. *Developmental Psychology, 41*, 885–901. doi:10.1037/0012-1649.41.6.885.

Manzi, J. (2012). *Uncontrolled: The Surprising Payoff of Trial-and-Error for Business, Politics, and Society*. New York: Basic.

Reynolds, A. J., Temple, J. A., White, B. A., Ou, S.-R., & Robertson, D. L. (2011). Age-26 cost–benefit analysis of the Child–Parent Center Early Education Program. *Child Development, 82*, 379–404. doi:10.1111/j.1467-8624.2010.01563.x.

Shindler, H. S., Fisher, P. A., & Shonkoff, J. P. (2017). From innovation to impact at scale: Lessons learned from a cluster of research-community partnerships. *Child Development, 88*, 1435–1446. doi:10.1111/cdev.12904.

Thompson, R. A. (2014). Stress and child development. *The Future of Children, 24*, 41–59. doi:10.1353/foc.2014.0004.

Wadsworth, M. E., Evans, G. W., Grant, K., Carter, J. S., & Duffy, S. (2016). Poverty and the development of psychopathology. In D. Cicchetti (Ed.), *Developmental Psychopathology*, 3rd Ed., *Vol. 4. Risk, Resilience, and Intervention* (pp. 136–179). New York: Wiley.

Zigler, E. G. & Hall, N. W. (2000). *Child Development and Social Policy: Theory and Applications*. New York: McGraw-Hill.

15 Methodological Considerations in Collaborative Memory and Aging Research

Michelle L. Meade, Summer R. Whillock, and Katherine M. Hart

Introduction to the Topic

The vast majority of memory research examines memory as it occurs in individuals in isolation. Yet, most information in our everyday life is presented and remembered in a social context, and past experiences are often shared and re-created with others. Social memory is a growing field (see Rajaram, 2011 for a review), but relatively little is known about social influences on older adults' memory performance. One approach to understanding social influences on memory is to determine the outcome when two or more individuals collaborate on a memory task, compared to individual performance on the same task. With respect to age, some researchers have found collaboration to impair memory performance in older adults (e.g., Johansson, Andersson, & Ronnberg, 2000), while others have found collaboration to benefit memory (e.g., Dixon, 1999). In the current chapter, we discuss the contradictory findings in relation to measurement and design issues and highlight how methodological considerations inform the role of collaboration on older adults' memories.

The current chapter provides a selective overview of methodological considerations surrounding collaborative memory and aging research (see Meade, Harris, Van Bergen, Sutton, & Barnier, 2018 for a more comprehensive discussion). We focus on measurement and design issues that bear directly on whether or not collaboration benefits or disrupts memory, namely measuring the effects of collaboration at the individual and group level, and measuring both accurate and false memories. We also discuss complementary measures of collaboration such as collaborative process variables (how individuals exchange information during collaboration) and metacognitive judgments (individuals' beliefs about collaboration). We discuss the advantages and limitations of each measurement, as well as the issues surrounding age-related differences in original learning, error production, and metacognitive judgments. The methodologies discussed highlight experimental issues relevant to future research on aging and collaborative memory.

Summary of the Topics

Memory is a multifaceted construct that encompasses several processes and/or systems (see Schacter, Wagner, & Buckner, 2000). Accordingly, the relationship between aging and memory is multidirectional. For example, semantic memory, or general world knowledge, increases with age presumably due to older adults' greater range of experience and acquired information (e.g., Park et al., 2002). In contrast, episodic memory, or memory for our personal episodes that we mentally time travel back to re-experience, declines with age. In the current chapter, we focus exclusively on age-related changes in episodic memory and specifically the role of collaboration in mediating age-related changes in episodic memory.

Past research on collaborative memory and aging has revealed that collaboration can both benefit and disrupt individual memory performance. On one hand, some studies have shown that collaboration benefits older adults' memory such that they remember additional information when remembering with a partner (e.g., Dixon, 1996, 1999; Gould, Trevithick, & Dixon, 1991). Collaborative benefits can be explained by the fact that older adults generally have more experience collaborating with others (Dixon, 1996) and are more adept at relying on other people as retrieval cues (cf. Craik & McDowd, 1987). On the other hand, many studies have shown that collaboration impairs memory in older adults, such that those remembering in collaborative pairs recall less than their predicted individual potential (individuals in collaborative groups recall less than the combined output of the same number of individuals recalling alone). This pattern of results is known as collaborative inhibition (Weldon & Bellinger, 1997). Collaborative inhibition can be explained by the retrieval strategy disruption hypothesis which suggests that working with another person distracts and disrupts individual retrieval strategies, thus resulting in lower recall (Basden, Basden, Bryner, & Thomas, 1997). Importantly, the magnitude of collaborative inhibition effects are equivalent for both young and older adults (Blumen & Stern, 2011; Henkel & Rajaram, 2011; Meade & Roediger, 2009; Ross, Spencer, Blatz, & Restorick, 2008), suggesting any disruptive effects of collaboration are age-invariant.

Considered together, current research demonstrates that older adults suffer declines in episodic memory and that collaboration can both benefit and disrupt memory performance. Measurement and design considerations are crucial to understanding age-related changes in collaborative remembering, and specifically how and when collaboration benefits and or disrupts older adults' memories.

Possible Measurement and Designs

Research on collaborative memory and aging includes a range of measurement and design choices that reflect the various questions asked and bear directly on the results. We outline below a selection of measurement and design issues that are particularly relevant to collaborative memory and aging research, including the level of measurement, and an overview of the different measures collected (accurate and false memory, collaborative process variables, and metacognitive judgments). We end this section with a cautionary tale regarding cross sectional comparisons that highlights the need for future longitudinal research (see Meade et al., 2018 for a more comprehensive consideration of factors and dimensions of collaborative memory research).

Individual and Group Level Analyses

One measurement issue central to understanding collaborative memory and aging is the choice of comparison group. Some researchers measure the effects of collaboration at the group level. This is most commonly used in the cognitive aging literature and involves comparing memory performance of a single individual to the combined output of a collaborating group. Consistent with the old adage that "two heads are better than one", group level collaborative memory studies generally find that collaborative groups produce more information than individuals working alone. Importantly, however, measuring individual recall against collaborative recall has a base-rate problem, and does not directly compare the performance of an individual performing on his or her own with the performance of an individual remembering in a group.

To examine how individual memory differs when recalling alone relative to recalling in a group, researchers can measure the effects of collaboration at the individual level. This approach is most commonly used in the cognitive psychological literature, and it involves comparing collaborative recall to nominal group recall. Nominal groups refer to the pooled unique items produced by individuals who had performed on their own, such that performance between two/three people recalling together is compared against performance of two/three people who recalled on their own. In this way, the base-rate problem is controlled, and one can determine the relative impact of collaboration on individual memory. Essentially, if collaboration has no impact on individual memory, there should be no difference between collaborative and nominal groups. However, instead, research that compares collaborative groups against nominal groups generally finds collaborative inhibition; individuals recall less when working with others than they do when working alone.

Broadly speaking, collaborative groups recall more than individuals but less than nominal groups. The level of measurement is thus critical to understanding how collaboration both benefits and disrupts older adults' memory. It is important to note, however, that individual level and group level analyses are not the entire story, as researchers have shown memory improvement while using nominal group comparisons (e.g., Meade, Nokes, & Morrow, 2009).

See Practice Exercise 15.1 for a more concrete example of group and individual level analyses and instructions for computing individual, collaborative group, and nominal group recall.

Accurate and False Memory Measurements

Collaborative memory studies generally present participants with information to be remembered and then compare individual and group performances in terms of the content of what is remembered and also whether or not the information remembered is correct or erroneous. Experimenters can determine both accurate and false memory because the experimenters presented the information and so know what was studied. Measuring both accurate and false memory is important to understanding how collaboration influences age, as the few studies that have directly compared collaborative inhibition effects between young and older adults have found different effects for accurate and false memory. Specifically, the impact of collaboration on accurate recall does not vary with age, but the results regarding errors are inconsistent across studies such that sometimes collaboration reduces errors (Henkel & Rajaram, 2011; Ross et al., 2008), and sometimes collaboration increases errors (Meade & Roediger, 2009). Several additional methodological factors are likely related to whether or not collaboration reduces errors or increases errors, including collaborative recall style (turn taking or free for all collaborative recall (cf. Thorley & Dewhurst, 2007)) and the relationship between collaborators (e.g., Harris, Keil, Sutton, Barnier, & McIlwain, 2011; see Meade, Perga, & Hart, in press, for discussion). Still, differentiating the method of measurement (accurate or false memory) is an important aspect of understanding when and how collaboration influences memory.

Considered together, age differences in collaborative memory may differ across accurate and false memory and so it is crucial to examine both measures. It is important to note, however, that some materials are easier than others to score as accurate and false. For example, when scoring information recalled from a word list, researchers can easily determine if the word was recalled or not. In contrast, when scoring information recalled from a story or a more complex event, participants do not remember the information verbatim, and so experimenters must determine if the information is conceptually similar to the original event and/or if it is a distortion of previously presented information (cf. Bergman & Roediger, 1999). See Practice Exercise 15.2 for a more concrete example of how to determine accurate and false memory and instructions for comparing accurate and false memory coding across different types of materials.

Collaborative Process Variables

In addition to measuring the content of what is remembered (and whether or not the content is accurate or erroneous), many collaborative memory studies examine collaborative process variables, or the manner in which people talk about their memories. The manner in which information is exchanged during collaboration may influence the relative gains and losses from the collaboration, as individual contributions are rejected or incorporated into the group (e.g., Meade, 2013). For example, Meade et al. (2009) tested expert and novice pilots on their memory for aviation scenarios and demonstrated that the reason the expert pilots were able to overcome inhibition and, in fact, benefit from collaboration, was that they acknowledged their partner's suggestions and also elaborated on the content (see too Harris et al., 2011; Meade & Gigone, 2011; Ross et al., 2008). Collaborative process variables may shed light on the mechanisms underlying collaborative performance and are generally assessed in addition to content and accuracy of information recalled.

Metacognitive Measures

Also in addition to accuracy and the content of what is remembered, collaborative memory researchers may include measures of metacognition. That is, participants may be asked about their beliefs regarding the effects of collaboration on memory. As one example, Henkel and Rajaram (2011) asked young and older adults how helpful it was to remember in a group. Those individuals who had recently collaborated rated collaboration as more helpful than those who had recently remembered alone. Importantly, there were no age differences, suggesting both young and older adults found collaboration beneficial. Metacognitive measures offer insight into collaborative memory because older adults generally think collaboration helps them, although in reality, collaboration can be both beneficial and disruptive (Dixon, de Frias, & Backman, 2001; Henkel & Rajaram, 2011).

Cross Sectional Vs. Longitudinal

Finally, one important note about collaborative memory and aging designs is that the field is almost exclusively based on cross sectional designs. Typically, young adults' (usually aged 18–25 years old) memory is compared to older adults' (usually at least 65 years old) memory on the same tasks. Cross sectional studies allow important discoveries regarding age differences in how collaboration influences memory; however, future longitudinal research is necessary to examine possible age changes in how individuals rely on collaboration across the lifespan.

Core Methodologies Used

Each of the design and measurement issues outlined above has advantages and limitations that intersect with the nature of the task and research questions. Further, there are important age-specific considerations-based age-related changes observed in the individual episodic memory literature. In this section, we outline the various advantages and limitations to individual and group level analyses, measurement of accurate and false memory, collaborative process variables, and metacognitive judgments, and specifically highlight how changes associated with individual memory performance are relevant to designing experiments and measuring collaborative memory and aging.

Individual and Group Level Analyses

The choice of comparison group depends on the research questions of interest; specifically if researchers are more interested in group level vs. individual level comparison. The individual level comparison has the advantage of controlling for base-rate differences and measuring individual memory; however, it suffers ecological validity concerns. To date, there are no age-specific considerations here, as both group level and individual level comparisons have been successfully examined in both young and older adults. Again, see Practice Exercise 15.1.

Accurate and False Memory Measurements

As mentioned above, measuring accuracy varies along with the type of material, as recall of some materials can be more cleanly scored as accurate compared to recall of other materials (again see Practice Exercise 15.2). In addition, there are several age-related changes in individual memory that are relevant to measuring accurate and false memory in collaborative memory experiments. First, it is important to consider differences in original learning associated with age-related declines in memory. Specifically, if older adults start out recalling less information than young adults, then any further change or difference in the manipulations (e.g. the effect of collaboration on young and older adults' memory) is confounded with original learning and/or scaling artifacts. More precisely, if young and older adults' recall is mismatched to begin with, then it is difficult to interpret the magnitude of any effects, as a 5% difference when starting at 40% recall is not equivalent to a 5% difference when starting at 60% recall (Craik & McDowd, 1987; Meade & Roediger, 2009).

Measuring age differences in collaborative errors is also complicated in light of the research showing that older adults are more likely to make errors on individual memory tests (see Jacoby, 1999). Specifically, on individual tests of memory, older adults have been shown to rely on different processes than young adults when making memory judgments, such as the gist or plausibility of an item (e.g. Reder, Wible, & Martin, 1986), or on the general ease with which an item is generated (e.g. Jacoby & Hollingshead, 1990). Judgments of gist and fluency have been shown to increase older adults' errors in a variety of paradigms (Jacoby, 1999; Koustaal & Schacter, 1997) and may have important implications for understanding age differences in collaborative errors especially across different materials.

Further, older adults may be more likely than young adults to guess on memory tests (Huff, Meade, & Hutchison, 2011). On tests of recall, it is important to determine if a response was produced from memory, or if it was produced as a guess. Guessing biases are especially problematic on tests of related items such as categorized word lists because participants may produce a categorical exemplar simply by guessing. To correct for guessing, researchers have proposed counterbalancing which exemplars are presented vs. excluded from the study list. This allows a comparison of how likely the item is to be produced when it was actually studied relative to how likely the same item was to be produced from guessing (e.g., Meade, Geraci, & Roediger, 2012; Roediger, 1973; Whillock, Meade, & Tsosie, in preparation), although such corrections are not widely used.

Collaborative Process Variables

There is growing evidence that collaborative process variables, or the manner in which information is exchanged and incorporated (or not) into the group output, influences how disruptive or beneficial collaboration is to memory. One advantage of collaborative process variables is that they allow a more nuanced, and idiosyncratic view of how information gets incorporated or rejected by the group and so shed light on the mechanisms underlying collaborative memory and age. However, it is also the case that collaborative process variables are typically presented as supporting examples, rather than manipulated. Further, collaborative process variables are somewhat inconsistent in how they are operationalized and measured across studies. Specifically, collaborative process coding schemes draw heavily on the mother–child scaffolding literature in developmental psychology (e.g., Reese, 2018), and also on the verbal protocol literature in cognitive psychology (e.g., Clark & Wilkes-Gibb, 1986). Because the schemes draw from various literatures, extra care is required to carefully define terms and describe coding procedures.

Metacognitive Judgments

Metacognitive judgments offer a complementary assessment of the role of collaboration on memory. In addition to the content of what is recalled, individuals may prefer (or not) to work with others on memory tests. Importantly, there are important age-related differences in how well calibrated accuracy and metacognition are. For example, Jacoby (1999) demonstrated that not only did older adults produce higher rates of erroneous or false items, but that they were also more likely to report "remembering" specific recollective details about the erroneous items, presumably because they were relying on a different criterion for assessing recollection. The consideration of such age-related biases in metacognitive judgments are critical to understanding age-related considerations in metacognitive judgments. Nonetheless, older adults' metacognitive feelings regarding the influence of a partner may offer important insight into older adults' perceptions of when and how collaboration influences memory and aging.

Considered together, the evidence presented here highlights the importance of considering age-related changes in episodic memory as a factor in understanding age differences in collaborative memory. It is also important to consider the advantages and limitations of the various design and measurement choices, as the advantages and limitations direct the pathway forward to future research on collaborative memory and aging. For example, there is a great need for more experiments that measure a wider range of outcomes (for example measuring accuracy in addition to both collaborative process variables and metacognitive judgments). There is also a need for more tests of generalizability across tasks and groups (e.g., are the same processes underlying age differences when recalling artificial lab materials as when recalling life experiences?). Finally, there is a great need for longitudinal research. Longitudinal studies would greatly contribute to the literature as they could examine age-related changes and track across time the influence of collaboration in relation to individual episodic memory declines.

Innovations

Memory and aging has been studied almost exclusively in isolation and collaboration is a recent innovative approach (e.g., Rajaram, 2011). Researchers are still working out the precise conditions in which collaboration helps vs. hurts memory performance in both young and older adults. However, researchers have started to highlight and promote the potential benefits for older adults. To the extent that older adults benefit from external retrieval cues, relying on another person is a readily available and free memory aid. Relying on others to scaffold memory is well supported in the literature examining group level analyses of collaboration (see Dixon, 1999; Dixon, Gagnon, & Crow, 1998). The idea is also gaining traction in the individual level (e.g. Blumen, Rajaram, & Henkel, 2013; Blumen, 2018). However, there are still many questions regarding how such scaffolding might operate at the individual level (see Barnier, Harris, & Congleton, 2013; Dahlstrom, Danielson, Andersson, & Ronnberg, 2013; Dixon, 2013; Hirst, 2013; Meade, 2013; Wright, 2013).

Also important is that research on collaborative memory and aging is steadily becoming more interdisciplinary in that the dialogue across and within related research perspectives has increased (see Meade et al., 2018). This has resulted in more mixed methods and measures that have moved the field forward in terms of how the effects of collaboration are measured and assessed. For example, in addition to the measures addressed in this chapter (accuracy, collaborative process variables, metacognitive judgments), researchers are also examining the function of collaboration, or why individuals remember together (e.g., Fivush, Zaman, & Merrill, 2018; Pasupathi & Wainryb, 2018). In addition, researchers are also examining the effects of collaboration across a wider range of contexts (for example collaboration in clinical settings, McVittie & McKinlay, 2018), organizational settings (e.g., Bietti & Baker, 2018), and as a means to scaffold memory for Alzheimer's patients (e.g. Blumen, 2018; Hyden & Forsblad, 2018). With these new mixed methods and increasing interdisciplinary dialogue, the field is steadily progressing toward a more thorough and nuanced understanding of the role of collaboration on older adults' memory. People remember together frequently and understanding how and when collaboration helps and/or disrupts memory performance has important implications for both young and older adults.

References

Barnier, A. J., Harris, C. B., & Congleton, A. R. (2013). Mind the gap: Generations of questions in the early science of collaborative recall. *Journal of Applied Research in Memory and Cognition*, 2, 124–127.

Basden, B. H., Basden, D. R., Bryner, S., & Thomas, R. L., III. (1997). A comparison of group and individual remembering: Does collaboration disrupt retrieval strategies? *Journal of Experimental Psychology: Learning, Memory, and Cognition*, 23, 1176–1189.

Bergman, E. & Roediger, H. L., III (1999). Can Bartlett's repeated reproduction experiments be replicated? *Memory & Cognition*, 27, 937–947.

Bietti, L. M. & Baker, M. J. (2018). Multimodal processes of joint remembering in complex collaborative activities. In M. L. Meade, C. B. Harris, P. Van Bergen, J. Sutton, & A. J. Barnier (Eds.), *Collaborative Remembering: Theories, Research, and Applications* (pp. 177–196). Oxford, UK: Oxford University Press.

Blumen, H. M. (2018). Collaborative memory interventions for age-related and Alzheimer's disease-related memory decline. In M. L. Meade, C. B. Harris, P. Van Bergen, J. Sutton, & A. J. Barnier (Eds.), *Collaborative Remembering: Theories, Research, and Applications* (pp. 422–435). Oxford, UK: Oxford University Press.

Blumen, H. M., Rajaram, S., & Henkel, L. (2013). The applied value of collaborative memory research in aging: Behavioral and neural considerations. *Journal of Applied Research in Memory and Cognition*, 2, 107–117.

Blumen, H. M. & Stern, Y. (2011). Short-term and long-term collaboration benefits on individual recall in young and older adults. *Memory & Cognition*, 39, 147–154.

Clark, H. H. & Wilkes-Gibbs, D. (1986). Referring as a collaborative process. *Cognition*, 22, 1–39.

Craik, F. I. M. & McDowd, J. M. (1987). Age differences in recall and recognition. *Journal of Experimental Psychology: Learning, Memory, and Cognition*, 13, 474–479.

Dahlstrom, O., Danielson, H., Andersson, J., & Ronnberg, J. (2013). The applied value of collaborative memory research in aging—some critical comments. *Journal of Applied Research in Memory and Cognition*, 2, 122–123.

Dixon, R. A. (1996). Collaborative memory and aging. In D. Hermann, C. McEvoy, C. Hertzog, & M. K. Johnson (Eds.), *Basic and Applied Memory Research: Theory in Context* (pp. 359–383). New York: Lawrence Erlbaum Associates.

Dixon, R. A. (1999). Exploring cognition in interactive situations: The aging of N + 1 minds. In T. M. Hess & F. Blanchard-Fields (Eds.), *Social Cognition and Aging* (pp. 267–290) Academic Press.

Dixon, R. A. (2013). Collaborative memory research in aging: Supplemental perspectives on application. *Journal of Applied Research in Memory and Cognition*, 2, 128–130.

Dixon, R. A. de Frias, C., & Backman, L. (2001). Characteristics of self-reported memory compensation in older adults. *Journal of Clinical and Experimental Neuropsychology*, 23, 650–661.

Dixon, R. A., Gagnon, L. M., & Crow, C. B. (1998). Collaborative memory accuracy and distortion: Performance and beliefs. In M. J. Intons-Peterson, & D. L. Best (Eds.), *Memory Distortions and their Prevention* (pp. 63–88). New York: Lawrence Erlbaum Associates.

Fivush, R., Zaman, W., & Merrill, N. (2018). Developing social functions of autobiographical memory within family storytelling. In M. L. Meade, C. B. Harris, P. Van Bergen, J. Sutton, & A. J. Barnier (Eds.), *Collaborative Remembering: Theories, Research, and Applications* (pp. 38–54). Oxford, UK: Oxford University Press.

Gould, O. N., Trevithick, L., & Dixon, R. A. (1991). Adult age differences in elaborations produced during prose recall. *Psychology and Aging*, 6, 93–99.

Harris, C. B., Keil, P. G., Sutton, J., Barnier, A. J., & McIlwain, D. J. F. (2011). We remember, we forget: Collaborative remembering in older couples. *Discourse Processes*, 48, 267–303.

Henkel, L. A. & Rajaram, S. (2011). Collaborative remembering in older adults: Age-invariant outcomes in the context of episodic recall deficits. *Psychology and Aging*, 26, 532–545.

Hirst, W. (2013). Commentary on: Helena M. Blumen, Suparna Rajaram, and Linda A. Henkel's "The applied value of collaborative memory research in aging: Behavioral and neural considerations". *Journal of Applied Research in Memory and Cognition, 2,* 118–119.

Huff, M. J., Meade, M. L., & Hutchison, K. A. (2011). Age-related differences in guessing on free and forced recall tests. *Memory, 19,* 317–330.

Hyden, L.-C. & Forsblad, M. (2018). Collaborative remembering in dementia: A focus on joint activities. In M. L. Meade, C. B. Harris, P. Van Bergen, J. Sutton, & A. J. Barnier (Eds.), *Collaborative Remembering: Theories, Research, and Applications* (pp. 436–455). Oxford, UK: Oxford University Press.

Jacoby, L. L. (1999). Ironic effects of repetition: Measuring age-related differences in memory. *Journal of Experimental Psychology: Learning, Memory, and Cognition, 25,* 3–22.

Jacoby, L. L. & Hollingshead, A. (1990). Reading student essays may be hazardous to your spelling: Effects of reading incorrectly and correctly spelled words. *Canadian Journal of Psychology, 44,* 345–358.

Johansson, O., Andersson, J., & Ronnberg, J. (2000). Do elderly couples have better prospective memory than other elderly people when they collaborate? *Applied Cognitive Psychology, 14,* 121–133.

Koustaal, W. & Schacter, D. L. (1997). Gist-based false recognition of pictures in older and younger adults. *Journal of Memory and Language, 37,* 555–583.

McVittie, C. & McKinlay, A. (2018). Collaborative processes in neuropsychological interviews. In M. L. Meade, C. B. Harris, P. Van Bergen, J. Sutton, & A. J. Barnier (Eds.), *Collaborative Remembering: Theories, Research, and Applications* (pp. 216–230). Oxford, UK: Oxford University Press.

Meade, M. L. (2013). The importance of group process variables on collaborative memory. *Journal of Applied Research in Memory and Cognition, 2,* 120–121.

Meade, M. L., Geraci, L. D., & Roediger, H. L., III. (2012). Neuropsychological status in older adults influences susceptibility of false memories. *American Journal of Psychology, 125,* 449–467.

Meade, M. L. & Gigone, D. (2011). The effect of information distribution on collaborative inhibition. *Memory, 19,* 417–428.

Meade, M. L., Harris, C. B., Van Bergen, P., Sutton, J., & Barnier, A. J. (Eds.). (2018). *Collaborative Remembering: Theories, Research, and Applications.* Oxford, UK: Oxford University Press.

Meade, M. L., Nokes, T. J., & Morrow, D. G. (2009). Expertise promotes facilitation on a collaborative memory task. *Memory, 17,* 39–48.

Meade, M. L., Perga, V. A., & Hart, K. M. (in press). Memory and aging in social contexts. In A. K. Thomas, & A. Gutchess (Eds.), *Handbook of Cognitive Aging: A Life Course Perspective.* Cambridge University Press.

Meade, M. L. & Roediger, H. L., III. (2009). Age differences in collaborative memory: The roleof retrieval manipulations. *Memory & Cognition, 37,* 962–975.

Park, D. C., Lautenschlager, G., Hedden, T., Davidson, N. S., Smith, A. D., & Smith, P. K. (2002). Models of visuospatial and verbal memory across the adult life span. *Psychology and Aging, 17,* 299–320.

Pasupathi, M. & Wainryb, C. (2018). Remembering good and bad times together: Functions of collaborative remembering. In M. L. Meade, C. B. Harris, P. Van Bergen, J. Sutton, & J. Barnier (Eds.), *Collaborative Remembering: Theories, Research, and Applications* (pp. 261–279). Oxford, UK: Oxford University Press.

Rajaram, S. (2011). Collaboration both helps and hurts memory: A cognitive perspective. *Current Directions in Psychological Science, 20,* 76–81.

Reder, L. M., Wible, C., & Martin, J. (1986). Differential memory changes with age: Exact retrieval vs. plausible inference. *Journal of Experimental Psychology: Learning,Memory, and Cognition, 12,* 72–81.

Reese, E. (2018). Encouraging collaborative remembering between young children and their caregivers. In M. L. Meade, C. B. Harris, P. Van Bergen, J. Sutton, & A. J. Barnier (Eds.), *Collaborative Remembering: Theories, Research, and Applications* (pp. 317–333). Oxford, UK: Oxford University Press.

Roediger, H. L., III. (1973). Inhibition in recall from cueing with targets. *Journal of Verbal Learning and Verbal Behavior, 12*, 644–657.

Ross, M., Spencer, S. J., Blatz, C. W., & Restorick, E. (2008). Collaboration reduces the frequency of false memories in older and younger adults. *Psychology and Aging, 23*, 85–92.

Schacter, D. L., Wagner, A. D., & Buckner, R. L. (2000). Memory systems of 1999. In E. Tulving & F. I. M. Craik (Eds.), *The Oxford Handbook of Memory* (pp. 627–643). Oxford, UK: Oxford University Press.

Thorley, C. & Dewhurst, S. A. (2007). Collaborative false recall in the DRM procedure: Effects of group size and group pressure. *European Journal of Cognitive Psychology, 19*, 867–881.

Weldon, M. S. & Bellinger, K. D. (1997). Collective memory: Collaborative and individual processes in remembering. *Journal of Experimental Psychology: Learning, Memory, and Cognition, 23*, 1160–1175.

Whillock, S. R., Meade, M. L., & Tsosie, M. D. (in preparation). Age of collaborating partners influences false recall in the collaborative inhibition paradigm.

Wright, D. B. (2013). Commentary on Blumen, Rajaram, and Henkel. Adding "simulate" to their steps. *Journal of Applied Research in Memory and Cognition, 2*, 131–132.

Index

acquisition: of EEG 75–7; of language 91, 108, 113–14; of language in robots 116–18; of nouns and verbs 104–5; of number learning in robots 118–19
adolescents 4, 16, 26, 43, 45–7; and gender 166; and peers 135–7,142, 149; prosocial and moral development of 178, 182–3
aging 162, 200–1, 203–6
aggression 148–9, 152–4, 163, 172, 180, 183–4, 196
altruistic *see* prosocial behavior
animal models 51; avian 52, 54, 59–63; ovine 52–3; rodent 52, 53, 59, 61
antisocial 172, 184, 195
artificial intelligence 113, 115
assent 43 45, 106, 194
assessment 73, 75, 114; of stereotypes 164
attachment 12, 72, 74, 190, 195; ABC+D model 123–30; Ainsworth, M. 12, 123–6; Bowlby, J. 12, 122–3; Dynamic-Maturational Model of Attachment and Adaptation 123–31; future directions in attachment research 127–31; methodologies 125–31
attribute: adoption 162–4, 166; self-perception 159–61
atypical development 53, 63, 80
auditory 62, 63, 85–7, 86, 89, 118–19
Autism Spectrum Disorders (ASD) 84, 92, 119

baby robot platforms 114, 116, 119; *see also* iCub; NAO humanoid robot
Bayesian modeling 116
behavioral: enactment studies 106–7; reports 162, 180, 183; studies 74
bias: ethnocentric 175; intergroup 165; item 177; response 154; selection 194; social desirability 153
biological 79–80, 127–9, 157–8, 163, 165
biological sex *see* sex
biology 70, 72, 79, 84, 195
brain activity 74, 77, 93

brain activity measurement: fMRI 74; fNIRS 74, 85, 97, 96–9; MRI 73–4; PET 74; *see also* EEG; ERP
brain development 53, 73; EEG association with neurohormones 75; patterns 74, 96
bullying 150, 172; *see also* aggression; victimization

CFA *see* confirmatory factor analysis
child psychology experiments 117–19
Child Study Movement 2, 4–5, 8
clinical applications 75
cognition 7, 12, 74, 78, 85, 92, 96, 99, 111, 113, 114, 115, 116, 118, 119
cognitive: architectures 115–18; (*see also* Epigenetic Robotic Architecture (ERA)); modeling 115–16; processes 75, 80, 172
cognitive development: moral reasoning and 172
coherence: of EEG 78
common-method variance 154
comparative development 50, *51*, 99
confirmatory factor analysis (CFA) 176
conformity: of gender 164–6
confound 72, 161, 184
construct validity 177, 180, 183
content analysis 13
contextual factors 164, 173
convergent validity 179–80, 182–3
core methodologies *see* designs
cortisol 57, 74–5; analysis 78–9; reactivity 75, 197
cross-cultural 171–84
cross-sectional 105; gender development 162; and rodent models 52
cross-sequential 71
cross-sex 161, 166
cultural/ethnic groups: Argentinian 179; Brazilian 182, 184; European 175, 178–79, 181; Italian 182; Mexican 175, 179, 181, 183; non-European 173–74; Spanish 179, 182–83; Taiwanese 181, 183; Turkish 182

culturally diverse 174, 178, 183–84
culture-centered theories of moral development 173; ecocultural stress-based model 173–74
culture-related mechanisms of 171, 173

Darwin, C. 50
designs 22–3, 28, 33, 44, 52, 64, 71–2, 75, 80, 105–6, 136, 161–2, 191, 194, 201, 203; behavioral 52, 61, 71, 73–5, 80, 87, 106, 113–14, 136, 151, 162, 173, 197; behavioral reports 162, 180, 183; biological 196; case studies 161–2, 171, 174, 177; correlational 79; exploratory 161, 176; field research 195–6; interviews 162, 175, 181–3; observational 127, 138–9, 141, 161; randomized control trials 194–5
discriminant validity 179–80, 182–3
diversity 14–7, 22–3
dopamine 53, 60, 88

ecocultural stress-based theory of moral development 173, *174*
ecological momentary assessment 142
Electroencephalograms (EEG) 75–8; acquisition of 76–7; analysis of 77–8; artifact in 77, 93; asymmetry 78; brain development and 53, 73; coherence of 78; and core methodologies 75–8, 96; data collection 77; power of 78
Electromyography (EMG) 53, 55, 77
emergentist cognitive modeling 116
emotion-regulation 61
empathy 171–2
emulation 159–61
epigenetics 72, 80
Epigenetic Robotic Architecture (ERA) 116
ethics 40, 193; Nuremberg Code 41
ethnicity 14, **19–21**, 175, 177; *see also* race
event-related potentials (ERP) 76, 93–4
evolutionary theory 122, 157, 171
exploratory factor analysis (EFA) 176
external validity 181
externalizing 135–6, 148, 180, 189, 191, 197
eye-tracking 87, 89–92, *90*, 108–11

faces 84–98, *86, 89, 91, 95, 98*, 159; processing 84, 94, 97–8
factor analysis 176–7, 179
family systems 71–2
fetal behaviors *60–1*; high frequency **51**; low frequency **51**
fetal studies *see* prenatal studies
fetus 50–64, 70–4, 79
fetus-to-infant 73–4, 79

gender 157–9; conformity 164–6; contentedness 160, 165–6; membership knowledge of 160–1, 165; nonconformity 148; role 165; stereotypes 158–67; typicality 159, 161, 165–6
gender development 162–3; biological theories of 157; genetic research 63; in infant research 79–80; Kohlberg's theory of 158; secondary analysis of longitudinal datasets 197
Gender Schema Theory (GST) 158; Self-Socialization Model (GSSM) 159–62; *see also* theory
gender-typed 158–60, 162
genetic 53; expression 70; mutation 59
guinea pig *see* rodent

habituation/dishabituation 85, 87–9, *88, 89*, 92
heart rate variability 73
hormone 53–4, 59, 62, 73–5, 79; *see also* neurohormones
hybrid cognitive modeling 116

ICC *see* item characteristic curve
iCub *114*, 114–15, 117–18
in utero 73
incentives 44, 46
individual differences 36, 73, 159–60, 163–6, 173
informed consent 41–45, 47
innovations: in animal research 61–2; biological measures 196–7; in child and family policy research 196; developmental psychopathology research 196; eye tracking devices 108–10; function of collaborations 206; in gender development research 162; in infant developmental research 79–80; in memory and aging research 206; in overimitation research 31; in peer relationship research 154; in studying neighborhoods 134, 141–2; secondary analysis of longitudinal datasets 197; spatial analytic methods 141–2
Institutional Review Board (IRB) 41–2
intercorrelations 176
interdisciplinary 113
interference tasks 117
intergroup bias 165
internalizing 135, 148–50, 166, 180, 189, 191, 197–8
interventions 70–1
interview 182–3
IRT *see* item response theory
item characteristic curve (ICC) 150, 177
item response theory (IRT) 177

Index

knowledge-manipulation 115
Kohlberg, L.: and moral development stage theory 172; and theory of gender development stages 158, 165

language 13, 28, 44–5, 84, *86*, 87, *91*, 104–8, 110, 118–19, 126, 138, 161, 174–5, 18, 179, 192, 195; learning 27, 113–14, 116–18; and noun acquisition 104–11
Likert scale 178
longitudinal design: and avian models 52–3, 55; and gender development 162; and rodent models 57–8
looking behavior 85, 87–9, *88*

manipulations 54, 59
maternal stress 53, 72
measurement equivalence 175–7, 179, 184; functional 179; item 175–6
measurement: in animals 58–63; behavioral 40, 44, 50, 52, 54, 57, 59, 60, 61, 71, 73–5, 80, 87, 106, 113–14, 135–6, 150–1, 158, 173, 180, 197; behavioral reports 162, 180, 183; cultural-sensitive 174–5; focus groups 45, 175, 178; interview 11, *12*, 43, 47, 105, **125**, 126, 162, 175, 181–3, 192, 194; parent reports 162; physiological 18, 59, 71, 72–5, 77–80, 99, 190–1; postnatal 59–63; prenatal 58–9; Prosocial Reasoning Objective Measure (PROM) 181–3; Prosocial Tendencies Measure (PTM) 178–81; self-report 130–1, 140, 148, 153–4, 162, 164, 180; teacher reports 140, 153, 162
mechanisms: cognitive 30, 99, 111, 113, 116, 119, 162, 171–2, 203, 205; culture-related 28, 171–3; molecular 63; of neighborhood effects 135–7; neural 94, 99; memory 63, 78, 92, 94, 115, 118, **125**, 126, 200–6
mental health 166
metacognitive 200–1, 203–6
mice *see* rodents
minimal risk 43
models: Bayesian 116; cognitive 115; cognitivist 116; computational 113; emergentist 115–16; environmental exposure 53; hybrid 115–16; item response theory (IRT) 176–7; robotics 116–19; *see also* common animal models
monkeys *51*
moral behaviors 172–3, *174*
moral development: of adolescents 178, 182–3; culture-center theories 173; ecoculture stress based theory 173–4; stage theory 172
moral emotions 172; empathy 180–1; guilt 183–4
moral judgements 172

moral socialization theory 172
morality 171–2
mother-infant 74, 79

NAO humanoid robot 115
naturalistic *see* methods: observational
neighborhood effects: defining and measuring 136–43; on parenting 135; on peer relationships 135; on physical health 136; and poverty 191; on self-regulation 136, 189
neural networks 93, 116, 118, 127
neural plasticity *see* plasticity
neurocognitive 72, 118
neurodevelopmental 71, 73–5, 78
neurohormones 74–5, 78–9
norepinephrine 74
number learning 118–19

observational 127, 134–8, 141–2, 161
observational learning 158
ontogeny 50, *51*; 70
oxytocin 75, 79

paradigm 61, 171; cognitivist 115; connectionist neural networks 116; developmental robotics 118; emergentist 116; evolutionary 157; gender self-socialization 159; hybrid 115–16; "periodic oddball" 95; puzzle box 32; social-rival 74; Strange Situation 12; symbolic 115
peers 29–30, 34, 43, 45, 134–5, 137, 142, 158, 164–6, 180–1, 195; peer nomination inventory (PNI) 148; and perceived popularity 152; and reference groups **149**; *see also* aggression; victimization
perception 84–5, 92, 94, 96, 97–9, *98*, 140, 152, 159–60, 164, 167; in development 7, 84–5, 89–90, 92, 113; discrimination and learning 61, 63
physiological *18*, 59, 71–5, 190–1; factors 77–8; functioning 80; regulation 79
plasticity 80; experience-dependent 71
postnatal 54–5, 59–63, 70, 73–4, 79–80
prenatal behavior: in animals 55–9; development alterations 53–5; measuring 58–9; observing 55–8; studies 73–4
PROM *see* Prosocial Reasoning Objective Measure
prosocial behavior 178, 180, 181, 183
Prosocial Reasoning Objective Measure (PROM) 181–3; Tendencies Measure (PTM and PTM-R) 178–181
protective: behaviors 75; factors 79, 189, 191; influences 196; relationships 127; self- **125**, 128; strategies 126, 129
psychometric 176, 183–84

race 10, 13, 14, *15*, *17*, 22, 23, 42, 89, 138, 143; *see also* ethnicity
Randomized Controlled Trial (RCT) *see* designs
reasoning 171–3
  approval-oriented 181–3; empathic and internalized 181; hedonistic 181–3; needs-oriented 181–2; prosocial moral 176–7, 180–1; stereotypical 181
recall 201–6
recruiting 46, 106
reliability 73, 76–7, 182, 192; internal 138, 179, 182; interrater 30, 58, 139; test-retest 179, 182
response bias 154
retrieval cues 201, 206
risk factors 136, 189–91, 196
rodents 52, 56, 63

same-sex 31, 57, 150, 158, 160, 164
self-concept: and gender 157, 159, 161–2, 165
self-esteem 166
Self-Organizing Map (SOM) 116 –17
self-report 130, 140, 148, 154, 162, 164, 180; and demand characteristics 153
self-socialization 159, 165–7
sensory development 55, 63, 74, 84, 96, 99
sex 36, 157, 164–7; biological 163, 165; differences 33–5, 159, 164–5, 167; mixed 164; sex-typed 37, 160, 163–7
sheep *see* animal models, ovine
simulation 113–15
sleep-wake cycles 53, 72–3
social cognition 74, 92; method 162; socio-cognitive 180, 183; theory 172–3
social desirability 153, 163, 180, 183
social interaction 34, 73, 119, 137, 139
social learning 26, 29–31, 33–6, 113, 158, 162
social policy 191
socialization 72, 172–3, 180; agents 180, 183; collective 139 *see* self-socialization
Society for Research in Child Development (SRCD) 8–9, *10–13*, 14, *15*, 23
socio-emotive 180, 183
sociometric 43; method 148; status categories 150–4
SOM *see* Self-Organizing Map
spatial analytic methods 141–2
spontaneous movement 55, 58–9
standardized 22, *60*, 139; assessments 5, 71, 192
statistical analysis 63, 78, 141, 150, 152, 177, 192, 197; confirmatory factor analysis (CFA) 176; digital coding and analysis 58–9; exploratory factor analysis (EFA) 176; item response theory (IRT) 176–7, 179; factor analysis 176–7
stereotype flexibility 163–4
stress 35, 53–54, 71, 173, *174*, 189–90, 196; fetal 72; hormones 192; maternal 53; reactivity 75, 191–2, 197; regulation 72, 75
symbol-manipulation 116, 118–19
sympathy 183–4

tasks 40, 77; Baldwin object-label mapping 117; behavioral 180; emotion regulation 61; framing 29, 32, 35; Interference Posture Change Task 117; memory 204; overimitation 26–9; perceptual discrimination 61; prosocial behavioral 180; puzzlebox 27, 28, 30–5; social 61; tool-based 32
teacher: nomination 153–4; reports 140, 162
temperament 12, 73–4 79, 128
teratogen 53–4
theory 113, *124–5*, 127–8, 130–1, 137; ABC+D 123, *124–5*; Ainsworth's ABC theory of attachment 123, 126; attachment 12, 122–3, 127; biological 157–8; Biosocial Theory 158; Bronfenbrenner's bio-ecological model 134, 142; culture-centered 173–4; -driven 1; Dynamic-Maturational Model of Attachment (DMM) *123*, *124–5*; ecocultural stress-based theory 173, *174*; evolutionary 157, 171; Gender Schema Theory (GST) 158; Gender Self-Socialization Model (GSSM) 159–61; item response theory (IRT) 176–7; Kohlberg's gender development 158; Kohlberg's moral stage 172, 184; of mind 118; moral socialization theory 172; social cognitive 172–3; social learning 158; socio-constructivist 119; of structural alignment 111; theory method 13
traits 34–5, 163; agentic 164–6; communal 165–6; intrapersonal 154, 173
translational science 189–95, 198
trends 5, **19**, **21**; historical 9; research 9–16, 21–3; secular *10–11*, *15*

ultrasound **51**, 56–7, *58*

validity 29–30, 73, 173–5; construct 76, 150, 177, 180–1, 183; convergent 76, 179–80, 182–3; cultural 173–4; discriminant 180, 183; ecological 204; external 30, 181; face 175, 179; internal 30; predictive 73, 138
victimization 148, 150, 152–4
visual 85–7, *86*, 89, 92, 94 95, 99, 107, 116–18
vulnerable 43–7, 71, 190, 194

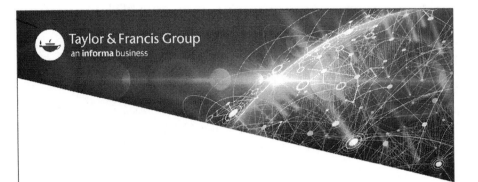